Ken Sakamura (Ed.)

# TRON Project 1988

Open-Architecture Computer Systems

Proceedings of the Fifth TRON Project Symposium

With 134 Figures

Springer-Verlag
Tokyo Berlin Heidelberg New York
London Paris

KEN SAKAMURA
Leader, TRON Project
Department of Information Science
Faculty of Science
University of Tokyo
Hongo, Tokyo, 113 Japan

ISBN 978-4-431-68083-3      ISBN 978-4-431-68081-9 (eBook)
DOI 10.1007/978-4-431-68081-9

# Foreword

It has been almost 5 years since the inauguration of the TRON project, a concept first proposed by Dr. K. Sakamura of the University of Tokyo. The TRON Association, which was founded as an independent organization in March 1988, has been taking over the activities of the earlier TRON Association, which was a division of Japan Electronic Industry Development Association (JEIDA). It has been expanding various operations to globalize the organizations activities. The number of member companies already exceeds 100, with increasing participation from overseas companies. It is truly an awaring historical event that so many members with the same qualifications and aims engaged in the research and development of the computer environment could be gathered together.

The TRON concept aims at the creation of a new and complete environment beneficial to both computer and mankind. It has a very wide scope and great diversity. As it includes the open architecture concept and as the TRON machine should be able to work with various foreign languages, the TRON is targetted to be used internationally.

In order for us to create a complete TRON world, although there are several TRON products already on the market, continuous and aggressive participation from as members together with concentration as further development are indispensable. We, the TRON promoters, are much encouraged by such a driving force.

At this opening of the Fifth TRON Symposium, I hope that people will come to understand the concept TRON thoroughly through their participation in the symposium and that diffusion of such understanding will contribute significantly to the development of the computer industry in the world.

TAKUMA YAMAMOTO

Chairman, TRON Association
President, FUJITSU LIMITED

# Preface

It is my pleasure to chair the Fifth TRON Project Symposium. The TRON project started in 1984 and is now into its fifth year of development. The first target date of the TRON project 1990, is approaching quickly. The project has already produced results to make us believe that we can achieve our first goals by 1990.

The project's long-term objective is to design and develop the highly functionally distributed system (HFDS). In order to achieve this final goal, design concepts, system architecture, interface definitions, and real implementation methods have been vigorously studied. The core of the TRON computer architecture, the 32-bit VLSI CPU, has been designed and manufactured for sampling. ITRON has been commercialized and has many users now. Prototype systems based on BTRON and CTRON are being implemented. The research on MTRON, to connect many intelligent objects together in order to build, the HFDS, has proceeded steadily.

One important feature of the TRON architecture is to allow independent and yet compatible implementation of TRON-based systems. The open and accessible interface definitions of various layers of the computer system architecture are very important. One good example of independent, compatible implementation is TRON VLSI CPU. Several manufacturers have separately developed VLSI CPU, and yet these chips assure the operation of the same binary instruction. The interface definitions will be available to the public in accordance with the spirit of the TRON project. Never before in the history of computing has the need for such open standard architecture been felt as strongly as it is today. I think the TRON project has contributed much in this regard.

In 1988, the TRON Association became incorporated and now has more than 100 members. I would like to acknowledge the help of many organizations in promoting the TRON project, and hope that the TRON computer architecture can contribute to the welfare of the many members of the society in the 1990s.

KEN SAKAMURA

# Table of Contents

**Chapter 1: TRON System Architecture**

TRON Universal Language System
K.SAKAMURA. With 1 Figure ............................................ 3

Design of MTRON: Construction of HFDS
K.SAKAMURA. With 2 Figures ........................................ 21

**Chapter 2: ITRON**

HI8:A Realtime Operating System with $\mu$-ITRON
Specification for the H8/500
H.TAKEYAMA, T.SHIMIZU, M.KOBAYAKAWA. With 8 Figures ..... 35

MR7700: An Implementation of $\mu$-ITRON Specification on
16-bit Single-Chip Microcontroller
K.NAKATA, H.TSUBOTA, T.SHIMIZU, K.SAITOH, T.ENOMOTO.
With 5 Figures ......................................................... 55

An Integrated Embedded Systems Software Development
Environment for ITRON
J.READY, D.KALINSKY. With 5 Figures .............................. 67

**Chapter 3: BTRON**

TACL: TRON Application Control-Flow Language
K.SAKAMURA. With 4 Figures ........................................ 79

Natural Language Translation Services in BTRON
R.T.MYERS, K.SAKAMURA. With 7 Figures ........................ 93

A Study on Video Manager of the BTRON Specification
K.KAJIMOTO, M.SHIMIZU, Y.KUSHIKI. With 3 Figures ............ 109

The Type Mechanism of the TIPE/L Programming Language
H.TAKADA, K.SAKAMURA. With 1 Figure ........................... 119

## Chapter 4: CTRON

Perspectives on CTRON
J.D.Mooney. With 2 Figures ............................................ 135

CTRON Reference Model
T.Wasano, Y.Kobayashi, K.Sakamura. With 1 Figure ......... 145

Design of the CTRON Communication Control Interface
Y.Shimizu. With 3 Figures .............................................. 157

Design of CTRON Execution Control Interface
Y.Baba, M.Ohminami, H.Kusumoto, H.Kosugi.
With 6 Figures ............................................................. 167

Enhancement of the CTRON Kernel Interface
I.Kogiku, T.Okubo, M.Matsushita. With 9 Figures ............. 189

An Implementation of the CTRON Basic OS
M.Ishizuka, Y.Ikeda, M.Fukuyoshi, T.Ogawa, T.Sakuma,
M.Matsushita. With 10 Figures ........................................ 213

An Implementation of CTRON Basic OS on a Lap-Top
Workstation
K.Oda, N.Shimizu, N.Inoue, Y.Iba. With 2 Figures ............. 235

## Chapter 5: TRONCHIP

Architectural Features of OKI 32-Bit Microprocessor
N.Ito, H.Nojima, Y.Mori. With 6 Figures ......................... 247

Design Considerations of the Matsushita 32-Bit Microprocessor
for Real-Memory Systems
T.Kiyohara, T.Sakao, K.Adachi, O.Nishijima.
With 7 Figures ............................................................ 263

An Examination of the Fundamental Configuration of
the Microprocessor for Virtual Memory Systems
Y.Nishikawa, M.Deguchi, T.Sakao. With 4 Figures ............. 275

Implementation and Evaluation of the TRONCHIP
Specification for the TX1
J.Iwamura, H.Kishigami, A.Ishii, K.Usami.
With 9 Figures ............................................................ 285

A Floating Point Processing Unit for the Gmicro CPU
H.Kida, M.Watabe, T.Nakamikawa, S.Morinaga,
S.Kawasaki, H.Inayoshi. With 10 Figures ......................... 301

High Performance Bus Interface of Gmicro/300
T.Kitahara, M.Yuhara, A.Fujihira, M.Mitsuhashi, M.Itoh.
With 8 Figures ............................................................ 317

A 40 MB/s 32-Bit DMA Controller with 3411 Product Terms
PLA
M.KIMURA, T.IWASAKI, S.MORI, K.FUJITA, S.HAZAMA.
With 6 Figures ............................................................. 331

Development of a C Compiler for GMICRO Micro Processor
Based on TRON Architecture
Y.KASHIWAGI, H.CHAKI, M.NARUSHIMA. With 2 Figures ......... 341

Development Support System for TX Series
S.ISHIMARU, K.TAMARU. With 7 Figures ............................. 351

An Integrated Software Development Toolkit for
the GMICRO/200
A.BIGAZZI, J.E.LILLGE, D.E.JASKOLSKI. With 8 Figures ......... 363

List of Contributors ...................................................... 381

Keywords Index ........................................................... 383

# Chapter 1: TRON System Architecture

# TULS: TRON Universal Language System

## Ken Sakamura
Department of Information Science, Faculty of Science, University of Tokyo

**ABSTRACT**

In future computer systems based on TRON specifications, various interfaces will use programming languages. The basic specification for such languages in building these interfaces is TULS (TRON UNIVERSAL LANGUAGE SYSTEM).

This paper explains the motivation behind the use of programmable interfaces.

In this paper, the design of TULS is explained along its philosophy. An example of a TULS application is the physical data layout format of TAD (TRON Application Databus), which is described using TULS.

TULS is meant to provide programming capability for various types of interfaces.

The specification of the interfacing parts of computer systems can be dynamically changed for optimum load balancing using TULS.

This makes it possible to adapt the interfaces to new technologies that will emerge in the future, while maintaining compatibility over the long run.

TULS will be used for data representation, the human interface, network protocols, user programming interfaces, system program interfaces, etc. BTRON, ITRON, and CTRON will use TULS.

TULS is what makes the building of the MTRON environment possible.

**Keywords:** TULS, HFDS, MTRON, macro language, programmable interface, TAD

## 1. INTRODUCTION

The TRON project aims at building the HFDS (Highly Functional Distributed System).[1] In order to build the HFDS, we have started several subprojects to produce the basic components—ITRON (Industrial-TRON) for embedded computers,[1] BTRON (Business-TRON) for providing a good human-machine interface,[2] CTRON (Central-TRON) for server applications in networks,[3] and MTRON (Macro-TRON)[4] to manage the networks and use the HFDS effectively.[5]

The HFDS envisioned in the TRON Project is expected to contain computers numbering into the hundreds of millions, or even billions. This massive network will be truly open, and nodes will be added to, and deleted from it dynamically. The HFDS will manage cooperation among these nodes to provide sophisticated services.

It is desirable that the nodes in the HFDS follow a standard set of communication protocols. If we have to prepare programs to handle different communication protocols, the system will be too bulky. This is because it is impossible to have all the different interface codes necessary to handle different interface methods in computers of every size.

Therefore, we must provide a set of standards for the HFDS. The TRON Project aims at achieving long-term compatibility of standards, even if it is necessary to do away with an existing standard that has become outdated. Since it is impossible to anticipate future interface methods, we must also be prepared to incorporate future technological advancements smoothly.

What we need at each node is an expandable interface that retains compatibility as it grows by incorporating advances in technology.

Thus we need to supply a programmable interface nucleus to handle all the interface requirements of both existing and future network nodes. Here, the programmable interface is an interface that can be changed by reprogramming in specification language. Certain type of programmable interfaces have an abstraction mechanism to hide the internals of subsystems across the interface.

Supplying such a programmable interface has the additional merit of providing the system with a limited type of load balancing capability. For example, electronic utilities controlled by ITRON can also be used as a part of the BTRON human interface by reprogramming the interfaces of the ITRON-controlled electronic utilities.

The introduction of a programmable interface will also provide a solid foundation for TAD, which describes the data exchange format used in on-line and off-line data exchange.[2]

## 2. INTERFACE LAYERS

There are several interface layers in the TRON Architecture. The first task of designing a programmable interface to describe the interactions across these interface layers was to clearly identify the interfaces. This means we had to consider ITRON, BTRON, CTRON, and MTRON to define the interfaces. The interfaces defined in these TRON computer subarchitectures are considered sufficient to cover most of the conceivable computer applications.

## 2.1 Interactions

Basically speaking, there are four types of active elements in the HFDS—the human user, application programs, system programs, and hardware.

The interactions among these active elements must be analyzed.

Strictly speaking, human users and application programs never interact directly with each other, since what human users interact with are hardware devices such as the keyboard and display devices. However, from the point of view of information flow, human users can be thought of as interacting with the application programs.

Let us list the possible interactions among these elements, and also give some examples of what they entail.

- Human user and human user  (e.g., communication using E-mail)
- Human user and application program  (e.g., operating an application program)
- Human user and hardware.  (e.g., controlling hardware operations)
- Application and application  (e.g., data exchange between applications)
- Application and system program  (e.g., using system calls)
- Application and hardware  (e.g., executing a program on a CPU)
- System and system  (e.g., communication at the logical level)
- System and hardware  (e.g., using a CPU or other hardware resource)
- Hardware and hardware  (e.g., physical-level communication and hardware control)

## 2.2 Interfaces

We define the interface as the protocol for information flow between the elements discussed in section 2.1.

Based on this definition, we can list some major interfaces that exist among these elements.

- Natural language interface  (human and human)
- Human interface  (human and an application or system)
- User programming language/environment  (human and an application or system)
- Device design  (human and machine)
- Data description format  (application and application)
- System call  (application and system)
- Application programming language/environment  (application and system, application and hardware)

6

- Network protocol (system and system)
- System programming language/environment (system and hardware)
- Physical level interface (hardware and system)

Among the above interfaces, device-design interface and physical-level interface are not programmable in nature, and thus are not discussed here.

A programmable interface is an interface that can adapt to changes in specifications through reprogramming, and that is not limited to being a programming language*.

If interaction among the elements of the HFDS is done only through a fixed programming language/environment, then the interface is not programmable.

3. IMPLEMENTATION

After considering these interface needs, we decided to adopt an interface description language that is also an executable specification language. We will now describe this language, which we will call "language 0" for the time being.

3.1 Language Compilability

Language 0 has to be compilable, as well as being executable purely for reasons of efficiency. This is because many interfaces require real-time response. Therefore, if we want to use an interface description that is also an executable implementation, it is necessary to perform compiling.

Although we made the decision to introduce this compiling capability to language 0, we had to observe the currently defined interfaces for ITRON, BTRON, and CTRON, which are written in machine language. Thus the compiler for language 0 had to be compatible with the present interface routines of ITRON, BTRON, and CTRON, and extensions of these routines that are likely to be implemented in the future.

---

\*  Please note that the programmability of programming language/environment interfaces are not directly related to the programming language itself. What is at issue is the programmability of the interface specification and not the language.

However, as you can see in later sections, we have opted for an executable specification language and the distinction is blurred in this case.

**3.2 An Interactive Language**

We required language 0 to be an interactive language in the sense that we should be able to dynamically change its description. The system we have in mind is a compilable language system with interpreter support. A language system like this that allows editing, interpreting, and compiling in its own environment is called an interactive language.[6]

An interactive language also has the advantage of achieving good code density with efficiency when compiling takes place in strategic portions of programs written in the language.[7]

**3.3 A Resource Model for von Neumann Computers**

Language 0 also had to have a rich set of programming data resources in order to program the human interface, data formats, and other languages. Since language 0 is used to describe both languages and interfaces run on von Neumann computers, it was necessary for language 0 to have provisions to allow programmers to write efficient code for von Neumann computers.

**3.4 Real-time Control**

In the TRON Project, special emphasis is placed on real-time response in computer systems. In order to support this real-time processing, we decided to adopt a procedural paradigm as the control in language 0.

**4. TULS**

The name we have given to language 0 is TULS (TRON UNIVERSAL LANGUAGE SYSTEM), which, as described above, is an interactive language system for the standardization of interfaces.

As a result of analyses and requirements carried out up to now, we have decided that TULS should have the following features.

**4.1 A Resource Model**

TULS has a data resource model that reflects the memory model in von Neumann computers. Since there is no distinction between data and program in a von Neumann computer, TULS' storage mechanism can store anything in it.

There are two types of storage in TULS. One is called "dictionary" and is volatile; the other is called "real object"[2] and is persistent. Data in dictionary storage is referenced by searching with macronames, while real objects are directly specified by real object pointers. Both types of storage handle strings, numbers, text, figures, virtual objects[2], fusen[2], and TULS programs.(*Fig. 1*)

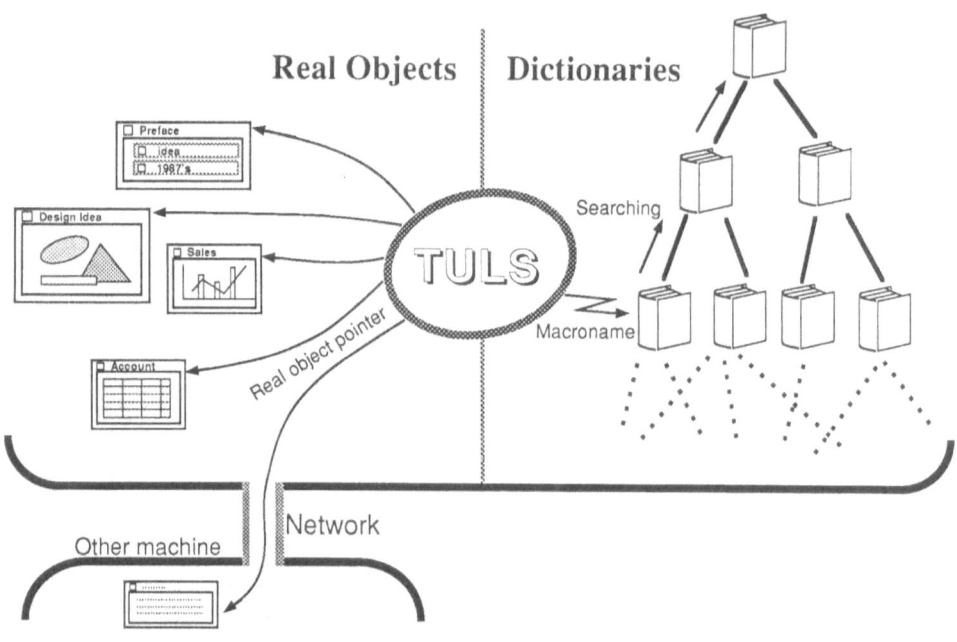

*Fig. 1 Real object and Dictionary.*

### (a) Dictionary

Dictionary storage in TULS is volatile because it is created by a process (the smallest unit of control flow in TULS) and is destroyed when the process ceases.

Dictionary storage has a scope associated with it. There are parent-child relations among dictionaries in keeping with the relations among the processes that create the dictionaries. The child dictionary is smaller in scope, and the searching of dictionaries proceeds from the child dictionary to its parent. Hence, the scope and the parent-child relation can be used to define data that is accessible only within a process, such as the automatic local variables in conventional programming languages.

A dictionary consists of entries that are made up of a macroname and its corresponding macrobody. The macroname is a character string, and the macrobody is a variable length of data that can contain any TULS data or program. The dictionary entries can be dynamically inserted and deleted.

The dictionary system in TULS reflects the dynamic memory management system in computers. We do not specify how the dictionary should be implemented. As far as the semantics for the TULS interpreter is concerned, any implementation method suffices.

**(b) Real Object**

A real object is a persistent storage in TULS. The real object continues to exist unless it is explicitly destroyed.[8] This is in clear contrast to the dictionary. TULS has primitives for creating, duplicating, and destroying real objects.

Real objects play the role of system files in conventional computer systems. They consist of variable length records and can store any TULS data.

A real object is accessed with a real object pointer, which is unique to that real object. This means that no matter where a reference comes from in the computer system or network, it always goes through the same real object pointer to get to the real object attached to it.

A real object and its real object pointer play the role of global variables in conventional programming languages.

Since there is only one copy of a real object its unique real object pointer, real objects can be used to build a consistent database for multiple clients. If data in the form of real object is changed, the change is reflected in all references to the data in the computer network.

The method for implementing real objects is not specified in TULS.

**(c) Shadow Object**

When using a system based on real objects, there is an implementation overhead connected with their semantics, because changes must always be reflected in every reference to a real object. Thus we introduced the concept of a "shadow object." Essentially, a shadow object is a copy of a real object on which changes are made. These changes are then written back into the real object in an atomic transaction. As a result, it is not necessary to continually access the real object to make changes on it.

For example, a word processor can work on a real object by first making a shadow object of it. After changes have been made to the shadow object, they can be transferred from the shadow object to the real object.

**4.2 CONTROL FLOW**

TULS is based on the procedural control flow usually seen in macro programming languages.

**(a) Macro Expansion.**

TULS uses macro expansion as its evaluation mechanism.[9] Macro expansion proceeds by substituting a macro call for its macrobody. A macrobody in TULS can contain any data or program.

**(b) Dictionary Search**

In TULS, a combination of a macroname and a macrobody is stored as an entry in a dictionary. Dictionary search is performed to expand macro calls.

Since the dictionary system in TULS is a hierarchy based on a parent-child relationship, it is possible to have many leaf dictionaries in the hierarchy. Thus there can be several choices when it comes to dictionary search starts. The choice is made according to the interface extension requirements of TULS. However, if the search does not find the entry that corresponds to the macro call in the child dictionary, it then proceeds to its parent until it finds the entry.

The macroname is used as the search key, and when a dictionary entry is found, its macrobody stored in the body part of the dictionary entry is substituted for the macro call. If there are further macro calls found in the macrobody, these calls are searched for until all the macro calls are processed.

The dictionary system with the parent-child relationship in TULS can be used to introduce an inheritance mechanism in macro processing. Also, searching in the dictionary system can be augmented by limiting the search to certain dictionaries, or by specifying access controls to the dictionaries.

**(c) Event-Driven Paradigm**

TULS is used with applications that respond to both external and internal events. External events such as the movements of the digitizing pen and keys, and internal events such as window resizing and software signals, are treated by TULS as requests for prespecified macro execution. These requests are stored in a queue and are processed by the macro processor.

Since external events occur at unexpected times and often require real-time processing, TULS has a mechanism to process these events in a concurrent fashion.

TULS can fork processes along different control paths, run those processes in parallel, and synchronize the processing they do. In addition, conditional generation of new events is also possible with TULS.

Events can be grouped and given a group name. These names are used for specifying a job name. A job is a collection of control paths that are meant to work cooperatively to perform a task.

**(d) Real-time Data**

An event-driven macro processor is at the core of real-time processing in TULS.

However, the features discussed above can only handle the successor/predecessor relation and synchronization of control in TULS. In order to handle deterministic real-time processing, we introduced the concept of an event with a time stamp.

This time stamp specifies the time in absolute terms. The time stamp concept is used to define a series of events at a specified time. By using this concept, it is possible to describe the events on an absolute time scale.

This concept of a time stamp is useful in describing the motion in an animated film, the sound generated in music, and the real-time control of robots arms.

## 5. TAD

TAD (TRON Application Databus) is a common data format in the TRON Project. ITRON, BTRON, and CTRON use TAD for data exchange. The main objective in using TAD is to achieve data compatibility among applications.

TAD is based on the TULS concept. TULS allows for a flexible description of the data format. Furthermore, it allows for future extension of the data format while maintaining compatibility. This is ideal for TAD.

From a physical standpoint, TAD defines a stream of variable length records. Each record contains a TULS macro call, and is merely considered a segment in the TAD scheme.

### 5.1 The Data Segment

Although a record that contains data is referred to as a segment when talking about it in terms of TAD, from the viewpoint of TULS, the segment is nothing more than a macro call used to display the contents of the data record. This display feature was added to TULS during the building TAD.

The data thus displayed is text, a figure, or real-time events to be generated at a specified time using the time stamp. Future extension is planned to segments with three-dimensional data.

### (a) Text Data Segment

A text data segment is a linear sequence of data. Text is an example of such. Other examples are voice data represented by phonetic symbols, and very simple musical notes expressed with musical symbols.

**(b) Graphic Data Segment**

A graphic data segment is a two-dimensional collection of data. A figure is one such example. This type of data has attributes such as planer position, color, and other graphics attributes.

**(c) Real-time Data Segment**

A real-time data segment is a series of events in time. The time stamp feature of TULS is used to specify when the event takes place. A real-time data segment can describe either a serial or parallel series of events. It can also describe some repetition or loop in an event. A TULS macro that describes the passage of time can be used to describe an event that occurs with a certain delay after another event takes place.

**5.2 Virtual Object Segment**

The virtual object segment has a real object pointer and associated housekeeping data. TAD shows a virtual object segment as a rectangular shape on the screen.[9] TAD also defines the macro processing that handles human-interaction when a user points at the rectangle on the screen.

**5.3 Fusen Segment**

TAD segments that are neither data nor virtual object segments are called fusen segments. Fusen segments can contain non-TAD data, or special macros for application programs.

**5.4 Programming in TAD**

**(a) Definition and Repetition**

In TAD, you can define and register an often used sequence as a macro and then call it back later with a macro call. Non-standard character symbols such as those found in Japanese are handled this way.

If a macro is defined so that it takes arguments, you can call the macro with different arguments to achieve different results. For instance, if you define a macro to draw a pattern on the screen that requires argument to move or tilt the pattern, you can achieve dazzling effects by repeatedly calling the macro with slightly different arguments.

**(b) Packaging of Operations**

Data compatibility is increased by packaging operations that handle a piece of data, and then exchanging the package of operations together with data.

If somewhat esoteric data has to be displayed in a certain way, the sender of the data can write the algorithm to display this data in a meaningful way in TAD (or TULS) and send the display operation together with the data itself. The receiver can run the operation on his or her machine to take a look at the data.

The above scenario is made possible because TULS, on which TAD is based, is extensible.

In the TRON Project, the separation of the display algorithm and other parts of an application is encouraged.

TAD provides the mechanism to automatically pass these operations together with the data itself, thus increasing compatibility. The TAD system inquires about the environment, and then loads the display algorithm if the algorithm is missing.

### (c) Automatic Processing

Macros embedded in TAD data can be used to run applications automatically. Thus, for example, an automatic demo presentation of the data becomes possible when it is referenced on the screen.

In this way, TAD offers advanced hypertext and multimedia processing that may not be entirely possible by the real/virtual object model alone.[2]

Please remember that the features of TAD discussed above do not have to be implemented in TULS. They can be implemented using whatever practical methods are available, including machine language coding, as long as the future compatibility with TULS is assured.


### 5.5 MULTI-LANGUAGE PROCESSING

Natural language processing must be handled in the TRON Project, since the HFDS is envisioned in the project aims at increasing the level of communication among people throughout the world.

First , the local language of every society must be supported. Computers now have the power to do this.

However, multi-language processing is easier said than done. Displaying the local character set is only part of the problem. Some languages are written from right to left, others from left to right, and still others in a mixed manner. There are also languages written vertically, and there can be different presentations or forms of characters according their positions in sentences. In short, there is a multitude of problems. In order to handle these idiosyncrasies of languages, a language processing environment is provided in the TRON Architecture.

The mere switching of language environment is not enough to incorporate texts from two or more different languages in the same document. Thus programming in TAD offers the solution by incorporating the necessary formatting operations in a package.

Natural language translation to facilitate communication between cultures is an attractive target. In the TRON Project, we intend to use a pivot approach for this. Instead of devising translators for all possible pairs of languages, we define a pivot, or an intermediate language, to which the translator from the natural language is built. The pivot language is called Language ∅[11].

In principle, we can construct, for example, an English-to-Japanese translator by combining the English-to-Language ∅ translator and the Language ∅-to-Japanese translator.

If the translator from a natural language, say Japanese, to Language ∅ can be packaged in a TAD (or TULS) operation package, it then becomes possible to send out the original, natural-language document together with the operation package to another BTRON computer. Thus the original Japanese-language document can be compared against the translation made by the translator from Language ∅ to the receiver's native language.

Of course, this scheme is still in the research stage. Language ∅ must be capable of defining the semantics of natural languages. We have been studying the possibility of extending TULS to define the semantics necessary for natural language translation.

## 6. OTHER BENEFITS

The original goal behind the introduction of TULS into the TRON Architecture was to achieve standardization in the network environment, but there are added benefits to TULS.

### 6.1 TULS as a systems programming language

TULS can be used as a systems programming language that can access particular machine resources defined as macros, in addition to operating system resources.

### (a) Intermediate Language

Since TULS can access both low-level computer system details and high-level computer resources (real objects, for example), it is an ideal choice as an intermediate language in which to include a compiler that can generate output code from high-level languages such as Pascal, C, Fortran, and Modula-2.

If such compiler is made, then we can share the application programs written in such languages on different computer systems.

### (b) Program Portability

TULS can be used to increase program portability in the following way. A TULS environment can be interrogated to see if it has the necessary functions for running a program. If the environment is an older installation written in TULS that needs some extensions, these can be carried along with the program, since TULS allows for extensions to existing facilities.

A mechanism in TAD to interrogate the environment and copy missing functions will be used for this purpose.

### (c) Intelligent Device Control

Many external devices, such as printers, have become intelligent devices due to built-in CPUs and large program memories.

The TULS approach of using programmable interfaces has the merit of moving functions of devices across interfaces during run-time. This is desirable because the best way to partition the functions among different subsystems is not known during the design phase. It is ideal then if we can move the functions from one system to the other to achieve better performance.

For example, if an intelligent display controller can receive pieces of TAD programs and execute them locally, window system functions such as frame drawing and menu display can be done in the display controller. This reduces the load on the main CPU. Similar off-loading to intelligent communication processors in networks is often seen today.

TULS will provide a uniform framework for this type of load balancing.

### 6.2 TULS as a Macro Language

BTRON computer end users can use TULS as a macro language processor system. The language system based on TULS is called TACL (TRON APPLICATION CONTROL-FLOW LANGUAGE) and provides the human interface for BTRON.[12]

### (a) OS Command Line Interpreter

The lowest line on the BTRON screen[2] is a window where users can write TACL interpreter statements. This window is called the system message panel. It displays error messages from the interpreter and on TACL job status.

All macro processing triggered by events can be initiated by writing down the macro calls here.

## (b) Application Macro Language

BTRON application programs are built in such a way that some of their functions can be accessed from TACL. BTRON programs are ideally build as a collection of functions that are combined with TACL macros at the top level.

It is possible to call the application program as a whole TACL macro, even if its functions cannot be invoked from TACL. By writing down a sequence of suitable TACL macros, we can achieve batchlike processing of multiple programs.

It is possible to write an application solely to enhance TACL library as well.

## (c) User Programming Language

Since TACL is an interactive language, it can be used to write short programs. TACL is typeless and has a relatively high-level view of data such as real objects. Therefore, programming in it should be relatively easy.

Programming using fusen segments, which contain TACL macros, will also be easy. In many cases, it is only necessary to fill in the parameters of the fusen on the screen[12] and then group them together. The result is a full-fledged program instruction.

## 7. IMPLEMENTATION OF TULS

At present, TULS exists as a standard model. Hardware technology is not yet mature enough to allow for efficient operation of TULS.

However, an initial study of implementation is under way. A TULS interpreter for the TRON VLSI CPU is being designed. This will take advantage of high-level instructions, such as string search of the TRON VLSI CPU.

Our long term goal is to use TULS to describe every interface of TRON computer systems. It would be desirable to implement TULS in microprogramming for this goal.

TACL has been designed and will be offered as a BTRON user environment and programming language, The advantage of TULS as interactive language is apparent for TACL.[12] However, TACL implementation cannot wait for efficient TULS implementation. Thus TACL has been implemented as a standalone interpreter compiled into machine code.

The current BTRON human interface has been described in TACL to verify its descriptive power and test its efficiency.

Although the implementation of TULS has yet to be achieved, its power as specification language has already been proved during the design of TACL and in other research.

## 8. SUMMARY

TULS is a language system to be used as an executable specification language for von Neumann computers.

Our approach to TULS design has been necessitated by the demand for uniform compatibility in a wide range of computer systems. TULS has been designed to be extensible, but it can also accommodate existing standards, such as ITRON, BTRON, and CTRON, without any loose of compatibility.

Many functions offered in TRON interfaces will be described in TULS and will be extensible in the future.

Our approach is very practical in the sense that TULS functions can be offered in machine language routines, as long as each routine is compatible with the TULS runtime system. By defining the interface specification from the beginning as a guideline, we assure future compatibility. When technology advances to the point where it becomes possible to recode the functions in TULS for more efficient execution, we will enjoy extensibility with compatibility intact.

In graphics, BITBLT operation has become a basic and important primitive that captures the essence of graphics operations. TULS primitives are meant to play similar role for von Neumann computers.

We expect TULS to become the most versatile programming language for the von Neumann architecture, which the TRON Project tries to elevate to its ultimate form.

## REFERENCE

[1]  K. Sakamura, "ITRON: An Overview," TRON Project 1987 (Proc. of the Third TRON Project Symposium), Springer-Verlag, 1987, pp.29-34.

[2]  K. Sakamura, "BTRON: An Overview," TRON Project 1987 (Proc. of the Third TRON Project Symposium), Springer-Verlag, 1987, pp.75-82.

[3]  K. Sakamura, "CTRON: An Overview," TRON Project 1987 (Proc. of the Third TRON Project Symposium), Springer-Verlag, 1987, pp.153-156.

[4]  K. Sakamura, "Design of MTRON: Construction of HFDS," TRON Project 1988 (Proc. of the Fifth TRON Project Symposium, this volume), 1988.

[5]  K. Sakamura, "The Objectives of TRON Project," TRON Project 1987 (Proc. of the Third TRON Project Symposium), Springer-Verlag, 1987, pp.3-16.

[6] M. P. Atkinson, O. P. Buneman, "Types and Persistence in Database Programming Languages," ACM Computing Surveys, Vol.19 (2), 1987.

[7] T. Pittman, "Two-Level Hybrid Interpreter/Native Code Execution for Combined Space-Time Program Efficiency," Proc. of the SIGPLAN'87 Symposium on Interpreters and Interpretive Techniques, pp.150-152, 1987.

[8] P. J. Brown, Macro Processors and Techniques for Portable Software, John Wiley & Sons, Ltd., 1974.

[9] K. Sakamura, "BTRON: Human-Machine Interface," TRON Project 1987 (Proc. of the Third TRON Project Symposium), Springer-Verlag, pp.83-96, 1987.

[10] K. Sakamura, "Multi-language character Sets Handling in TAD," TRON Project 1987 (Proc. of the Third TRON Project Symposium), Springer-Verlag, pp.97-111, 1987.

[11] R. Myers and K. Sakamura, "Natural Language Translation Services in BTRON," TRON Project 1988 (Proc. of the Fifth TRON Project Symposium, this volume), Springer-Verlag, 1988.

[12] K. Sakamura, "TACL: Tron Application Control-flow Language," TRON Project 1988 (Proc. of the Fifth TRON Project Symposium, this volume), Springer-Verlag, 1988.

**Ken Sakamura** is an associate professor in the Department of Information Science, University of Tokyo. He received his Ph.D. in electrical engineering from Keio University (Yokohama) in 1979. As one of Japan's foremost computer architects, he has been the driving force behind the TRON Project, which he started in 1984 to build a new computer architecture for 1990s and beyond. The TRON Architecture he designed for this purpose has now expanded to include applications in buildings and furniture.

Sakamura serves on the editorial board of *IEEE Micro*, a magazine published by the Institute of Electrical and Electronics Engineers (IEEE), and he heads the project promotion committee of the TRON Association. He is also a member of the Japan Information Processing Society (JIPS); the Institute of Electronics, Information and Communication Engineers (IEICE); the Association for Computing Machinery; and he is a senior member of IEEE. He has received the best paper award from IEICE twice; the JIPS best paper award once, the IEEE best annual article award, in addition to other awards from Japanese and overseas organizations.

The above author may be reached at Department of Information Science, Faculty of Science, University of Tokyo, 7-3-1 Hongo, Bunkyo-ku, Tokyo, Japan.

# Design of MTRON: Construction of the HFDS

## Ken Sakamura
Department of Information Science, Faculty of Science, University of Tokyo

**ABSTRACT**

MTRON (Macro-TRON) is the network architecture for building the HFDS (Highly Functional Distributed System) in the TRON Project. Nodes with embedded microprocessors in an MTRON network are called intelligent objects The HFDS is designed to be scaled into a very large network consisting of vast numbers of such intelligent objects. The HFDS needs various forms of data and real-time communication services, which MTRON is designed to provide using a composite layered architecture approach. Applications in the HFDS include management of buildings. In order to handle the position-dependent processing of intelligent objects inside a building, MTRON is specifically designed to handle the concept of the physical position of a node. In order to communicate with the large number of nodes that will be connected to networks in the future, communication protocols are defined dynamically using TULS (TRON UNIVERSAL LANGUAGE SYSTEM).

**Keywords:** MTRON, HFDS, intelligent object, network architecture, intelligent building/house, TULS.

## 1. INTRODUCTION

The ultimate goal of the TRON Project is to build the HFDS (Highly Functional Distributed System) in which a great number of computer-controlled objects are connected and work cooperatively to perform various services. The number of these computer-controlled objects, called intelligent objects, can reach into the billions.[1]

The HFDS as envisioned in the TRON Project requires a very versatile communication network. The communication is in real time for the majority of applications, and information transfer takes place in many forms, such as digitized sound, video images, and others. Because the HFDS is to be used to control so-called intelligent objects, real-time communication must be provided.

In this paper, we refer to MTRON as the architecture of the HFDS. This is a network architecture in which real-time communication is done in hierarchical layers of network nodes.

An MTRON network is different from existing networks in that the nodes on it determine their behavior depending on their physical location. In comparison to the position transparency provided by the logical node names in the conventional networks, the physical location of each node in an MTRON network plays an important role in how it passes information and provide various services.

Nodes that comprise the MTRON-based HFDS include both computers and computer-controlled objects, the latter of which are called intelligent objects. Examples of intelligent objects include telephones, various electronic devices, and among other intelligent objects used in modern buildings, air conditioners and interior lighting systems. These computer-controlled systems will be part of the MTRON-based HFDS as nodes. (*Fig. 1*)

In the TRON Project, we have approached the goal of building the HFDS by providing building blocks. Since the range of applications covered by the computers and intelligent objects is so vast, we decided to design a series of different computer architectures to support the needs of these applications. ITRON (Industrial-TRON) is designed for embedded industrial applications, BTRON (Business-TRON) is designed to provide a good human interface, and CTRON (Central-TRON) is designed for servers in computer networks. A TRON VLSI CPU architecture has also been designed to support these operating systems and applications efficiently. All of these computer architectures have been designed and some prototype systems have already been built.

The MTRON network architecture will control distributed systems based on ITRON, BTRON and CTRON, which will be connected in large computer networks. The MTRON architecture is a network structure consisting of the MTRON interface definition, the MTRON communication protocol standard, and the MTRON operating system architecture. In this paper, we use the term MTRON generically to refer to the architecture, interface definition, and protocol, as far as it presents no confusion.

Below, we will identify the basic problems which must be solved to construct the MTRON-based HFDS. Since an MTRON network is a distributed computer network, we must solve many of the same problems that appear in the design and construction of a conventional distributed network. However, such problems are not discussed in detail here.

In order to present the special problems of the MTRON-based HFDS, we use examples of applications in the HFDS, such as those consisting of intelligent objects and intelligent buildings, and a large network of such intelligent buildings.

These applications in the HFDS would pose very interesting problems in a civil engineering project or urban planning. The physical location of each node elements plays

23

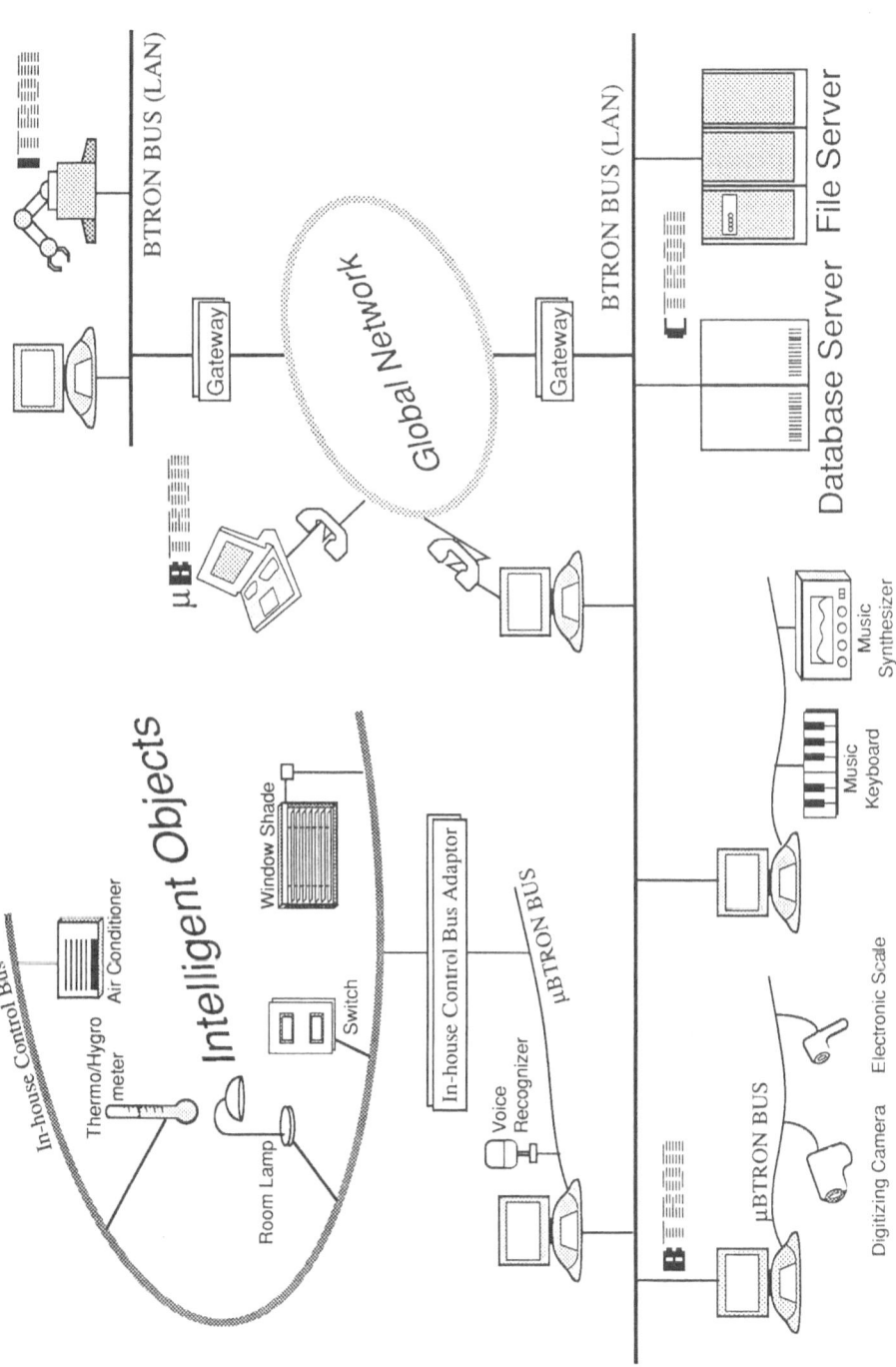

Fig. 1 HFDS (Highly Functionally Distributed System)

an important role. Thus we discuss the location of properties introduced into the HFDS, and how TULS (TRON UNIVERSAL LANGUAGE SYSTEM)[2] handles these problems.

## 2. THE STRUCTURE OF MTRON NETWORKS

In this section, we review the various types of network architectures that will be used in conjunction with the MTRON network. We classify these networks according to what type of application they will handle in the MTRON network.

First, networks can be classified into two types depending on whether they perform switching or non-switching functions. Switching networks cannot be used to broadcast messages. For example, you cannot call all the subscriber telephones of the world from your telephone at the same time.

We can classify the non-switching network into two types of networks according to how tight the coupling of the network node elements are—these are the tightly coupled network and the loosely coupled network. A multiprocessor bus is one example of tightly coupled network.

We can subdivide the loosely-coupled network into two types from the viewpoint of control; these are the master-slave network and the symmetrical network.

Whether a network is symmetrical or master-slave type influences how the network nodes are seen from outside the network. In a symmetrical network, all nodes can be seen from the outside, whereas only master nodes are to be seen from the outside in a non-master-slave network.

The symmetrical network is further divided into the position-dependent type and the position-independent type. Here position means the physical location of the network node. In MTRON, physical location of network nodes plays an important role. Conventional networks are position-independent in that they try to establish location transparency.

In the following, we look into the details of these network types.

### (a) The multiprocessor system as a tightly-coupled network

A multiprocessor system is a very primitive network in the sense that it consists of multiple CPUs connected over a system bus. Usually, it has shared memory and a fast system bus to connect the CPUs. Distributed processing at the task level, or even at instruction level is performed in such systems.

From the viewpoint of the MTRON architecture, we regard these tightly coupled multiprocessor systems as just one node. So the whole system is regarded as one unit.

Similarly, backup systems for fault tolerant systems are regarded as part of one computer system, and are treated as such.

## (b) The master-slave type network

A master-slave type network is one in which master-slave relation(s) exist among groups of network nodes at one time or another.

Since our interest in the network is inter/intra-network communication, the gateway to connect to outside network always brings in master-slave relation as far as inter-network communication is concerned.

One good example of a master-slave type network is seen in the case of a BTRON-based computer and electronic stationery goods connected via the µBTRON bus.[3] Electronic stationery goods are intelligent objects for office use, such as image scanners, electronic scales, and voice recognition devices.

On the µBTRON bus, a BTRON-based computer (multiple computers can be used on the µBTRON bus) can exclusively command a group of electronic stationery goods for a period of time. The BTRON-based computer is a master, and the electronic stationery goods are slaves.

In this configuration, only the BTRON-based computer is directly responsible for external communication, and it handles all traffic, so the electronic stationery goods are seen as part of the BTRON-based computer node from the viewpoint of MTRON.

## (c) The position-dependent symmetrical network

The term symmetrical here refers to the fact that every intelligent object has equal status as far as communication is concerned. There is no central authority. The method of communication is usually of broadcast type.

However, a group concept is introduced to lessen the overhead of broadcast reception in the MTRON network. The physical position or location of the nodes is used to limit the broadcasting in order to eliminate unnecessary traffic in parts of the network.

In MTRON, this type of network is used to manage buildings and houses. We call buildings and houses managed by intelligent objects under the control of MTRON "MTRON intelligent buildings" and "MTRON intelligent houses."

Intelligent objects used in this type of application include air conditioners, interior lighting systems, audio-visual devices, electrically controlled bathrooms, and electrically controlled windows and doors. These intelligent objects are connected to an in-house control bus and can talk to BTRON-based computers, which are used by human operators to control the management of the building. They can also obtain information from sensors on the bus, which monitor temperature, humidity, atmospheric pressure, wind strength, noise, brightness, the status of many switches on the walls, and even the movement of human bodies.

It should be noted here the relationship between the intelligent objects and the BTRON and CTRON computers on the in-house control bus is symmetrical.

A typical application in MTRON intelligent houses is air conditioning. When a temperature sensor passes the temperature information to the in-house control bus, an intelligent air conditioner either heats or cools a room according to a built-in program. A very intelligent controller that controls simple air conditioners can control several rooms by building an optimum strategy and controlling the dumb air conditioners by sending them explicit commands to set the air temperature at the outlets.

### (d) The position-independent symmetrical network

Conventional local area networks (LANs) can be included in this category. The nodes that make up these networks are computer systems such as BTRON, ITRON, and CTRON-based machines. The addresses of the nodes are logical in the sense that the physical location of the node has nothing to do with its logical address.

The transactions done in this network are just like the ones on a conventional network. Inter-network communication at this level will be as popular as it is today.

This type of LAN can be connected to the MTRON intelligent network via a TRON-based gateway so that the information from, say, an MTRON intelligent building can be passed on to other intelligent buildings, other LANs, or sent into global network.

### (e) The switching network

This is essentially the global telecommunication network of today. The switching network is used for long distance communication among intelligent buildings, or places geographically separated by a long distance. It will be an important part of the MTRON-based HFDS.

An MTRON network combines the above mentioned networks in a hierarchical manner. (*Fig. 2*)

### 3. MTRON COMMUNICATION PROTOCOLS

It is imperative that every intelligent object on an MTRON network follow a set of standard communication protocols. Otherwise, the HFDS will not be able to offers sophisticated services.

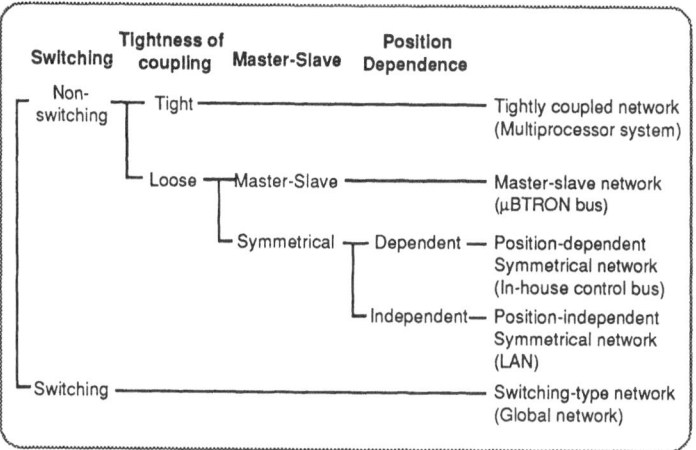

*Fig. 2  MTRON network structure*

The communication protocol of MTRON must support a wide range of applications, from simple ITRON-based embedded computers[4] to highly complex artificial-intelligence-based servers.

It is probably possible to meet this variety of applications by providing a set of protocol programs for computers. In other words, if you have protocol drivers for different devices such as BTRON-based personal computers, CTRON-based database servers, or ITRON-based embedded computers, you can possibly control them in a network today.

However, such an ad-hoc approach breaks down when handling new devices added to networks such as MTRON networks, which are open networks. A node can be added or deleted during the operation of an MTRON network. Unless we specify that all nodes follow a standard set of network protocols, it is impossible to keep the network open.

In deciding on the set of communication protocols, we have come to the conclusion that we cannot satisfy future application needs by providing a statically fixed protocol. This is because trying to accommodate all application needs will increase the size of protocol and we can't possibly foresee all the needs of future applications in 1990s. ITRON-based embedded computers cannot have all the necessary drivers for different protocols.

So instead of providing for fixed interface specifications, we have decided on a dynamically specifiable and programmable interface using TULS (TRON UNIVERSAL

LANGUAGE SYSTEM)[2]. The approach is to design (or specify) all interfaces using an underlying specification language. TULS is the first step taken in this direction.

Static specifications, of course, are very important at this time, and TULS can work with static specifications. On the other hand, an approach based on a dynamically specifiable interface can bring much execution overhead. Thus it should be stressed here that this approach has been taken to bring flexibility in the future.

By using TULS, it is possible to reconfigure an interface in order to balance the load between two sub-systems. Also, it offers a good way to assure the compatibility of different implementations that follow the *TRON Design Guidelines*.

MTRON communication protocols will be described in TULS. A data format rule, a derivative of TULS, is the TRON Application Databus (TAD) and application programs are expected to use the TAD data format. Aside from ordinary data such as text or figures, TAD has special rules to describe physical locations inside buildings so that MTRON can be used to manage buildings.

## 4. THE HFDS AND THE PHYSICAL ENVIRONMENT

Intelligent objects used in MTRON intelligent buildings or houses offer services to make the physical surroundings hospitable.

In order to do this, intelligent objects must sense environmental conditions such as temperature, humidity, atmospheric pressure, wind strength, wind direction, noise level, and luminosity. By using MTRON, intelligent objects exchange this data so that they can control the environment in cooperation with each other as they actively changing the state of the environment based on the data of sensors.

For an air conditioning system, it could be argued that current air conditioners that sample locally are sufficient.

However, in complex modern buildings, we must deal with unexpected situations involving interactions among many computer-controlled objects. For example, the following situation can occur. A standing lamp is moved to a new location. It so happens that a temperature sensor is located near the lamp. Instead of monitoring the average room temperature, the sensor picks up the heat from the lamp, and, as a result, the air conditioner places the room temperature at an undesired level.

In an MTRON environment, the movement of lamp is detected if the lamp is an intelligent object, and the air conditioner can handle the local disturbance caused by the heat generated from the lamp.

In order for an MTRON network to handle the above situation, it is necessary that for the computers to be able to reflect the physical surroundings faithfully. Thus we had to introduce the concept of physical location and physical distance between the intelligent objects in the management of MTRON-based systems.

Incorporating the concept of, and information from the physical position of the node makes it possible to handle the above-mentioned situation, if the controller is capable of deducing that the lamp is too close to the temperature sensor so that it can make the proper adjustment.

Another simple example in which the concept of physical location plays an important role is turning down the volume of televisions (or audio devices) during a telephone call. By knowing that the handset is off the hook and a call is being made, an MTRON network can instruct the television set to turn down its volume. How quiet it becomes depends on the physical distance between the telephone and television. If the call is routed to other room, the television can return to its original volume. This operation also requires that information on the physical location of the active nodes must be available on the MTRON network.

The notion of the physical location of active nodes extends to human users as well. Each user has a set of preferences, say, in the case of building control. Some people in a jointly occupied room want cooler air, while others want to have warmer air, for example.

By monitoring the location of all the human beings, it becomes possible to control the surroundings of each human being according to that person's set of preferences registered in the MTRON network. Such preferences are a natural extension of the preferences that are handled in each BTRON—namely, the choice of language, the keyboard layout, function key assignment, etc. Thus we literally take the notion of personalizing the environment from the limited world of computer desktop, and extend it to the living environment.

## 5. THE PROPAGATION OF INFORMATION

The information flow inside an MTRON network has interesting features suited to the application area for which MTRON is meant.

### (a) Non-uniform format

In order to reduce unnecessary traffic, we use different data communication formats for the different layers of an MTRON network. This is due to the different requirements of each layer. We do not intend to provide transparent logical address space in which the same communication format is used for all the nodes. In a small MTRON network, it makes sense to use a specialized data format, say, for transferring sensor data in realtime. So we change the format according to both the purpose and the part of network in which the data flows.

**(b) Group addressing in network**

Many MTRON networks use broadcasting. For example, an in-house control bus for intelligent buildings uses broadcasting. We use the notion of group addressing so that data packets on the network are screened according to type. When group addressing is used, receivers read in only the data packets that have the group address of that receiver.

The reason we use group addressing is to reduce the overhead on the receivers. This scheme is also intended to reduce the overhead incurred by simple broadcasting.

A receiver usually has to be in many groups. For example, in the case of an intelligent building, an intelligent air conditioner may have to be in two groups—one for receiving outdoor temperature readings, and another for receiving the status of doors and windows. We use a bit table to specify the group to which a particular receiver belongs.

A newly added node can have all its group bits set when it is installed in a network. Later, the application running in the node can gradually reset these group bits to eliminate the handling of unnecessary information.

**(c) Location information**

Intelligent objects identify themselves and also report their locations to the MTRON network. Each MTRON local network retains a database on the position, the identity, and the functionality of its nodes. When a new node is installed, a managing function is invoked to update the necessary database information, and, if necessary, the intelligent objects affected by the new nodes are notified by this managing function. Thereafter, the nodes will communicate with each other to offer desired services such as keeping the room temperature at acceptable level.

**(d) Seeping**

Some of the data on MTRON networks will be sent and received without using active application programs. This is because data is vital in certain basic applications, such as the control of MTRON intelligent buildings. We refer to the sending of data in this way as the "seeping of data."

Seeping is essentially broadcasting in a position-dependent local area network or a global network. The MTRON system takes care of what information to send and where to send it. In the case of building management, the MTRON network takes care of seeping through the in-house control bus, local area network, and the global network that is connected to them.

## 6. Summary

The design of MTRON has to satisfy the needs of various applications while assuring real-time responsiveness. We have taken a hierarchical network approach to achieve this. TULS is used to describe interface specifications in MTRON in a flexible manner. Intelligent objects in MTRON-based networks will be used as office and home equipment, as well as parts of our living environment–MTRON intelligent buildings and houses. Intelligent objects networked by MTRON are destined to play an important role in the computerized society of the future.

## REFERENCES

[1]   K. Sakamura "The Objectives of the TRON Project," TRON Project 1987 (Proc. of the Third TRON Project Symposium), pp.3-16, Springer-Verlag, 1987.

[2]   K. Sakamura "TRON UNIVERSAL LANGUAGE SYSTEM," TRON Project 1988 (Proc. of the Fifth TRON Project Symposium, this volume), Springer-Verlag, 1988.

[3]   K. Sakamura, K. Tsurumi and H. Kato "μBTRON Bus: Design and Evaluation of Musical Data Transfer," TRON Project 1987 (Proc. of the Third TRON Project Symposium), pp.127-138, Springer-Verlag, 1987.

[4]   K. Sakamura "ITRON: An Overview," TRON Project 1987 (Proc. of the Third TRON Project Symposium), pp. 29-34, Springer-Verlag, 1987.

**Ken Sakamura** is an associate professor in the Department of Information Science, University of Tokyo. He received his Ph.D. in electrical engineering from Keio University (Yokohama) in 1979. As one of Japan's foremost computer architects, he has been the driving force behind the TRON Project, which he started in 1984 to build a new computer architecture for 1990s and beyond. The TRON Architecture he designed for this purpose has now expanded to include applications in buildings and furniture.

Sakamura serves on the editorial board of *IEEE Micro,* a magazine published by the Institute of Electrical and Electronics Engineers (IEEE), and he heads the project promotion committee of the TRON Association. He is also a member of the Japan Information Processing Society (JIPS); the Institute of Electronics, Information and Communication Engineers (IEICE); the Association for Computing Machinery; and he is a senior member of IEEE. He has received the best paper award from IEICE twice; the JIPS best paper award once, the IEEE best annual article award, in addition to other awards from Japanese and overseas organizations.

The above author may be reached at Department of Information Science, Faculty of Science, University of Tokyo, 7-3-1 Hongo, Bunkyo-ku, Tokyo, Japan.

# Chapter 2:  ITRON

# HI8: A Realtime Operating System with μITRON Specifications for the H8/500

Hiroshi Takeyama,Tsuyoshi Shimizu, Manabu Kobayakawa
Hitachi Ltd.

**ABSTRACT**

The ITRON specification was originally designed for general-purpose 16-bit microprocessors. Recent years, however, have seen the appearance of ASICs incorporating 8- and 16-bit microprocessors and supporting modules on a single chip with an application-specific architecture. To accommodate these single-chip microcomputer devices, the TRON project has created a subset of the ITRON specification, designated as the μITRON specification.

Hitachi Ltd. has implemented the μITRON specification for its H8/500 Series of single-chip microcomputers which feature a 16-bit CPU core. Designated HI8, the implementation is part of Hitachi's HI Series of operating systems. HI8 is targeted particularly at system-on-a-chip configurations. This paper discusses the design philosophy and performance of HI8 and its method of implementing the μITRON specification.

**Keywords** : ITRON, μITRON, Single chip microcomputer, Interrupt, Kernel

## 1. THE HI SERIES

Intended for embedded applications, the HI Series of realtime operating systems implements the ITRON specification on both the 68000 microprocessor [1] and the H Series. The H Series is a series of 8- to 32-bit microprocessors and microcomputers with an original architecture.

As shown in *Table 1*, the HI Series includes both operating systems (designated HIxx) conforming to the ITRON specification [2] [3] [4], and file management systems (designated HIxxA) conforming to the ITRON/FILE specification [5].

Files created by file management systems conforming to the ITRON/FILE specification are designed to be compatible with files created by file management systems conforming to the BTRON specification [6] [7], subject to certain restrictions. Accordingly, when

BTRON-specification computers are implemented, it will be easy to migrate these files onto those computers.

The H8/500 Series of microcomputers are designed for control of medium-scale office, industrial, and consumer equipment. Their main purpose is to provide high-speed processing in a compact package, so file management is not supported.

Table 1  *HI Series and ITRON Specifications*

| HI Series | | 68000 | H Series Microprocessors | | |
|-----------|--|-------|------|-----|---------|
| | | | H8/500 | H16 | H32/200 |
| HIxx: | operating systems conforming to the ITRON specification | ● | ● | ● | ○ |
| HIxxA: | file management systems conforming to the ITRON/FILE specification | ● | — | ● | ○ |

●: Now available  ○: Being developed  —: Not supported

The realtime operating systems of the HI Series are designed to take advantage of the features of the processors on which they run.

The H8/500 chips are high-performance, single-chip microcomputers with on-chip memory, timer, and I/O functions in addition to their high-speed CPU core with an internal 16-bit architecture. The HI8 operating system is highly compact so that it can operate in the single-chip mode (using only on-chip ROM and RAM).

The HI16 operating system is designed to take advantage of the switchable register banks of the H16.

The H32 chips support special instructions for high-speed execution of operating system functions. The HI32 operating system uses these instructions to enhance its realtime capabilities.

The HI Series of operating systems provide not only compatibility with the ITRON specifications but also compatibility within the series, so application programs can easily be ported among HD68000, H8/500, H16, and H32 environments. *Fig.1* shows how the HI Series of operating systems are interrelated.

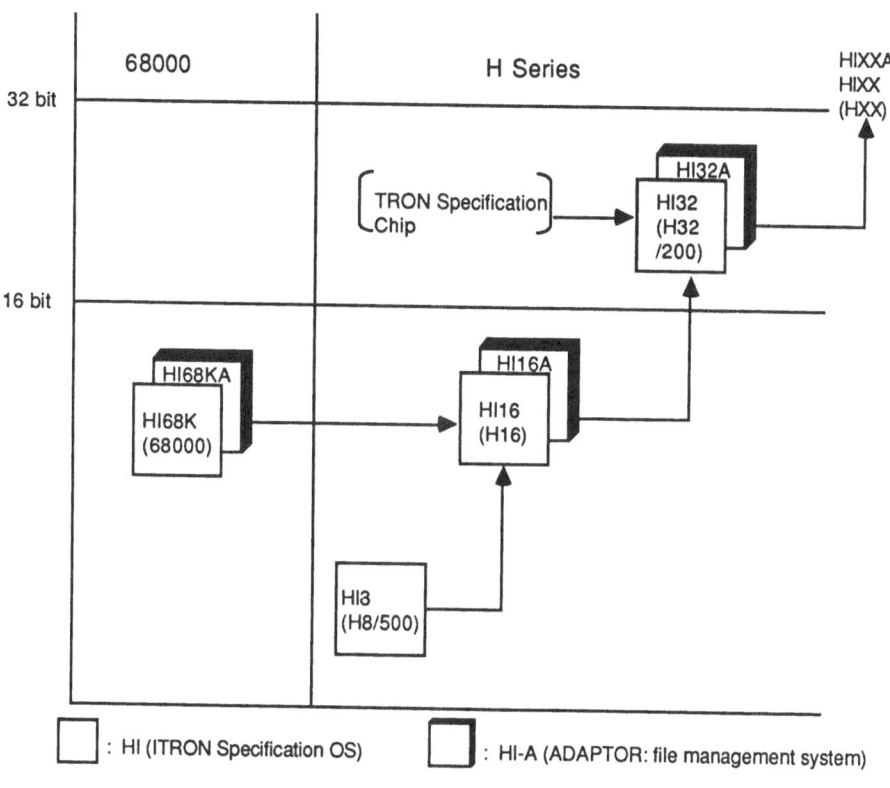

*Fig.1  HI Series of Operating Systems*

## 2. H8/500 ARCHITECTURE

The H8/500 single-chip microcomputers share a common CPU core with an internal 16-bit architecture, but differ in the size of their on-chip ROM and RAM and the configuration of their I/O ports, timers and other peripheral modules. An instruction prefetch function and 16-bit access to the on-chip ROM and RAM contribute to the high speed of these chips. Minimum instruction execution time is 0.2μs (at 10 MHz). Multiply and divide instructions execute in 1.6 to 3.0μs. The address space depends on the operating mode of the chip. The single-chip mode uses only the on-chip ROM and RAM. The expanded modes allow access to external memory, enlarging the address space to up to 64K bytes in the expanded minimum mode and 1M byte in the expanded maximum mode. *Fig.2* shows a memory map of the H8/532 chip in these three modes. HI8 operates in the single-chip mode and expanded minimum mode.

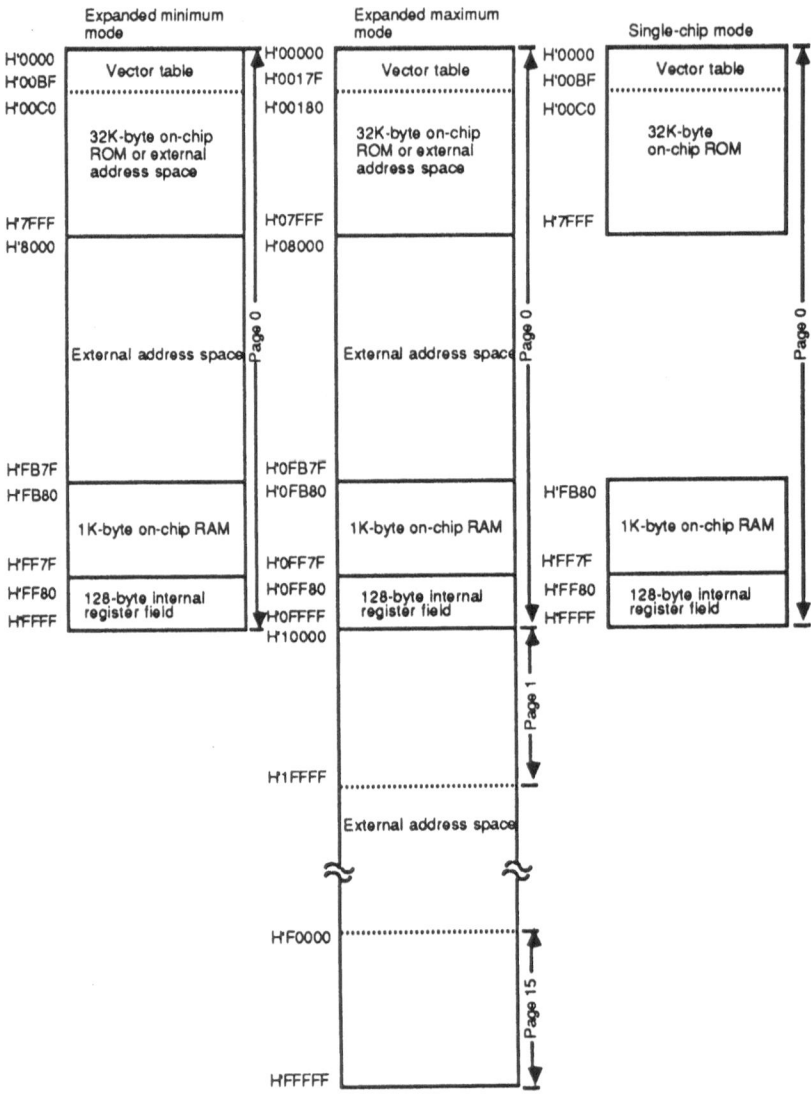

*Fig.2  H8/532 Memory Map in Each Mode*

## 2.1 CPU PROGRAMMING MODEL

*Fig.3* shows the H8/500 register configuration. There are eight 16-bit general registers (R0 to R7), two 16-bit control registers (PC and SR/CCR), and five 8-bit control registers. The general-register architecture simplifies programming because the registers can store either addresses or data. R7 also acts as the stack pointer, and R6 as the frame pointer.

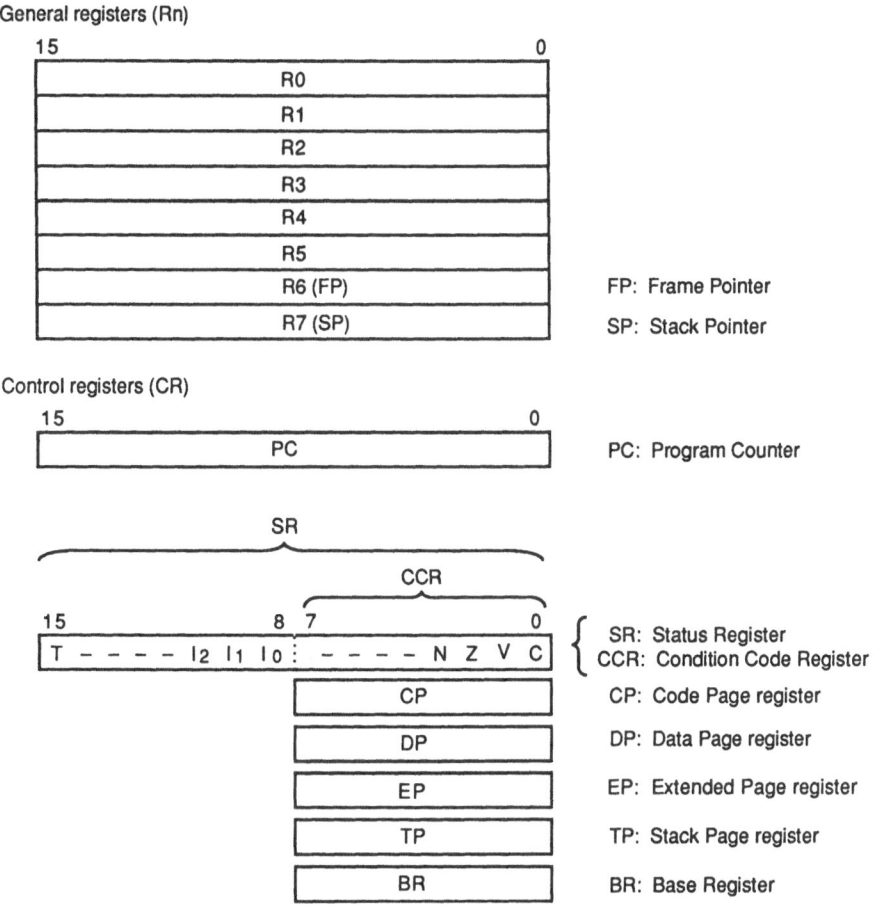

General registers (Rn)

FP: Frame Pointer
SP: Stack Pointer

Control registers (CR)

PC: Program Counter

SR: Status Register
CCR: Condition Code Register
CP: Code Page register
DP: Data Page register
EP: Extended Page register
TP: Stack Page register
BR: Base Register

*Fig.3  H8/500 Programming Model*

The status register (SR) indicates the internal state of the CPU. The lower half of the SR is referred to as the condition code register (CCR). Its 8 bits can be accessed as a 1-byte condition code.

Bits 10 to 8 are the interrupt mask, which indicates the priority of the program currently executing, from 7 (high) to 0 (low). Interrupt requests of the indicated priority level or lower are not accepted.

The base register stores the base address (upper 8 bits of an address within page zero) used in the short absolute addressing mode. The base address can be located on any 256-

byte boundary. The short absolute addressing mode specifies an offset with respect to the base address.

The page registers are used in the expanded maximum mode to expand the address space up to 1M byte. They contain the upper 8 bits of a 24-bit address.

## 2.2 INSTRUCTION SET AND ADDRESSING MODES

General instructions support 1.5-orthogonal addressing modes; that is, they support register-register and register-memory operations, and permit the data size and addressing mode to be specified independently. The orthogonality of the instruction set is another feature that simplifies programming. Special instructions such as LNK and UNLK support high-level languages.

## 2.3 ON-CHIP SUPPORTING FUNCTIONS OF THE H8/532

The H8/532 is the first of the microcomputers in the H8/500 Series. *Table 2* lists its on-chip supporting functions. The chip comes with 32K bytes of electrically-programmable or masked ROM and 1024 bytes of RAM. It is well supplied with timers, including three 16-bit free-running timer channels, one 8-bit timer channel, three PWM (Pulse-Width Modulation) timer channels, and a watchdog timer. It is also well endowed with I/O facilities, including one SCI (Serial Communication Interface) channel, an eight-channel A/D converter with 10-bit resolution, and a DTC (Data Transfer Controller).

## 3. HI8: AN H8/500 OPERATING SYSTEM CONFORMING TO THE μITRON SPECIFICATION

## 3.1 DESIGN PHILOSOPHY

Practically all applications of single-chip microcomputers require some sort of realtime operating system. In the past, most system houses developing single-chip microcomputer application software also developed their own operating systems, because no standard, compact, high-performance operating system was available. The HI8 design targets were accordingly to:

1) completely satisfy the standard μITRON realtime operating system specification [8].

2) minimize interrupt response time and the time during which interrupts are masked by the operating system—two critical factors in realtime systems.

*Table 2  H8/532 Specifications*

| CPU | H8/500 CPU (internal 16-bit architecture) |
|---|---|
| ROM | 32K Bytes (PROM or masked ROM) |
| RAM | 1024 Bytes |
| Timers | 16-Bit free-running timer module—3 channels |
| | (three input capture pins, six output compare pins) |
| | 8-Bit timer module—1 channel (two compare registers) |
| | PWM timer module—3 channels |
| | Watchdog timer—1 channel |
| SCI | 1 Channel (asynchronous and synchronous modes) |
| A/D | 10-Bit resolution, 8 channels (single and scan modes) |
| INTC | 3 External interrupts |
| | 19 On-chip interrupts |
| | 8 Priority levels |
| DTC | On-chip data transfer controller |
| WSC | On-chip wait-state controller |
| I/O ports | 57 Input/output pins |
| | 8 Input-only pins |
| Package | 84-Pin PLCC |
| | 84-Pin windowed PLCC |
| | 80-Pin QFP |
| Process | CMOS, 1.3μm |

3) reduce the size of the object code sufficiently to enable both the operating system and application software to execute in the on-chip ROM (32K) and RAM (1K) of the H8/532.

## 3.2 FEATURES

As the following summary shows, besides implementing the μITRON specification, the HI8 operating system provides a number of additional features.

### (a) Emphasis on realtime capabilities

A realtime operating system must be fast enough to respond immediately to requests originating in external devices or the microcomputer itself. HI8 provides submillisecond response to asynchronous external interrupt requests and requests for process (task) switching.

Realtime speed can be further enhanced by eliminating the OS checks of system call parameters.

Although HI8 is a compact operating system designed for single-chip architectures, it employs double-linked lists throughout to ensure a fixed OS processing time independent of the scale (number of tasks and other objects) of the user system. The ready queues are managed using bit-mapped tables and a binary search algorithm to minimize the maximum overhead time, ensuring that task switching can be completed within a fixed time horizon. The net result of this and other measures is a high-speed realtime operating system with the performance criteria listed in *Table 3*.

*Table 3 HI8 Performance Criteria*

| Performance criteria | Value |
|---|---|
| Interrupt-masked time | Max. 15µs |
| Task dispatching time* | Max. 24µs |

* Time required to find the next task to be executed, switch from the current task context to the next task context, and dispatch the next task.

**(b) Complies with level 3 of the µITRON specification**

Compliance with level 3 of the µITRON specification simplifies the porting of application programs to or from other operating systems conforming to the ITRON specification.

**(c) Supports system configurations using only on-chip ROM and RAM**

HI8 has a building-block structure with functional modules that can be selected as required by user systems. The operating system itself is highly compact, with a size that ranges from 1.9K bytes (minimum) to 4.7K bytes (maximum) depending on the modules selected. The on-line debugger is structured to require only 2.5K bytes (minimum) to 5.0K bytes (maximum) of memory. The OS work memory includes a fixed region of 18 bytes and a table region which varies according to the system. One task ready queue table is created for each task priority level; the space occupied by these tables depends on the number of task priority levels in the system. Additional tables are needed for managing tasks, mailboxes, and other objects, but only the necessary number of tables are created. The size of the stack used by the operating system depends on the number of interrupt levels employed. All OS work areas are thus proportioned to the scale of the user system. *Table 4* lists the sizes of the tables used for managing various objects.

*Table 4 Size of Object Management Tables*

| Object | Table size |
|---|---|
| Task | 16 Bytes |
| Event flag | 4 Bytes |
| Semaphore | 6 Bytes |
| Mailbox | 6 Bytes |
| Memory pool | 8 Bytes |

The H8/532 has 32K bytes of on-chip ROM and 1K byte of on-chip RAM. In small systems, this provides sufficient space for both HI8 and the application programs. The on-chip timers and I/O ports enable an entire system to be configured on a single chip.

HI8 can operate in either the single-chip mode or expanded minimum mode of the H8/532. The single-chip mode provides a maximum of nine parallel I/O ports. If the system will not fit into the on-chip ROM and RAM, however, external ROM or RAM can be added to accommodate the system configuration.

### (d) Standard on-line debugger

An efficient, on-line debugger is supplied as a standard feature of HI8. The debugger enables an arbitrary task to be debugged on-line in the multitasking environment of the user application system without affecting other tasks currently executing. It provides seventeen debug commands for controlling task execution, setting breakpoints, and obtaining task status information.

### (e) Quick, easy evaluation using an H8/532 evaluation board

The ZTAT (Zero Turn-Around Time) versions of the H8/532 chip are user-programmable. With an H8/532 evaluation board, the user can evaluate HI8 performance easily by running HI8 from RAM on the evaluation board instead of from the H8/532's on-chip ROM.

### 3.3 IMPLEMENTATION LEVEL OF THE μITRON SPECIFICATION BY HI8

The ITRON specification is basically designed for a 16-bit processor, but the μITRON specification is intended to cover a wide variety of microcomputer systems, including 8-bit microprocessors and single-chip microcomputers with limited memory space. The μITRON specification therefore demands less functionality than the ITRON specification, allows considerable freedom in implementing the system call specifications, and permits subsetting of functions at the OS level. The system calls are classified into levels from 1 to 5, representing different levels of indispensability.

Level 1 defines the minimum set of mandatory functions required by the μITRON specification. Only three tasks statuses are implemented: ready, wait, and run. Level 2 implements four tasks statuses: ready, wait, run, and dormant. Level 3 supports all the task statuses defined in the μITRON specification.

*Table 5* lists the HI8 system calls. HI8 supports a superset of level 3 of the μITRON specification, including all the level-3 system calls and additional task termination handler and exception handler functions that are defined in the ITRON specification but excluded from the μITRON specification. The basic difference between HI8 and the original ITRON specification is that HI8 does not support dynamic generation of objects or dynamic definition of handlers.

To permit the OS size to be optimized for the application system, HI8 is divided into functional modules. The basic module (1.9K bytes) supports the three task statuses required at the minimum μITRON level. The priority manipulation module, status reference module, timer management module, task termination module, exception handling module, task start/end module, and other functional modules can be selected as needed. (See *Fig.4*)

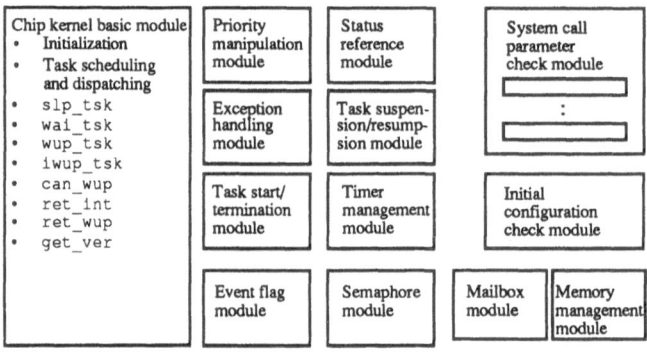

*Fig.4  Chip Kernel Module Configuration*

*Table 5 HI8 System Calls (μITRON Specification Level 3)*

| No. | Key word | System call | Function |
|-----|----------|-------------|----------|
| | Task control | | |
| 1 | Start | sta_tsk | Start task |
| 2 | Exit | ext_tsk | Exit task |
| 3 | Terminate | ter_tsk | Terminate task |
| 4 | Priority | chg_pri | Change task priority |
| 5 | | ichg_pri | |
| 6 | Queue | rot_rdq | Rotate ready queue |
| 7 | | irot_rdq | |
| 8 | Status | get_tid | Get task identifier |
| 9 | | tsk_sts | Get task status |
| | Task synchronization | | |
| 10 | Suspend | sus_tsk | Suspend task |
| 11 | | isus_tsk | |
| 12 | Resume | rsm_tsk | Resume task |
| 13 | | irsm_tsk | |
| 14 | Wait | slp_tsk | Sleep task |
| 15 | | wai_tsk | Wait for wake up task |
| 16 | Wake up | wup_tsk | Wake up task (with queuing) |
| 17 | | iwup_tsk | Wake up task (non-task) |
| 18 | Cancel | can_wup | Cancel wake-up task |
| 19 | Set | set_flg | Set event flag |
| 20 | | iset_flg | Set event flag (non-task) |
| 21 | Clear | clr_flg | Clear event flag |
| 22 | Wait | wai_flg | Wait for event flag to be set |
| 23 | Poll | pol_flg | Poll event flag |

*Table 5 HI8 System Calls (μITRON Specification Level 3) (cont.)*

| No. | Key word | System call | Function |
|-----|----------|-------------|----------|
| | Semaphore control | | |
| 24 | Signal | sig_sem | Signal semaphore (V operation) |
| 25 | | isig_sem | Signal semaphore (non-task) |
| 26 | Wait | wai_sem | Wait on semaphore (P operation) |
| 27 | Get | preq_sem | Poll and request semaphore |
| | Mailbox control | | |
| 28 | Send | snd_msg | Send message to mailbox |
| 29 | | isnd_msg | Send message to mailbox (non-task) |
| 30 | Wait | rcv_msg | Receive message from mailbox |
| 31 | Receive | prcv_msg | Poll and receive message |
| | Interrupt handling | | |
| 32 | Return | ret_int | Return from interrupt handler |
| 33 | | ret_wup | Return and wake up task |
| 34 | Mask | chg_ims | Change interrupt mask |
| 35 | Status | ims_sts | Get interrupt mask status |
| | Exception handling | | |
| 36 | Return | ret_exc | Return from exception handler |
| | Memory management | | |
| 37 | Wait | get_blk | Get fixed-length memory block |
| 38 | Get | pget_blk | Poll and get fixed-length memory block |
| 39 | Release | rel_blk | Release fixed-length memory block |
| | Timer Management | | |
| 40 | Set | set_tim | Set time |
| 41 | Get | get_tim | Get time |
| | Miscellaneous | | |
| 42 | Version | get_ver | Get version NO |

## 3.4 HI8 SYSTEM ARCHITECTURE

*Fig.5* shows the HI8 system architecture. The chip kernel provides functions for task management, task synchronization, inter-task synchronization and communication, interrupt handling, exception handling, memory management, and timer management. The debugger and I/O drivers are controlled by the chip kernel and execute as tasks, similar to application tasks.

The interrupt handlers and some of the exception-handling functions of the chip kernel can be generated by the user to suit the application system.

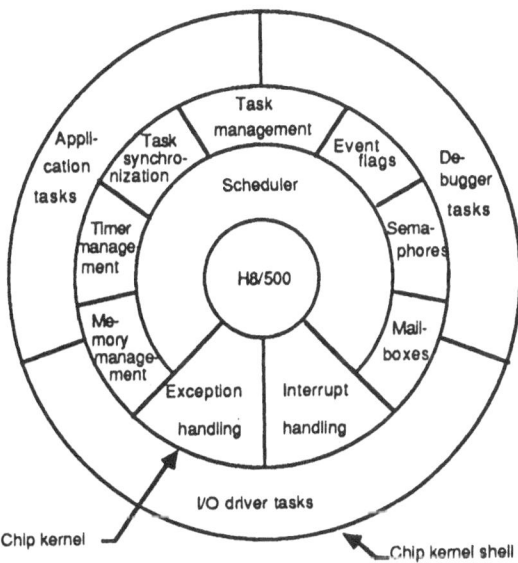

*Fig.5  HI8 System Configuration*

## 3.5 CHIP KERNEL FUNCTIONS

### (a) Task Management

HI8 can manage up to 64 tasks. *Fig.6* shows the task status transitions when the full HI8 configuration is used.

Shading indicates the task statuses supported by the minimum HI8 configuration, equivalent to level 1 of µITRON.

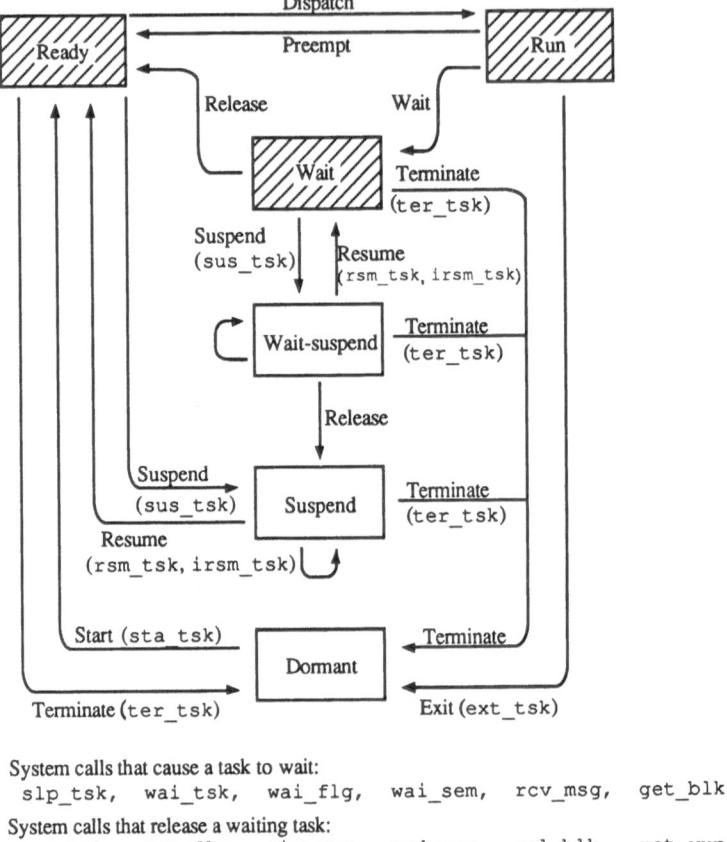

System calls that cause a task to wait:
`slp_tsk, wai_tsk, wai_flg, wai_sem, rcv_msg, get_blk`
System calls that release a waiting task:
`wup_tsk, set_flg, sig_sem, snd_msg, rel_blk, ret_wup,`
`iwup_tsk, iset_flg, isig_sem, isnd_msg`

*Fig.6 Task Status Transitions*

The task status transitions are equivalent to those of the ITRON specification except that there is no "non-existent" state. All tasks are initially in the dormant state. As a result, a task becomes dispatchable immediately on request, and application program size can be reduced. Tasks are generated by specifications made when the system is configured.

The scheduler dispatches ready tasks in order of task priority, which is denoted by a number from 1 to 32. Priority can be adjusted dynamically by the `chg_pri` system call. Tasks with equal priority are queued in a separate ready queue for each priority level. In standard scheduling the ready queue is a first-in-first-out (FIFO) queue. User-defined round-robin scheduling is also possible, in which the ready queue is rotated by a `rot_rdq` system call, enabling tasks on the same priority level to be scheduled on an equal basis.

For each task, a task termination handler can be provided to perform termination processing when the task is terminated by the operating system due to an event such as an exception or the start of another task.

### (b) Task synchronization

The task synchronization function performs basic task synchronization by executing the `wai_tsk`, `slp_tsk`, and `wup_tsk` system calls, and can suspend or resume tasks with the `sus_tsk` and `rsm_tsk` system calls. Systems that do not require complex forms of synchronization can operate using these functions alone. The `wai_tsk` system call can be used to execute tasks at controlled times.

### (c) Inter-task synchronization and communication

Three types of inter-task synchronization and communication are supported: event flags, semaphores, and mailboxes. The system can accommodate a maximum of 64 of each of these types of objects. They must be built in when the system is configured.

1) Event flags

    The μITRON specification offers a choice between single-bit and multiple-bit event flags. Single-bit event flags conserve memory space, but HI8 opts for multiple-bit event flags, since these permit synchronization to be based on combinations of events. Taking advantage of the internal 16-bit architecture of the H8/500, a single event flag can control 16 events (the number of bits in the event flag). A system call can cause a task to wait for one or all of a specified subset of the 16 bits to become true.

2) Semaphores

    Semaphores are used for allocating resources to tasks. A semaphore is essentially a counter (0 – 65, 535) indicating the number of units of a resource currently available. When a task needs a unit of the resource it performs a P operation: a system call stating that one unit is required. If a unit is available, the semaphore is decremented by one. If no unit is available, or if another task is already waiting for the resource, the requesting task must queue up until the resource becomes available.

3) Mailboxes

    Mailboxes are used for synchronization that involves an exchange of data between tasks. The sending task specifies a mailbox and sends a message to it. The receiving task specifies the same mailbox to receive the message.

In the ITRON specification, when a system call causes a task to wait for one of the above three objects, a parameter can be specified to limit the maximum waiting time. The waiting time must then be monitored by the operating system. In μITRON, to reduce the size of the operating system the waiting time monitoring function is removed from these inter-task synchronization and communication functions. In its place, a simpler function is added that monitors these objects by polling. Systems that require it can implement time monitoring by using this polling function and the `wai_tsk` system call.

### (d) Memory management

HI8 allocates and deallocates blocks of memory requested by tasks from continuous memory extents called memory pools. The memory block size can be specified separately for each memory pool when the system is configured.

### (e) Interrupt handling

One of the features of the H8/500 is its powerful built-in interrupt controller that can control eight levels of interrupts. The interrupt sources are three external signals (IRQ0, IRQ1, NMI), and the on-chip supporting modules (timers, SCI, A/D), each of which has its own set of interrupts. An arbitrary interrupt level can be assigned to each interrupt source. *Fig.7* shows the hardware sequence executed at an interrupt.

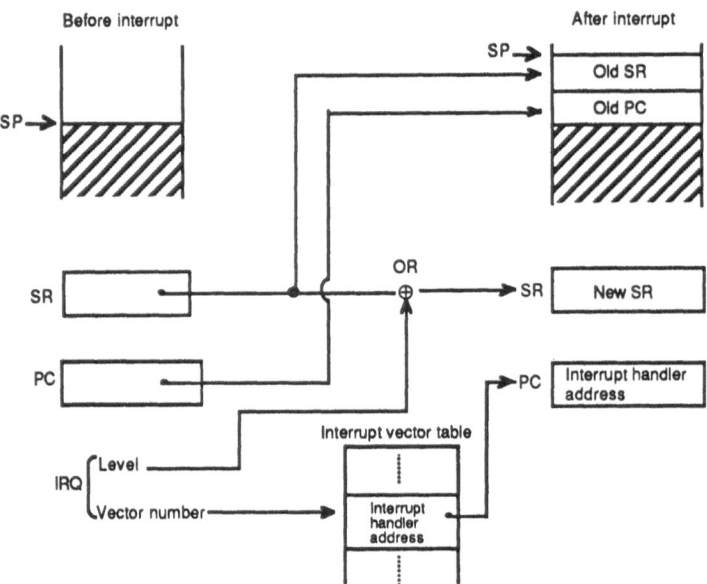

*Fig.7  H8/500 Hardware Interrupt-Handling Sequence*

When the CPU accepts an interrupt, the current PC and SR contents are saved on the stack and the address of the interrupt handler for the specific interrupt is fetched from the interrupt vector table and loaded into the PC. At the same time, the interrupt mask bits in the SR are set to mask further interrupts of the same or lower level. HI8 uses the innate interrupt features of the H8/500 and does not interfere with interrupts in any way. The OS overhead in interrupt handling is therefore essentially zero. User-coded interrupt handler routines are also spared the overhead of mask setting, because interrupts of equal or lower level are masked automatically when the interrupt is accepted.

To reduce the size of ROM code, the addresses of interrupt handlers are obtained directly from the vector table; they are not generated dynamically by system calls. Accordingly, the user must store the handler addresses in the vector table.

An interrupt handler is terminated by the `ret_int` system call, or by the `ret_wup` system call which combines the functions of `ret_int` with task wake-up. To guarantee execution of interrupt handler with the highest priority, the operating system does not switch contexts while an interrupt handler is executing, even if task statuses change. The task switch is instead performed after the interrupt handler has terminated. The same rule is applied to tasks that manipulate the interrupt mask. When a task masks interrupts, the operating system will not switch tasks until the interrupt mask is released, thus guaranteeing the status of the CPU interrupt mask bits during this interval. (See *Fig.8*)

### (f) Exception handling

If an exception occurs while a task is executing, normally the operating system terminates the task, but for the H8/500 exceptions listed below, an exception handler can be created for each task. The exception handler is executed if the exception occurs during that task.

It is also possible to provide a program that analyzes the cause of an unrecoverable exception or undefined interrupt that occurs during execution of nontask processing, or takes action to abort system operation.

If the exception handling module is excluded from the system configuration, user-coded exception handlers are executed directly from the exception vector table without OS intervention.
 − Address error
 − Invalid instruction
 − Zero divide
 − TRAP/VS (Trap If Overflow) instruction
 − Trace
 − TRAPA (Trap Always) instruction

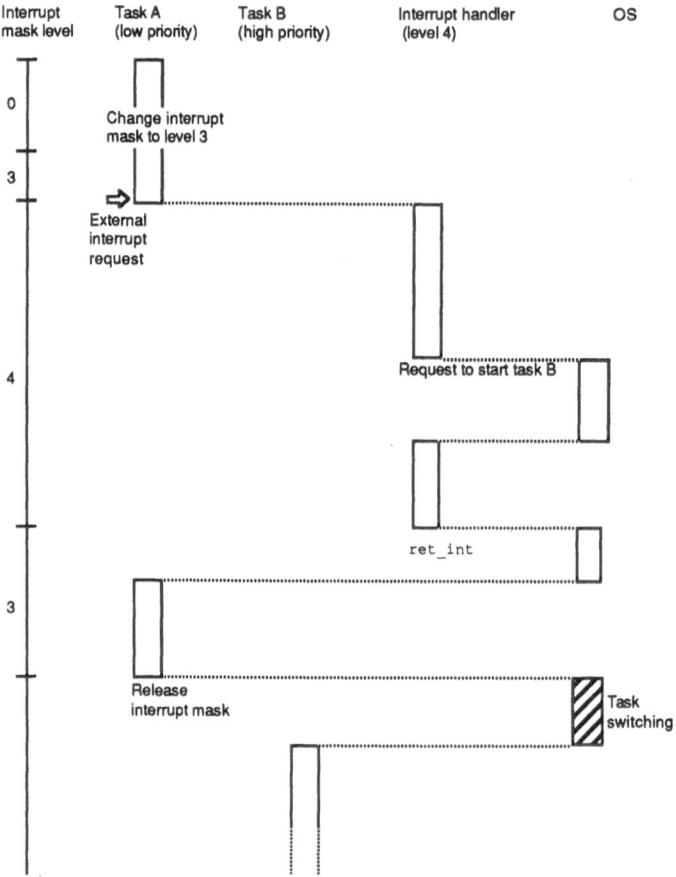

*Fig.8  Interrupt Mask and Task Switching*

## 4. CONCLUSION AND ACKNOWLEDGEMENT

HI8 is a compact operating system based on the μITRON specification that has been developed for the H8/500 Series of single-chip microcomputers.  HI8 fully implements level 3 of the μITRON specification.

Concerning two critical parameters in realtime operation, HI8 has been confirmed to have a maximum interrupt-masked time of 15.0μs and maximum task dispatching time of 24.0μs.  The OS object code has been compressed to a size of 1.9K bytes to 4.7K bytes, leaving ample space for application programs to operate in the on-chip ROM (32K bytes) and RAM (1K byte) of the H8/532.

It is anticipated that realtime operating systems conforming to the μITRON specification will come into use in the single-chip application field. Current plans call for HI8 to be expanded to support levels 4 and 5 of the μITRON specification.

The authors would like to express their gratitude to Dr. Ken Sakamura of the Department of Information Science, Faculty of Science, The University of Tokyo for his guidance in the development of HI8, and to members of The TRON Association for their cooperation in standardizing the external specifications.

REFERENCE

[1]  Hitachi Ltd. (1987) Real-time Operating System HI68K, Personal Media Co. Japan

[2]  K. Sakamura (1984) ITRON Real-time Operating System, Operating System Study Group, Japan, pp 24-34

[3]  K. Sakamura (1985) ITRON Real-time Operating System, Vol. 3 No. 5, J. Robotics Soc. Japan, pp 41-48

[4]  K. Sakamura (1988) Introduction to ITRON, Iwanami-shoten, Japan

[5]  H. Takeyama, T. Shimizu, H. Horikoshi (1987) The HI Series Operating Systems with ITRON. K. Sakamura (ed) TRON Project 1987. Springer-Verlag, Tokyo, Berlin, Heidelberg, New York, London, Paris, pp 57-70

[6]  K. Sakamura (1988) The TRON Project, IEEE Micro, April: 8-14

[7]  K. Sakamura (1987) making of TRON, Kyoritsu Shuppan, Japan

[8]  K. Sakamura (1988) [μITRON], Vol. 1 No. 1, TRON Study Group, Japan

**H. Takeyama** joined Hitachi, Ltd. in 1969 and is now a senior engineer in the Microcomputer System Engineering Dept. at the Musashi Works of Hitachi's Semiconductor Division. Since 1983 he has participated in research and development of realtime operating systems for microcomputers and incircuit emulation software, and in product planning for microcomputer support tools. He received his BA in electronic engineering from Fukuoka Institute of Technology in 1969.

**T. Shimizu** joined Hitachi, Ltd. in 1978 and is now an engineer in the Microcomputer System Engineering Dept. at the Musashi Works of Hitachi's Semiconductor Division. He is currently engaged in research and development of realtime operation systems for microcomputers. He received his BA in informatics from the University of Osaka in 1976 and his master's degree from the same school in 1978.

**M. Kobayakawa** joined Hitachi, Ltd. in 1985 and is now an engineer in the Microcomputer System Engineering Dept. at the Musashi Works of Hitachi's Semiconductor Division. He is currently engaged in research and development of realtime operation systems for microcomputers. He was graduated from Hitachi Keihin Technical college in 1988.

Above authors may be reached at: Musashi Works, Hitachi Ltd., 5-20-1, Josuihon-cho Kodaira, Tokyo, 187 Japan.

# MR7700: Implementation of μ-ITRON Specification on 16-Bit Single-Chip Microcontroller

Kiyoshi Nakata, Hideo Tsubota, Toru Shimizu,
Kazunori Saitoh, Tatsuya Enomoto
Mitsubishi Electric Corporation

**ABSTRACT**

μ-ITRON is a specification of real-time operating system developed in the TRON project for 8 or 16-bit single chip microprocessor and positioned as a subset of ITRON specification. MR7700 is an implementation of the μ-ITRON specification to the Mitsubishi original MELPS7700 series microcontroller, which is a 16-bit single chip microprocessor with some memory and some peripheral circuits. This paper describes the MR7700's design concept, implementation and evaluation of its performance.

**Keywords:** Real-time operating system, Single-chip microcontroller, μ-ITRON specification, MR7700, MELPS7700

## 1. INTRODUCTION

The advance of semiconductor technology makes a microprocessor more powerful and makes it possible to integrate a single chip microprocessor which contains memory and some peripheral circuits in it. Such a single chip microprocessor is called microcontroller and used in many applications such as air conditioners, audio-visual equipments and automobile engines. μ-ITRON real-time operating system specification is established for these single chip microcontrollers embedded in application systems.

MR7700 is the first implemented real-time operating system based on the μ-ITRON specification. It is implemented on MITSUBISHI's MELPS7700 series microcontroller, which is a 16-bit microcontroller containing RAM, ROM, timers and serial I/O's. This paper describes the MR7700's design concept, implementation and its evaluation.

## 2. DESIGN CONCEPT

The advantage of using microcontroller is ability to control several equipments with only a single chip without any other external memory and peripheral chips. We have three major goals in designing MR7700 real-time operating system. First goal is small memory size occupation. MR7700 should be designed small enough to run only on on-chip ROM and RAM with application program code. After evaluating some application programs, MR7700 code size should be less than 6K bytes and data size should be less than 256 bytes.

Second goal is real-time response to coming outer events. An operating system gives some overhead time to an application program. Based on the evaluation of the application programs, task switching time should be less than 100 micro seconds.

Third goal is a flexibly reconfigurable operating system. An embedded real-time controller has wide range of applications. Therefore, flexible reconfiguration of the operating system provides system adapted to each of the application.

The target chip of MR7700 is a MELPS7700 series microcontroller, which has 32K-byte on-chip ROM and 512-byte on-chip RAM. The MELPS7700 microcontroller has some peripheral circuits such as timers, serial I/O's and A/D converters. It has 16-bit wide internal bus and 8 or 16-bit wide external bus. It is driven by 16MHz external clock and the shortest instruction execution cycle is 250 nano seconds.

## 3. MR7700 IMPLEMENTATION

### 3.1 Specification

The μ-ITRON specification is classified into 5 levels, called implementation levels. The relation between implementation levels and task states is shown in *Table 1*.

*Table 1  μ-ITRON Implementation Levels*

| Level | Task States |
|-------|-------------|
| 1 | RUN, READY, WAIT |
| 2 | RUN, READY, WAIT, DORMANT |
| 3-5 | RUN, READY, WAIT, DORMANT, SUSPEND |

MR7700 provides level 1-3 system calls and has 5 task states, RUN, READY, WAIT, DORMANT and SUSPEND, which are enough for wide range of applications. MR7700 includes some system calls of level 4 or 5. For example, REL_WAI system call of level 5 is implemented to avoid endless waiting in the synchronization, because μ-ITRON specification of level 3 does not have time-out mechanism. Timer functions for cyclic handler and alarm handler, which are of level 4, are also implemented on the same reason. *Fig.1* shows system configuration of MR7700. *Table 2* is a table of MR7700 system calls.

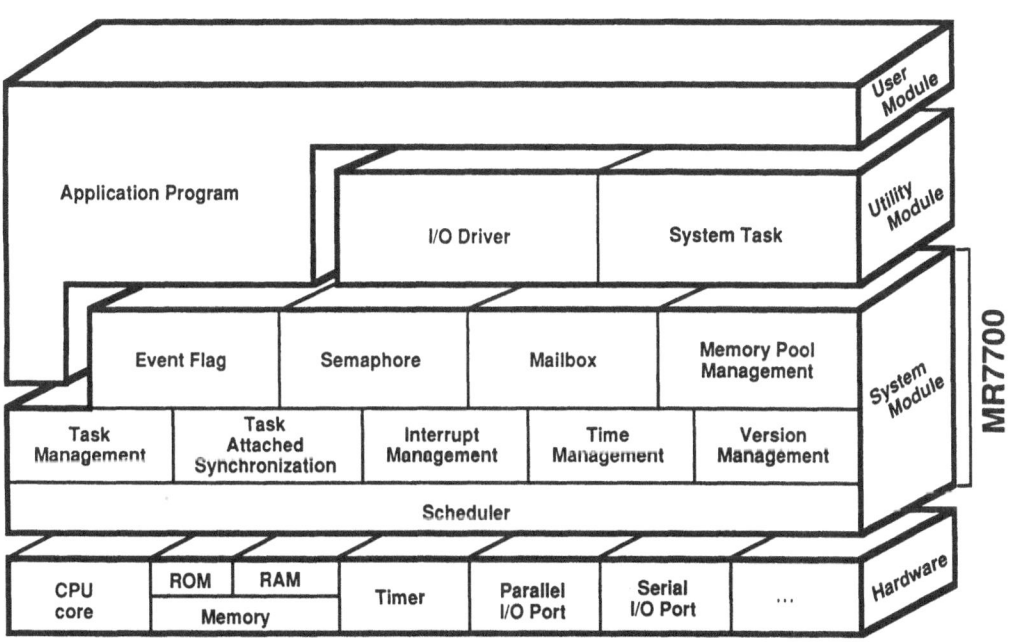

*Fig.1 MR7700 System Configuration*

Table 2  MR7700 System Calls

| System Call | Function |
|---|---|
| 1. Task Management | |
| sta_tsk | Start Task |
| ext_tsk | Exit Task |
| ter_tsk | Terminate Task |
| chg_pri | Change Task Priority |
| ichg_pri | Change Task Priority(For Task Independent Portion) |
| rot_rdq | Rotate Ready Queue |
| irot_rdq | Rotate Ready Queue(For Task Independent Portion) |
| rel_wai | Release Task Wait |
| irel_wai | Release Task Wait(For Task Independent Portion) |
| get_tid | Get Self Task ID |
| tsk_sts | Get Task Status |
| 2. Task Attached Synchronization | |
| sus_tsk | Suspend Task |
| isus_tsk | Suspend Task(For Task Independent Portion) |
| rsm_tsk | Resume Task |
| irsm_tsk | Resume Task(For Task Independent Portion) |
| slp_tsk | Sleep Task |
| wai_tsk | Wait for Wakeup Task |
| wup_tsk | Wakeup Task |
| iwup_tsk | Wakeup Task(For Task Independent Portion) |
| can_wup | Cancel Wakeup Task |
| 3. Interrupt Management | |
| ret_int | Return from Interrupt Handler |
| ret_wup | Return Interrupt and Wakeup Task |
| chg_ipl | Change IPL |
| ipl_sts | Get IPL |
| 4. Memory Pool Management | |
| pget_blk | Poll and Get Memory Block |
| rel_blk | Release Memory Block |
| mpl_sts | Get Memory Pool Status |

*Table 2  MR7700 System Calls (cont.)*

| System Call | Function |
|---|---|
| **5. Synchronization and Communication** | |
| set_flg | Set 1bit EventFlag |
| iset_flg | Set 1bit EventFlag(For Task Independent Portion) |
| clr_flg | Clear 1bit EventFlag |
| wai_flg | Wait 1bit EventFlag |
| cwai_flg | Wait and Clear 1bit EventFlag |
| pol_flg | Poll 1bit EventFlag |
| cpol_flg | Poll and Clear 1bit EventFlag |
| flg_sts | Get 1bit EventFlag Status |
| sig_sem | Signal Semaphore |
| isig_sem | Signal Semaphore(For Task Independent Portion) |
| wai_sem | Wait on Semaphore |
| preq_sem | Poll and Request Semaphore |
| sem_sts | Get Semaphore Status |
| snd_msg | Send Message |
| isnd_msg | Send Message(For Task Independent Portion) |
| rcv_msg | Receive Message |
| prcv_msg | Poll and Receive Message |
| mbx_sts | Get Mailbox Status |
| **6. Time Management** | |
| set_tim | Set Time |
| get_tim | Get Time |
| act_cyc | Activate Cyclic Handler |
| cyh_sts | Get Cyclic Handler Status |
| alh_sts | Get Alarm Handler Status |
| **7. Version Management** | |
| get_ver | Get Version No. |

## 3.2 Optimization of Memory Access Time

MELPS7700 series support 8-bit address space and 24-bit address space. The 8-bit address space, called direct page, enables faster access to the on-chip RAM compared with 24-bit address space. Access time of the direct page is four machine cycles and access time of the 24-bit address space is six machine cycles. Effective use of the direct page is important for operating system performance.

MR7700 uses the direct page for operating system's working variables and TCB's (Task Control Blocks), which provides fast system calls. Also, each of the TCB address is fixed in direct page, and a TCB can be addressed without any address translation overhead. *Fig.2.* shows the memory map of MR7700.

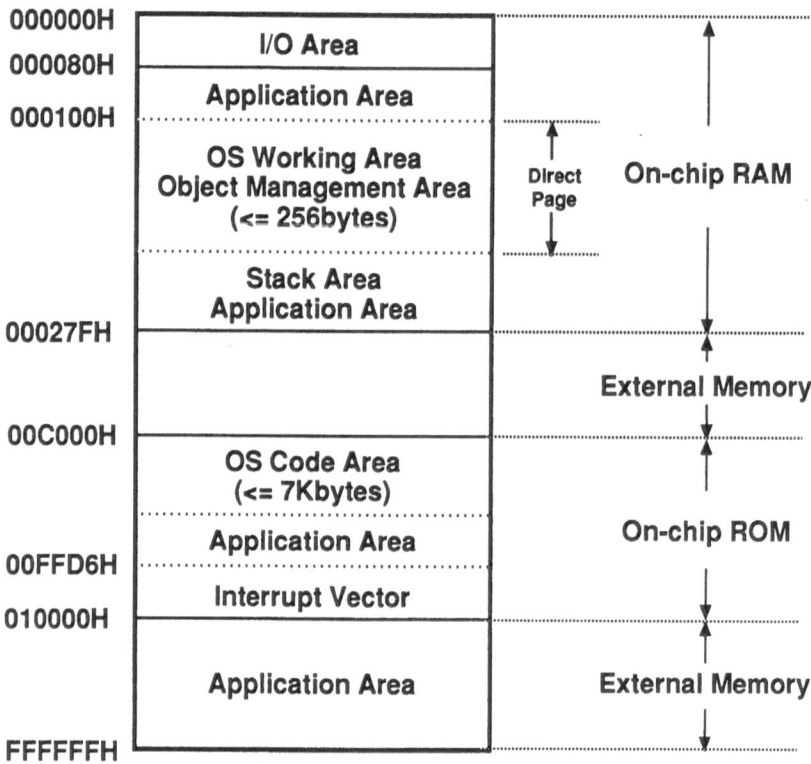

*Fig.2  Memory Map of MR7700 (for M37700M2)*

### 3.3 Optimization of Memory Size

Using the direct page for the operating system's working area, the operating system code size also becomes compact because the instruction code of the direct page access is two bytes in the shortest case.

Run-time generation of an interrupt handler, a cyclic handler and an alarm handler would require extra RAM data area. MR7700 does not have handler generation system calls to minimize the use of RAM area used by the system, but allows handler definition in the ROM area at system initialization time. MR7700 allows users to indicate the number of priority levels to be used in order to minimize the task management area. Additional one priority level requires 1 byte increment of the system area. MR7700 does not have queuing function for suspended tasks to minimize the size of a TCB by recording the suspended state by 1 bit flag.

### 3.4 System Configuration

All system calls of MR7700 are implemented as subroutines and supplied as a program library, so system calls which are used by an application program are collected and linked with the application program code automatically by a linkage editor. MR7700 kernel is also a set of subroutines, so system reconfiguration by a linkage editor is applied the kernel itself. This means automatic optimization of the operating system transparent to users. Users can make an application program only making an initialization data file without complicated system generation procedure.

### 4. EVALUATION

*Table 3* shows memory size of MR7700. ROM size depends on the number of system calls used by an application program. Maximum ROM size becomes 7K bytes when all (51) system calls are linked. Minimum RAM size is 16 bytes and increases with the number of task priority levels (1-63) specified in the initialization phase. The TCB size is 9 bytes. Stack area needs more than 16 bytes for each task.

*Table 3 MR7700 Memory Size*

| ROM | | | |
|---|---|---|---|
| Code | Kernel | | 0.5Kbytes |
| | Kernel + Level 1 | | 2Kbytes |
| | Kernel + Level 1,2 | | 3Kbytes |
| | Maximum (51 System Calls) | | 7Kbytes |
| RAM | | | |
| System Variables | | | $(16 + 1 \times \#\text{priority})$ bytes |
| Tables | Task | | 9 bytes/Task |
| | EventFlag | | 2 bytes/EventFlag |
| | Semaphore | | 3 bytes/Semaphore |
| | Mailbox | | 4 bytes/Mailbox |
| | Maximum Size | | $\leq 256$ bytes(Direct Page) |

For example, 6 task system with 3 event flags, 3 semaphores and 4 priority levels requires 259 bytes RAM area as shown in *Table 4*. In this case, operating system occupys half of the on-chip RAM, so application program can use the rest half for its own use.

*Table 4   RAM Size for a Sample Case*

|  | RAM Size |
|---|---|
| System working area<br>For six tasks<br>For three event-flags<br>For three semaphores | 16 + 4 (for priority) + 20 (for system stack)<br>{ 9 + 25 (for stack) } × 6<br>2 × 3<br>3 × 3 |
| Total | 259 bytes |

*Table 5* shows performance of MR7700 compared withe the performance of MR32, which is an operating system based on ITRON (not μ-ITRON) specification for National Semiconductor's NS32000 series microprocessors. Task switching time by wakeup task system call is 29 micro seconds and interrupt masking time in that case is 20 micro seconds. The interrupt masking time does not depends on the number of tasks. MR7700 is about four times faster than MR32.

*Table 5   Task Switching Time*

| Task wakeup time | MR7700<br>(M37700M2 16MHz) | MR32<br>(NS32332 15MHz) |
|---|---|---|
| By WUP_TSK<br>(Interrupt masking time) | 29 μ sec<br>20 μ sec | 131 μ sec<br>70 μ sec |
| By EventFlag<br>By Semaphore<br>By Mailbox | 38 μ sec<br>30 μ sec<br>35 μ sec | 209 μ sec<br>206 μ sec<br>213 μ sec |

## 5. APPLICATION PROGRAM DEVELOPMENT TOOLS

MELPS7700 series has C compiler, assembler, linkage editor, librarian and emulator as application program development tools. MR7700 application programs are also developed by the tools. C language interface library for MR7700 is supplied in order to write programs in C language. (After preparing system initialization data, users can write application programs by C language with normal manner.) *Fig.3* shows the procedure of developing an application program. After compiling, assembling and linking application program, object code is down-loaded to the target system and debugged by emulator.

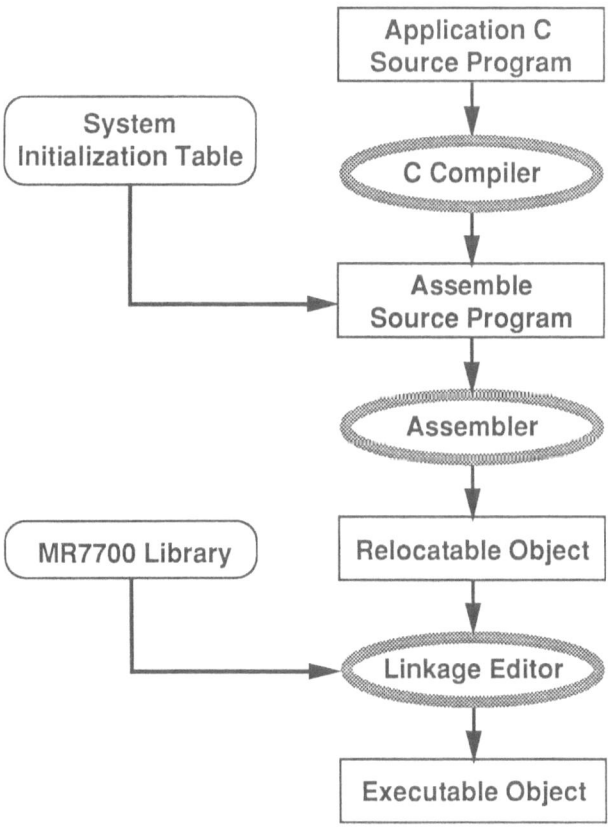

*Fig.3 Development of an application program for MR7700*

## 6. CONCLUSIONS

We successfully implemented the real-time operating system MR7700 based on the μ-ITRON specification on a single chip microprocessor with on-chip small memory and achieved good performance. Task switching time is optimized to be 29 micro seconds. With these results, we expect real-time operating systems based on the μ-ITRON specification will be implemented on many processors and used in various application fields.

The authors wish to acknowledge Dr. Ken Sakamura for his useful discussions and Tatsuya Kamei of Mitsubishi Semiconductor Software corp. for his helpful suggestion.

## REFERENCE

[1] Ken Sakamura, "Design Concepts of μ-ITRON", Proc. of TRON Technical Conference, vol.1, no.1, pp.1-17 (1988) (in Japanese)

**Kiyoshi Nakata:** He received his B.S. and M.S. degrees, both in physics, from Kob e University, Hyogo, Japan, in 1984 and 1986, respectively. He joined Mitsubishi Electric Corporation in 1986. Since then, he has been engaged in research and d evelopment of basic software for microprocessors at LSI Research and Development Laboratory.

**Hideo Tsubota:** He received his B.S. degree, in information technology, from the University of Shizuoka, Shizuoka, Japan, in 1983. He joined Mitsubishi Electric Corporation in 1983. Since then, he has been engaged in research and development of basic software for microprocessors at LSI Research and Development Laborator y.

**Toru Shimizu:** He received his B.S., M.S. and Ph.D. degrees, both in computer sci ence, from University of Tokyo, Tokyo, Japan, in 1981, 1983 and 1986, respective ly. He joined Mitsubishi Electric Corporation in 1986. Since then, he has been e ngaged in the research of VLSI microprocessor architecture and basic software fo r the microprocessor at LSI Research and Development Laboratory. Dr. Shimizu is a member of ACM, IEEE, the Institute of Electronics, Information and Communicati on Engineers of Japan, and Information Processing Society of Japan.

**Kazunori Saitoh:** He received his B.S. and M.S. degrees, both in electrical engin eering, from Waseda University, Tokyo, Japan, in 1975 and 1977, respectively. He joined Mitsubishi Electric Corporation in 1977. From 1977 to 1980, he was engag ed in the development of CAD and electron beam lithography technology at the VL SI Cooperative Laboratory. From 1980, he has been engaged in research and develo pment of VLSI process technologies and basic software for microprocessors at LSI Research and Development Laboratory.

**Tatsuya Enomoto:** He received his B.S. and Ph.D. degrees, both in electronics eng ineering, from University of Tokyo, Tokyo, Japan, in 1962 and 1980, respectively . He joined Mitsubishi Electric Corporation in 1962. From 1962 to 1977, he was e ngaged in wafer process engineering of MOS integrated circuits at Kita-Itami Wor ks. Since 1977, he has been engaged in research and development of VLSI process technologies, gate array design, and advanced microprocessors at LSI Research a nd Development Laboratory. Dr. Enomoto is a member of the Institute of Electroni cs, Information and Communication Engineers of Japan, and the Japan Society of A pplied Physics.

Above authors may be reached at: LSI R&D Laboratory, Mitsubishi Electric Corporation, 4-1 Mizuhara, Itami, Hyogo, 664, Japan.

# An Integrated Embedded Systems Software Development Environment for ITRON

James Ready, David Kalinsky
Ready Systems Corp.

**ABSTRACT**

As more and more software developers use the ITRON operating system nucleus as the basis for real-time application software development, it becomes necessary to apply a modern software engineering approach based on an infrastructure of computer-aided software development tools. This infrastructure should begin with front-end CASE tools which make it possible to model software requirements and real-time software designs using graphic workstations, in direct analogy to CAD and CAE systems for hardware.

Real-time software engineering toolsets contain a number of facilities which must be highly integrated with one another and must make use of special knowledge of the ITRON-based runtime software and hardware environment. Such a toolset would vastly increase the efficiency of development of large-scale embedded systems software using ITRON.

**Keywords:** ITRON operating system, Real-time, Multi-tasking, Software Design, Embedded Computer Systems Software

## 1. INTRODUCTION

During the 1980's it has become possible to have computerized support for structured software development. In particular, a number of CASE (Computer Aided Software Engineering) tools have become available for requirements specification and design. Unfortunately, standard CASE tools are oriented toward the development of data processing software such as Management Information Systems. Consequently they do not address many software engineering issues specific to industrial real-time software development with an operating system nucleus such as ITRON.

Among the issues which are crucial for real-time software development, but which are not normally addressed by CASE tools, are:

1) Software Interfaces to Specialized Hardware

2) Performance Requirements, such as Response Time

3) Identification of Concurrent Software Tasks

4) Intertask Communication and Synchronization Mechanisms

5) Timing Performance Analyses of Software Design

6) Detailed Design of Data and Logic, for critical software.

Ready Systems Corporation has created "CARDtools" as a CASE toolset specifically oriented to the development of real-time and embedded systems software. It integrates traditional CASE tool facilities with special facilities for addressing the above aspects of real-time systems. While initially developed for use with Ready Systems' VRTX and ARTX series of operating system nuclei, it is possible to extend CARDtools so as to support the development of ITRON-based software systems.

The following section of this article will take the reader through an embedded system software engineering cycle using the Ready Systems integrated tools technology for Computer-Aided Real-time Development ("CARD") as it might be extended to ITRON-based software. It will show that it is possible to capture extensive embedded real-time requirements and design information using specifically ITRON-oriented CASE tools. This information could be directly carried into the application coding and target hardware integration phases.

A later section will outline the information about the ITRON operating system nuclei which is needed in order to begin to extend CARDtools so as to support ITRON-based software development.


## 2. COMPUTER-AIDED EMBEDDED SYSTEMS SOFTWARE DEVELOPMENT:

### 2.1 System Requirements and Design

Embedded systems development projects originate in a systems engineering phase. In this phase, software issues are not yet addressed, since the entire system is conceptualized abstractly as a 'black box'. For instance in the application area of industrial control, the system may be thought of as an instrument with an attractive man-machine interface at its front panel and cables to sensors and industrial robotic equipment at its rear.

The systems engineer, in close consultation with application area experts, begins his work by analyzing system-level requirements. Functional requirements may be expressed using the graphic modelling techniques of structure charts or data/control flow diagrams, with the aid of the Ready Systems CARDtools CASE facilities. An example of such an initial functional 'decomposition' is shown in *Fig. 1*. Performance requirements may be associated with individual functions or chains of functions. For instance, a certain stimulus-response path may be assigned an upper limit of time in which it must respond to a trigger. In the system requirements phase, the systems engineer can perform modelling and timing calculations to evaluate the feasibility of his requirements.

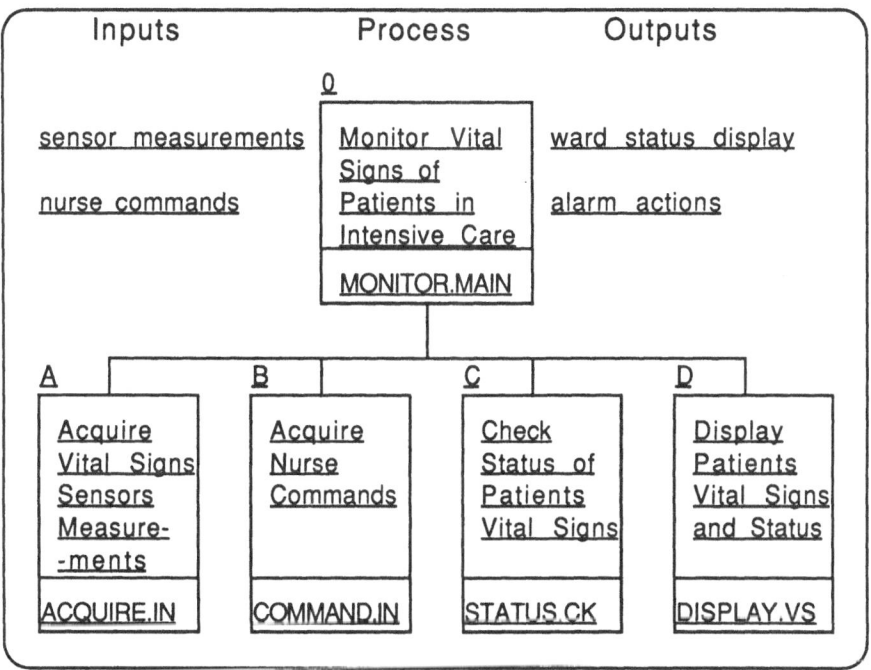

*Fig. 1 System Requirements model top level*

A second step in system-level activity is termed system design or functional allocation. In this activity, the systems engineer assigns the individual functions in his system requirements specification, to different technologies. For example, a function may be assigned to implementation in analog electronics, another to digital electronics, and others to perhaps electro-optics or even mechanical or vacuum technologies. Yet other system-level functions may be assigned to implementation as software on digital computers or microprocessors.

For example, in an industrial control system, raw materials detection may be assigned to an image analysis sub-system, processing information presentation to a series of video displays, and process and quality monitoring to software running on an embedded microprocessor.

## 2.2 Software Requirements Analysis

Once system-level allocation has taken place, and computer software has appeared in the system design, the work of the software engineer formally begins. The software engineer, in cooperation with systems engineers, must develop requirements for this software based on those system-level requirements allocated to it, and interface needs which have appeared in the system-level allocation.

The primary activity of the software engineer is to perform a functional analysis of the requirements for his software. These are usually modelled graphically using a data flow diagramming technique, in which functions are shown as bubbles and their data interconnections shown as arcs. Functional bubbles may be 'exploded' to show greater levels of functional detail. *Fig. 2* shows an example of a data flow diagram.

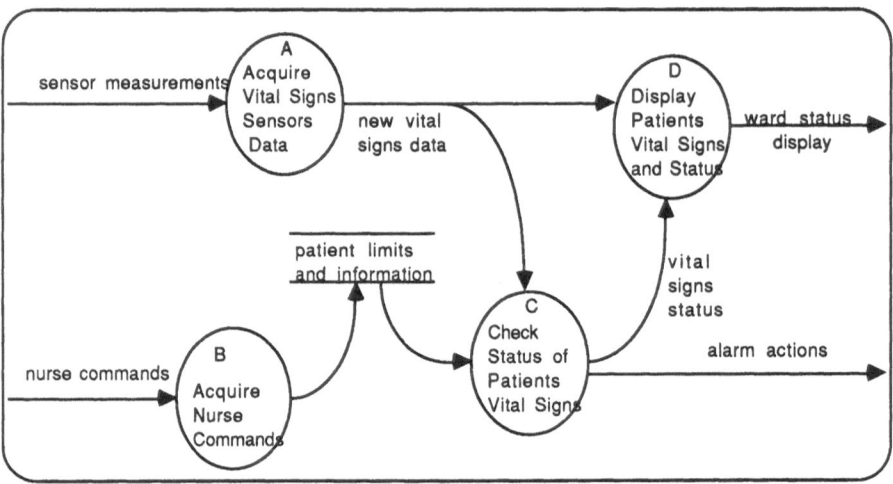

*Fig. 2 Software Requirement Model*

Together with the functional analysis, the software requirements engineer may need to describe the control interconnections between functions, and perhaps model special 'control centers' associated with certain of his data flow diagrams. State Transition Diagrams and tables are used to detail the control logic. CARDtools supports these functional and control modelling methods.

As part of the software requirements specification phase, all interfaces between computer software and its surrounding hardware must be specified fully. Such a specification becomes a detailed 'contract' between the software developer on the one hand, and the hardware developer on the other. Details down to the level of individual bits and interrupt addresses and timing constraints must be specified; for if not, the software to be developed will not correctly integrate with the specific hardware being developed in parallel. 'Interface Control' specifications are captured by CARDtools and are linked with the functional and control modelling methods of the tools.

## 2.3 Software Design

Once software requirements have been established, the software design process begins. In embedded systems software development, the structure of the requirements model developed earlier is not usually the same as the structure of a design model providing an implementation solution. Constraints such as timing requirements and special hardware-software interrelationships such as interrupts and DMA interfaces, are typical reasons for the differences in structure of requirements and design models. Hence the phase of high-level software design for real-time systems is an activity of major restructuring or even creating a new structure for the software solution.

This software solution model typically includes the identification of concurrent tasks within the software, and the selection of the appropriate mechanism for regulating each instance of intertask communication and synchronization. For example, in ITRON data might be passed between tasks via Mailboxes, resources allocated via Semaphores, and tasks synchronized by Event Flags -- but certainly information can not be passed freely between concurrent tasks, as this would cause random-appearing errors of mutual exclusion violation.

Requirements modelling tools and traditional CASE techniques, such as data and control flow diagrams, are not adequate or even appropriate for software **design** modelling. With such methods, much critical real-time design information such as identification of tasks and identification of intertask communication and synchronization mechanisms, can only be noted as informal comments -- or worse yet, they remain as decisions stored only in the mind of the designer.

The Task Maps Builder facility of CARDtools explicitly captures these real-time design decisions, in the form of a visual formalism which is both well-defined and easy to understand because of its graphic expression. An example of a Task Map, as it might be depicted for an ITRON-based software design, is shown in *Fig 3*. The symbols used in this ITRON Task Map are exhibited in *Fig 4*. These are a subset of the symbology which would have to be used to provide a complete graphic language for ITRON design.

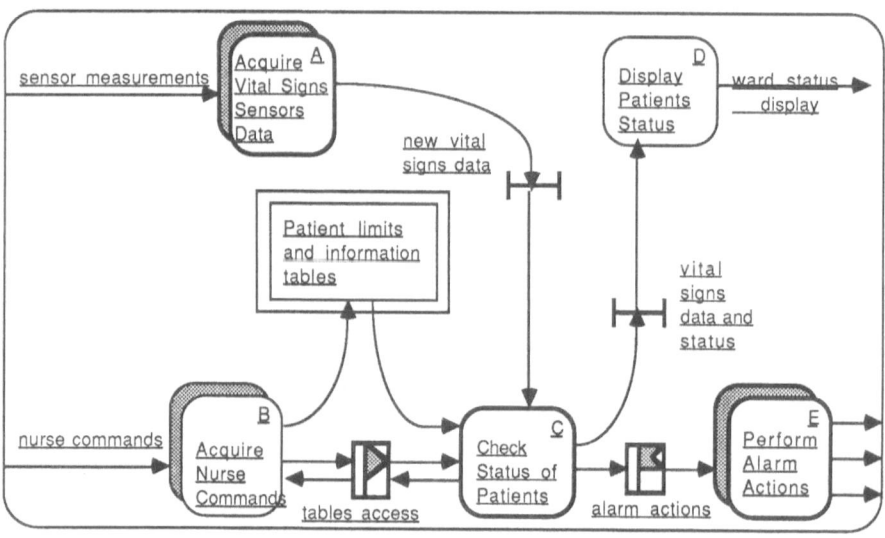

*Fig. 3  Task Map Example for Medical System*

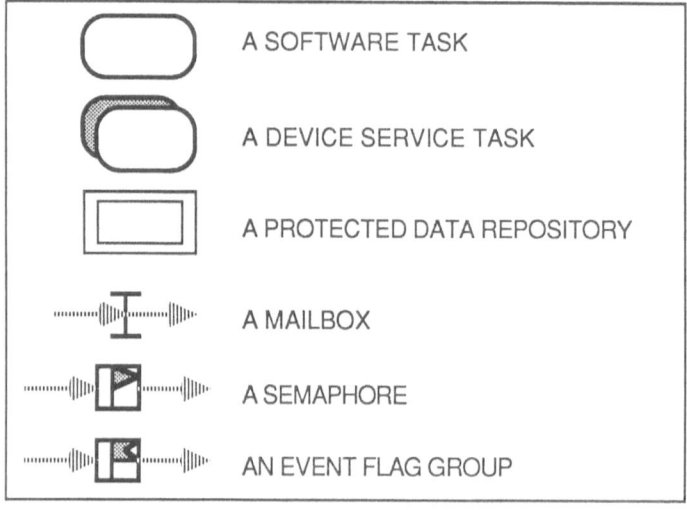

*Fig. 4  Part of Proposed Icon Language for ITRON Task Maps*

CARDtools also makes it possible to perform timing analyses of these visual depictions of high-level real-time designs. The basis for these analyses is intimate knowledge of the underlying ITRON run-time software and the hardware environment, which must be built into CARDtools. These tools will then provide the ability to do static timing calculations on these diagrams, in order to evaluate whether a software design will meet real-time constraints. The results of such a timing analysis are shown in *Fig. 5*.

## TIMING REPORT

| CRITICAL PATH : | Sensors to Alarms path | | |
|---|---|---|---|

| CPU TYPE | CLOCK (MHz) | OS VERS. | RAM | ROM |
|---|---|---|---|---|
| 1  68020 | 24.0 | HI68K | 1  2 | 0 |

TIME (microsec.)

| COMPONENT | CONSTRAINT | ESTIMATED | CALCULATED |
|---|---|---|---|
| Server: Acquire Vital Signs Sensors | 850 | 820 | 831 |
| Mailbox: New Vital Signs Data | 47 | 47 | 47 |
| Task: Check Status of Patients | 2000 | 1700 | 1751 |
| Event Flag: Alarm Actions | 63 | 63 | 63 |
| Server: Perform Alarm Actions | 1500 | 1200 | 1321 |
| High-priority task overhead | | 900 | 850 |
| **TOTALS** | **4460** | **4730** | **4863** |

*Fig. 5  CARDtools Timing Analysis Example*

Task Maps may be constructed and detailed using either hierarchical or object-oriented methods. Numerous tools today provide strong support for hierarchical methods, but CARDtools also provides support for object-oriented methods. The software designer can select his choice of method as it is most appropriate for each section of his project, and even design using combinations of methods.

### 2.4 Code and Debug

In the past, software engineers have manually translated individual pieces of a software design, into source code. This is not only tedious, but inevitably leads to a rift between the software design and the software code implementation.

CARDtools provides fully integrated consistent connections between high-level structural models such as task diagrams and low-level detailed specifications such as program design language (PDL). Tight connections may in the future be made to continue down to automatic translation of design specifications into source code skeletons, via data dictionary construction, task and function specifications and PDL.

In the sequential-programming world of data processing applications, automatic code generation is already a demonstrable reality. In the highly-constrained world of real-time software full realization of this goal is not yet practical, hence CARDtools will provide a Code Frame Generator which must, of necessity, sometimes provide only partial code generation.

## 3. EXTENSIONS TO CARDTOOLS FOR ITRON

A real-time CASE tool must be "knowledgeable" about the run-time operating system and underlying microprocessor, so that it can support real-time software design. In order to make CARDtools "knowledgeable" about ITRON, the following areas must be addressed:

### 3.1 Operating System Determinism

It must be shown that the behavior of the ITRON operating system, in its various implementations for different microprocessors and configurations, is always deterministic and never statistically distributed. This is necessary since the only timing response which is of interest to the real-time designer is worst-case timing. He must perform timing analyses so as to be convinced that in all cases, his software will meet its timing requirements. Statistically distributed timing behavior is unacceptable in real-time software design, since it would result in an occasional violation of timing requirements on a stochastic basis.

However, constant timing of operating system services, while acceptable, is also not necessary. All that is needed is a fixed algebraic formula describing the relation of an operating system service's time consumption, to those factors upon which it depends.

### 3.2 Graphic Symbolism and Rules

Conventions must be established for representing each kind of application software entity and each operating system entity. For example, *Fig 5* proposes graphic symbols for ITRON Mailboxes, Semaphores and Event Flag groups. The individual operations on each ITRON entity should also be differentiated graphically, if there is a danger of confusion. For example, the ITRON **rcv_msg** (Receive Message) call and **mbx_adr** (Get Mailbox Access Address) call must be represented differently.

Rules associated with ITRON system calls must also be supplied to CARDtools. For example, a Mailbox may pass its contents to an application task, but it may not pass it directly into a Semaphore. CARDtools can check adherence to these rules. In this way, CARDtools can both prevent errors in Task modelling representations, and detect many anomalies when they do occur in Task Maps.

### 3.3 Operating System Service Times

Once it has been established that all ITRON system call timings are deterministic, the actual formulae expressing these timings and their algebraic dependencies must be documented and supplied to CARDtools.

An algebraic formula must be given for each individual system call in ITRON. These formulae may well depend on such parameters as memory wait states, CPU clock speed, total number of tasks in the application software, or number of tasks pending for the service at the time of the system call.

Clearly, there will also be strong dependencies on the microprocessor which the ITRON version is serving. For example, we can expect ITRON's timing behavior to be different on the various Hitachi H Series microprocessors, and these different for ITRON for a Motorola 68000. It is recommended that timing formulae be provided separately for each microprocessor upon which ITRON can operate, for each system call.

### 4. SUMMARY AND CONCLUSION

Ready Systems' CARDtools is the first highly integrated CASE tool set specifically oriented to the development of real-time and embedded computer systems software. In order to provide software design support in the highly-constrained world of real-time, a software engineering tool set must have intimate knowledge of the characteristics of the hardware platform and the operating system nucleus underlying the application software. CARDtools today contains knowledge of the popular VRTX and ARTX series of operating system nuclei.

It is possible to extend CARDtools so as to be knowledgeable of the ITRON series of operating system nuclei, and thus bring the power of Computer Aided Real-time Design tools to the developer of ITRON-based applications.

Today coding is only a small fraction of the software engineer's effort. The real-time software engineer's main activities are modelling, testing and documentation throughout the life cycle. A real-time design oriented CASE tool such as CARDtools can bring both greater efficiency and greater reliability to the work of application developers with ITRON.

**James F. Ready**, President has more than a decade of experience with mini- and microcomputer applications. Before founding H&R in 1981, he was Z8000 product manager at Advanced Micro Devices. He had previously been software product manager of Rolm's Mil-Spec Computer Division. He holds a BS degree from the University of Illinois and an MA from the University of California, Berkley.

**David Kalinsky**, Director of Software Engineering Technologies at Ready Systems Corporation, co-founded MEDICOM Computer (Israel).,Ltd., a software company specializing in software engineering technologies and in the development of real-time software for embedded systems He served as director of the Software Engineering Division of Medicom. Before co-founding Medicom, he was with Israel Aircraft Industries with responsibility for technology transfer and usage of new software engineering tools and methodologies in real-time embedded systems. Prior to joining Israel Aircraft in 1979, he held positions responsible for the development of real-time software at M.G. Electronics Medical Computer Systems Division and at the Nuclear Physics Laboratories of the Weizmann Institute of Science. Kalinsky holds an A.B in Physics from Brown University and a Masters and Ph..D. in Nuclear Physics from Yale University.

Above authors may be reached at: Ready Systems Corp., Sunnyvale, CA 94086 U.S.A.

# Chapter 3:  BTRON

# TACL: TRON Application Control-flow Language

## Ken Sakamura
Department of Information Science, Faculty of Science, University of Tokyo

**ABSTRACT**

In the TRON Project, many interfaces are described in extensible manner using a language called TULS (TRON Universal Language System). TACL (TRON Application Control-flow Language), which provides a programming, environment on BTRON is based on TULS. The execution of TACL is done by the expansion of macros. It uses volatile dictionaries stored locally, and permanent storage in the form of real objects, which are the same as the real/virtual objects of BTRON data model. Macros are defined in the dictionaries. Display of data inside a window is done by interpreting the content of data as a TACL program. TACL handles external events, such as those from devices, as part of macro processing. the dictionaries used in TACL offer a versatile processing capability.

**Keywords:** TACL, TULS, BTRON, programming language, programming environment, macro language

## 1. INTRODUCTION

The HFDS(Highly Functional Distributed System), which is the ultimate goal of the TRON Project, encompasses many types of computer systems. In such systems, there are many interfaces, and they are defined by a programming language called TULS (TRON UNIVERSAL LANGUAGE SYSTEM).

The human-application interface, the human-system interface, and application-application interfaces are handled by the programming language/environment on BTRON. TACL (TRON APPLICATION CONTROL-FLOW LANGUAGE) is used in this environment.

TACL is based on TULS, and a basic knowledge of TULS[1] is assumed in this paper.

Since TACL handles the human-machine interface on BTRON-based computer systems, all processing done on a BTRON computer is understood as a result of TACL execution. This includes user input, and display of execution results.

TACL has the following features.

- It is an interactive language and some parts of it are compilable
- It has multiple focuses of control
- It is a typeless macro language
- It dose not distinguish between data and program
- It has two types of storage—real object (as in real/virtual object model) and dictionary
- A TACL macro can be defined anywhere in TAD (TRON Application Databus[1]) data
- User events are handled as macro invocation
- Input argument to a macro can be picked up from data such as a text object

## 2. LANGUAGE MODEL

TACL is a macro processing language, and all processing in it is done by macro expansion.

Initial invocation of a macro call is generated by an explicitly typed-in macro call by a user. Examples are display of a block of data that has a macro call in it, and events such as the clicking of digitizing pen or key input.

There is an evaluation window at the lowest part of the BTRON window system in order to explicitly call TACL macros  by writing the macro call in there.

Data described in TAD format can be considered as a TACL program and whenever data is displayed, macro calls embedded there is evaluated.

External events trigger macro calls after they are matched against dictionary entries.

Macro invocation triggers a search of the dictionaries which consist of macro definitions. A macro call is then substituted for the macrobody.  Each dictionary is a hierarchical dictionary system that has nested scopes.  When a new dictionary is generated, the new dictionary has the innermost scope.  If the macro is not found in the dictionary with the innermost scope, the hierarchy of the dictionary is scanned upward until the macro is found.

Macro calls can have arguments.  A macrobody is a TACL program.  Before the macrobody is substituted for the macro call, any macro calls that are defined in the macrobody are called first.  Hence, a macro call can act like the function call of other programming languages by replacing the body of a macro.

The TACL language model has inherited many of the features of TULS.

## 3. REAL OBJECT AND DICTIONARY

Real objects and dictionaries are the primary storage mechanism used in TACL.

### 3.1 Real Object

Real objects[1][2][3] form a global persistent storage in TACL.

Since real objects are persistent storage, they do not cease to exist unless an explicit operation is performed to remove them. Termination of programs, shutting the system power-off will not delete them. In this sense, real objects play the role of files in conventional systems.

Real objects are global storage in the sense that they can be addressed irrespective of where they are (either in the hierarchy of the objects, or on a local area network). Real objects in this sense can be used as a global variable in conventional programming languages.

A real object pointer is used to address and specify a particular real object. For example, the virtual object[2][3] of BTRON can be considered as a macro that has a real object pointer as its argument.

### 3.2 Dictionary

Dictionary in TACL is used as a local temporary storage.

#### (a) The Structure of Dictionary

A dictionary entry has three parts—macroname, arguments, and its body. You can store anything in the macrobody—strings, numbers (strings that can be interpreted as numbers), figures, virtual objects, TAD data, and TACL programs.

Dictionary is volatile in the sense that it can be dynamically created and destroyed during TACL execution. It corresponds to the automatic local storage of called functions in conventional programming languages.

#### (b) The Hierarchy of Dictionary

Dictionary can be created during the processing of data objects.

There is a parent-child relation between data introduced as a result of the order of operations. For example, if a virtual object in window A is opened into window B, then A is considered a parent of B. The nesting of segments in TAD data is also considered to introduce a parent-child relation. Dictionaries created during the processing of these data that have a parent-child relation inherit the parent-child relation.

If there is a dictionary that covers the scope of aggregate data, and if another dictionary is newly created that has only a limited scope of the original data, then the newly created dictionary is considered a child of the dictionary with the aggregate data. (*Fig. 2d*)

In the statically defined object network of the real/virtual object model, a child can have many parents. But the parent-child relation between dictionaries allows only one parent for each child.

| Macroname | Arguments | Macrobody |
|---|---|---|
| 2add | number | `#add(#add(number,1),1)` |
| 1dollar | | `125` |
| VirtualObject | Application ID<br>Real Object Pointer | `#createDictionary(),`<br>`#setup(...)` |
| EmergencyEvent | | `#createDictionary(),`<br>`#setup(pen up, , ##beep(..)),...` |

- '#' introduces a macro
- '`#createDictionary()`' is a primitive macro that defines a local storage with a scope limited only to the display-area argument
- '`#setup`' is used to make an entry to a dictionary
- '##' quotes a macro, not invoking it

*Fig. 1   An Example of Dictionary*

## 4. MACRO

A macroname is used to identify an entry in a dictionary. The macroname and the arguments that follow it make up a macro call. A TACL macro is always started with a special character and is clearly visible even when it is embedded in plain text. Macros are often represented as fusen in TAD.[1]

By redefining a dictionary entry, we can override it and change what happens when its macro is invoked.

### 4.1 Search by Macroname

Execution of TACL proceeds in the following manner. When a macro call is detected, its macrobody is searched for in the dictionaries (starting from the dictionary with innermost scope), and this corresponding macrobody is expanded if a matching entry is found.

When a macroname is not found in the dictionary with innermost scope, the search continues into its parents until the entry is either found, or all the ancestral dictionaries have been searched.

### 4.2 System Primitive Macros

When a system is started, a system dictionary is automatically created. This contains the macros that are necessary for TACL execution. Some of the macros can even be machine instruction routines. The existence of this system dictionary can be assumed during operation of BTRON.

It is possible to override the definition of system primitive macros within dynamically created dictionaries. Operations that look up these new definitions will use the new definitions instead of the system supplied definitions.

### 4.3 Macro Arguments

TACL macro calls allow for arguments. Thus macro calls act essentially like function calls in conventional programming languages.

The arguments are passed to the macrobody during macro expansion. You can define a default value for a parameter that is omitted during macro call.

There is a special way of specifying a macro argument for certain types of macros. This is called "display-area argument." Display-area argument is applicable only to data that is to be displayed on the screen. In the case of display-area argument, the argument can be fed to any number of macros that precede it.

In TACL, there is a mechanism to specify a display area as the argument of the physically preceding macro. This is done by a special mechanism that keeps track of the current display area of the argument specified by the macro call. This mechanism is used to define the area in which dictionaries are active.

The macros which can use display-area argument effectively are the ones that modify the display of the argument in some way, such as by underlining (*Fig. 2d*). Also, the macros used this way usually can be safely ignored if necessary. An underlining macro can be skipped over without decreasing the information content.

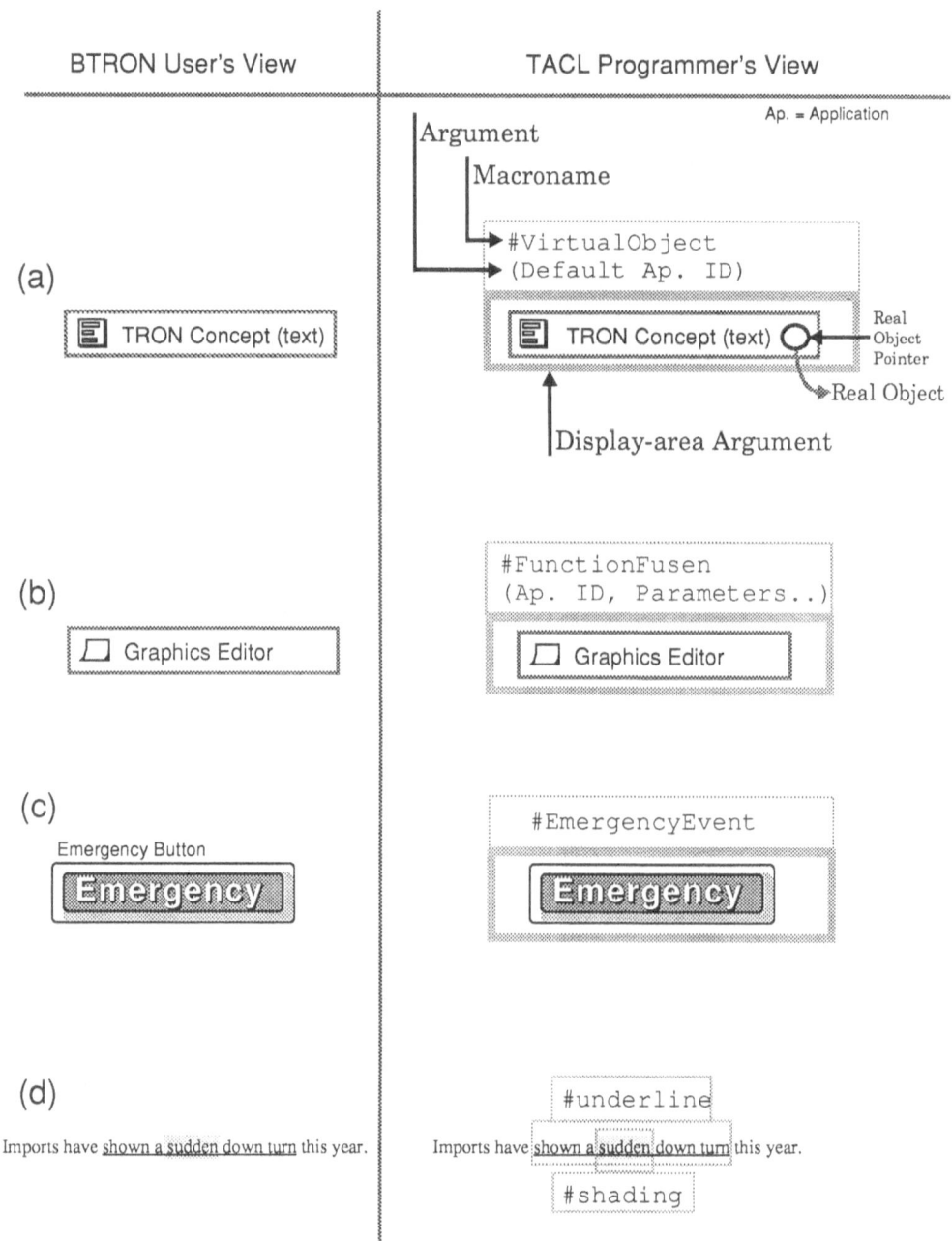

*Fig. 2 Macro with Display-area Argument*

85

If a macro expects an output from an underlining macro that has a display-area argument, and if the underlining macro does not work on a particular system, we still can pass the display-area argument to the preceding macro without doing anything with underlining macro.

Data can be a part of many display-area arguments. However, in such cases, the display-area arguments are nested in one another geometrically. Hence the nesting of the display-area will be a true parent-child relation.

### 4.4 Macro Expansion

Macro expansion is done sequentially.

During the expansion of the macro call of macro A, if there are macro calls in the macro arguments to macro A, the macro calls are first processed, and the results are fed back to the original macro call as arguments.

If the macrobody is simply a data segment, the macro call is substituted for the segment. This is the use of the macro as a constant.

If the macrobody contains further macro calls, these macro calls are first processed and reinserted into the macrobody before the original call is finished.

We provide for the quoting of a macro so that we can suppress the evaluation of a macro during macro expansion. For example, a macro call may want to register a macro in a dictionary instead of calling the macro itself. the example entry of `EmergencyEvent` in *Fig. 1* is such an example.


### 5. USE OF TACL IN BTRON

### 5.1 Event and Macro Invocation

In BTRON, external operations such as the up and down movements of the digitizing pen, redisplay of the screen, and resizing of windows are called events. These events can trigger certain processing by the BTRON computer. Usually, these events cause macro invocation of TACL.

Each event has some parameters associated with it. For example, a pen up event has its position as parameter. An event of window resizing has the old and new size, in addition to the location and the path name for the window, as its parameter.

These events are dynamically bound to TACL macros to trigger macro processing. The bindings are registered in the dictionary system. For events such as a pen moving up and down, the dictionary in which the event/macro binding is looked for can vary according to the position where the event takes place on the screen. So the same pen up and down movements can trigger different macro processing according to the position where they take place.

The event parameters can be extracted from within the macro that is bound to the event. Thus macro processing can use these parameters.

For an event that has a location parameter such as the up and down movements of the pen, the searching of event/macro pair starts within the dictionary that is active on the spot where the event takes place.

These flexible bindings of events and macros make various useful operations possible on BTRON systems.

For example,user data can define a locally scoped dictionary that is active only over the display area for the user text or figure segment. By changing the event/macro binding in the dictionary, the user can intercept the event, which is usually passed on to an application. The user can build a control part from any text and figure segments.

For example, a local dictionary defined on a button mark can have a different event/macro pair than that of the encompassing dictionary. This makes it possible for a program to intercept the button-up event on the button mark and take appropriate action. For example, the emergencyEvent macro defines the dictionary which is active only on the button mark. If a button-up event occurs there, a beep sound is generated. (*Fig. 1, Fig. 2c*)

We can regard the system supplied control parts as if they were built using TACL primitives in this way.

### 5.2 Display and Macro Processing

When application programs display data in BTRON windows, they actually evaluate the data as TACL macros.

Any macros embedded in the data are evaluated sequentially, starting from the beginning.

In BTRON, we can define a "display-area-hook" for a piece data. A display-area-hook is a list of macros that are evaluated when the piece of data is displayed. The data in this case is called display-area data. (The actual area of the display in which the data is shown vary dynamically.)

During the displaying of data, if a display-area-hook is defined for text or figures in the data, then the macros in the display-area-hook are evaluated.

If the mid-point is within the display-area data for which a display-area-hook is defined, then the macro must be evaluated.

Of course, if the display is done starting from the midpoint in the data, we can skip the evaluation of the macros that precedes the midpoint.

### 5.3 Fusen and Macro Processing

Fusen in BTRON[2][3] are built using TACL facilities. A fusen is a macro with a real object pointer that points at an application. From the user's point of view, all macros look like fusen.

### 5.4 Automatic Execution

The automatic execution available in the TACL/BTRON environment is essential for the user.

BTRON users carry out the automatic execution of programs with parameters set in fusen for each real object. By pointing to a suitable fusen pasted onto the real object, appropriate programs are automatically invoked to process the real object.

In real offices, the division of labor is used to handle various parts of a job. TACL supports the concept of division of labor through "delegation" (or *omawashi* in Japanese).[3]

Each real object has a special storage place called "fusen page," and fusen stored on it are responsible for processing the real object. This page is not evaluated when the real object is evaluated during processing.

In BTRON, user data are stored as real objects. You can think of fusen as stored instructions to specify tasks done on these objects.

For example, a fusen used to draw a graph and a fusen used to send a real object to someone else can be combined so that a drawn graph is sent out . (*Fig. 3*)

Fusen allow for multiple control flow and can invoke the system functions of BTRON.

An invocation via a fusen can be triggered by events or by another fusen. The flow of work in the real offices can be modeled using automatic invocation via fusen.

In BTRON, fusen used to call system functions are provided for the following operations.
- Arithmetic
- Conversion
- Control
- Input/output  (visual/audio, window/dialogue, and panel control)
- Setup
- List processing
- Others

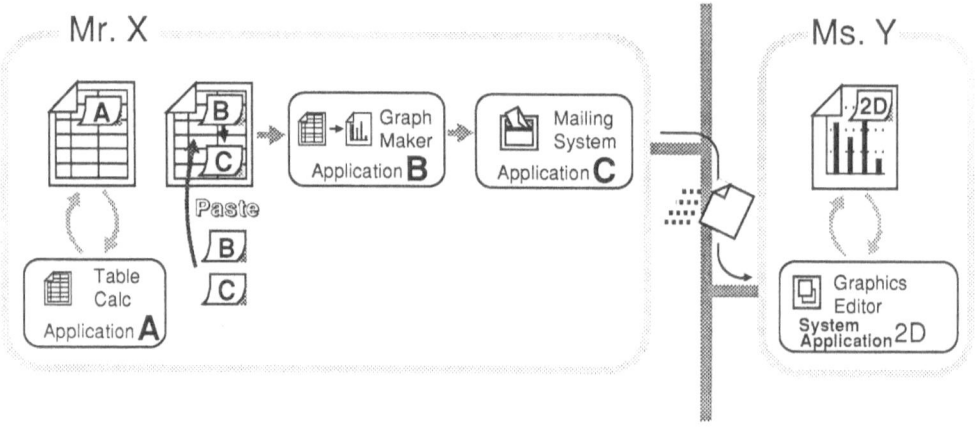

*Fig. 3   Automatic Execution(delegation) with Fusen*

Since new fusen can be installed by loading the corresponding applications, the user can enhance a system easily.

### 5.5 Programming Environment

From the user's point of view, fusen are just a combination of control panels. The control panels explain the function of each fusen and support orderly input. Control panels also support default value setting. For Office workers, programming using these control panels as a template in much easier than programming in conventional programming languages for office workers. (*Fig. 4*)

Of course, we also offer an ordinary programming interface based on a textual representation of programs, since there are applications with so many fusen that they are difficult to handle by control panels alone.

TACL allows for the capture of user interaction, such as keyboard input, and records it as a fusen. The fusen thus recorded can be executed to play back the user interaction. They can also be edited.

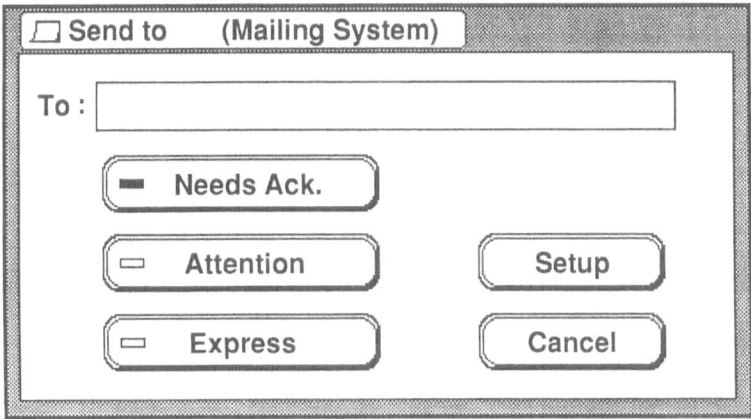

*Fig. 4  Fusen*

### 5.6  Fusen as an Application Interface

Fusen play two roles—one to allow access to data, and the other to offer functionality in an application.

#### (a) Access to data

A fusen can supply a macro to retrieve the internal data from a real object by using an application in a standard manner.

An example is a spreadsheet real object. A fusen can be defined to retrieve the data in the spreadsheet without regard to its internal presentation.

```
#CalcCell (data, column, row)
                value              the value of cell
data            reference          reference to a spreadsheet real object
column          expression         column number of spreadsheet (1-origin)
row             expression         row number of the spreadsheet (1-origin)
```

#### (b) Functions of an Application

It is desirable to integrate some of the functionality of the application program to the TACL environment. One way is to provide TACL macros that can use application program's functionality in fusen form.

Examples are search and replace functions of the basic text editor. These capabilities are now available in the TACL environment as fusen. TACL programmers can search for and replace words in a real object without invoking the basic text editor.

By providing fusen that offer the functionality of an application, it is possible use applications effectively from the TACL environment.

## 6. TACL IMPLEMENTATION

### 6.1 Primitive Compiler

A primitive compiler that compiles macros into machine language is also provided in TACL. The compiler is used to compile basic macros that must be executed quickly.

Macros coded in by machine language are compatible with the ideal TACL run-time system, that is, the real macro expansion system, and they maintain language compatibility both today and in the future.[1]

### 6.2 The Future of TACL

We will be able to use the TACL macros with reasonable speed in the future when the implementation technology becomes more advanced. TACL macros will be used extensively. User reprogramming of the TACL macros will occur often.

As for rewriting in TACL, we will be able to maintain compatibility in the future.

If someone writes a new TACL macro that does interesting processing, others can share the macro, and they can expect similar processing on their computer systems.

For example, special formatting macros for document processing can be shared as long as the format is done using standardized TACL. Everyone can print the document according his or her special style.

The addition of these new TACL macros is handled like additions to a dictionary. The management of such a dictionary should not pose any problems in the future.

## 7. SUMMARY

The human-machine interface of BTRON is implemented using TACL. The interface requires relatively slow speed compared to real-time industrial applications, for example. Thus we can use interactive programming systems with much benefit.

TACL is based on TULS, and it is the first such language to be investigated in the TRON Project. Real implementations of TACL will start soon.

From the user's point of view, TACL on a BTRON computer will provide for the automatic execution of various applications. Delegation and cooperative work in the offices can be modeled and easily carried out by writing into fusen or moving fusen around.

The simple dictionary mechanism and macro expansion in TACL (and also TULS) will encompass various implementation methods and will assure compatibility among many TRON-based systems. TACL is the base on which the construction of the HFDS will take place.

REFERENCE

[1]   Ken Sakamura, "TULS: TRON Universal Language System," TRON Project 1988 (Proc. of the Fifth TRON Project Symposium, this volume), Springer-Verlag, 1988

[2]   Ken Sakamura, "BTRON: An Overview," TRON Project 1987 (Proc. of the Third TRON Project Symposium), Springer-Verlag, 1987, pp.75-82

[3]   Ken Sakamura, "BTRON: The Business-oriented Operating System," IEEE Micro, April 1987, pp.53-65

**Ken Sakamura** is an associate professor in the Department of Information Science, University of Tokyo. He received his Ph.D. in electrical engineering from Keio University (Yokohama) in 1979. As one of Japan's foremost computer architects, he has been the driving force behind the TRON Project, which he started in 1984 to build a new computer architecture for 1990s and beyond. The TRON Architecture he designed for this purpose has now expanded to include applications in buildings and furniture.

Sakamura serves on the editorial board of *IEEE Micro,* a magazine published by the Institute of Electrical and Electronics Engineers (IEEE), and he heads the project promotion committee of the TRON Association. He is also a member of the Japan Information Processing Society (JIPS); the Institute of Electronics, Information and Communication Engineers (IEICE); the Association for Computing Machinery; and he is a senior member of IEEE. He has received the best paper award from IEICE twice; the JIPS best paper award once, the IEEE best annual article award, in addition to other awards from Japanese and overseas organizations.

The above author may be reached at Department of Information Science, Faculty of Science, University of Tokyo, 7-3-1 Hongo, Bunkyo-ku, Tokyo, Japan.

# Natural Language Translation Services in BTRON

Robert T. Myers, Ken Sakamura
Department of Information Science, Faculty of Science, University of Tokyo

**ABSTRACT**

An architecture for providing natural language translation services at the operating system level is presented. A component known as the Translation Manager is proposed as a way of structuring the interface between translators and their clients. Various examples of the use of such services, at both the system and the application level, are discussed. Finally, the design of a specific Japanese—English translator now under development is briefly presented.

**Keywords**: natural-language processing, machine translation, operating systems

## 1. INTRODUCTION

Recently there is a clear trend to extend the functionality offered by operating systems. Examples of such functionality are windowing and graphics systems, database capabilities, and communications. The **BTRON** operating system specification fits this pattern, offering, for instance, complete user interface and certain database capabilities at the operating system level. This paper describes the design for natural-language translation services embedded in **BTRON**.

The advantages of placing these services directly in the operating system, rather than packaging them as a separate application, are clear, and include the following:

- information input by the user in one language can transparently be provided to an application in another
- users can view messages, menus, on-line help, and so on displayed by the operating system or an application in their own language, translated dynamically
- information arriving over a communications network may be translated into and displayed in the user's language, in real time
- an operating system utility to view a text file, for example, would automatically gain the capability of displaying the file in another language

The natural language translation services can be thought of more generally as natural language processing services. Due to our adoption of a *pivot*-based architecture, all applications, in particular those involving natural-language processing aspects, such as databases with natural-language front ends, can avail themselves of the services, not necessarily strictly for translation.

Although these goals might be considered ambitious, they appear possible in the context of TRON. TRON attempts to shoot where the moving target of technology will be in the 1990s, rather than where it is today. In this case, "technology" refers not only to hardware and operating system technology, but also to machine translation technology. The expected improvements in functionality and cost-performance of memory and microprocessor technology are wholly adequate to handle the translation problem. And a wide variety of research is being done in linguistics, mathematics, philosophy and artificial intelligence which holds out true hope for finally nearing the goal of mostly-automatic, acceptable-quality translation.

In addition, details of the TRON project already underway are perfectly suited for the attempt of embedding natural-language translation services into the operating system. The horsepower of the TRON VLSI CPU is apparently adequate for machine translation. The virtual memory architecture of the TRON VLSI CPU eliminates much of the worry about the memory requirements of the translator. And the modular nature of **BTRON** makes it easy, as will be discussed below, to integrate the translation services into the operating system architecture.

Our research is divided into two parts. The first addresses how translation services should be incorporated into an operating system such as **BTRON**. This is the topic of this paper. In addition, we are doing research on machine translation itself; at the end of the paper, we give an overview of that research.

## 2. OPERATING-SYSTEM TRANSLATION SERVICES OVERVIEW

This section discusses the types of natural language translation services which will be provided by **BTRON**, and how they will be integrated into **BTRON**.

## 2.1. THE TRANSLATION MANAGER

As will be discussed below, translation services are to be invoked from a variety of locations within **BTRON**, as well as directly from applications. Furthermore, it is important to allow various translators, including those from third-parties, to be used and to function correctly when called from all of those locations. Our architectural solution to this is a new component of **BTRON**, the Translation Manager. It can be pictured as in *Fig. 1*.

All invocations of translation services from applications or operation system components are made through the Translation Manager. The Translation Manager in turn invokes one or more of the currently available translators.

The above approach requires fixing an interface between invokers of the Translation Manager and the Manager itself (the **BTRON** Translation Manager Interface, or BTMI), as well as between the Manager and the Translators (the **BTRON** Standard Translator Interface, BSTI). We have developed a preliminary draft of such interfaces. In the area of translation, because of the difference in approaches, it is important for the interface to be flexible and extendible.

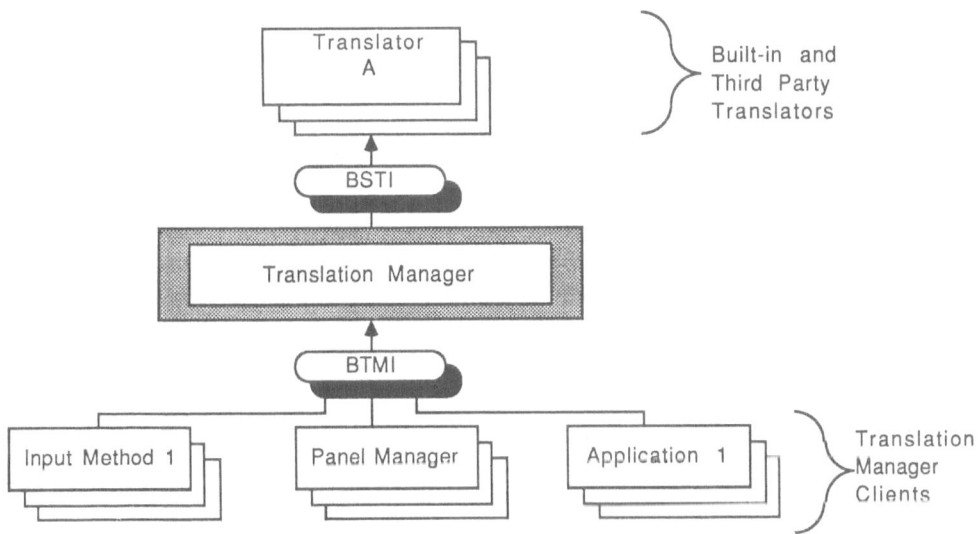

*Fig. 1  Role of the Translation Manager*

Translators are required to register themselves with the Translation Manager, in particular as to their target and source languages. The Translation Manager then takes care of determining which Translator to call based on the request made by the application or operating system component. But the Translation Manager does provide the following key, "pivot" services:

(1) Language Ø, which is the **BTRON** natural language pivot, discussed below.

(2) Pre-defined translators between Ø and Japanese, Japanese and Ø , English and Ø, and Ø and English.

In the most common case, a request for translation from English to Japanese will be handled by invoking the English—Ø translator, and passing the results to the Ø—Japanese translator. Alternatively, if a dedicated English—Japanese translator is available, it could also be used, depending on user preferences.

As described below, the interface between the Translation Manager and its users is based on the TAD specification[2]. This specification has been extended, in a way also described later, to include the definition of information represented simultaneously in many languages: the so-called *multiple-language text element*. When asked to perform a translation, the Translation Manager may realize that a version in the requested target language is already available; in such a case, that version is simply passed back. This is the simplest task that might be performed by the Translation Manager.

## 2.2. THE BTRON NATURAL LANGUAGE PIVOT

What is Ø, the **BTRON** natural language pivot?

The pivot approach to natural language translation can at best be considered to be unproven. A true pivot language, completely independent of any specific natural language, must be able to represent all vocabulary items, tense and aspect information, semantic relationships including case and sub- and superordination, and to some extent pragmatics (the flow of the discourse). Various attempts have been made to develop such a language; none can be said to have been truly successful.

However we believe that advances in linguistics and semantics will make a useful pivot language feasible over the next few years. Thus our architecture assumes the existence of a pivot language (but does not define it at present). In addition, the interface between the Translation Manager and the various Translators (BSTI) is based on a pivot model, even for dedicated Source Language—Target Language Translators. Finally, the pivot provides a standard interface for natural-language processing applications, such as a database system with a natural-language front end.

The definition of the **BTRON** natural language pivot is a topic for further research. Our intent is to first specify a pivot subset which can be used to code information relating to humans using **BTRON** workstations. This pivot will enable translation of input and output relating to the use of the computer itself. The definition of a full natural language pivot is a next stage.

The pivot is not only used as an intermediate stage in the translation of one natural language to another by the Translation Manager. It may also be used by applications, for example, to store messages for output directly. Translation of such messages stored in pivot format then may be accomplished in one step (pivot-to-target-language) rather than two (source-language-to-pivot-to-target-language). We also plan to develop an external, human representation for the pivot language. Users fluent in the pivot may then communicate directly.

The pivot services provided in the operating system are expected to be of great benefit in applications other than simply translation. As alluded to above, for instance, a natural-language interface to a database could request the Translation Manager to convert a user's query into the pivot; the retrieval portion of the application would then need only to be able to accept a query in the pivot.

## 2.3. MULTI-LANGUAGE TEXT ELEMENT FORMAT

Inter-application data transfer in **BTRON** occurs across the conceptual bus known as TAD, or TRON Application Databus. TAD sets forth a set of principles for representing arbitrary types of data, and applies them to define formats for particular types of data (text, graphics, etc.) of immediate interest (see [1]).

Previously published TAD specifications allowed the specification of the language of some data. But there was no way to associate directly multiple representations of the same information in multiple languages. Although in principle it would suffice to perform dynamic translation whenever necessary, in practice this would consume machine resources; and the application developer would have no way to insist that a particular second-language representation be used.

To avoid this problem, we have designed a *multi-language text element* format for TAD. When a string is passed to the Translation Manager for translation, a check is made to determine if a string in the desired target language is already present within the multi-language string; if it is, that string is returned. Only if the second-language string is not already present does dynamic translation occur. Once translated, the result might be added to the multi-language string, avoiding the necessity for retranslation later.

In addition, if the Translation Manager determines that a pivot representation is present in the multi-language text element format, it will direct the appropriate translator to create target language message information from the pivot representation.

A pictorial representation of this aspect of this aspect of the operation of the Translation Manager is shown in *Fig. 2* .

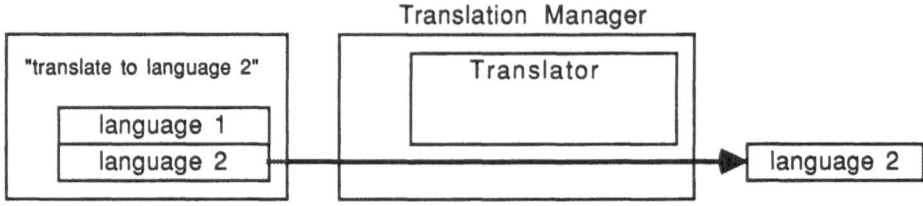

*Fig. 2  Translation Manager Operation (I)*
*Target Language Representation already Present.*

This is the case where the second-language representation was already present in the multi-language string. The Translation Manager simply passes the second-language string back as the result.

*Fig.* 3, on the other hand, shows the case where the desired target language representation was not present in the multi-language text element, and so the Translation Manager invokes one or more of the Translators to perform translation.

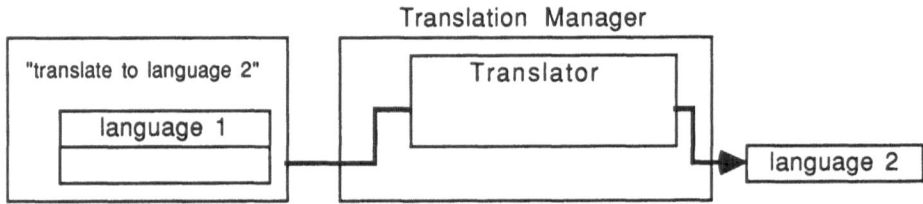

*Fig. 3  Translation Manager Operation (II)*
*Target Language Representation not Present.*

## 2.4.  INTERNATIONALIZING  AN  APPLICATION

The first requirement for an application to work harmoniously with the Translation Manager is that it register its native language. This permits the Translation Manager to verify the availability of Translators from that language to the pivot or to other target languages.

Below, we summarize the operation of the Translation Manager and the pivot language by giving approaches to internationalizing an application.

1) *do nothing.* Translation of input and output will occur dynamically. Speed will suffer, and quality may be uneven. The advantage is just that development time is zero.

2) *add multi-language text element format resources for the pivot language representation of menus, messages, help screens and so on.* Now translation of messages can be done in half the time, and with greater accuracy.

3) *add multi-language text element format resources for the desired target language.* At the expense of adding these resources, messages and menus will appear exactly as specified, and quickly, in the target language.

We propose that a utility in the development environment be made available to automatically translate message and menu text resources into the pivot or some target language. The developer could then check these translations manually.

**BTRON** supports parameterizable messages, also known as message templates. A problem with such templates is that the location of the slots for the parameters in the target language version might depend on the run-time information being placed in the slots. Therefore, such messages cannot necessarily be translated directly into a specific target language before-hand. The solution is to translate such message templates into the pivot language. The final translation into some specific language happens at application execution time.

## 3. OPERATING SYSTEM USAGE OF THE TRANSLATION SERVICES

### 3.1. TRANSLATION OF INPUT

Many cases of translation are best handled immediately upon input. Examples are:

-   typing messages or mail to a bulletin board or to another user in chat mode

-   typing comments to a computer program under development

**BTRON** contains a definition for *input methods* which allow a variety of conversions at input time.

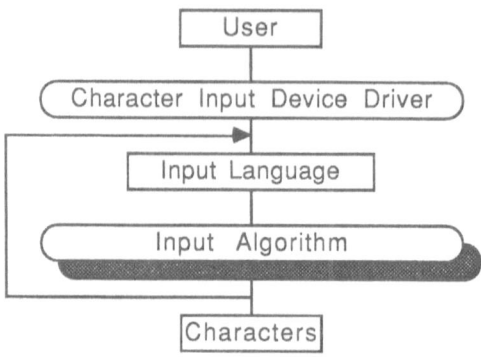

*Fig. 4  Role of BTRON Input Algorithms*

The diagram above gives the original version of **BTRON** input processing. Note that the loop may be repeated many times; originally, the design goal was for this repetition to permit conversion of romaji into kana, thence into kanji. It speaks well for the robustness of the original design that it works well as its stands for translation as well. Translators are nothing more than addition input algorithms. The user specifies automatic translation on input in the same way that he would otherwise specify some particular type of kana-kanji conversion, for example. Translation input methods invoke translation services through the Translation Manager.

### 3.2. TRANSLATION OF MESSAGES

One of the most common uses of the translation services in the operating system is expected to be in translating system and application messages.

In **BTRON**, such messages are displayed via a limited number of well-defined routes. For instance, the Panel Manager may often be used to display an advisory or warning message.

Translation of messages will thus be implemented via an extension to the Panel Manager to use the Translation Manager. As discussed above, the translation services extensions to the operating system include the definition of "multi-language text element format." An application may choose from among the different languages in which the text is present. When the Panel Manager calls the Translation Manager, the latter will first check to see if the message to be displayed is present in the desired language, and if so, return it. If not, dynamic translation will be invoked. Since most such message are limited in length, the delay for translation should be no more than one or two seconds. If it appears likely to be longer, a message will be displayed advising the user that translation is in progress.

No matter how well the translator functions, certain messages will probably be garbled. We envisage two solutions for this. First, as explained above, the application developer may provide a target or pivot-language version of just the most sensitive and/or garble-prone messages; those will be displayed, while other messages, for which no target-language version is available, will be translated.

The second solution is that the user may request that the message be redisplayed in the original language.

To show these ideas in diagrams, one-language operation works as follows:

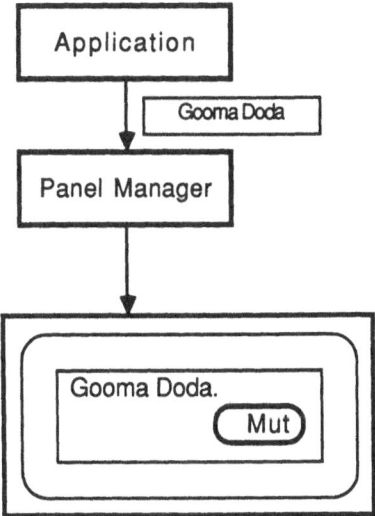

*Fig. 5  Panel Manager Operation*

This example assumes the native language is the mythical "Booma". In this language, "Gooma Doda" means "Disk Full", and "Mut" corresponds to "OK".

When automatic translation is invoked, we have the situation shown in *Fig. 6*.

The application has provided the single Booma-language string "Gooma Doda" to the Panel Manager. But the user has requested automatic translation to English. (The application itself has already registered its own native language as Booma.) Thus the Panel Manager invokes the operating system translation functions. The result is the string "Disk Full." This message is displayed in the resulting panel, along with the translation for OK, and the Booma-language string "Krb"; the Panel Manager has put this button there, which means "Original Text" is the Booma language. One assumes that only those that can understand enough Booma to know that Krb means Original Language would care to see the message in the original language in the first place.

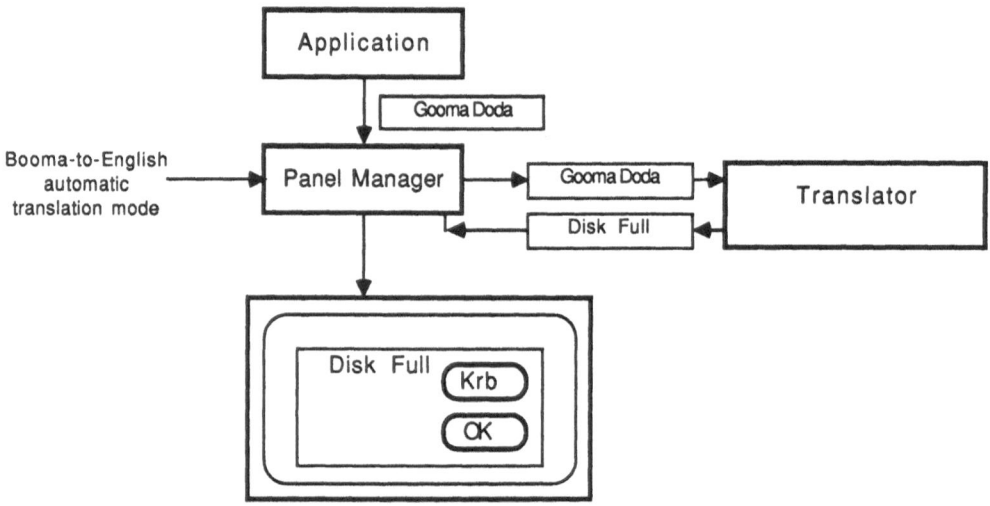

*Fig. 6   Example of Translation in the Panel Manager*

The above example shows an application which is relatively "ill-behaved," in that it has failed to provide a pivot-language representation, much less a target-language representation, of an important message like "Disk Full."

The above can be summarized in the form of the following flowchart, *Fig. 7*, which shows how the Panel Manager interacts with the Translation Manager:

103

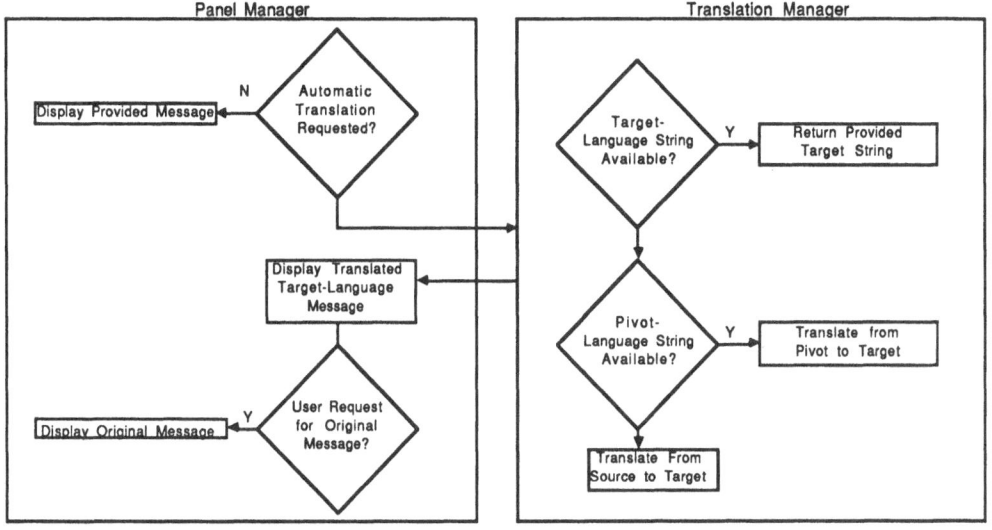

*Fig. 7   Panel Manager and Translation Manager Interaction*


## 3.3. THE TRANSLATOR SHELL APPLICATION

The kernel translation services in **BTRON** will also be made available as a stand-alone utility application. Since this utility will invoke the Translation Manager, users may use a variety of translators. In addition we have commenced the definition of another interface definition that allows users to interact with specific translators through the utility application (the **BTRON** Translator's User Interface). Thus users may take advantage, in a controlled way, of specialized capabilities available in individual translators.

Users for whom the automatic input and automatic translation modes are not sufficient, or who want more detailed control, will translate documents by means of this translation utility application.

The **BTRON** Specification defines a user language, TACL (TRON Application Control Language) and the concept of *fusen*, instructions to the operating system for certain actions to be performed automatically when a document is opened. The relationship between these and the Translator Shell is obvious. Fusens attached to documents might, for example, request that a document be automatically translated before being displayed on the screen.

## 4. APPLICATION USE OF THE TRANSLATION SERVICES

### 4.1. TRANSLATION OF COMMUNICATIONS DATA

A most attractive application of the natural language translation services in the operating system is to translate, in real-time, information coming in from or going out to the outside world, for instance through a communications network. Current estimates are that the expected performance of TRON VLSI CPU-based **BTRON** workstations will be able to accomplish such a feat for low-speed communication links. This capability will most likely be implemented through specialized communications programs which invoke the Translation Manager.

### 4.2. TRANSLATION IN THE DEVELOPMENT ENVIRONMENT

One subproject in the **BTRON** project is to specify a state-of-the-art program development environment. This environment, partially outlined in Takada[3], will provide a comprehensive set of globally optimizing compilers, custom editors, version managers, debuggers, documentation tools, and performance analyzers for **BTRON**. In this section, we discuss the user of the operating system translation services in this environment.

In practice, the development environment is simply an application. Accordingly, there is no special connection between the development environment and the translation services; this discussion is simply meant to illustrate how an ambitious application might make full use of the translation services.

### (a) Translation in Structured Program Editors

Comments in present-day Japanese software are often sparse (although becoming less so) because the programmer does not know enough English to write an English comment, but Japanese comments require entering a Japanese input mode, performing kana-kanji conversion and so on. In the **BTRON** development environment custom editors, a one-key capability will translate program comments. Once translated, the comments will be stored in the **BTRON** multi-language string format; the next time a second-language representation is requested, it will appear immediately.

### (b) Translation in the Documentation Tools

The Documentation Tools in the **BTRON** development environment use the **BTRON** real-object/virtual-object model to create a fully cross-referenced, networked, hypertext-like set of documentation for a software system. Our design is for these tools to be closely integrated with the translation services so that any portion of them can be viewed in any language at any time.

These capabilities are expected to greatly facilitate the flow of software across national boundaries and improve the effectiveness of multi-national software development.

## 5. A ENGLISH—JAPANESE TRANSLATION SYSTEM

The foremost requirement for the success of our project is that we be able to produce good quality translations fast enough. In order to establish the feasibility of this, we are doing research on machine translation itself. This section gives a brief overview of that work.

### 5.1. KEY FEATURES OF TRANSLATION APPROACH

As described above, the **BTRON** Natural Language Translation Services Architecture is based on the **BTRON** natural language pivot known as Ø. Initially a pivot subset for describing computer-usage-related actions is to be developed.

But due to the outstanding problems in designing a good pivot, pending further research on the pivot, our work on a translator itself has adopted a pseudo-pivot approach as described below.

We chose the English—Japanese problem.

### 5.2. THE META-ARCHITECTURE

Our architecture is based on a meta-architecture which views the translation process as a series of *experts* manipulating and converting information at several *representation levels*. Each expert makes use of a rule base of common format.

The architecture we are building now defines representation levels of English text, English lexical elements, English syntax structures, meaning, Japanese syntax structures, Japanese lexical elements, and Japanese text.

### 5.3. PRE-PROCESSING

Experts at the English text and English lexical element representation level include ones to break the input into sentences and words, and perform morphological analysis on the words to find plurals of nouns, past forms of verbs, and about ten other varieties of morphological variants. The morphological analysis is based on a fast, compact finite state table derived directly from symbolically-expressed morphological rules.

Additional experts expand contractions, identify abbreviations, find groups of words which represent numbers, and handle a variety of other English lexical phenomena.

## 5.4. ANALYSIS

Analysis can be broken down roughly into syntactic analysis, or parsing, and semantic analysis. Our approach is distinguished by how these two parts of analysis work closely in tandem. The parser is a deterministic, stochastic (probability-based) one. It is distinguished by its speed and robustness. Semantic analysis is carried out by means of a large (500-node) semantic network, used for both expressing parsing conditions as well as general-purpose lexical disambiguation, the latter carried out by taking semantic moving averages across the text.

## 5.5. TRANSFER

In the transfer stage, the result of the analysis phase, which takes the form of a series of linked syntax frames, is converted into a pure case representation. Cases are a way of categorizing the role which is played by a component in some larger language unit. A unique feature of our approach is to analyze all the components of any phrase, not only verb phrases, in terms of the cases at work. The resulting case frames are subjected to a series of manipulations known as case frame algebra. These manipulations are partially based on a limited number of categories of pure semantic information, and can result in case frames being added and deleted from the case frame structure.

The case frame representation is the pseudo-pivot. Currently, English-oriented case frames are built; they are then transferred into Japanese-oriented case frames. As the system moves closer to using a pure pivot, the amount of pure semantic information used in these frames will increase.

## 5.6. GENERATION

Generation is implemented by experts which convert the case frames resulting from the transfer phase into Japanese syntax frames, and thence into linearized text.

## 6. SUMMARY

Automatic natural language translation services are critically important for the international era; placing such services directly in the operating system is a natural extension of the trend towards increased functionality of all varieties in operating systems. Our approach provides a clean interface from and to the natural language translation services. By assuming a pivot architecture for the Translators, the groundwork is laid for the easy integration of the expected high-performance, pivot-based translation engines of the future.

REFERENCES

[1] Ken Sakamura "TRON UNIVERSAL LANGUAGE SYSTEM", Proceedings of the Fifth TRON Project Symposium (this volume), 1988

[2] Ken Sakamura "Multi-language character sets handling in TAD", Third Real-Time Architecture TRON Study Meeting, October 1987, Information Processing Society, 1987

[3] Hiroaki Takada, Ken Sakamura "The Type Mechanism of the TIPE/L Programming Language", Proceedings of the Fifth TRON Project Symposium (this volume), 1988

**Robert T. Myers** is a Foreign Research Scholar in the Department of Information Science, University of Tokyo. He is currently conducting research into issues of machine translation, particularly English-Japanese. Prior to his association with Tokyo University, he worked for many years for Interactive Data Corporation, then a subsidiary of the Chase Manhattan Bank, developing and managing large-scale systems for the delivery and analysis of financial data. Mr. Myers is fluent in Japanese. He received the BS degree in Mathematics of Computation from Rensselaer Polytechnic Institute, Troy, NY, USA, in 1972.

**Ken Sakamura** is currently an associate professor at the Department of Information Science, University of Tokyo. He holds Ph.D. in EE. Being a computer architect, he has been the leader of the TRON project which he started to build a new computer system architecture for 1990's since 1984. His promotion of the TRON architecture now extends to architecture of buildings and furniture. He servers on the editorial board of Institute of Electrical and Electronics Engineers (IEEE) MICRO magazine and is a chair of the project promotion committee of the TRON Association. He is a member of Japan Information Processing Society, Institute of Electronics, Information and Communication Engineers, ACM, and is a senior member of IEEE. He has received best paper awards of IEICE twice, of JIPS once, IEEE best annual article award, and other awards from Japanese and overseas organizations.

Above authors may be reached at Department of Information Science, Faculty of Science, University of Tokyo, 7-3-1 Hongo, Bunkyo-ku, Tokyo, Japan.

# A Study on Video Manager of the BTRON Specification

## Kazuo Kajimoto, Masahiro Shimizu, Yoshiaki Kushiki
Matsushita Electric Industrial Co., Ltd.

**ABSTRACT**

Personal computers have grown up to process high rate and huge data like video-data. But few systems provide rich human interface with video-data.

In this paper, it is insisted that video-data must be managed not by each application software, but by operating system. We call the video-data management part of operating system *Video Manager*.

The *Video Manager* has several features. The first feature is that the video-data is represented by *Video Descriptor* which identifies the video-data with uniform format regardless of media, video devices.

Another feature of *Video Manager* is *Logical Video Data Model (LVD)* as video interface model. The *LVD Model* consists of four layers. And the functions of *Video Manager* are defined as processes intra/inter these layers.

The *Video Manager* is implemented as extended kernel of BTRON specification operating system, adopting special hardware *Video Processor Unit*.

**Keywords:** Video Manager, Video Descriptor, Logical Video Data Model (LVD Model), Video Processor Unit, BTRON specification OS

## 1. INTRODUCTION

The progress of semiconductor technology allows personal computers to handle high rate and huge data like *Video-data*. As another phase, the environment that offers richer human interface using texts, graphics and video-data is eagerly demanded because video-data has huge information and gives familiarity.

But it has not been answered how to manage video-data, how to control video devices and what video interface model is good. In this paper, one of the answers is discussed.

## 2. VIDEO-DATA AND OPERATING SYSTEMS

There are some systems that are able to manage video-data[1]. One of the most important features of these systems is that video-data are managed by an application software, that is, the systems are independent of each other. So the compatibility of video data between such systems is never guaranteed.

Moreover on multi-task operating system, video-data inconsistency can occur. Suppose one application software displays the video-data "the life of lions" and at the same time another application software wants to display another video-data "the life of elephants" in the same video disk. Which video-data must have priority? How is the command sequence given to video disk player arranged? No one except operating system can negotiate with the cancellation of that inconsistency.

So, we insisted that operating systems must manage video-data. The merits of the management of video-data by operating systems are summarized as follows.

- Compatibility of video-data between application software
- Portability of video-data
- Ease to extend application software
- Ease to transport application software to other hardware
- Consistency of video-data management on multi-task operating systems
- Sharing main memory dominated by the video-data handling part of object code of each application software

The video-data management part of operating system is called *Video Manger*.

## 3. VIDEO DESCRIPTOR

In this paper, video-data is defined as follows.

| | |
|---|---|
| **Sub-video-data:** | A visible form data that is obtained by playing continuous range of a media on a video device. |
| **Scatter play:** | To Play more than one sub-video-data sequentially. |
| **Video-data:** | A visible form data that is obtained by scatter playing on a video device. |

Video-data can be classified into many classes according to media and video devices. If the representation of video-data depends on the media and video devices, there must be many representations. This means that the software for specific medium cannot be applied to other media.

So uniform video-data representation is needed. We propose that *Video Descriptor* as video-data representation. *Video Descriptor* is the information which can identify original video-data at syntax level. In the *Video Manager*, *Video Descriptor* is treated as video-data instead of real video-data. Using *Video Descriptor*, the management of video-data is done as follows:

1) An application software finds *Video Descriptor* in its file, then it registers the *Video Descriptor* in the *Video Manager*

2) The *Video Manager* interprets the *Video Descriptor*

3) The *Video Manager* controls video device and displays real video-data

In order to implement this function, *Video Descriptor* must include following information.

1) **Video device information**: the information which can identify the video device that plays video-data.

2) **Time address unit**: the unit which represents time address unit. *Table 1* shows examples of time address unit. In the *Video Manager*, every time address unit is interpreted into Frame.

3) **The list of start and end time address of sub-video-data**: As the definition of video-data, the video-data can be identified this list. *Fig. 1* show how to represent video-data by this list.

4) **Video media information**: Video-media ID (case of analog media) or the pointer to the video information which depends on media and devices (case of digital media). There exists some video devices that can identify analog media by writing/reading media ID. In near future, such video devices will be popular.

5) **Audio information**: Audio control information (case of analog media) or the pointer to the audio information which depends on media and devices (case of digital media).

*Table 1  Time Address Unit*

| Time Address Unit | Physical/Logical | Value | Video Device |
|---|---|---|---|
| Frame | Physical | 1/30 sec | LV, AV_File |
| Page | Physical | 2 frames | VHD |
| Time (min/sec) | Physical | time | LV, VHD |
| Time (minute) | Physical | time | LV |
| Time (hour/min/sec) | Physical | time | VTR |
| Chapter | Logical | 1 scene | LV, VHD |

**LV**: Laser Vision Video Disk Player     **VHD**: VHD Video Disk Player
**AV_File**: Optical Video Disk File Player     **VTR**: Video Taper Recorder

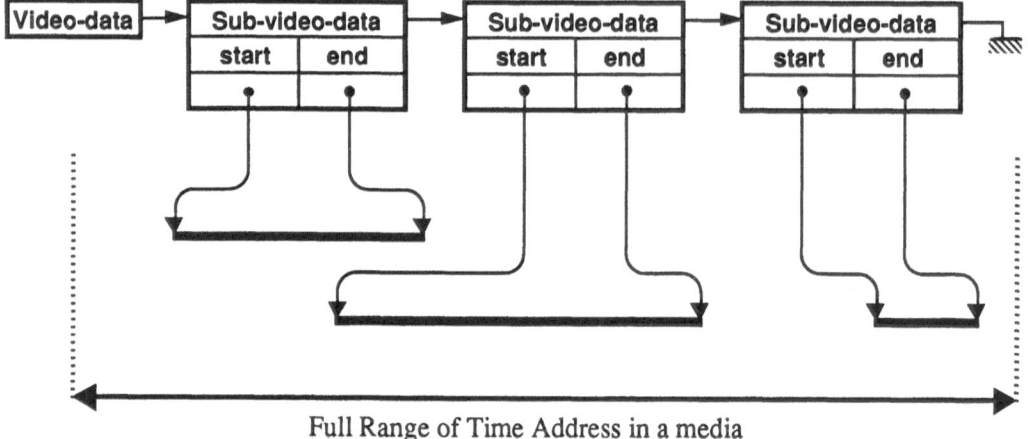

Full Range of Time Address in a media

*Fig. 1 Video-data and Sub-video-data list*

## 4. LOGICAL VIDEO DATA MODEL (LVD MODEL)

Using *Video Descriptor*, we can represent the video-data. Our next step is to provide video-data processing environment, that is, video interface model.

The video interface model must be decided by the following factors.

1) The model must offer rich human interface, especially it must match multi-window environment.

2) Although the standard model is independent of video processing hardware, the subset of the model can be implemented on all kind of video processing hardware. So we propose *Logical Video Data Model (LVD Model)*, which consists of four layers.
   - Standard video layer
   - Logical video plane layer
   - Graphic plane layer
   - Display layer

*Fig. 2* shows this *LVD Model*.

### 4.1 Standard Video Layer

In the *Standard video layer*, the original video-data is represented by *Video Descriptor*. The original video-data is treated to be sampled as standard size (for example 640 dots width * 480 dots height) and to be played as standard play speed (for example 30 frames/second). So the original video-data is called *standard video*.

This layer offers recording function. It is called *Bridge recording function*.

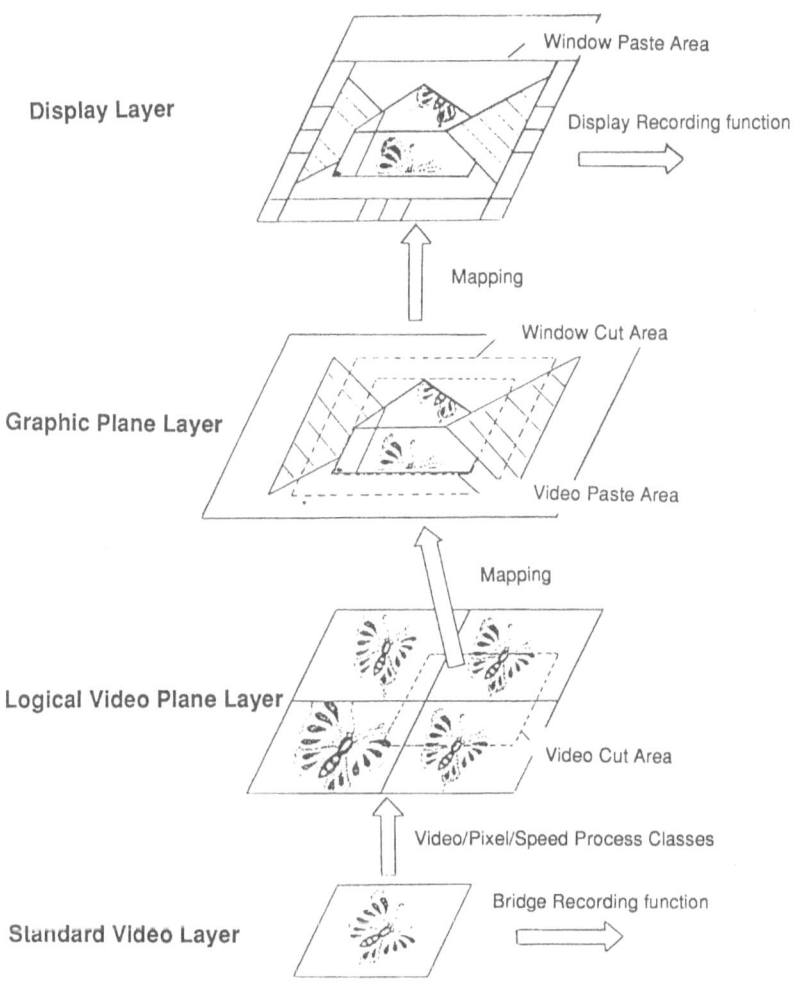

*Fig. 2 Logical Video Data Model (LVD Model)*

## 4.2 Logical Video Plane Layer

The *standard video* is mapped into *Logical video plane layer*. The mapped video-data is called *logical video plane*. The mapping function is classified into three classes:

- video process class
- pixel process class
- speed process class

The functions in the video process class process video-data itself like mosaic.

The functions in the pixel process class process pixels like color negation.

The functions in the speed process class process play speed like fast forward playing.

### 4.3 Graphic Plane Layer

A area is cut from the *Logical Video Plane* and mapped by window-viewport transformation and pasted into another area in the *Graphic plane layer*. In the *Graphic plane layer*, the pasted part of the *logical video plane*, texts and graphics are integrated. The integrated image is called *graphic plane*.

In the *Graphic plane layer*, *video transparent color* is defined. The *video transparent color* is treated as one of colors. Other colors are not transparent for the pasted part of the *logical video plane*. On the contrary, the *video transparent color* is transparent not only for other colors but also for the pasted part of the *logical video plane*. So if you draw some figures with this *video transparent color*, then video-data comes through the figures. In other words, you can use superimpose technique easily in the *Graphic plane layer*.

### 4.4 Display Layer

A area is cut from the *Graphic plane* and mapped by window-viewport transformation again and pasted into another area in the *Display layer*. In the *Display layer*, the mapped area is accompanied by window frame and is physically visible through a display device.

This layer offers recording function. It is called *display recording function*.

### 4.5 Video Manager Functions

*Video Manager* offers many functions and they are defined as processes intra/inter the layers of *LVD Model*. *Fig. 3* shows the relation between video manager functions and *LVD Model*.

### 5. AN IMPLEMENTATION OF VIDEO MANAGER ON THE BTRON SPECIFICATION

We have already developed the *Video Processor Unit* as a video processing hardware[2].

*Video Processor Unit* is optional hardware of the personal computer and provides following functions:

| LVD Model | Video Manager Functions |
|---|---|
| Display Layer | Dislpay Record etc. |
| ↑ | Redraw Video etc. |
| Graphic Plane Layer | Draw with Video Transparent Color etc. |
| ↑ | Mapping etc. |
| Logical Video Plane Layer | Get Play Time Address etc. |
| ↑ | Mosaic/Negation/Strobo etc. |
| Standard Video Layer | Regist Video Descriptor etc. |

*Fig.3 Video Manger Function and LVD Model*

- Scanning transformation of video signal (NTSC format)
- Digitization of video signal
- Superimpose
- Video display position control

Moreover we have also implemented the BTRON Specification operating system, which supports multi-window and multi-task functions[3]. In order to implement *Video Manager*, we adopted both of them.

Considering the ability of the *Video Processor Unit* and the demand of application software, we prepare three video modes:

1) Signal video mode

2) Multi video mode

3) Superimposer mode

These video modes are decided by configuration file. So users can choose one video mode according to his/her purpose.

*Signal video mode* offers most mapping functions from the *Standard video layer* to the *Logical video plane layer*, but only one video-data can be registered and displayed.

*Multi video mode* offers less mapping functions, but multiple video-data can be registered and displayed.

*Superimposer mode* simulates the cheaper hardware called *superimposer* which has the least functions for video-data processing. The application software which runs on this mode can be transported many other personal computers very easily because most of personal computers have their own cheap superimposer.

Regardless of video mode, there are following limitations of *LVD Model* in our implemented *Video Manager*.

1) The mapping form the *Logical video plane layer* to the *Graphic plane layer* is no zoom/reduction.

2) The mapping from the *Graphic plane layer* to the *Display layer* is also no zoom/reduction.

3) The coordinates of the *Graphic plane* is *Relative coordinates* defined in the BTRON specification OS.

4) The coordinates of the Display is *Absolute coordinates* defined in the BTRON Specification OS.

## 6. CONCLUSION

In order to treat video-data with personal computer, it is better that the operating system manages video-data. We call that part of OS *Video Manager*.

In the *Video Manager*, video-data is represented by *Video Descriptor* which identify the video-data.

The *Logical Video Data Model (LVD Model)* is proposed as video interface model. This *LVD Model* consists of four layers. And the functions of *Video Manager* are defined as processes intra/inter these layers.

The *Video Manager* is implemented adopting the *Video Processor Unit* as a video processing hardware and the BTRON specification OS. The *Video Manager* prepares three video modes, so a user can choose best mode according to his/her purpose.

**REFERENCE**

[1]   (for example) Y. Sotomura.et.al., "A Staudy on Motion Picture Retrieving/Editing System", 37th Proc. of IPSJ, 1988 (in Japanese)

[2]   T.Tatsumi.et.al, "Video Processor Unit for Personal Computer", PRoc. of ITEJ, 1988 (in Japanese)

[3]   Y.Imai et al, "An Implementation based on the BTRON specification", Proc of 33rd IEEE COMPCON, 1988

**Kazuo Kajimoto** was born in Osaka City, Japan, on January 26, 1962. He received the B.E. and M.E. degrees in information science from Kyoto University, Kyoto, Jpapan, in 1984 and 1986, respectively. He joined Matsushita Electric Industrial Co., Ltd. (MEI) in 1986. He has been engaged in the research and development of audio visual interface of computer. He is currently with MEI Infomation Systems Research Laboratory, Kadoma, Osaka, Japan. He is a member of the IPSJ, IEICEJ and the ASJ.

**Masahiro Shimizu** was born in Himeji City, Hyogo Prefecture, Japan, on December 8, 1948. He recieved the B.E. degree in engineering fron Kyoto University, Kyoto, Japan, in 1970. He joined Matsushita Electric Industrial Co., Ltd. (MEI) in 1970. From 1981 to 1982, he was a Visiting Scholar at the Electrical Engineering Department of University of California, Davis. He has been enaged in the research and development of digital image processing and pattern recognition. He is a member of IEICEJ and the IPSJ.

**Yoshiaki Kushiki** was born in Tokushima Prefecture, Japan, on Januaru 17, 1946. He received the B.E. degree in electronic engineering from Kyoto University, Kyoto, Japan, in 1968. He joined Matsushita Electric Industrial Co., Ltd. (MEI) in 1968. He has been engaged in the research and development of office system architecture, such as OS, DB, HMI and AI. He is currently with MEI Information Systems Research Laboratory, Kadoma, Osaka, Japan. He is a member of the IEEE, ACM, IEICEJ and the IPSJ.

Above authors may be reached at : Matsushita Electric Industrial Co., Ltd. Information Systems Research Laboratory Task Force 1, Kadoma, Osaka, 571, Japan

# The Type Mechanism
# of the TIPE/L Programming Language

Hiroaki Takada, Ken Sakamura
Department of Information Science, Faculty of Science, University of Tokyo

**ABSTRACT**

We have designed a programming language named *TIPE/L*, which is the base language of a general-purpose software development environment for BTRON machines called the *TIPE System* (TRON Integrated Programming Environment). The major features of TIPE/L are: a module structure based on the *real object/virtual object model* of BTRON for supporting software development by many distributed programmers, a powerful type mechanism to facilitate the construction of program components, and a TRON CPU dependent part of the language specification clearly separated from the CPU independent part. This paper describes the type mechanism of TIPE/L, which is the most important feature of the language.

The most attractive features of the type mechanism are *parametric types* and *type arguments*. Type parameter passing is realized by a method named *call-by-signature*. Types and functions with type arguments and *signatures* are powerful enough to make a library including various useful data structures and related algorithms. Moreover, TIPE/L supports *self-contained types* and user-defined *implicit type conversions*. This paper also outlines the means to implement the TIPE/L with reasonable efficiency.

**Keywords:** BTRON, TULS, TIPE system, parametric type, signature, self-contained type

## 1. INTRODUCTION

With the rapid progress of computer hardware, software systems are growing both in scale and in number, and the increasing cost of the development and maintenance of software systems is emerging as a serious problem. In order to solve this problem, we are constructing the *TIPE System* (TRON Integrated Programming Environment), which is a general-purpose software development environment for use on BTRON machines, as one of the sub-projects of the TRON project.

Our primary notions in the TIPE sub-project are the following.

1) As the scale of software systems grows, it becomes more important that many software engineers, who may work at different locations, be able to cooperate on one system.

2) In order to improve the productivity of respective engineers, the reuse of software components should be encouraged.

To facilitate development by distributed programmers, the development environment should be network-based. Project management and communication tools should also be integrated with other software tools. A database of software components must be the kernel of the environment to make software reuse convenient.

Above all, the most important feature is that the environment should facilitate a software system constructed modularly. All modules of the system should be strongly independent of each other, to permit development by many programmers and to make use of software components. The TIPE System provides a powerful and structured module mechanism exploiting the *real object/virtual object model*, which is a powerful data model of BTRON [1].

It is also important to integrate the TIPE System with the TRON total architecture. Hence, the TIPE System takes advantage of many useful features of BTRON machines, such as the uniformity of the human interface and the data transportability. It is also possible to utilize many other tools provided as a part of the BTRON architecture. For example, it is very easy to embed figures in a program text as comments.

Though the TIPE System is an environment independent from programming languages, the facility for constructing module-structured systems heavily relies on programming languages. We also plan to design a series of standard languages for the TRON projects. This language system is called TULS (TRON Universal Language System), and covers a wide application area with several languages for different purposes [2]. Hence, we have designed a programming language for professional programmers which strongly supports modular programming and matches with the TRON total architecture. This language, named *TIPE/L*, is applicable both to system programming and to some applications which require efficiency in execution time. This paper introduces the TIPE/L programming language and its type mechanism, the most important feature of the language.


## 2. TIPE/L PROGRAMMING LANGUAGE

TIPE/L is a clean extension of conventional procedural programming languages. The reason why we choose procedural paradigm is that this paradigm agrees well with von-Neumann machines and is more efficient compared with any other paradigm. TIPE/L also adopts some useful features from other programming paradigms, such as object-oriented programming and polymorphism, in order to increase the descriptive power of the language.

The major features of TIPE/L are discussed below.

### (a) Module structure utilizing the real object/virtual object model of BTRON

TIPE/L divides a module into two parts: a *definition part* and an *implementation part*. The definition part of a module is also called a definition module, and the implementation part is called an implementation module. Each part constitutes a real object in BTRON machines (a file in conventional machines) and becomes a compilation unit. This module structure is primarily the same as that of other modular languages, such as Modula-2 [3]. The definition part of a module comprises declarations (interface definitions) of objects (variables, functions, types, etc.) which are defined in the module and should be exported to others. The implementation part of the module gives the actual implementation of the objects together with some other objects which are local to the module and are hidden from other modules. Moreover, a mechanism to regard a set of modules as a single *composite module* is provided. The definition part of a composite module exists in order to export some declarations to other modules. Its implementation part includes some virtual objects pointing to the modules (which are contained in real objects) constituting the composite module. Composite modules should constitute a hierarchical structure and provide a mechanism for hierarchical information hiding.

Configuration management and version control (source code control) are important issues in developing a large software system. We have proposed a simple but powerful mechanism for configuration management and version control as a part of the TIPE System [4]. The method utilizes the real object/virtual object model and is language-independent. TIPE/L is equipped with the mechanism in the language specification.

TIPE/L also enables division of a program text into small parts. If a program text includes a virtual object, it is expanded to the real object pointed to by the virtual object when complied. A virtual object can be opened and the real object pointed to by the virtual object is displayed, as set forth in the BTRON user interface guideline. This method greatly improves the readability of the program text. It is also effective to attach some documentation at the top of each real object. Although a similar approach is adopted in the WEB system [5], our approach presents more structured organization.

#### (b) Powerful type mechanism

In recent years, many new programming paradigms have been proposed to provide programming languages with stronger descriptive power. Among them, object-oriented programming has drawn wide attention, and many languages which adopt the object-oriented paradigm have been designed and implemented [6] [7]. It has been demonstrated that object-oriented languages are effective for modular programming and software components through systems such as Smalltalk-80 [8]. However, object-oriented languages, especially object-oriented languages with static type checking, are not necessarily good for constructing a software component library of various useful data structures and related algorithms.

Take the case where we want to make a component realizing the B-tree structure. In an object-oriented language, the B-tree structure should be realized as a class (we will call it the class B). As for the data structure which is managed in the B-tree, however, it also should be defined as another class (we will call it the class A). Thus, the B-tree structure managing the class A is a class derived from the class B and has some instance of A as instance variables (this class is called BA). In this method, the definition of the class BA is quite complex, and the class B is incomplete as a software component (*Fig. 1(a)*). Lately, in order to remedy this defect, mechanisms for multiple inheritance have been extensively studied. Although this approach makes the mechanism very complex, it has not necessarily succeeded in making the expressive power strong enough to describe such a complex data structure as B-tree (*Fig. 1(b)*).

We consider that the mechanism to naturally express such a data structure is not based on object-oriented paradigm but on polymorphism [9], though some features of object-oriented languages are also useful. The

Ada programming language has a mechanism called a generic unit [10], which is a module template with some arguments including types. The CLU programming language also has parameterized modules [11], and the where clause of CLU is a similar mechanism to the *signature* of TIPE/L. However, these languages do not have any mechanism for type inheritance or self-contained types, which are types including all necessary operations on values of the types in them. TIPE/L lays importance on *parametric types* (generic types), and also adopts some useful features of object-oriented languages, such as *type inheritance* and *self-contained types (Fig. 1(c))*.

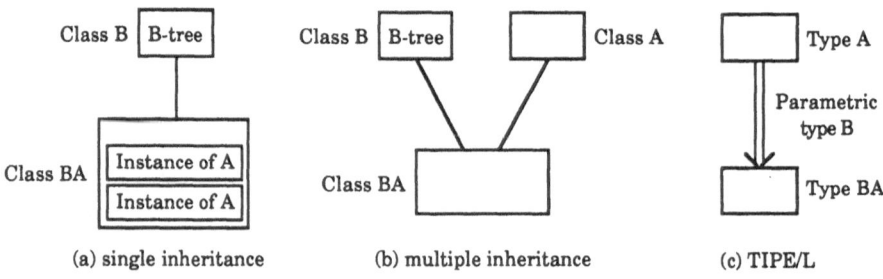

(a) single inheritance          (b) multiple inheritance          (c) TIPE/L

*Fig. 1    Type/class structure of object-oriented languages and TIPE/L*

### (c) TRON CPU dependent facilities

TIPE/L is good at describing system programs, such as the kernel of ITRON and BTRON and the various managers of BTRON. Thus, it is important to make the most of all instructions of the processor. For this purpose, TIPE/L provides the TRON CPU dependent language specification, in which facilities to write assembler instructions as a part of TIPE/L programs (in-line assembler facility) and to explicitly assign variables and arguments to registers are provided.

This facility is powerful when it is used together with the type mechanism. For example, in order to utilize the queue manipulation instructions of the TRON CPU, it is sufficient to provide a (parametric) type for the queue structures and some queue handling functions in the program library which are defined using in-line assembler facility and are compiled to code using queue manipulation instructions. Then, programmers who are not acquainted with the instruction set of the TRON CPU can generate efficient object code only by using the type and the functions prepared in the library. Providing another implementation of such a function without using in-line assembler facility maintains the portability and the readability of the program. It is even possible that programmers define some basic data types such as the integer type, which are usually provided as a primitive type in other languages.

## 3. TYPE ARGUMENTS AND PARAMETRIC TYPES

### 3.1 FUNCTION OVERLOADING

TIPE/L has a *function overloading* facility. Functions with the same function name but with different numbers or types of arguments (formal arguments) can be defined at the same time. In this case, the function name is said to be overloaded. Which function is actually called is determined by the type of the parameters (actual arguments) alone according to the function selection rule of TIPE/L [12].

Examples of functions with an overloaded name and their sample usage are presented below.

**Example 1** (function overloading)

```
val min(n,m:int):int                /* function (a) */
{
    return(n<m ? n : m)
};

val min(x,y:float):float            /* function (b) */
{
    return(x<y ? x : y)
};

val n:int;
val r:float;

n = min(3,4);                       /* (a) is called */
r = min(3.0,4.0);                   /* (b) is called */
n = min(3.0,4);                     /* causes type check error */
```

In TIPE/L, a procedure is realized as a function whose return value is of type void. Thus, the overloading mechanism described above is also applied to procedures. TIPE/L also allows programmers to overload predefined operators, which include infix operators, such as + and = (assignment), prefix operators, such as − (negation) and ! (not), and postfix operators, such as [ ] (indexing). These operators are in fact defined as functions. Precedence among those operators is defined in the language specification and cannot be altered by programmers. Together with the TRON CPU dependent facilities described in Section 2, the overloading facility enables users to define some primitive types, such as the integer type, and various operators on them.

### 3.2 TYPE ARGUMENTS AND CALL-BY-SIGNATURE

One of the most important features of the TIPE/L type mechanism is that a type can be passed as an argument. It is also possible to take a value of the parameter type (the type which is passed to a type argument) or some type constructed from the parameter type (such as the pointer type of the parameter type) as an argument. A value of such a type can also be returned as a return value.

We will show some examples of type arguments.

**Example 2** (signatured function with a type argument)

```
signature lessSig(type t) = sig {
                             val op<(n,m:t):bool
                 };

val min(type ty:lessSig(ty);x,y:ty):ty
{
    return(x<y ? x : y)
};

n = min(int,3,4);
```

The function `min` declared above takes three arguments, the first of which is a type argument. Trailing two arguments are value arguments of the type `ty`, which is passed as the first argument. The function returns a value of type `ty` as a return value. `lessSig(ty)` is called a signature and declares that the function `min` uses some functions which depend on the type argument `ty` in its implementation. The definition of `lessSig` states that only the function named `op<` is required (`op<` is the functional form of the binary operator `<`) and that it takes two arguments of type `ty` and returns a Boolean value.

In general, functions with type arguments demonstrate their expressive power when they contain some operations depending on the parameter type. In this case, the parameter type can be considered as completely characterized by these operations. Thus, passing a type as an argument is equivalent to passing these operations.

TIPE/L is a modular programming language, and a function with type arguments and a function which calls the former one may be compiled independently. More strictly, the called function must be compiled by itself, and the calling function must be compiled by referring only to the declaration (interface definition) of the called function. (Inter-module optimization described in Section 6 aims at further optimization by removing this restriction.) In order to compile them independently, it is necessary to enumerate all parameter dependent operations used in the called function as a part of its declaration.

In TIPE/L, all the operations on values are presented as functions. Therefore, in order to enumerate the operations, it is sufficient to give a set of function names and the types of their arguments and their return values. This set is called a *signature*, and a set of actual functions corresponding to a signature is called a *signature instance*. In TIPE/L, a parameter type is passed to a function by passing a signature instance instead. This parameter passing method is named *call-by-signature*, and a function with a signature is called a *signatured function*.

In the above example, the function `min` requires three arguments, but the first argument is determined by the type of the trailing parameters and can be omitted as below.

**Example 3** (signatured function with a type argument)

```
val min(x,y:(type ty:lessSig(ty))):ty
{
    return(x<y ? x : y)
};

n = min(3,4);
```

## 3.3 PARAMETRIC TYPES

In TIPE/L, types may have arbitrary arguments. A type with arguments is called a *parametric type*, in contrast with a type without arguments. A parametric type enables handling a class of types which have the same outer structure but include different components as one type. For example, all doubly linked queues have a common structure; each node has a link pointing to the previous node as well as to the following one and includes some items which are managed by the queue structure. The data structure of the items varies with the use of the queue. In this case, it is suggested to define a type for queue structures using the parametric type mechanism.

**Example 4** (parametric type)

```
type queue(type elt) = struct {
                            val next:*queue(elt);
                            val last:*queue(elt);
                            val elem:elt
                        };

type intQueue = queue(int);
```

The first definition above states that the type `queue` is a parametric type with one type argument, which is the data type of items managed by the queue structure. It also defines the type as consisting of two pointers and the item data. `*queue(elt)` represents a type of pointers to the type `queue(elt)`. The second definition gives another name `intQueue` to the type `queue(int)`. It is noteworthy that the type `intQueue` is defined totally independently of the structure of the type `queue`.

It is also possible to define a function which is applied to a value of a parametric type. As an example, a function named `insert` which inserts a new node in a queue is described below. The doubly linked queue handled here constitutes a ring structure as a whole, and has a queue header node which indicates the start and the end position of the queue.

**Example 5** (function on parametric type)

```
val insert(p,q:*queue(type elt)):void
// insert *q in the next position of *p
{
    q->next = p->next;
    q->last = p;
    p->next->last = q;
    p->next = q
};
```

Though it is not described in detail in this paper, the function `insert` and certain other queue operations can be realized efficiently by using the queue manipulation instructions of the TRON CPU together with the CPU dependent facilities of TIPE/L.

**Example 6** (TRON CPU dependent facility)

```
inline val insert(p,q:*queue(type elt)):void
asm {
    QINS q,p
};
```

# 4. IMPLICIT TYPE CONVERSIONS AND SELF-CONTAINED TYPES

## 4.1 IMPLICIT TYPE CONVERSIONS

For a language with a powerful type mechanism like TIPE/L, *type conversion* is also an important feature. Type conversion is a mechanism to construct a value of a type from values of other types. Almost all programming languages provide some language-defined type conversions such as a conversion from an integer type to a real number type. Some languages also allow programmers to define type conversions.

TIPE/L provides some language-defined conversions, and allows programmers to define conversion functions called user-defined conversions. Because a user-defined conversion which uses a language-defined one in its implementation can override the language-defined conversion, two constructs to describe conversions are provided. One of them is a primitive operator named `convert` in which only language-defined conversions are represented and cannot be overridden by user-defined ones. The other is to use a type name as a conversion function. This kind of conversion functions represent language-defined conversions until they are overridden by user-defined ones.

TIPE/L also supports *implicit type conversion*. In case that a type conversion is implicit one, the conversion function can be omitted. Some language-defined conversions are defined as implicit. A user-defined conversion is implicit if keyword `implicit` is added before the declaration of the conversion function. There is one restriction that an implicit conversion function must have only one argument.

## 4.2 TYPE INHERITANCE AND TYPE `void`

TIPE/L realizes a simple type inheritance mechanism as a syntax-sugaring of the implicit type conversion.

**Example 7** (type inheritance)

```
type titledWindow = struct {
                    super val w:window;
                    val      t:titleInfo
               };
```

The keyword `super` in the above example has the same effect with two language-defined implicit type conversions: a conversion from the type `titledWindow` to the type `window` and one from the type `*titledWindow` to `*window`. In this case, the type `window` is called a *parent type* of the type `titledWindow`. Thus, every function with an argument of the type `window` can be applied to a value of the type `titledWindow`. It is also possible to have more than one parent types by attaching `super` to many fields.

The type `void` is a parent type of all other types. In other words, there are implicit type conversions from all types to the type `void` and conversions from all pointer types to the type `*void`. On the other hand, conversions from the type `*void` to all other pointer types are provided as explicit language-defined conversions.

## 4.3 SELF-CONTAINED TYPES

In Example 2 and Example 3, signatures are attached to functions. Therefore, all data structures must be homogeneous. In the case of doubly linked queue, the item data in each node must be of the same type. However, one often must handle a heterogeneous queue, each node of which may have different types of items. This kind of structure is called heterogeneous.

One approach to manipulate such a structure is to make a new data type in which some different types of data are admitted. Such a type is realized as a union of the C language or a variant record of Pascal. TIPE/L also supports a union, which is quite different from that of the conventional languages [12]. However, these constructs have a limitation that the all possible types (of the item data, in the case of queue) must be listed in advance, and they are not good at constructing program components beforehand.

Another approach to handle heterogeneous data structure is to include all necessary information about the data in itself. This approach is usual in object-oriented languages. Since any kind of information about a type can be presented as a signature in TIPE/L, the facility to have a signature in a data structure is sufficient to handle heterogeneous structures.

**Example 8** (heterogeneous queue)

```
signature printSig(type t) = sig {
                                val print(x:*t):void
                             };

type printQueue(type elt) = struct {
                                val next,last:*printQueue(void);
                                val elem:elt
                             }:printSig(elt);
```

By attaching a signature to a type definition as the above example, a signature instance is included into each value of the type `printQueue`. It is acceptable to consider that a field for the signature instance is added. (In fact, a field for a pointer to the signature instance is added in normal implementation.) This kind of type is called a *self-contained type*, since the type includes all necessary information about itself in form of a signature instance.

When an assignment to one of the fields which have some influence on the signature occurs, a new signature instance is also assigned to the signature field (a possibly virtual field which contains a signature instance or a pointer to a signature instance). In order to make the signature assignment possible, the following restrictions are imposed.

1) All the fields that have some influence on the signature instance must be assigned at the same time.

2) The type of the value which is assigned to such a field must be statically determined, or the signature can be constructed from another signature on the type of the value.

# 5. OTHER FEATURES OF THE TIPE/L TYPE MECHANISM

## 5.1 MULTIPLE RETURN VALUE

TIPE/L provides a mechanism to facilitate a function with multiple return values. The TRON CPU and many other microprocessors today have many registers with the same functionality. In order to utilize such registers, programming languages may well support functions with multiple return values and should naturally express them.

**Example 9** (function with multiple return values)

```
val divide(x,y:int):(int,int)
{
    return(x/y,x%y)
};

val a,b,c:int;

(a,b) = divide(10,4);
(c,_) = divide(20,3);
```

The function `divide` in this example takes two integers and returns two integers. For efficiency, this function should be implemented with a machine instruction which computes the quotient and the remainder of two integers at the same time using in-line assembler facility. `_` is a pre-defined variable of type `void` and is used when some of the return values are not necessary.

## 5.2 POINTERS AND ARRAYS

In TIPE/L, pointers and arrays can be explained as parametric types. A pointer type takes one type argument, and an array type takes a type argument and an integer argument. Of course, these types cannot be defined from any other types, and they are called *primitive parametric types*.

Because an array type is characterized as a parametric type, how to handle arrays is quite different from that of the C language. A variable name of an array type does not express a pointer to the first element of the array, but the whole contents of it. And, a function which takes an array as an argument also takes the number of its elements.

**Example 10** (function on array type)

```
val sum(a:*(int[val n:int])):int
// calculate the sum of the integer array (*a)
{
    val s,i:int;

    for (s = i = 0; i<n; i++) {
        s += (*a)[i];
    };
    return(s)
};
```

In this example, $t[n]$ represents the array type whose base type is $t$ and the number of elements is $n$, where $t$ is a type and $n$ is a value of integer.

## 6. IMPLEMENTATION AND EFFICIENCY

### 6.1 NAIVE IMPLEMENTATION VS. INSTANTIATION

There are two approaches to implement signatured functions. The first approach is a naive implementation of call-by-signature. When a signatured function is called, a signature instance is passed with other parameters. When the signature includes many function declarations, it is suggested to pass the pointer to the signature instance. In this case, the number of memory accesses increases by one (when the pointer to the signature instance is on a register) or two (when the pointer is on the stack), whenever one of the functions listed in the signature is called. When the function has an argument of a parametric type the size of which varies, the size and the address of the argument in the stack must also be passed. Some extra costs must be paid to access such an argument. It also causes some inefficiency that the signature must be reconstructed when a signatured function calls another function with a different signature.

The other approach is to implement by instantiation. Whenever a signatured function is called with different types of parameters, the object code for the function is created for the respective type. In execution time, the object code generated by this method has the same efficiency as the code of a function which is written respectively for each non-parametric type.

This implementation approach is further divided into two methods: instantiation by the compiler and instantiation by the linker. The first method is used in Ada compilers. However, when a signatured function and another function which calls the former one reside in different modules, the object code of the latter function depends on the former function, and dependency relations among modules become complex. The second method, instantiation by the linker, imposes some extra burden on the linker. This kind of linker is called an instantiation linker, which is described in 6.2.

The signatured functions of TIPE/L are carefully designed to be implemented by both approaches described above. It is also possible to combine the two approaches. It depends on the situation as to which approach should be chosen. Though it is ideal that the optimizer chooses the better one, it is also permissible to provide some mechanism to let the programmer determine whether each function should be instantiated for a type or not.

## 6.2 INSTANTIATION LINKER

An instantiation linker generates some instances of an object according to an *object template* obtained from a relocatable object file created by compilers. A directive to generate an instance and some additional information are also included in the relocatable object. When this mechanism is used for the instantiation of a signatured function, the template is a function template and the additional information is a signature instance. Therefore, it can be said that the call-by-signature is performed at linking time in this implementation method. Of course, this kind of linker is more inefficient compared with a conventional linker, but this method is a good trade-off between the efficiency at execution time and the efficiency at development time.

By extending the notion of an instantiation linker, the implementation body of an in-line function no longer need to be written in a definition module, and the amount of storage required by the compiler can be reduced.

## 6.3 INTER-MODULE OPTIMIZATION

TIPE/L is a modular language, and each module should be independently compiled in principle. This characteristic is important for efficient development, especially for debugging. However, it is also important to optimize a whole program ignoring this characteristic, that is, the independence of the respective modules. This kind of optimization is called *inter-module optimization.*

Suppose we implement a signatured function by instantiation by the compiler, then it becomes necessary to refer to the implementation part of another module. This belongs among applications of inter-module optimization. Heterogeneous data structures realized by self-contained types can also be optimized by enumerating all types whose values are assigned to the related fields of the types. As all modules must be scanned to enumerate those types, this task also requires inter-module optimization mechanism. It is also possible to make some signatured functions take a common signature, or to share a signature instance among modules. Global register allocation also becomes possible.

## 7. CONCLUSION

We have designed a programming language named TIPE/L, which is equipped with some useful features to facilitate modular programming and software components. Type arguments, parametric types, signatured functions, implicit type conversions, and self-contained types are central concepts within the type mechanism of TIPE/L. We have also presented some basic ideas for efficient implementation of the language. The actual implementation and the evaluation of TIPE/L remains as future works.

**REFERENCES**

[1] K. Sakamura, "BTRON: the business-oriented operating system", *IEEE Micro*, Apr. 1987, pp. 53-65.

[2] K. Sakamura, "TRON UNIVERSAL LANGUAGE SYSTEM", *Proc. of the Fifth TRON Project Symposium* (this volume), Springer-Verlag, Tokyo, 1988.

[3] N. Wirth, *Programming in Modula-2*, 3rd ed., Springer-Verlag, Berlin, 1985.

[4] H. Takada and K. Sakamura, "Configuration management and version control in TIPE system", *Proc. of the 2nd TRON Technical Study Group Meeting*, Oct. 1988, pp. 21-31 (in Japanese).

[5] D. E. Knuth, "Literate programming", *The Computer Journal*, vol. 27, no.2, 1984, pp. 97-111.

[6] B. Stroustrup, *The C++ Programming Language*, Addison Wesley, Reading, Mass., 1986.

[7] B. J. Cox, *Object-Oriented Programming*, Addison Wesley, Reading, Mass., 1987.

[8] A. Goldberg and D. Robson, *Smalltalk-80: The Language and its Implementation*, Addison Wesley, Reading, Mass., 1983.

[9] L. Cardelli and P. Wegner, "On understanding types, data abstraction, and polymorphism", *Computing Surveys*, vol. 17, no. 4, Dec. 1985, pp. 471-522.

[10] *The Programming Language Ada: Reference Manual*, ANSI/MIL-STD-1815A-1983, LNCS 155, Springer-Verlag, Berlin, 1983.

[11] Barbara Liskov, et.al., *CLU Reference Manual*, LNCS 114, Springer-Verlag, Berlin, 1981.

[12] H. Takada and K. Sakamura, "The TIPE/L programming language reference manual", in preparation.

**Hiroaki Takada** is a Ph.D. course student of Department of Information Science at the University of Tokyo. He is now, under the supervision of Dr. Sakamura, engaged in research on software development environment and programming language for the TRON project. Takada is also interested in hypertext systems. He received the B.S. and M.S. degrees in information science from the University of Tokyo. He is a member of ACM, IEEE, Information Processing Society of Japan, and Japan Society for Software Science and Technology.

JUNET: hiro@spica.is.s.u-tokyo.junet
CSNET: hiro%spica.is.s.u-tokyo.junet@japan.cs.net

**Ken Sakamura** is currently an associate professor at the Department of Information Science, University of Tokyo. He holds Ph.D. in EE. Being a computer architect, he has been the leader of the TRON project which he started to build a new computer system architecture for 1990's since 1984. His promotion of the TRON architecture now extends to architecture of buildings and furniture. He servers on the editorial board of Institute of Electrical and Electronics Engineers (IEEE) MICRO magazine and is a chair of the project promotion committee of the TRON Association. He is a member of Japan Information Processing Society, Institute of Electronics, Information and Communication Engineers, ACM, and is a senior member of IEEE. He has received best paper awards of IEICE twice, of JIPS once, IEEE best annual article award, and other awards from Japanese and overseas organizations.

Above authors may be reached at Department of Information Science, Faculty of Science, University of Tokyo, 7-3-1 Hongo, Bunkyo-ku, Tokyo, Japan.

# Chapter 4: CTRON

# Perspectives on CTRON

## James D. Mooney
Dept. of Statistics and Computer Science, West Virginia University

**ABSTRACT**

Unlike other TRON software components, CTRON is designed to run on various CPU architectures, including existing, large-scale computers as well as microprocessors. It is expected that various implementations of CTRON should provide common support for suitable applications in spite of differences in software and hardware architecture. Thus CTRON may be viewed as a standard for an interface between operating systems and applications, and between operating systems and CPU architectures.

Such a standard must be robust, to be useable in many different environments. It also should be in harmony with other standards that may exist for similar or related elements of the distributed system which TRON envisions. This paper reviews some principal interfaces that exist in a typical computing system and significant formal and de facto standards for these interfaces, and examines CTRON's role among these standards. The review is based on experience in the development of the IEEE MOSI standard, which has many similarities with CTRON, and on an ongoing study of CTRON itself.

Based on this review, some suggestions are offered for the fine tuning and evolution of CTRON, which may help the specification to best fulfill its intended purposes.

**Keywords:** CTRON, Operating System Interfaces, Portability

## 1. INTRODUCTION

The CTRON Operating System Specification is designed to enhance the portability of applications across a variety of multitasking environments. An important class of applications which CTRON must support are those providing service in a high-performance TRON distributed network. Some of these applications have strong realtime behavior requirements. The combined objectives of application portability and realtime performance in a multitasking environment present CTRON with ambitious challenges not faced by other projects.

The design concepts of CTRON, developed to meet these challenges, have been well described by others [Ohkubo et al 1987, Wasano et al 1987]. Many of the initial

---

This work is funded in part by grants from Nippon Telephone and Telegraph and from the TRON Association.

specification documents have also been published. This paper is intended to assist in the refinement of these concepts and specifications by examining CTRON, in view of its objectives, and in relation to some related OS specifications and standards. Although the CTRON objectives differ significantly from those of other projects, much can be learned from examining both the differences and the similarities.

Since 1980 I have participated in the MOSI standard project of the IEEE Computer Society, and since 1985 I have chaired the MOSI working group. This project has resulted in development of an operating system interface standard with many similarities to CTRON (The MOSI standard was approved in 1985 for Trial Use [IEEE 1985], and a revised version is now in the final stages of approval). A number of lessons learned during the MOSI project are described in [Mooney 1986a], and CTRON is examined in this paper using the perspective of these lessons.

While working with MOSI I have studied the work of other projects, including POSIX [IEEE 1986] and the new international initiatives of JTC-1. I am now performing a study of CTRON and its relation to other OS interface projects, sponsored by NTT and the CTRON Committee. This study is still in progress; a detailed review has been completed only for the CTRON Kernel. This paper is based on all these experiences. A detailed presentation of the results of the study so far is beyond the scope of the paper, but the principal conclusions are identified and discussed.

The next section identifies some unique aspects of CTRON that distinguish it from related projects. We then review the principal responsibilities of common types of operating systems, and the various interfaces which may exist between an OS and other system elements. These reviews provide perspectives to determine if CTRON is well-focused on a suitable subject area. The paper next compares CTRON with several related system interface standards, and consider whether its relationship to those standards is consistent and complementary to an appropriate extent. The important issue of language-level standards (language bindings) is examined in the following section. Finally, we provide some summary comments on aspects of the CTRON resource models, and some recommendations for future development.

## 2. Unique Aspects of CTRON

The central problem addressed by CTRON is the design of a standard interface between operating systems and application programs, to simplify the job of transporting programs among different operating systems running on processors with different architectures. Stated in this way, this objective is shared by a number of other projects, including the TRON subprojects ITRON and BTRON. However, CTRON's goals differ from those of ITRON and BTRON in several respects:

1. CTRON is intended to run on more powerful microprocessors than ITRON or BTRON, and also on larger mainframes;

2. CTRON must support concurrent tasks which do not necessarily cooperate;

3. Unlike BTRON, CTRON does not provide direct support for a human-computer interface.

Several other projects exist for the development of OS interface standards, and several widely-used operating systems provide interfaces which may be viewed as *de facto* standards. Some of these interfaces share at least the first two attributes listed above, but CTRON differs from them in other ways:

1. CTRON is planned fundamentally for support of realtime processing requirements;

2. Because of these requirements, CTRON is intended for the development of new operating systems, not for grafting onto existing ones.

## 3. OPERATING SYSTEM TYPES AND RESPONSIBILITIES

To assess the suitability of the general functional areas addressed by CTRON, let's examine the responsibilities of common types of operating systems. General-purpose OSs fall into a few fundamental categories, and largely share a common set of responsibilities. It is reasonable to say that the primary purpose of most operating systems is *to manage a collection of resources,* and that the objectives of this management are *to protect resources from unauthorized use* and *to make resources more convenient to use.*

As described in Lane & Mooney [1988] and other textbooks, the principal resources managed by a typical OS include:

PHYSICAL RESOURCES: CPU, memory, I/O devices, storage devices, timers

LOGICAL RESOURCES: Jobs, processes or tasks, files, information in memory, system services

Jobs and processes, along with users, may also be viewed as "active resources" on whose behalf the other resources are managed. These resource types lead to the OS responsibilities listed below:

| | |
|---|---|
| User Interface Management | Error Handling |
| Process/Task Management | Reliability |
| Job/Session Management | Security |
| I/O & Storage Device Management | Monitoring |
| Timer Management | Accounting |
| Memory Management | System Management |
| File Management | |

The fundamental OS categories that strongly determine system structure are Batch, Interactive, and Realtime. The category of an operating system establishes the importance of the various responsibilities; for example, batch systems have limited task or timer management, while realtime systems may be less concerned with accounting or the user interface. No OS specification can cover all categories at once, and the natural domain of CTRON is the realtime system.

As a realtime system specification, CTRON addresses all the responsibilities in the left column except Job/Session and User Interface Management. It places appropriate emphasis on Error Handling, Reliability, and Security, although its security mechanisms could be strengthened. CTRON does not define aspects of the specialized functions of Monitoring, Accounting, and System Management. This omission is appropriate, since these functions are not expected to be accessed by portable applications. Thus CTRON addresses all of the appropriate functional areas for its intended domain.

## 4. OPERATING SYSTEM INTERFACES

A computing system contains a number of important interfaces between its various components. In this section we discuss the principal interfaces, and identify those with which CTRON is and should be concerned.

Figure 1 illustrates the principal interfaces that may be of concern when a typical application program is running with a typical operating system. Some of these interfaces (shown by solid arrows in the figure) are direct connections between two system components; others (shown as dashed arrows) are indirect interfaces, logical connections which are mediated by other components. All of these interfaces are described more fully in [Mooney 1986b].

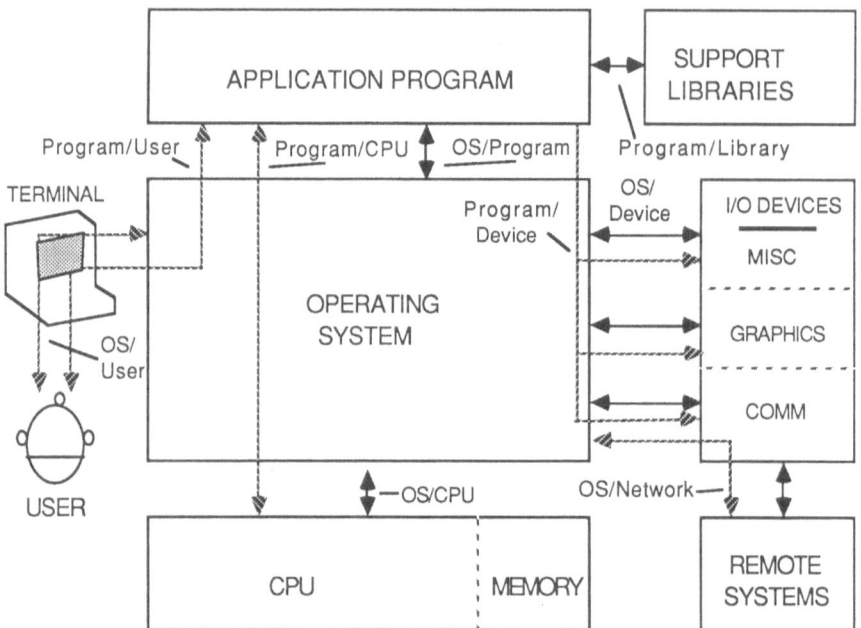

Figure 1. Operating System Interfaces

Standardizing any of these interfaces can contribute to the portability of applications, operating systems, and other system components. Most have been given some attention by formal or informal standardization groups. CTRON is concerned with application portability, and focuses especially on the OS/Program interface.

A realtime system standard must also provide access to low-level system functions, bypassing OS overhead when necessary. CTRON meets this need by specifying portions of the Program/CPU interface (such as interrupts and the architecture-dependent "black box") and by providing a Program/Device interface for low-level access to I/O Devices. Finally, in keeping with its special role in communication and switching control, CTRON establishes an indirect "Program/Network" interface, providing low-level access to the more traditional OS/Network interface shown in the figure.

## 5. FORMAL AND DEFACTO STANDARDS

The objective of CTRON is to develop a standard for certain system interfaces. A number of other standards have been established for most of the interfaces described above, and additional ones are being developed. The CTRON specification will be most useful if it does not compete and conflict with widely-accepted standards in addressing similar concepts. Instead it should focus on areas that are not yet well standardized. When concepts are included that are addressed by other standards, moreover, CTRON should introduce differences only for good reason. This section reviews some important standards related to CTRON, and assesses CTRON's objectives in the perspective of those standards. Many of these standards are further discussed in [Mooney 1986a].

Standards may be classified broadly as formal and *de facto*. A formal standard is established after study and agreement by a standard-making committee, usually sponsored by an official organization. Such a committee ideally represents most of the parties who may be interested in using such a standard. A *de facto* standard, in contrast, is established unilaterally by a single supplier. If that supplier is a dominant one, other suppliers may copy the standard and users may have little choice but to conform to it.

Most standards, in computing and other fields, primarily address an *interface* between elements of a system. The elements themselves are not unduly constrained, since the purpose is to enable differing elements to fit together in a common fashion. Early standards for nuts and bolts defined the form of the threads but not the shape and color of the bolts. In similar fashion, a standard for operating system interfaces is more useful than one which defines the structure of the operating system itself.

The principal organizations which develop and sponsor formal standards in the computing field fall into three major groups:

1. Professional organizations, especially the IEEE and its Computer Socicty;

2. National bodies, such as ANSI in the U.S. and JISC in Japan;

3. International organizations, especially ISO, IEC, and CCITT.

The formal standards of most concern to CTRON are those that address the four interfaces identified in the previous section. Of primary concern is the OS/Program interface; this is addressed by the IEEE MOSI and POSIX standards as well as CTRON. A joint committee of ISO and IEC, JTC-1, has begun a broad study of standards issues for software system interfaces and application portability; this work is still in an exploratory stage.

No established standards exist for the aspects of the Program/CPU interface covered by CTRON. The Program/Device interface is defined to some degree by MOSI and POSIX, and also by a variety of standards for specific device types (e.g. ASCII for terminals, GKS for graphic devices). The OS/Network interface is comprehensively defined by the OSI model standardized by the ISO. Let us compare CTRON with each of these standards:

MOSI: CTRON and MOSI address many similar areas, but have somewhat different objectives. MOSI is concerned with the portability of general-purpose applications in small system environments. The revised version of MOSI gives more attention to realtime constraints, but does not meet a full spectrum of realtime requirements. CTRON addresses a class of realtime applications on systems which may be small or large. CTRON models are highly consistent with MOSI models, although not always identical, when similar needs are addressed.

POSIX: The primary goal of POSIX is to formalize the *de facto* standard OS/Program interface implemented by UNIX® operating systems, and to resolve inconsistencies among UNIX versions. This interface serves general-purpose applications, especially interactive software tools. UNIX is fundamentally a non-realtime system. New POSIX subprojects address realtime issues but are still at an early stage. POSIX makes use of the very effective UNIX model for hierarchical file systems; CTRON file management uses a model which is consistent with POSIX though less detailed.

PROGRAM/DEVICE STANDARDS: Standards for accessing I/O devices vary greatly in the generality of the device model. The choice ranges from simple operations applicable to almost any device type, to models and operations that apply to a very specific device. ASCII and GKS define complete sets of control functions for fairly specific device classes. POSIX defines a very detailed terminal interface. MOSI and CTRON both take a generic approach. MOSI defines only a few operations applicable to all devices. CTRON follows this strategy and goes on to identify operations for important device classes. This was also a goal of MOSI, but due to resource limitations it was not completed.

THE OSI MODEL: The OSI seven-layer communication model is well known and widely followed. The model itself does not include detailed system interface definitions for most layers. CTRON defines a comprehensive program interface for four of the layers; this interface is not addressed by any other formal standard.

Although formal standardization is valuable even where de facto standards exist, there are several de facto standard OS/Program interfaces which should be examined in relation to CTRON. UNIX is probably the most widely used; its interface has been addressed by POSIX. VAX/VMS is widely used in medium-scale environments, and includes a rich collection of mechanisms for realtime support. Some of these VMS models (e.g. cyclic task scheduling, exit handlers) are followed closely by CTRON.

MS-DOS is a clear *de facto* standard in small environments, and OS/2 is a potential one. OS/2 includes some facilities for realtime support, but neither of these systems provides an interface comprehensive enough to meet all the needs envisioned for CTRON applications. There are several commonly used OSs which are designed primarily as realtime executives (such as VRTX, iRMX, etc.), but none of these appears to have gained the dominance necessary for a *de facto* standard.

We can thus conclude that CTRON on the whole does not conflict with other standards, and is reasonably consistent where it should be. In addition, it fills some gaps in functional areas that have not been addressed by other OS/Program interface standards. The principal gap is in support functions necessary for certain realtime applications. In addition, CTRON is unique in addressing the Program/Network interface, and the Program/Device interface for specific device classes.

Although it is somewhat surprising in a realtime oriented context, CTRON also defines mechanisms for managing indexed files, and is expected to address higher level data management issues. Both of these were also unattained MOSI goals, and have not been effectively handled by other standards.

## 6. LANGUAGE LEVEL STANDARDS

The OS/Program interface is specified by CTRON and other standards in the form of a collection of "system calls." This type of definition is important but incomplete. We must remember that programs are generally written in high-level programming languages, and it is within programs in these languages that the interface functions must actually be invoked. A system interface standard provides little help for portability if the language mechanisms for accessing it remain unspecified. To be effective, such a standard *must* include language bindings.

When considered over its full development cycle, the interface between a program and the operating system actually includes several "translation interfaces" along with the direct OS/Program interface. These interfaces are shown in Figure 2. They represent the translation of a program from source language form to object form by a compiler or interpreter, and then to executable form by a relocating and linking loader.

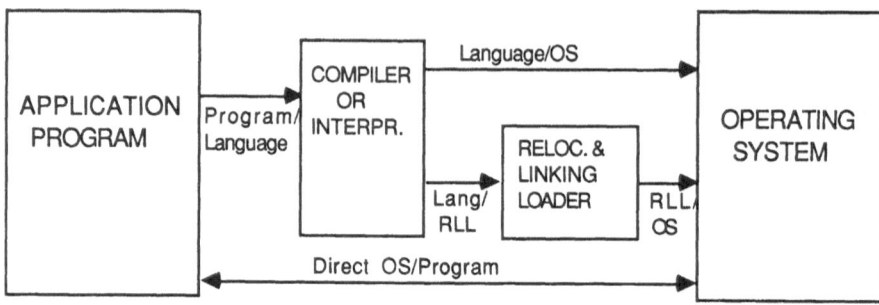

Figure 2.  Translation Interfaces

Important standards are associated with these interfaces as well.  The most important are programming language standards.  Formal standards have been established for most of the popular languages.  A recent IEEE standard addresses the object code representation as well.

Every language standard differs in the mechanisms it provides for access to system resources.  COBOL has elaborate file management built in; Pascal has almost none.  Mechanisms for timing, intertask communication, exception handling and memory management vary greatly.  Some of the OS interface is implicit in language statements; some may be completely unusable (e.g., memory allocation in FORTRAN), and the rest must generally be accessed by procedure calls.  In this case a collection of standard procedures may also be defined, such as the Standard Library of C or the standard packages (and extended environments like CAIS) defined for Ada®.

A number of principles for development of language bindings for a system interface standard are listed and discussed in [Mooney 1986a].  Most of these principles can be summarized in a single rule: *Fit the standard to the language, not the language to the standard.*  We must remember that the interface standard is to be used by programmers who are most familiar with the language and its conventions, not with the standard.  For this reason, built-in mechanisms should not be replaced or duplicated;  interface elements should be expressed in forms and types appropriate to the language, and the entire binding should be developed or reviewed by experienced programmers in that specific language.

As is usually the case for an emerging standard, the CTRON language bindings are at an earlier stage of development than the base standard.  A consistent set of languages has also not yet been chosen.  It will be important to keep these principles in mind as the language bindings are finalized.

## 7. CONCLUSIONS AND RECOMMENDATIONS

In the preceding sections we have examined CTRON from the perspective of general OS structures, system interfaces, and existing standards.  Here we will present some conclusions and make some recommendations for the future development of the CTRON specification.

143

On the whole, CTRON is well focused on an important and appropriate subject area: support of applications for communication, switching and other services in a highly distributed network. Such applications have realtime requirements not addressed by other standards. CTRON complements existing standards with few avoidable conflicts or redundancies.

In its detailed specification of task states and attributes, scheduling algorithms, and other system aspects, CTRON places more constraints on OS implementation than similar standards. However, its unique realtime objectives make these constraints necessary. My study of CTRON's Version 1 specifications leads to a variety of minor criticisms which cannot be detailed in this paper. If there is a possible overall weakness, it must be only that CTRON is very ambitious. Many subjects are addressed that other standards groups have found difficult to define. The CTRON solutions in these areas will need to be validated and refined through implementation and use. The broad-based membership of the TRON Association and the CTRON Technical Committee creates a high likelihood of a successful standard. A modular structure is essential, with extended features viewed as options, and this is indeed the approach that has been taken in the CTRON specifications.

The following recommendations may help to guide the refinement and continued development of CTRON:

1. Maintain consistent models throughout the standard. Consistency should apply across all documents as well as within documents, and should extend to presentation and naming as well as system call structure.

2. Modularize wisely. Package mechanisms that will not always be necessary in optional modules, but don't create choices so extensive that no two CTRON-based systems will really support the same applications.

3. Don't underestimate language bindings. Choose suitable and consistent languages throughout; consult experienced users of each language; and fit the standard to the language, not the language to the standard.

## REFERENCES

IEEE [1985]. IEEE Trial-Use Standard Specifications for Microprocessor Operating Systems Interfaces. IEEE Std 855-1985.

IEEE [1986]. IEEE Trial-Use Standard: Portable Operating System for Computer Environments. IEEE Std 1003.1-1986.

Lane, M.G., and Mooney, J.D. [1988]. A Practical Approach to Operating Systems. Boyd & Fraser, Boston MA, 1988.

Mooney, J.D. [1986a]. Software Interface Standards: Lessons from the MOSI Project. *Proc. IEEE Computer Standards Conf.,* 1986. Revised version published as Lessons from the MOSI Project, *Computer Standards & Interfaces,* vol. 5, 1986, pp. 201-210.

Mooney, J.D. [1986b]. The MOSI Standard for Operating System Interfaces. Published electronically on the BIX information system by BYTE Magazine, 1986. Available from the author.

Ohkubo, T., Wasano, T., & Kogiku, I. [1987]. Configuration of the CTRON Kernel. IEEE Micro, vol. 7, no. 2, April 1987, pp. 33-44.

Wasano, T., Ohminami, M., Kobayashi, Y., Ohkubo, T., & Sakamura, K. [1987]. Design of CTRON. *TRON Project 1987 (Proc. of 3rd TRON Project Symposium),* Springer-Verlag Tokyo, 1987.

**James D. Mooney** was born in Jersey City, New Jersey, U.S.A. He received the B.S. degree in electrical engineering from the University of Notre Dame in 1968, and the M.S. and ph.D. degrees from the Ohio State University in 1969 and 1977. He has worked in the typesetting industry, and is currently an associate professor in the Department of Statistics and Computer Science of West Virginia University, where he teaches courses in operating systems and computer architecture. he has been active in IEEE standards committees, and was chairman of the MOSI standard working group. He is a member of IEEE, ACM, Tau Beta Pi, Eta Kappa Nu, and Upsilon Pi Epsilon.

Above author may be reached at : Dept. of Statistics & Computer Science West Virginia University Morgantown, WV 26506 U.S.A.

# CTRON Reference Model

## Tetsuo Wasano, Yoshizumi Kobayashi
NTT Network Systems Development Center

## Ken Sakamura
Department of Information Science, Faculty of Science, University of Tokyo

ABSTRACT

CTRON is an operating system interface that provides functions which can be applied commonly to a variety of nodes in an information communication network, and is designed to contribute to software portability improvement. As a way of ensuring a common conceptualization of CTRON functions and configuration among both users and system designers, a CTRON Reference Model has been devised, giving an overview of the interface configuration. The present paper discusses the configuration of this Reference Model and the concepts that went into its design, focusing on the following points.

1) Requirements for creation of the CTRON Reference Model.

2) Configuration of the CTRON Reference Model, and detailed structure within interface classes.

**Keywords**: CTRON, reference model, operating system interface, information communication networks, software portability

## 1. INTRODUCTION

CTRON[1][2] is an operating system interface designed for application to each of the fields involved in implementing network services, including switching processing, communication processing and information processing. It aims to promote software portability across these different fields and different node equipments. For this OS interface to be commonly applicable to each field, standardization is required of terminology and concepts; moreover, a common approach to OS functions and configuration must be fostered. Further, for the standardization work to proceed smoothly, it is necessary to divide OS functions into a number of units which can be studied in parallel. In addition, to enhance applicability to a variety of different fields, and also make it easier to incorporate future technological advances, the interface must be subdivided into units which can be removed or combined as needed.

To help meet these needs, a CTRON Reference Model was devised to show the structure of the CTRON interface as a whole. The aim of this Reference Model is to establish a common basis to guide CTRON users and designers. The present paper discusses the configuration of the CTRON Reference Model and the design concepts it incorporates.

## 2. REQUIREMENTS OF THE CTRON REFERENCE MODEL

The following requirements had to be fulfilled in devising the CTRON Reference Model.

(1) It must represent an OS capable of common application to each of the service nodes in a network for switching processing, communication processing, and information processing.

(2) To improve software productivity, portability across different fields and different node equipments must be possible not only of application programs (APs) but also of part of the OS.

(3) t must contribute to realization of a software configuration featuring outstanding portability.

(4) To make possible creation of an OS offering excellent performance in different applications, subsetting is necessary, allowing interfaces to be put together from a choice of optional functions to match particular applications.

(5) It must be flexible enough to permit addition of a new interface or localized modifications of an existing interface in line with future technological advances.

## 3. CONFIGURATION OF THE CTRON REFERENCE MODEL

### 3.1 Basic Configuration

The relation between the requirements noted above and the CTRON Reference Model are as follows. (See *Fig.1.*)

1) To satisfy requirements (2) and (3) above, the overall CTRON configuration is based on a two-layer OS interface.

(a).Basic OS Interface: The role of this interface is to hide differences in hardware architecture. Software running on a Basic OS conforming to these interface specifications can be made portable across the hardware of different manufacturers.

(b).Extended OS Interface: This interface is situated above the Basic OS Interface, and provides a higher level of OS interface functions.

2) To satisfy requirement (1), OS functions are classified and systematized as shown in *Table 1*, into groups of common interface functions, or interface classes, corresponding to the various resources controlled by the OS.

(a).The Basic OS consists of two interface classes — a kernel interface for hiding differences in processor architecture , and an input/output control interface for hiding differences in input/output device architecture.

(b).The Extended OS consists of seven interface classes, corresponding to different resources. To satisfy requirement (5), the division of functions is made in such as way as to ensure a high degree of independence between each interface. There is also room for addition of new interface classes to meet future technological advances.

*Table 1  CTRON Interface Classes and Resources*

| Layer | Interface classes | Resources |
|---|---|---|
| Basic OS | Kernel | Processors, memory |
| | Input/output control | I/O devices |
| Extended OS | Data storage control | Files, databases |
| | Communication control | Communication path |
| | Execution control | Objects of execution (programs, etc.) |
| | HMI control | Pointing and display resources |
| | Switching network control | Switching network path |
| | Maintenance and operation control | Device resources |

3) To satisfy requirements (3) and (4), a grouping is made of system calls, which are the smallest interface configuration units. Conditions are stipulated for use of these interface units in combination (subsets) for various applications. This subsetting approach allows CTRON as a whole to be made large enough to cover a wide range of application fields, while at the same time letting users select only the particular set of functions needed in a given field.

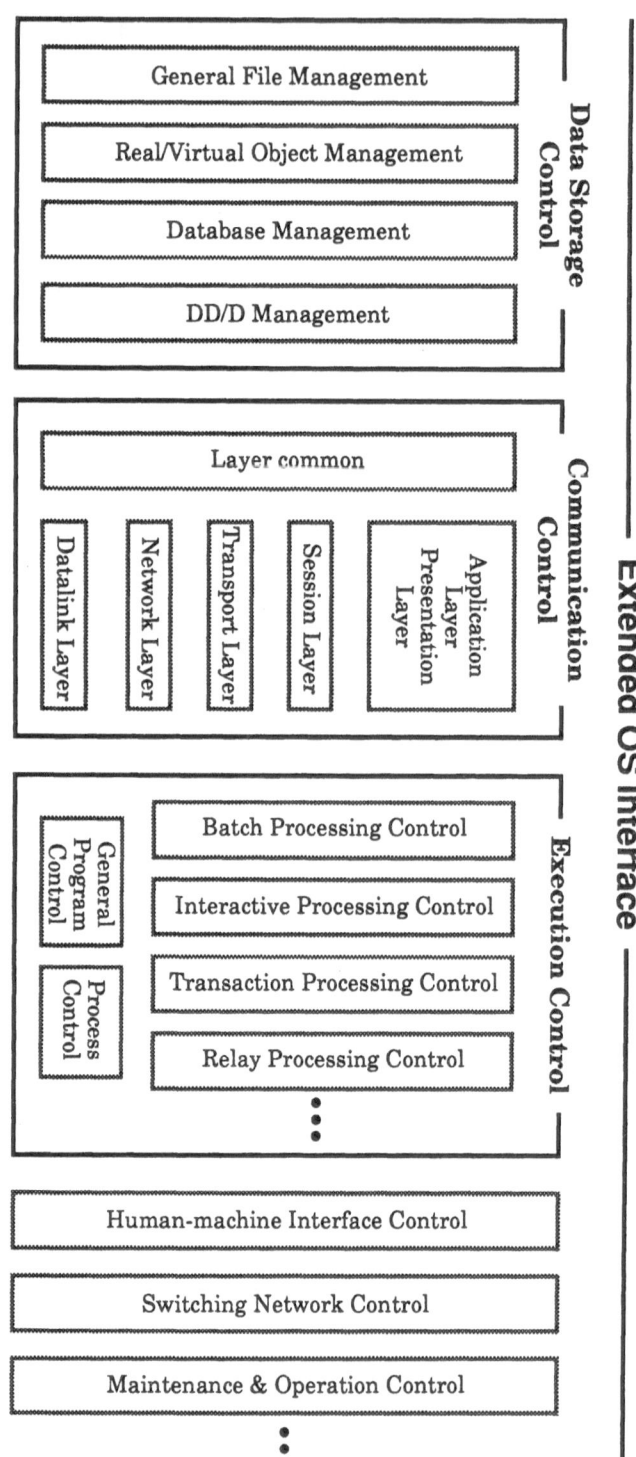

Fig. 1  CTRON Reference Model

## 3.2 Configuration of each interface class

The interfaces in each class are provided for interface to other interface classes above it or at the same level. This approach is followed even when there is a hierarchy within an interface class; however, the semantics of the hierarchy are defined independently in accord with the characteristics of the resources to which the interface applies. This section will outline the interface configuration within each class.

### (a) Kernel

The kernel hides differences in architecture relating to processor resources, such as processors and memory. Its role is to provide a common interface independent of individual architectures. Processor resources are modeled in the kernel, and an interface is designed on that basis[3] (see *Table 2*). Specifically, units of parallel processing assigned to processors are defined as tasks, and the functions necessary for execution of those tasks are specified.

In addition, subsets are specified so that the interface functions can be provided to the full range of systems in network nodes, from small embedded communications devices to large-scale switching, communications and information processing devices, while at the same time assuring upward compatibility of software used in these systems.

### (b) I/O control

Input/output control[4] provides a common access interface to input/output devices that hides differences in architecture. At the same time, since input/output devices are objects of processing by programs, programs must be able to perform this processing in a way that takes maximum advantage of the features of each device. For this purpose, logical devices are defined for each type of device, such as magnetic disks, magnetic tape, etc., based on the general device characteristics. For each of these logical devices an access interface and control interface is specified (see *Table 3*). A logical device is called a BIO (Basic I/O). Some types of input/output devices, however, are subject to rapid technological advances, so that in some cases this kind of typification is not feasible. An example is image I/O devices. For such cases, an interface is provided that allows users to define logical devices. This is called GIO (General I/O).

Table 2  *Kernel Interface*

| Name | Function |
|---|---|
| Task management | Control and state control of tasks assigned to processors |
| Intertask communication and synchronization | Intertask communication, synchronization, and exclusive control of shared resources |
| Interrupt management | Notifying interrupts, which are asynchronous events to processors |
| Exception management | Notifying exceptions, which are asynchronous events to tasks. |
| Timer management | Getting and setting time, etc. |
| Memory management | Allocating and releasing memory; memory pool management |
| Statistical data management | Management of data on processor and memory utilization, etc. |
| Basic program control | Load and unload functions for nonresident system programs |
| Basic system control | Functions for system initialization and termination, and fault processing |

Table 3  *I/O Control Interface*

| Access to logical devices | |
|---|---|
| BIO access control | Access control of logical devices for which I/O data format and device control functions are predefined |
| GIO access control | Access control allowing free instructions to devices |
| Access request cancelation | Functions for canceling an access request |

| Control of logical devices | |
|---|---|
| Logical device connection and disconnection | Functions enabling or disabling device recognition |
| Logical device activation and deactivation | Functions enabling or disabling access to a device |
| Acquisition and modification of device attributes | Functions for acquiring and modifying device attributes |
| Asynchronous notification | I/O requests and asynchronously occurring notification functions from devices |

**(c) Data storage control**

The data storage control interface is for access to and management of information in files, databases and the like. It is configured of the following elements.

**a. General file management enabling realtime or high-speed processing of files[6]**
General file management has to do mainly with file location and access methods. The interface is designed to meet the requirements of information communication networks for realtime processing in a multiuser environment, and for physical distribution of network functions (see *Table 4*).

**b. Real and virtual object management specified in BTRON[5]**
Since a network incorporates both CTRON and BTRON nodes, real and virtual files created on a BTRON node should be usable by CTRON nodes. It should also be possible for the results to be sent back to BTRON nodes for editing and processing. For this purpose CTRON also specifies a real and virtual object management interface.

**c. SQL database management featuring ease of operation and a high degree of conformity to international standards**
This interface adheres closely to existing or certain-to-be-adopted international standard specifications for an SQL database. Additional specifications are made where further definition is required to assure software portability.

**d. DD/D management for centralized control of data format, location, generation, utilization, and interrelationships, etc.**

*Table 4 General File Management Interface*

| Name | Function |
|---|---|
| Directory management | Tree-shaped directory management for keeping track of file location |
| Acquisition and modification of file attributes | Functions for acquiring and modifying file attributes of files and logical devices |
| File security management | Functions for checking access privilege to files and directories |
| Control of basic organization files | Access functions to files in which I/O is performed in bytes, records or blocks |
| Control of indexed sequential files | Access functions to files organized for ease of record search, insertion, and deletion using keys |
| Control of distributed files | Functions for manipulating files in other system in the network |

**(d) Communication control**

The CTRON communication control interface is based on the seven-layer OSI (Open Systems Interconnection) model, and also conforms to CCITT recommendations on communications protocol systems. Layer 1 is normally implemented in hardware, and therefore is not specified as an OS interface. OS interfaces are specified for each of Layers 2 through 5,[7] enabling high performance to be built into communication control programs while at the same time assuring application to a wide range of communication control hardware. For Layers 6 and 7, separate OS interfaces are specified for FTAM, MOTIS, ISDN user control and other such fields. In addition a buffer management interface common to each layer is specified to allow efficient message exchange among layers.

As a result of this approach, interfaces for ISDN are specified with the same OS interface system as that for other communication functions, making it possible to merge information processing with switching processing techniques.

**(e) Execution control**

Objects of execution on computers include the tasks specified in the kernel. In execution control,[8] however, a higher level unit of parallel processing is defined, called a process. A process allocates programs, files and other logical resources to tasks, making possible efficient development of various information communication services. Execution control consists of a process control interface, which allocates resources to and controls processes, and a general program control interface, which controls programs running on processes, as well as interfaces for batch processing control, interactive processing control, transaction control, relay processing control and other control functions required by information communication services.

**(f) Other interface classes**

The human-machine interface (HMI) control interface provides functions by which users give instructions to systems and systems display information to users. In line with the approach adopted in the overall TRON architecture,[9] this is based on the BTRON HMI functions. Also incorporated are CGI and other results of international standardization efforts.

Design of other interfaces is now in progress. These include a switching network control interface for obtaining and controlling a switching network path, and a maintenance and operation control interface for system operation, fault processing, maintenance and testing.

## 4. CONCLUSIONS

CTRON studies are being carried out by the CTRON Technical Committee of the TRON Association, which is an open organization. The interface specifications which are being produced as a result of these studies are being made available to the public worldwide. Publication has already been made of specifications for the kernel and input/output control interfaces of the Basic OS, and for the general file management, communication control, and general program control interfaces of the Extended OS. The first round of design work on the remaining interfaces is to be completed during 1989, with specifications published as they are ready.

At the same time development work on OS products and systems based on these publicly offered specifications is under way by numerous developers and manufacturers. CTRON promises to contribute greatly to improved software portability as it comes into wide use as a new operating system interface.

### ACKNOWLEDGMENTS

The authors wish to express deep appreciation for the continuing guidance offered in the course of CTRON studies by CTRON Technical Committee Chairman Dr. Fukuya Ishino. Thanks are due also to participating members of Fujitsu Ltd., NEC Corp., NTT Corp., Northern Telecom Japan Inc., Oki Electric Industry Co. Ltd., and Toshiba Corp.

### REFERENCES

[1]   T. Wasano, M.Ohminami, Y. Kobayashi, T. Ohkubo and K. Sakamura, "Design Principles and Configuration of CTRON", Proc. FJCC '87, Dallas, pp.159-166, Oct. 1987.

[2]   T. Wasano, M. Ohminami, Y. Kobayashi, T. Ohkubo and K. Sakamura, "Design of CTRON", TRON Project 1987, pp.157-172, 1987.

[3]   T. Ohkubo, T.Wasano and I. Kogiku, "Configuration of the CTRON Kernel", IEEE Micro, pp.33-44, April 1987.

[4]   S. Narimatu, "Design of CTRON Input-output Control Interface", TRON Project 1987, pp.183-196, 1987.

[5]   K. Sakamura, "BTRON: The Business-oriented Operating System", IEEE Micro, pp.53-65, April 1987.

[6]   K. Kumazaki, "Design of the CTRON File Management", TRON Project 1987, pp.173-182, 1987.

[7]   Y. Shimizu, "Design of CTRON Communication Control Interface", TRON Project 1988.

[8]   Y. Baba, M. Ohminami, H. Kusumoto and M. Kosugi, "Design of CTRON Execution Control Interface", TRON Project 1988.

[9]   K. Sakamura, "The TRON Project", IEEE Micro, pp.8-14, April 1987.

**Tetsuo Wasano**: a executive engineer at NTT Network Systems Development Center. He is presently engaged in computer architecture strategy planning. Since joining the laboratory in 1970, he has been engaged in development research on DIPS operating systems and in research into artificial intelligence. He graduated from Tokyo University in 1970 with the BS degree. He is a member of the Institute of Electronics, Information and Communication Engineers of Japan(IEICE) and of the Information Processing Society of Japan(IPS).

**Yoshizumi Kobayashi**: a senior engineer at NTT Network Systems Development Center. Since joining the company in 1973, he has been engaged in the research and development of compilers and operating systems. He has played role in construction of principles required for the CTRON design and in the design of program control interface within CTRON. He received the BS degree in 1971 and the MS degree in 1973 at Osaka University. He is a member of the IEICE, the IPS and the Computer Society of the IEEE.

Above authors may be reached at:2-1, Uchisaiwai-cho 1-chome, Chiyoda-ku, Tokyo, 100 Japan

**Ken Sakamura** is currently an associate professor at the Department of Information Science, University of Tokyo. He holds Ph.D. in EE. Being a computer architect, he has been the leader of the TRON project which he started to build a new computer system architecture for 1990's since 1984. His promotion of the TRON architecture now extends to architecture of buildings and furniture. He servers on the editorial board of Institute of Electrical and Electronics Engineers (IEEE) MICRO magazine and is a chair of the project promotion committee of the TRON Association. He is a member of Japan Information Processing Society, Institute of Electronics, Information and Communication Engineers, ACM, and is a senior member of IEEE. He has received best paper awards of IEICE twice, of JIPS once, IEEE best annual article award, and other awards from Japanese and overseas organizations.

Above author may be reached at Department of Information Science, Faculty of Science, University of Tokyo, 7-3-1 Hongo, Bunkyo-ku, Tokyo, Japan.

# Design of CTRON Communication Control Interface

Yutaka Shimizu
NEC Corporation

Abstract

The communication control functions are considered as an important matter in the CTRON functions. The reason is that the communication control functions have become essential not only on the communication processing nodes, switching nodes and gateway nodes but also on the host computers and workstations according to the development of the information communication networks.

This paper discusses the design principles of the CTRON communication control interface and then describes the configuration and interfaces.


Keywords : CTRON, Communication Control, Open Systems Interconnection

1.  Introduction

The CTRON [1,2,3] is an operating system applicable to the wide range of application fields, such as switching and communication processing, information processing, and workstations.

CTRON has been designed to be independent of processor architecture and to assure excellent portability of operating system components implementing CTRON specifications, and of application programs. This aim is achieved by means of a two-layer configuration, consisting of what are called the basic operating system and extended operating system .

Operating system interfaces are provided for each of these two layers. The basic operating system consists of a kernel interface, which provides the processor control functions, and an I/O control interface, providing functions for control of communication equipment and peripheral equipment.

The extended operating system is located above the basic operating system, and provides application programs with the means of access to logical system resources.

The CTRON communication control is one of the extended operating system components, providing communication services for application programs and other extended operating system components.

This paper describes the design principles, interface configuration and the outline of specification of the CTRON communication control interface.


2. Design Principles

Design principles of the CTRON communication control interface are shown as follows.

(a) Accordance with OSI

Since the standardization of the various communication services and protocols —OSI(Open Systems Interconnection) [4] — has been developed within the ISO and CCITT for more than a decade, OSI becomes widespread for many computer systems. The CTRON is applicable to multi-vendor network environment in which OSI should be mandatory, therefore the accordance with OSI should be a matter of importance in the CTRON. The CTRON communication control is designed to provide the interface based upon the OSI reference model.

(b) Adoption of functional standards

In OSI world, now a second level of standardization called functional standards is in progress. The aim of functional standards is to select and define the combination of OSI services and protocols including optional facilities and parameter values so that each system may communicate one another effectively with high interoperability. In the CTRON communication control, subsetting of interfaces is based upon these functional standards.

(c) Flexibility for the proliferation of protocols

As abovementioned, communication services and protocols are being developed within ISO/CCITT and new protocols may appear hereafter. The CTRON communication control is designed to be flexible for the proliferation of new protocols.

(d) Software portability

Software portability is one of the most important design principles in the CTRON. In order to realize and promote software portability in the CTRON communication control, interfaces are defined for each layer based upon the OSI reference model. Furthermore, each layer function is divided into two functional modules. The one is the CCL (Communication Controller) which executes protocol function, including the related management service function and the other one is the OAM (Operation Administration and Maintenance) which executes the management functions dependent to each system.

(e)  Expansibility for non-OSI protocols

Although the OSI standards become widespread rapidly, there are still many non-OSI products in various systems represented by asynchronous dumb terminals, TCP/IP and vendor dependent network architecture products etc. From these backgrounds, the CTRON communication control is designed to be expandable for non-OSI protocols.

3.  Interface Configuration

3.1  Configuration of the CTRON Communication Control

Since various processors exist in the CTRON environment, communication functions differ in each processor. For example, a gateway or router includes up to the network layer function or the transport layer function.  In case that a dedicated application protocol or a non-standardized protocol is used in the application layer, up to the session layer function is needed. In another case there exists an equipment which uses only the data link layer function with non-OSI protocols above it.

From these backgrounds, the CTRON communication control interface is prescribed for each layer so that the application programs and/or other extended operating system components may use each layer function.
As regarding the implementation of the CTRON communication control, both the set of a single-layer implementation with accessible interfaces in each layer and the multi-layer implementation with non-accessible interfaces in intermediate layers are possible. In the latter case, intermediate layer interfaces are the matter of implementation.

The CTRON communication control is defined as one of the extended operating system components located above the basic operating system, which consists of each OSI layer function and common function to each layer. Figure 1 illustrates the functional reference model of the CTRON communication control interface.

3.2  The Relationship with the Communication Devices

The CTRON communication control makes use of the function of communication device via the input-output control in the basic operating system.  The coverage of communication function in the communication devices varies from device to device.  Consequently the functional boundary between the CTRON communication control and the communication device depends upon each system. For example, a

communication control unit generally supports up to the data link layer function
and a front end processor includes up to the network layer or the transport
layer.

Whatever types of communication device are equipped, application programs
or extended operating system components are able to use unified communication
control interfaces, regardless of the function of communication device. Figure
2 illustrates the relationship between the CTRON communication control and the
communication device.


## 3.3 The Classification of Interface

As abovementioned in chapter 2, from the viewpoint of software portability
and functional division, the CTRON communication control consists of two
functional modules-CCL and OAM.

The CCL provides the OSI service primitive interfaces and additional
management interfaces, which are called I-1 interfaces and I-2 interfaces,
respectively. The OAM executes the layer management function in the OSI
reference model using I-2 interfaces provided by the CCL.

The CCL and the OAM exist in each layer. Application programs, other
extended operating system components and upper layer CCLs use the CCL function
via I-1 interface. Although the OAM manages the CCL within the same layer via
I-2 interface, interfaces with the other layer's OAM and/or application programs
are considered to be dependent to each implementation, therefore they are not
defined. The details of I-1 and I-2 interfaces are described in chapter 5.
Figure 3 shows the classification of the CTRON communication control interface.

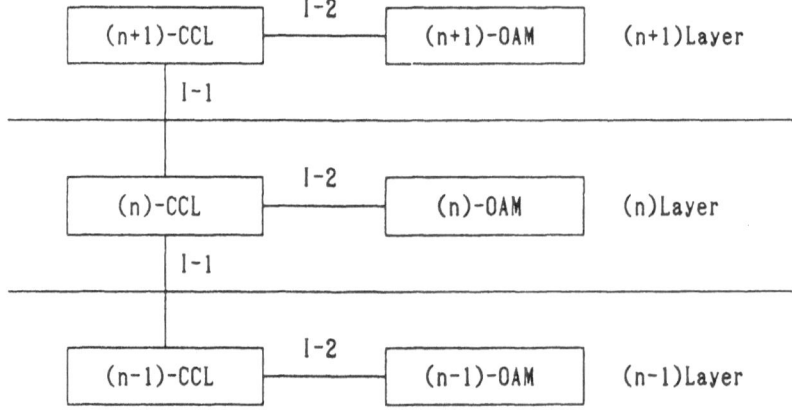

Figure 3    Classification of the CTRON communication control
            interface.

4. Services and Protocols

   The CTRON communication control prescribes interfaces in order to be applicable to various network configurations and application services. Services provided by each layer in the CTRON communication control and related protocols are listed as follows.


(a) The data link layer

Two types of services are supported. One is the connection type and the other one is the connectionless type.

   1) Connection type
      - X.25  (LAP(Link Access Procedure)-B)
      - T.71  (LAP-X)
      - MTP   (Message Transfer Part) level 2
      - I.441 (LAP-D)
   2) Connectionless type
      - DIS 8802-2 (LLC(Logical Link Control) type1)


(b) The network layer

Two types of services are supported. One is the connection type and the other one is the connectionless type.

   1) Connection Type
      - X.25 (packet level)
      - T.70 (CSDN)
      - MTP level 3
      - SCCP (Signaling Connection Control Part)
      - I.451
   2) Connectionless Type
      - ISO 8473 (CLNP(Connectionless Network Protocol))


(c) The transport layer

   The connection type service is supported.
   1) Connection type
      - ISO 8073 (COTP(Connection Oriented Transport Protocol))
         —class 0, 2, 4

(d) The session layer

The connection type service is supported.
  1) Connection type
    - ISO 8327 (COSP(Connection Oriented Session  Protocol))

(e) The presentation layer and the application layer

Following services are supported.

  1) CASE/P (Common Application Service Elements/Presentation layer)
    - ACSE (Association Control Service Element)
    - RTS  (Reliable Transfer Server)
    - ROSE (Remote Operation Service Element)
    - CCR  (Commitment, Concurrency and Recovery)

  2) MOTIS (Message Oriented Text Interchange System)
    - MTA/UA (Message Transfer Agent/User Agent)
    - MS   (Message Store)
    - NS   (Name Server)

  3) FTAM (File Transfer, Access and Management)
    - FPM (FTAM Protocol Machine)
    - NS  (Name Server)
    - TS  (Transfer Service)

  4) ISUC (ISDN User Control)
    - DSS (Digital Subscriber Signaling system)
    - TC  (Transaction Capability)
    - ISUP(ISDN User Part)

These protocols have close relationship with network configuration as depicted in Table 1.


5. Interface Specification

    The CTRON communication control interface consists of two forms. The one is the request system call issued by users and its confirmation by the CCL. The other one is the asynchronous notification to users by the CCL and its response system call issued by users. The former corresponds to the request and confirm service primitives and the latter corresponds to the indication and response

Table 1   Relationship between protocols and network configuration

| network configuration | P S D N, leased line | L A N | P S T N, C S D N | I S D N | |
|---|---|---|---|---|---|
| | | | | NO.7 | user network |
| Transport Layer | class 0,2 | class 4 | class 0,2 | — | — |
| Network Layer | X.25 | CLNP | T.70 CSDN | MTP level 3 SCCP | I.451 level 3 |
| Data Link Layer | LAP-B | LAP-B | LAP-X | MTP level 2 | LAP-D |

Table 2   Message Boxes

| Name of Message Box | Use |
|---|---|
| message-box-1 | completion of system call |
| message-box-2 | reception of data |
| message-box-3 | asynchronous event |
| message-box-4 | incoming call |
| message-box-5 | reception of connectionless data |
| message-box-6 | trace data |
| message-box-7 | statistical data |
| message-box-8 | failure event |
| message-box-9 | reception of expidited data |
| message-box-10 | not applicable |
| message-box-11 | not applicable |
| message-box-12 | SLSAP failure event |
| message-box-13 | buffer overloaded |

service primitives in terms of OSI. Furthermore, these interfaces are divided into two types— common interface and layer dependent interface. Message boxes, which are general interface information blocks within CTRON operating system, are used for interface from the CCL to user programs. Table 2 shows the kind of message boxes.


## 5.1  Common Interface

The CTRON communication control prescribes interfaces which are commonly used by each layer in relation to the communication function.

Common interfaces consist of buffer management and time management. Although these interfaces are provided by the kernel in the basic operating system, their functions are too simple and primitive to be used in the CTRON communication control.  Therefore the CTRON communication control enhanced these functions so that they may be easy to use from the viewpoint of performance and efficiency of implementation.

Concerning the buffer management, the length of transmitted and/or received data and the change of data traffic are, in general, unpredictable in the CTRON communication control environment.  Consequently the mechanism of buffer block chaining and notification of buffer management information is necessary. The buffer management provides these functions.

In relation to the time management, the application layer function is likely to use the UTC(Universal Time Co-ordinated) time and/or local time, especially within the MOTIS. Therefore the CTRON communication control provides the mechanism of conversion of time value provided by the kernel into the UTC/local time. These common interfaces are listed in Table 3.


## 5.2  Layer Dependent Interface

Layer dependent interfaces are classified into two types, I-1 and I-2 as abovementioned. Both interfaces are designed to be unified through all layers as much as possible.

I-1 interface mainly corresponds to the OSI service primitive and the most of interfaces are unified, such as connection establishment/release, data transmission/reception, SAP (Service Access Point) initialization/termination, etc.

I-2 interface corresponds to the layer management function and the most of interfaces are unified similarly to the I-1 interface, such as CCL activation/deactivation, trace start/stop, collection of statistical information start/stop, flow suspension/resumption, etc.

Layer dependent interfaces are listed in Table 4.

Table 3    Common Interface

| Classification | System Call Name | Function |
|---|---|---|
| buffer management | create-buffer-pool | get buffer pool area and define buffer management table |
| | delete-buffer-pool | free buffer pool area and delete buffer management table |
| | allocate-buffer | allocate specified number of buffers from specified pool |
| | free-buffer | return chained buffers to the pool |
| | get-buffer-pool-information | get buffer management information such as buffer block size, available number of buffer blocks etc. |
| Time management | get-UTC-time | get UTC time information |
| | get-local-time | get local place time information |

## 6.  Subset of Interface

Within the CTRON communication control, all of the interfaces are not mandatory for implementation for the reason that various fields of application and network configurations exist.

As is wellknown, functional standards in OSI can be divided into two large groups whose boundary is located at the transport layer service. The lower part, namely from the physical layer to the transport layer, relates to the network configuration, and the upper part, namely from the session layer to the application layer relates to the application service. Therefore the CTRON communication control prescribes the subset of interface in accordance with the abovementioned principles.

## 7.  Conclusion

This paper describes the design principles, interface configuration and interface specification for the CTRON communication control and so on. At present, concerning from the data link layer to the session layer, interface specifications have been completed for each layer. With regard to the presentation layer and the application layer, specifications are now under development for the following application profiles    —    FTAM, MOTIS, CASE/P and ISUC.

   In near future we are going to expand and refine these specifications according to the trend of OSI standardization and development of networking technology.


## Acknowledgements

   The author wishes to thank Prof. Ken Sakamura, Dr. Fukaya Ishino and the members  of CTRON technical committee for their helpful advice in the study of the CTRON communication control.


## References

[1] T.Wasano, M.Ohminami, Y.Kobayashi, T.Ohkubo and K.Sakamura,  "Design Principles and Configuration of CTRON  " , FJCC'87, October 1987
[2] T.Ohkubo, T.Wasano and I.Kogiku, "Configuration of the CTRON Kernel" , IEEE Micro, April 1987, pp.33-44.
[3] K.Sakamura,  "The TRON Project" , IEEE Micro, April 1987, pp.8-14
[4] ISO, TC97 Information Processing  — Open Systems Interconnection — Basic Reference Model. ISO 7498, 1984

Yutaka Shimizu : is a systems manager of Common Carrier Systems Division, NEC Corporation. He joined the company in 1972 after graduating from the University of Tokyo with a B.E.degree. He is a member of the information Processing Society of Japan.

Above author may be reached at : Network Engineering Department, Common Carrier Systems Division, NEC Corporation,11-5, Shibaura, 2-Chome, Minato-ku, Tokyo 108, Japan.

# Design of CTRON Execution Control Interface

Yasuhiko Baba,  Masato Ohminami
NTT Electrical Communications Laboratories


Hiromi Kusumoto,  Hiroshi Kosugi
FUJITSU LIMITED

**ABSTRACT**

CTRON provides an operating system interface that is not dependent on hardware architecture.   The aim is to assure excellent portability of OS components implementing CTRON specifications, and of application programs. To achieve this aim, the design is based on a two-layer OS configuration, consisting of a Basic OS and Extended OS. CTRON execution control belongs to the Extended OS. The execution control interface, which provides execution environments and controls program execution, greatly influences overall performance. The CTRON execution control interface assures high performance by adopting a combination of resources from the kernel in the Basic OS and from other parts of the Extended OS.

**Keywords:** CTRON, Execution Environment, Process Control, Program Control, Virtual Processor

## 1. INTRODUCTION

CTRON (Central and Communication TRON) specifies a common operating system (OS) interface for physical processors, in order to enhance portability of application programs and of the OS itself. To this end, CTRON adopts a two- layer OS configuration, consisting of a Basic OS and Extended OS. The Basic OS provides a logical interface which hides differences in the physical interfaces of computers and peripheral devices. The actual object of portability is the Extended OS, which functions above the Basic OS and provides high-level interfaces to application programs.

CTRON Execution Control belongs to the Extended OS. Its role is to provide execution environments for different services or users, and to control program execution. An execution environment is a particular combination of computer resources of various kinds. Execution control functions are directly involved in program execution, and play an integral role in various services that are offered. For this reason these functions must satisfy a number of diverse and often contradictory requirements, such as high performance, universality, flexibility, and ease of use.

An OS designed for a specific physical processor can take advantage of that processor's particular characteristics, and in that way assure high performance.If OS portability is not a concern, there is no need to adopt a two-layer configuration. In an embedded system, for example, which provides only a specific service, a fixed execution environment can be built in at the design stage. A two-layer OS, on the other hand, while making possible OS portability among different types of physical processors, is theoretically at a performance disadvantage compared with a single-layer OS. A key to designing the CTRON execution control interface is to devise specifications that will achieve portability while assuring high performance in implementations.

The approach adopted in CTRON execution control is to combine resources from various sources, including those of the Basic OS as well as file management and other resources provided by the Extended OS. In this way an interface is specified which assures high performance and ease of use.

The present paper begins by summarizing the relation between the OS and computer resources, and the roles of execution control. It then discusses the provision of virtual processors and execution environments in the two-layer OS, the relation between virtual processors (tasks) provided by the Basic OS and those (processes) provided by execution control, and the relation between tasks and programs. In this way the paper attempts to clarify the policies and approach adopted in designing the execution control interface so as to assure high-performance implementations. In addition a brief overview is presented of the interfaces for general program control and process control, for which specifications have already been devised, and the specific approach taken in these specifications is indicated.

## 2. THE ROLE OF EXECUTION CONTROL

Execution control provides an environment in which program execution can take place. This execution environment consists of a combination of various computer resources. From a physical standpoint these include the CPU (Central Processing Unit), memory, peripheral storage devices, communication devices, and the like. Logical resources include those provided by the Basic OS, as well as those resources other than execution control provided by the Extended OS, such as file management and communication control. Here the role of execution control is explained by summarizing the relationship of the OS to the computer resources that constitute the execution environment, and outlining the necessity and configuration of the execution environment.

### 2.1 Relation between Computer Resources and Operating Systems

The role of the OS is to turn the physical resources provided by computers into logical resources. Its basic functions are configured in accord with the kinds of physical resources that are provided. Specific ways in which logical resources are created are by changing physical resources into virtual, multiple,or shared resources. The OS consists of functions for each central resource (CPU and real memory) and for each peripheral resource (peripheral storage device, communication device, etc.). A general summary of the roles of the OS is presented in Table 2-1 based on the logical resources provided. The ways in which various computer resources are changed to logical resources are summarized below.

1) CPU

Virtual processors are provided by multiplexing the CPU (physical processor). Virtual processors are units of conceptual parallel processing, and make possible shared use of a CPU. A virtual processor is generally called a task or process.

2) Real memory

Large-capacity virtual storage, realized by virtualization of physical memory, is then multiplexed into a number of logical memory spaces, resulting in multiple virtual storage. Provision is further made of memory shared among virtual processors, and of memory pools for specific applications. There are also real storage systems which do not provide virtual storage.

3) Peripheral storage devices

Files are provided as logical resources by virtualizing and multiplexing of peripheral storage devices and media.

*Table 2-1. Roles of the operating system, and the resources it provides.*

| | | Role | Functions | Provided resources |
|---|---|---|---|---|
| Central resources | CPU | Makes sure the CPU does not become idle. (when there is competition for passive resources) | Virtual processor creation, starting, synchronization, communication, interrupts and exceptions. | Virtual processors, timers, message boxes, semaphore, programs. |
| | Real memory | Provides large-capacity memory. | Allocation, release, and reservation of logical memory; allotment of real memory. | Logical memory, memory pools, memory shared by virtual processors. |
| Peripheral | Storage devices | Virtualizes and multiplexes storage devices and media. | File location, definition, access, and sharing control. | Files and directories. |
| | Communication devices | Virtualizes and hierarchizes devices and networks. | Connection and data transfer. | Logical terminals, communication nodes, and networks. |

### 4) Communication devices

Communication control procedures (data link layer), connecting paths (network layer), ..., message communication (application layer), etc. are provided as hierarchical functions and resources. In this way it is possible to take into account the modularization of communication programs and the level of advancement of communication devices.

## 2.2 Provision of Execution Environments

The OS provides logical resources and functions in line with the provided physical resources. Fundamentally, these can be used to write programs and build systems. This section discusses the necessity of providing execution environments combining various resources, examines the configuration of execution environments, and describes the approach to assuring a high functional level in CTRON.

### (a) Necessity of Execution Environments

In an embedded system, for example, where only certain specific services are provided, for which the kinds, amount, and range of resources to be used can be predicted, the necessary resources to be shared by the system as a whole can be allocated at the design stage. In this way a fixed execution environment can be set. On the other hand, in a multi-user, multi-service system, or one in which many diverse programs are to be executed in parallel, the following considerations dictate that independent execution environments be provided for different kinds of programs.

### 1) Improving productivity

Individual users should not have to be aware of the address or location of available resources among the overall system resources. Moreover, when a system is developed by several people, or when functions are likely to be added on later, programming efficiency is improved by providing an execution environment for each function or service. For instance, a system allocates a specific memory space and file directory path to the user as an execution environment, within which the user accesses resources by referring to their names or other identifiers.

### 2) Avoiding monopolization of resources

When certain users or services monopolize large amounts of resources, throughput of the system as a whole is lowered significantly. To prevent this, a limit is placed on the amount of resources that can be used by each execution environment.

### 3) Assuring reliability

The resources of each user or service are kept independent, to prevent willful or inadvertent referencing or destruction by other users or services.

## (b) Configuration of Execution Environments

From the standpoint of application programs, the objects of execution environment allocation are users and services. From the standpoint of the resources provided by the OS, virtual processors, which are units of CPU execution, are chosen as units (bases) of execution environment allocation. An execution environment consists of a virtual processor and the resources allocated (attached) to that virtual processor.

### 1) Virtual processors

Virtual processors are allocated to services and users. A virtual processor is allocated for each session and command in the case of interactive processing, for each job and job step in the case of batch processing, and for each service or each terminal or communication line in the case of transaction processing. These are then units of parallel processing.

### 2) Allocated resources

All resources other than virtual processors are objects of allocation to virtual processors. In the case of memory and files, the resources are allocated with limitations placed on amount and range. Programs are also executed on virtual processors. Communication resources allocated include those for communication within a computer and those for designating remote systems.

## (c) Achieving High-level Functions

High-level OS functions are achieved by providing execution environments consisting of virtual processors and the resources allocated to them. The approach taken in CTRON execution control to providing high-level OS functions is outlined in *Fig 2-1*. Central resources consist of a combination of resources provided in the Basic OS kernel. In the case of peripheral resources, the input output control supervisor converts the physical interfaces of devices to logical interfaces, which are raised in level by the file management and communication control facilities of the Extended OS. Execution control thus needs only to allocate these peripheral resources to virtual processors.

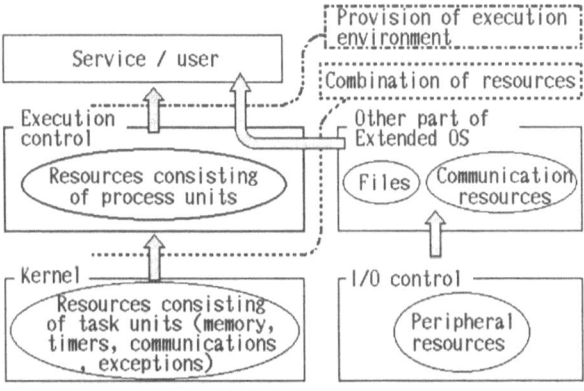

*Fig.2-1. Approach to assuring high level of functions.*

## 3. REQUIRED CONDITIONS AND DESIGN POLICY

As noted above, CTRON adopts a two-layer OS configuration. This section looks at the correspondence of this design to existing two-layer concepts, and compares two-layer OS approaches. It then discusses the way in which Basic OS kernel functions are made more advanced, and notes the conditions required in application fields, configuration of CTRON execution control, and other design policy aspects.

### 3.1 Assuring High Performance in a Two-layer Configuration

#### (a) Existing Two-layer Concepts

Existing concepts and products adopting a two-layer configuration include the Virtual Machine[1], examples of the Multiple Virtual Storage System[2], and Virtual Operating System[3], among others. The attempt has also been made to further virtualize the OS at the programming language level[4]. These approaches are summarized in *Table 3-1*. Among them, those that can be compared with CTRON from the standpoint of two-layer OS operation in actual service are the Virtual Machine and Multiple Virtual Storage System. Both of these, however, require specific computer architectures for the sake of high performance, so that neither concept can be incorporated as is into CTRON.

*Table 3-1. Relation of two-layer hierarchy concepts to CTRON.*

|  | Concept and features | Problems for incorporating into CTRON |
|---|---|---|
| Virtual Machine | Multiple OSs are run on one computer. Used for OS debugging, system replace, background running of batch processing, etc. | Requires hardware support for high-performance computer allocation. |
| Multiple Virtual Storage System | Multiple logical memory space is provided. Performs scheduling of executable logical memory space and multiple virtual processors executable in that space. | Requires specific computer architecture to realize high-performance memory management mechanism. |
| Virtual Operating System | Provides common interfaces for database access, file I/O, memory allocation and other functions needed for execution of software development support program, etc. | Performance suffers since execution is via mechanism for mapping on actual OS functions. |
| Virtualization in programming language | Provides virtual machine in the form of programming language and monitor, for application program scheduling, resource allocation, etc. | OS user is responsible for hierarchization when designing program, and in development of monitor, etc. |

#### (b) Virtual Processors in a Two-layer Operating System

The following two approaches can be taken to provision of virtual processors in a two-layer OS. The first is to provide virtual processors by first multiplexing physical processors in the lower layer. The virtual processors provided by the lower layer are then further multiplexed in the upper layer[5]. This approach necessitates two stages of scheduling for allocating physical processors to virtual processors, or a two-stage dispatch mechanism. The second approach is to multiplex processors only in the lower level. The upper layer then combines resources, consisting fundamentally of virtual processors provided by the lower layer. The difference between these two approaches, then, is whether the role of the upper layer is for further multiplexing virtual processors or for combining resources. The former approach is taken by the Virtual Machine. The advantages and disadvantages of these two approaches are summarized in *Table 3-2.*

*Table 3-2. Comparison of two-layer virtual processor methods.*

| | Performance | Applicability | Specification system | Compatibility with other functions |
|---|---|---|---|---|
| Multiplexing | Two-step scheduling of virtual processors. | Effective when number of simultaneous users increases in interact-ive processing. Not geared to transaction processing. | Results in duplicate functions for virtual processor control, synchronization, communication, etc. | Requires division of kernel resources consisting of task units. |
| Combination | High performance is made possible by multiple-task configuration. Tasks can be shared among processes. | Applicable to all services. | High-level functions essential to application programs and service control are added on. | For functions of limited necessity, kernel functions can be used directly. |

CTRON execution control adopts the second of the two approaches, that of combining resources in the upper layer. The main reasons are to avoid two- step scheduling, which results in poorer realtime performance -- a primary consideration in CTRON -- and to avoid duplication of similar functions.

Virtual processors provided by the Basic OS kernel are called "tasks," while those provided by execution control are called "processes." A "process" in CTRON is defined as a unit of parallel processing accompanying an execution environment. A process may be made up of one or more tasks.

### 3.2 Combination of Kernel Resources

OS functions are made more advanced by combining resources. The Basic OS kernel provides primitive functions, permitting application to small-scale systems and distribution of functions with the Extended OS. The following specific measures are taken to combine kernel resources and functions.

## (a) Linking of Tasks to Programs

In the kernel, tasks and programs, which are closely involved in execution control, are treated as independent concepts, and program loading is never handled by task management. Accordingly, the user must perform task creation and program starting, which involve the following steps.

- An initiator is loaded into memory shared by the creating task (A) and created task (B).
- Task B is created and started by task A, with control being passed to the initiator.
- The initiator allocates resources for use in task B and starts the program.

From the user's standpoint, however, it would be unnecessarily complex to write such a program. Creating a new task and invoking a program are performed frequently by the OS and application programs. For this reason, execution control provides composite functions, which are able to be designated all at once, for provision and loading of an initiator, for task creation, and for resource allocation and program invoking by the initiator. The unit created by composite functions, which is executed in parallel, is a process. In this process, resources are allocated by the initiator as an execution environment, and programs are executed in that environment.

Basic program management functions in the kernel are provided only for loading and unloading system programs. Program management functions for non-system (general) programs are then provided in execution control.

## (b) Control of Task Groups

Tasks are capable of parallel execution, and from the standpoint of CPU allocation are basic, independent units. On the other hand, units of work looked at from application programs consist of a series of functions, including system-provided functions, user-written routines, normal system functions, error processing functions, etc. As a result of performance improvements, functional distribution, modularization and the like, these consist of and are executed as a number of separate tasks.

Composite processing functions are required for groups of tasks that are closely interrelated. Execution control provides functions for task group control. These are intended mainly for controlling various service formats, for application to batch deletion and termination of related tasks in application programs, and for garbage processing.

## 3.3 Requirements of Different Application Fields

Next the requirements of various services are noted, based on differences among application fields.

CTRON is for application to many diverse fields, including switching processing,communication processing, information processing, and workstations. Among these, the main application fields of execution control are information processing and workstations. Fields like switching and communication processing, on the other hand, require vastly more multiplicity and speed of response, on the order of tens or hundreds of times greater than information processing or workstation applications[6]. In many cases these performance requirements are best met by designing an execution environment for the system as a whole, in the form of a specialized extended OS. Where programming efficiency and ease of functional expansion are important considerations, however, CTRON execution control may be applied to these fields as well.

Processing formats in information processing and workstations include interactive processing, batch processing, and transaction processing. The characteristics of each, and their demands on execution control, are listed in *Table 3-3*. Interactive and batch processing require provision of an execution environment for each user, and outstanding ease of use. Transaction processing requires separation of preprocessing and execution in order to realize high-speed response.

*Table 3-3. Processing formats and required conditions.*

| Processing format | Features | Role and requirements of execution control | |
|---|---|---|---|
| | | Provision of execution environments | Program execution control |
| Interactive ; batch processing | Many, indeterminate users ; processing content and amount indeterminate. | Resources allocated to each user; automatic garbage processing. | Ease of program invoking and parallel processing. |
| Transaction processing | Processing content known; high-speed response. | Pre-allocated. | Separation of prepro- cessing from execution. |

## 3.4 Configuration of Execution Control

All processing formats require allocation of virtual processors and execution environments, and program execution. On the other hand, such matters as the method for input of processing, input interpretation, scheduling (starting at a fixed time, deadlines, etc.), processing content, and output of results, etc. differ depending on the service. To make possible application to different services and assure portability, functions common to all services are separated from service-dependent functions. The configuration of execution control is shown in *Fig.3-1*.

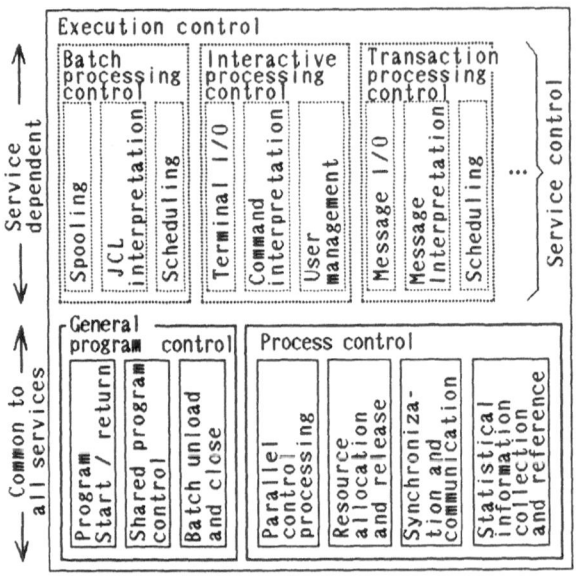

*Fig.3-1. Configuration of CTRON execution control.*

## (a) Functions Common to All Services

The basic framework for virtual processors and allocation of execution environments is provided in the form of process control. The basic framework for program execution is specified as general program control.

Program execution can be divided into parallel execution and sequential execution. Parallel execution normally requires an independent execution environment, so this control is made the responsibility of process control. General program control provides functions for successive program invoking in one task or process.

## (b) Service-dependent Functions

The procedures and methods used for input of processing, input interpretation, work scheduling, results output, etc. differ from one service to another. It is possible, however, to standardize these procedures for each of the typical processing formats, such as interactive processing, batch processing, and transaction processing. They are specified as part of service control.

# 4. OUTLINE OF CTRON EXECUTION CONTROL INTERFACES

The aspects of execution control for which specifications have been devised so far are General Program Control (Ver. 1) and Process Control (Draft). The following is a brief outline of these interfaces and the approach taken.

## 4.1 General Program Control Interface

The basic functions of general program control are those for loading program files to memory and starting them, which are essential for program invoking. Here an important requirement is the ability to invoke programs in line with the service and the program execution format.

## (a) Separation and Composition of Basic Functions

Among the functions necessary for invoking programs, those that require a certain amount of time include opening the program files, loading them into memory, and interpreting addresses. In transaction processing, where the starting of a program can be anticipated in advance, for programs requiring high-speed response it should be possible to perform the more time-consuming tasks ahead of time. With interactive processing, on the other hand, indeterminate numbers of programs are invoked at random times, making preprocessing unnecessary as well as impossible. To handle these differences in execution format, basic functions have been prescribed both separately and in composite system calls. The specific approach taken to the separation and combination of functions is outlined below. The patterns by which system calls are issued are shown in *Fig.4-1*.

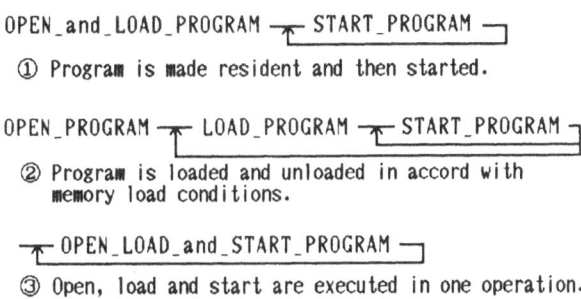

OPEN_and_LOAD_PROGRAM ⟶ START_PROGRAM ⟶

① Program is made resident and then started.

OPEN_PROGRAM ⟶ LOAD_PROGRAM ⟶ START_PROGRAM ⟶

② Program is loaded and unloaded in accord with memory load conditions.

⟶ OPEN_LOAD_and_START_PROGRAM ⟶

③ Open, load and start are executed in one operation.

*Fig.4-1. Patterns in which system calls are issued.*

- A separation is made first of all between preprocessing functions (program open and load) and execution (start).

- Program open and load functions are further separated, in order to allow control over the amount of preprocessing in accord with the execution format. Where necessary, for example, to avoid too great a demand on memory, only program opening is carried out as preprocessing. In other cases, loading and unloading of programs is performed in line with memory load conditions.

- Composite functions are provided for cases where preprocessing is unnecessary. These are aimed at improving programming efficiency and performance.

### (b) Making Functions Optional where Alternatives Exist

Program management functions include nested program invoking, multiple program loading, dynamic linking, and tree-structured program control (program overlay).

When these are considered as one program dynamically invoking another program, the following two methods are possible. These methods are alternatives in that the processing result is the same in each case.

- A number of programs are controlled in one task space, using program management functions.
- Each time a program is invoked, a new task is created and started.

The first method normally requires memory relocation. The second requires task creation, but relocation can be avoided by allocating a new memory space for each task, and loading the program to a fixed address (start address, etc.).

In execution control, general program control functions and process control functions are considered as alternatives. Accordingly, in general program control the implementation of nested program invoking and multiple program loading is not compulsory but optional. As for dynamic linking and tree- structured program control, there is minimal need for implementation of a dynamic interface in general program control; moreover, the method of detecting occasions for execution is dependent on computer architecture. For this reason these functions are not specified.

### (c) Program Control Information Format

To promote portability of general program control, compilers, and linkage editors, it would be desirable to standardize the program control information format, which is their common interface. There are major disadvantages to doing so, however, especially since this would prevent implementations from taking full advantage of particular architectures. The amount of programming effort that would be saved by such portability is also small. For these reasons, only items prerequisite to system call specification are given.

### (d) Program Residency

General programs are not objects of Initial Program Loading, and do not have resident/nonresident attributes. After a system call for loading has been issued, and until an unload system call is issued, they are considered to be resident.

Paging of program load space (on-demand paging) is handled as follows. Since there is little need for a dynamic interface, and the control method is system dependent, the possibility of paging is specified in program control information. System-dependent resource management, etc. then performs paging in reference to that information.

### 4.2 Process Control Interface

The role of process control is allocation of virtual processors and execution environments as required by different services or users. The basic functions involved are process creation and deletion, process starting and termination, allocation of resources to processes and their release, and program starting.

### (a) Process Configuration and Control

Process configuration, and the flow of control by system calls provided by the process control, are illustrated in *Fig.4-2*. Fundamentally a process consists of the three aspects of preprocessing, execution, and postprocessing. An initiator takes care of such preprocessing as allocation of an execution environment when a process is created and started. A user program is the program which a user of process control wishes to execute on a process. A terminator handles garbage processing and other postprocessing. An error processing routine performs necessary postprocessing on the user side when an error occurs in a user program.

A process consists of one or more tasks; but no specification is made as to the number of tasks, or such matters as whether the initiator and user program are separate tasks, since these depend on the system and service. Possible ways of configuring tasks in a process are as follows. A process made up of one task is called a "single-task process." A process consisting of multiple tasks is called a "multi-task process." A single-task process is implemented using only the process control functions. On the other hand, a multi-task process is implemented using task management functions in the user program.

1) Single-task process

The single-task process is the most fundamental form for linking task and programs. The initiator, terminator, user program, and error processing routine are executed in the same task.

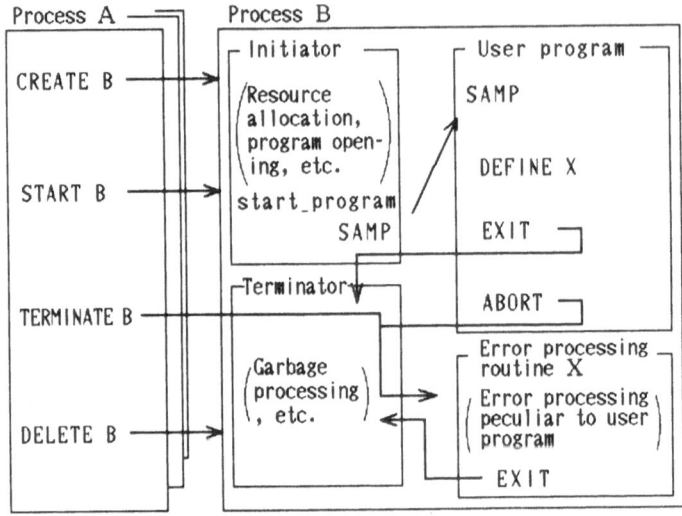

*Fig.4-2. Process configuration and flow of control.*

2) Multi-task process

A typical configuration of a multi-task process is shown in *Fig.4-3*. The initiator, terminator, and user programs are each given their own tasks. There are a number of user programs, which are also given their own tasks. The initiator allocates resources which are shared among those user programs.

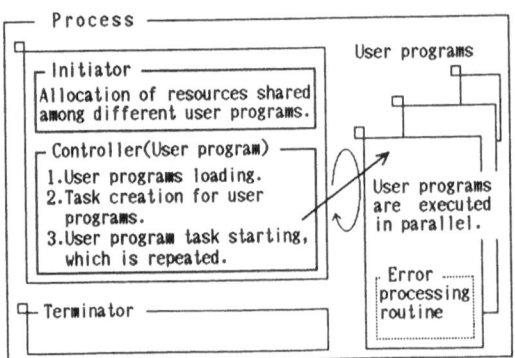

*Fig.4-3. Configuration of multi-task process.*

The multi-task process is applicable to services requiring a high level of realtime performance, in which multiple user programs are frequently invoked, and initiator and terminator processing is standard among user programs. In this case, however, the implementor must be aware that resource amounts may fluctuate as resources are allocated to other user programs. Provision must also be made for information (resource) protection among user programs, since resources are shared among different programs. Accordingly, the multi-task configuration is applicable to cases where the amount of resources to be used can be predicted, there is much common information among user programs, and the interfaces between programs are clear.

One good example of multi-task configuration applicability is to banking processes, in which the processing of deposits, withdrawals, and bank transfers, which take place all the time, are given respective tasks. In batch processing, likewise, it is possible for job input (reader), execution (application program), and output (writer) to be given respective tasks, but these are best made up of different processes, since they are independent of each other and need different execution environments.

(b) **Process States**

There are three process states, non-existent, dormant, and active. A non- existent process has either not been created or has been created and then later deleted. A dormant process has been created and allocated resources, and either not yet started or else started and then later terminated. An active process is one that has been started, and the user program is now executing. A different user program may be specified for each process start.

Process control does not provide system calls for controlling waiting state, so as to avoid duplication of functions provided by task management. Instead, the necessary functions are provided for inter-process communication, waiting for termination of a child process, dynamic resource allocation in the user program and the like, among which task management functions are used to control the waiting state.

(c) **Process Attributes**

1) Process identification

When a process is created, process control returns a process identifier. This identifier is used thereafter to reference the process. It is also possible to give a process a name when it is created, for easier control of processes whose creation is anticipated ahead of time, and to simplify inter-process communication.

2) Group identification

A concept expressing a group is that of parent-child relationship. This relationship can be understood in one of two ways. One is the natural relationship whereby the creating side is "parent" and the created side is "child." The other approach is to define the meaning of parent-child, and specify at the time of creation which is parent and which is child.

In CTRON execution control, applications of parent-child attributes are in handling of child processes (descendants) when a parent process (ancestor) is deleted or terminated, and in determining the scope of garbage processing. When each type of process is to be created at the service control level, it is not necessarily true in every case that deletion of a parent process means the automatic deletion of child processes, considered on a creator-created basis. For this reason CTRON specifies that parent and child are to be designated when a process is created. The processes designated as parent and child are called "master process" and "servant process," respectively.

When a master process is deleted, servant processes (including the descendants) created by that master process are also deleted. As a process is made up of tasks, a process group in a master-servant relationship is also a task group. Accordingly, when a master process is deleted, all tasks making up the processes in the master-servant relationship are also deleted.

3) Specifying roll-in/roll-out

A process, like a task, is a unit of parallel processing, to which the concept of roll-in/roll-out (swapping) can be applied. Such matters, however, as the way of selecting order of priority and other attributes, or the actual time of roll-in/roll-out, are dependent on the system or service. They are thus left to management by system-provided initiators or resource management, and are not specified as part of the process control interface.

4) Scheduling attributes

As a process is located between application program and task, it is conceivable that process control would provide two kinds of scheduling interfaces, one for starting of application programs (user program), and the other for CPU allocation to application programs that have already been started.The former is long-term scheduling, while the latter is short-term.

The scheduling of application program starting, however, depends greatly on service processing formats, and it is impossible to make a common interface covering all services. For this reason, such an interface is not specified in process control. If necessary, the interface is specified as part of service control.

The scheduling attributes of a process are for CPU allocation to the user programs. As a process is made up of tasks, scheduling of processes can be the responsibility of task management. The attributes given to processes are the same as those of task management, namely execution level (pre-emption index) and priority within that level.

**(d) Resource Management**

Resources that can be allocated as part of the execution environment include all those provided by the kernel and by other parts of the extended OS, except for tasks. Involving process control in all these resources would result in huge overhead. Since the initiators provided are usually determined by the service, the resources allocated when a process is created or started are designated by parameters in the form of a list, and the initiator allocates resources to a process in reference to the parameters. In this way a diversity of resources can be allocated, and resource allocation overhead due to the two-layer configuration is alleviated. There are also cases where memory, etc. is to be allocated dynamically in the user program, so a resource reference interface is specified.

1) Resource list

An initiator allocates different resources in reference to a resource list. Initiators and terminators are designed in pairs, making garbage processing possible as well. The basic approach to memory is allocation of pools, so that a limit may be placed on the amount of use. Files may be allocated by extracting subdirectories for use by users or services from the overall system directory.

2) Dynamic resource allocation method

A system call for resource reference is specified for space allocation from memory pools in user programs, for assigning of logical file names and directory path names by commands, and other cases where resource allocation cannot be specified at the time of process creation or starting. The steps involved in resource list designation and resource allocation in the user program are summarized below. An example of resource allocation using a resource list is shown in *Fig.4-4*.

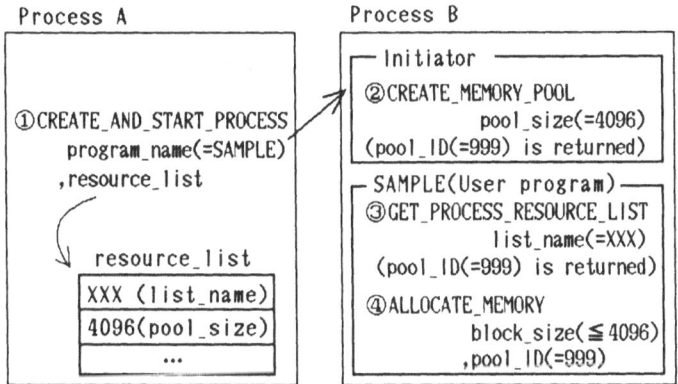

*Fig.4-4. Example of resource allocation with resource list.*

- A resource list is designated as a parameter in process creation.
- The initiator allocates resources to the process according to the resource list.
- The resource identifier, size, attributes, and other information are obtained by designating the resource list name (in GET_PROCESS_RESOURCE_LIST system call), which is predefined in accord with the kinds of resources or the purpose of use.
- Resources are allocated or accessed by means of the identifier. Resources allocated arbitrarily by the initiator without a resource list are accessed by means of a predefined resource name.

## 5. CONCLUSION

The CTRON execution control interface has been designed fundamentally by combining resources provided by the Basic OS kernel and by the Extended OS. The specific approaches being taken in devising specifications can be summarized as follows.

Functions common to services are separated from service-dependent functions in order to assure applicability to and portability among various services. General program control includes system calls for both separate and composite functions, and treats functions for which alternatives exist as optional. In this way performance can be tailored to different program execution patterns. The process control interface achieves outstanding ease of use as well as high performance by providing virtual processors and execution environments that do not require two-step scheduling.

Reduced performance due to combining resources fundamentally involves a tradeoff with productivity. However, in multi-user and multi-service processing such as in information processing or workstations, allocation of execution environments by initiators, and combining of resources, require implementation by some sort of functions at the service control level. Reduction in performance is thus not as great as when Basic OS functions are used directly.

Detailed specifications are now being considered as to resource list content, dynamic resource allocation, inter-process communication and other aspects of process control. Future study will also be carried out regarding the service control interface, such as the necessary recovery processing for assuring reliability in transaction processing, and handling of distributed processing.

## ACKNOWLEDGMENTS

The authors wish to express sincere appreciation to Dr. Ken Sakamura and Dr. Fukuya Ishino for their valuable opinions and guidance in consideration of the CTRON execution control interface. Thanks are due also to members of Hitachi Ltd., Mitsubishi Electric Corporation, NEC Corporation, Oki Electric Industry Co. Ltd., and Toshiba Corporation who studied, discussed and wrote the specifications in the CTRON Execution Control Working Group, General Program Control Subworking Group, and Process Control Subworking Group.

## REFERENCES

[1]  Creasy,R.J.(1981):The Origin of the VM/370 Time-sharing System, IBM J. Res. Dev., Vol.25, No.5, pp.483-490.

[2]  Auslander,M.A., Larkin,D.C. and Scherr,A.L.(1981):The Evolution of the MVS Operating System, IBM J. Res. Dev., Vol.25, No.5, pp.471-482.

[3]  DoD.(1980):STONEMAN, Requirements for Ada Programming Support Environments, Feb.

[4]  Baker,T.P. and Scallon,G.M.(1986):An Architecture for Real-Time Software Systems, IEEE Softw., May, pp.50-58.

[5]  Janson,P.A.(1985):OPERATING SYSTEMS Structures and Mechanisms, pp.72-75, Academic Press.

[6]  Wasano,T., Ohminami,M., Kobayashi,Y., Ohkubo,T. and Sakamura,K.(1987): Design Principles and Configuration of CTRON, Proc. FJCC'87, pp.159-166.

**Yasuhiko Baba:** Senior research engineer at NTT Communications and Information Processing Laboratories, where he is presently engaged in research on operating system architectures. Since joining the company in 1969, he has been engaged in developmental research on DIPS language processors and operating systems. He received the BE degree from Sophia University at Tokyo in 1969. He is a member of the IPS.

**Masato Ohminami:** Senior research engineer, project team leader at NTT Communications and Information Processing Laboratories, where he conducts research into operating system architectures. Since joining the company in 1972, he has been engaged in developmental research on DIPS operating Systems. He received the BE and ME degrees from Tohoku University at Sendai in 1970 and 1972, respectively. He is a member of the IPS.

Above authors may be reached at: 1-2356 Take, Yokosuka, 238 Japan.

**Hiromi Kusumoto:** Engineer of 1st Software Section in Software Development Department, Systems Engineering Division 4 at FUJITSU LIMITED, where he is engaged in development of operating systems since joining the company in 1979. He received the BE degree in electronic engineering from Hiroshima University in 1979.

**Hiroshi Kosugi:** Manager of 2nd Software Section in Software Development Department, Systems Engineering Division 4 at FUJITSU LIMITED, where he is engaged in development of operating systems since joining the company in 1972. He received the BE degree in electronic engineering from Tokyo Institute of Technology in 1972. He is a member of the IPS.

Above authors may be reached at: Systems Engineering Division, FUJITSU LIMITED, 1-4-1 Kitasaiwai, Nishi-ku, Yokohama, 220 Japan.

# Enhancement of the CTRON Kernel Interface

Ichizo Kogiku, Toshikazu Ohkubo
NTT Electrical Communications Laboratories

Masayoshi Matsushita
Oki Electric Industry Co., Ltd.

## ABSTRACT

An overall revision has been made of the CTRON kernel interface specifications with the aim of assuring even wider applicability of CTRON. The revisions center on subset designations and on specification of the architecture-dependent interface. The result is an easy-to-understand subset system, simplified to just five subsets, including the microsubset. Also, a detailed study is made of interface models for architecture-dependent features, and these models are the basis for a more thorough specification.

**Keywords:** CTRON, Kernel, Interface specifications, Subsetting, Architecture-dependent

## 1. INTRODUCTION

CTRON is a set of operating system interface specifications designed for common application to each of the service nodes in an information communication network[1][3][4][5][14]. CTRON adopts a hierarchical OS interface consisting of a Basic OS and Extended OS. Specifications for the CTRON kernel interface, which is part of the Basic OS, were published and offered to the public in November 1987. Since then, an overall revision has been made of these specifications with the aim of assuring even wider applicability of CTRON. The revisions center on subset designations and on specification of the architecture-dependent interface. This paper discusses the design approach and methodology applied to enhancement of the kernel interface.

Among the service nodes of an information communication network are many small-scale systems, including communication controllers as well as transmission controllers and other network components. When CTRON is applied to these small systems, the requirements in terms of performance and price are even more demanding than in the case of switching systems or workstations. To meet these demands, the new specification includes a CTRON kernel interface microsubset for application to small systems. The emphasis in choosing microsubset functions was chiefly on assuring portability of application programs and the Extended OS within the CTRON family.

Fundamentally, the CTRON kernel interface is designed to hide differences in architecture. Nonetheless, there are certain aspects, such as system configuration-dependent control, memory protection control, and interrupt-related control, in which architecture makes its presence known, and for which a physical interface must therefore be provided. In Version 1 of the Kernel Interface Specification, only partial specification was made of the system call names for such an architecture-dependent interface. More detailed interface models for these features have been devised for the new version, and the specifications have been more complete in this regard.

## 2. MAIN PROBLEMS IN VERSION 1

Since publication of Version 1 of the CTRON Kernel Interface Specification in November 1987, numerous requests and comments have been received. Many of these deal with specific items in the specifications. The largest overall problems pointed out, however, have to do with subsetting and with the treatment of architecture-dependent aspects.

### 2.1 Subset applicability

Upward portability of software is assured by strictly forbidding any departures from the CTRON kernel specifications; that is, implementations must not add to or delete from those specifications. The specified OS functions, however, include optional subsets, with different subset series designated for providing the functions required, depending on the application field and system scale. In Version 1, six subsets and two subset series (for switching systems and data processing systems, respectively) are designated (see *Fig. 1*). However, as implementations are now being readied based on application to actual products, the following points have been raised.

1) The common interface unit [C] is the smallest subset, but the specifications are rather cumbersome for application to small-scale systems such as transmission controllers, communication controllers, and the various supervisory equipment found in an information communication network, to which CTRON is supposed to apply. If CTRON is to find widespread application, it would be better to specify slimmed-down subsets for use with these small systems. These subsets should assure portability of application programs and the Extended OS, while satisfying the memory capacity and critical performance requirements of small equipment.

2) The "transaction control functions" included in the optional interface unit for task management [S] are special functions for conventional switching software implementations. In the future software should be created by means of a standardized programming style based on parallel (concurrent) tasks, and therefore these functions should be deleted.

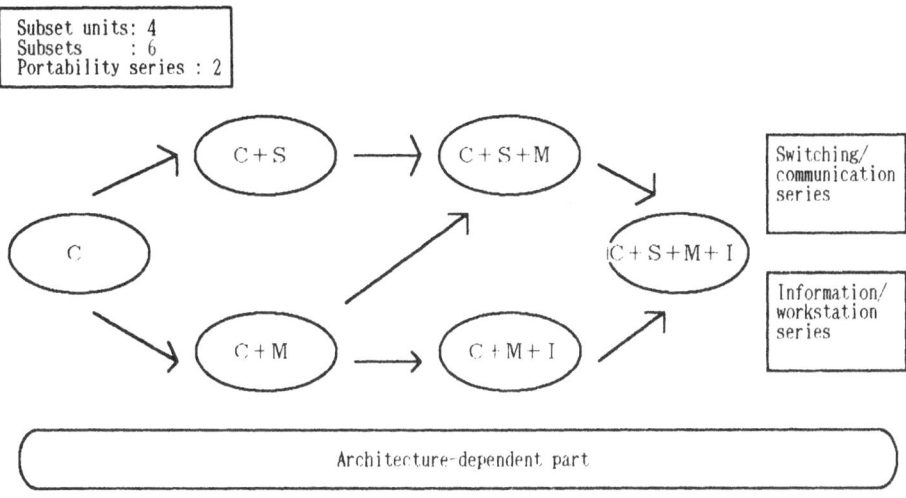

| Name of subset unit | Functions | Number of System call |
|---|---|---|
| C<br>Common interface unit | Task management<br>Task synchronization<br>         and communication<br>Interrupt management<br>Exception management<br>Timer management<br>Memory management<br>Statistical information management | 84 |
| S<br>Optional interface unit for task management | Cyclic procedure control<br>Transaction control<br>Task cyclic start control | 24 |
| M<br>Optional interface unit for task synchronization and communication | Rendezvous control<br>Message selection and<br>         reception control<br>Private timer control | 12 |
| I<br>Optional interface unit for memory management | Virtual memory control<br>Roll in/roll-out control<br>Basic program control | 22 |

*Fig. 1  Subsetting of Version 1*

3) When the optional interface unit for memory management [I] is implemented in the kernel so as to incorporate virtual memory functions into a system, the specifications require implementation also of the optional interface unit for task synchronization and communication [M] as well as the task management optional interface unit [S] added to [M]. This is an excessive interface for implementing, say, a microprocessor with built-in memory management unit (MMU). For such applications a subset should be specified consisting simply of the common interface unit [C] and memory management optional interface unit [I].

4) A presupposition of Version 1 was optimization of subsetting for each target application field. The emphasis was on minimizing the number of subsets in a kernel, which is the most basic element of a CTRON OS, from the standpoint of portability of the Extended OS and application programs. These subsets should be rearranged from the standpoints of functional level as well as portability.

## 2.2 Treatment of architecture-dependent aspects

In principle, CTRON kernel interface system calls are designed to be independent of any system architecture. It is difficult, however, to overcome differences among systems in respect to features such as system configuration-dependent control, memory protection control, and handling of interrupts. In the case of memory protection control, for example, interface models for ring methods and key methods are mutually exclusive (see *Fig. 2*). Also, interrupt-related control and system configuration control cannot be given common specifications without virtualizing them to the point where it may no longer be possible to assure a practical level of performance. In such cases, forcing these functions into a common mold would not serve the interests of gaining widespread acceptance for CTRON. In Version 1, no detailed specifications were provided for the functions or interface of these architecture-dependent aspects, and only some of the system call names were specified. Instead, when software is to be transplanted to different applications, this is done simply by using a source program editor or the like and mechanically extracting the places making use of the architecture-dependent interface. This is called a black box model (see *Fig. 3*).

As progress has been made, however, in devising the Extended OS interfaces[12][13][15][16], and also as the kernel implementations have begun to take shape[6][7][8][9] the following points have been made.

(a) Key protection method (▨ indicates difference from ring method)

| accessing side \ accessed side | 0 | 1 | 2 | 3 (No protection key) |
|---|---|---|---|---|
| 0 (Master protection key) | OK | OK | OK | OK |
| 1 | NG | OK | NG | OK |
| 2 | NG | NG | OK | OK |
| 3 | NG | NG | NG | OK |

(b) Ring protection method (▨ indicates difference from key method)

| accessing side \ accessed side | 0 | 1 | 2 | 3 |
|---|---|---|---|---|
| 0 | OK | OK | OK | OK |
| 1 | NG | OK | OK | OK |
| 2 | NG | NG | OK | OK |
| 3 | NG | NG | NG | OK |

*Fig. 2   Differences between memory protection schemes*

193

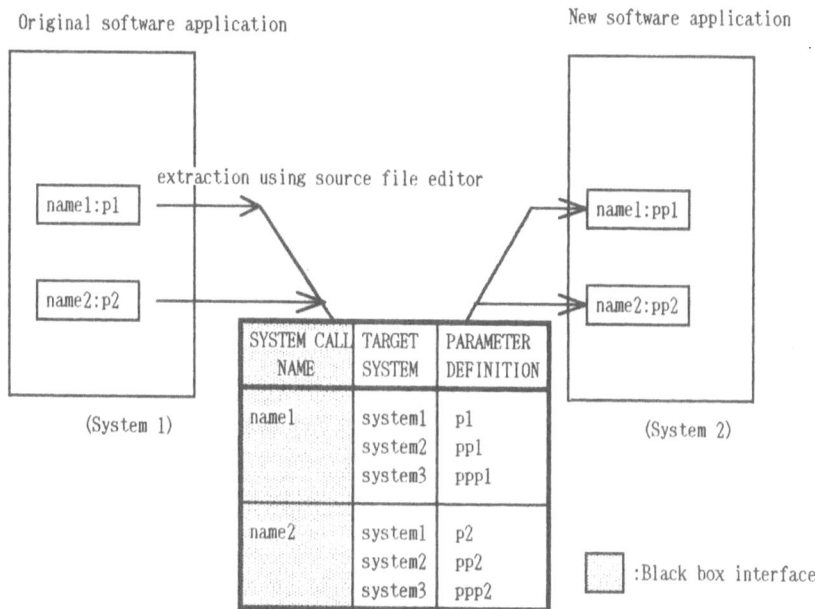

Fig. 3 *How software portability is achieved using black box function*

1) Even if it is difficult to devise a single interface model, it should be possible to come up with a number of typical patterns.

2) It should be possible to make not only partial specification of system call names but complete specification of the names as well as the parameter names.

These observations call attention to the need for a greater effort to standardize the architecture-dependent interfaces, and to promote increased software portability by specifying these interfaces in as much detail as possible.

## 3. REVISION OF SUBSETS

Based on the comments noted earlier, a revision of subset units, subsets and portability series was undertaken for Version 2 of the Kernel Interface Specification, from the standpoints of promoting the spread of CTRON and assuring portability of the vast amount of software (Extended OS and application programs) that is developed in the future.

## 3.1 Basic conditions

The basic conditions on which the revision was premised are as follows.

1) A subset is a kernel combining various groups of interface primitives specified as subset units for specific purposes, and must assure upward compatibility of the Extended OS and application programs.

2) The number of subsets should be kept to a minimum from the standpoint of Extended OS and application program portability.

3) Classification of subset units should stress Extended OS and application program portability over ease of implementation.

4) Extended OS and application program portability across all fields is enhanced by classifying subset units, subsets and portability series on the basis of function, and by ordering them in an upward direction from smaller to larger functions.

5) The smallest subset should be applicable even to the various embedded equipment found in a network.

6) The common interface unit [C], which is a subset unit, as a kernel should consist of common interface primitives not geared to any particular application field, and should itself be a standard subset.

## 3.2 Results of subset revision

As a result of the subset review premised on the above basic conditions, the subsetting shown in *Fig. 4* was specified in Version 2.

### a) Subset units

The common interface unit [C] consists of commonly applicable functions as in Version 1. For application to small equipment in the network, however, a slimmed down version of the common interface unit [C] is newly specified as a microsubset [mC] of minimum required functions. The high-level optional interface unit [M] is a functional merging of the optional interface units for task management [S] and task synchronization and communication [M] in Version 1. This represents a strengthening of common interface unit [C] primitives. The "transaction control functions" in the Version 1 task management optional interface unit [S] have been transferred to an architecture-dependent interface, since these functions are based on a specific software architecture. This maintains the validity of the specifications for existing implementations while easing the load of new implementations. The optional interface for virtual memory [I] consists of interface primitives for implementing a virtual memory system, based as in Version 1 on use of a memory management unit.

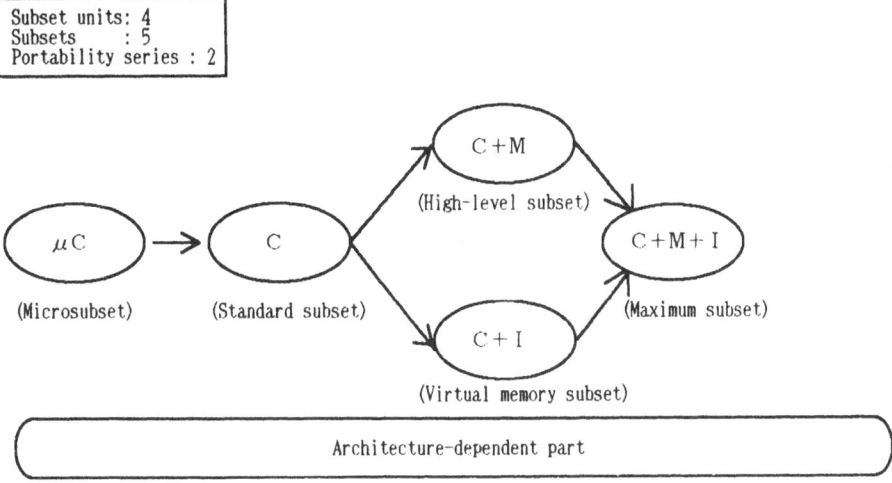

```
Subset units: 4
Subsets     : 5
Portability series : 2
```

μC → C

C + M
(High-level subset)

C + I
(Virtual memory subset)

C + M + I

(Microsubset)   (Standard subset)   (Maximum subset)

Architecture-dependent part

| Name of subset unit | | Functions | Number of System call | |
|---|---|---|---|---|
| C | μC (micro subset) | Task management<br>Task synchronization<br>and communication<br>(event flag, message box)<br>Interrupt management<br>Timer management<br>Memory management | 44 | 84 |
| | (Common interface unit) | Task synchronization<br>and communication<br>(semaphore, serially reusable resources)<br>Exception management<br>Statistical information management | | |
| M (High-level optional interface unit) | | Cyclic procedure control<br>Task cyclic start control<br>Message selection and reception control<br>Rendezvous control<br>Private timer control | 19 | |
| I (Virtual memory optional interface unit) | | Virtual memory control<br>Roll-in/roll-out control<br>Basic program control | 22 | |

*Fig. 4   Subsetting of Version 2*

## b) Subsets and portability series

Subsetting in Version 1 was aimed at optimizing of interfaces for specific application fields.  In Version 2, subsetting is functionally based, and aims to permit a selection of kernel functions with an optimal functional level for the scale of the implementation system.  Subsets range from the microsubset [mC] to the maximum subset [C+M+I].

Specifying of portability series for the Extended OS and application programs is also done on the basis of function. Each series is built around [C] as the standard subset. The microsubset [mC] is slimmed down from [C], while [C] is expanded in the high-level subset [C+M] for real memory systems, [C+I] for introduction of virtual memory systems, and [C+M+I], the maximum subset containing all the kernel functions.

The result is an easy-to-understand subset system, simplified to just five subsets. Upward portability is assured for extended OS and application software implementations based on the CTRON kernel, from the minimum subset [mC] to the maximum subset [C+M+I].

### 3.3 Introduction of a microsubset

The microsubset [mC], newly specified in Version 2, is outlined below.

#### (a) Purpose of specifying a microsubset

While maintaining upward compatibility of the Extended OS and application programs within CTRON systems, the slimming down of the standard subset [C] functions expands application to small-scale network equipment.

#### (b) Position of the microsubset

1) Range of application: The microsubset is for application to equipment used as components of information communication networks. It is not intended for standalone equipment, but for small-scale components connected to main equipment like exchanges and host computers, which are controlled by higher subsets. The microsubset assumes processors of 16 bits or more which can form an embedded-system OS.

2) Relation to ITRON: ITRON, for industrial applications, is an embedded kernel aimed at high performance in equipment control. The CTRON microsubset is a minimum subset of the "CTRON kernel" for use in network information and communication processing applications. This kernel subset is concerned mainly with assuring software portability within CTRON systems. Also, ITRON is applied to a signle-user environment, but the CTRON microsubset is applied to a multi-user environment. The different roles played by ITRON and the CTRON microsubset are illustrated in *Fig. 5*.

#### (c) Criteria for system call selection

The slimming down of common interface unit [C] system calls in microsubset [mC] was done from the following standpoints.

1) System call parameter levels guarantee upward compatibility of the Extended OS and application programs in a higher subset environment.

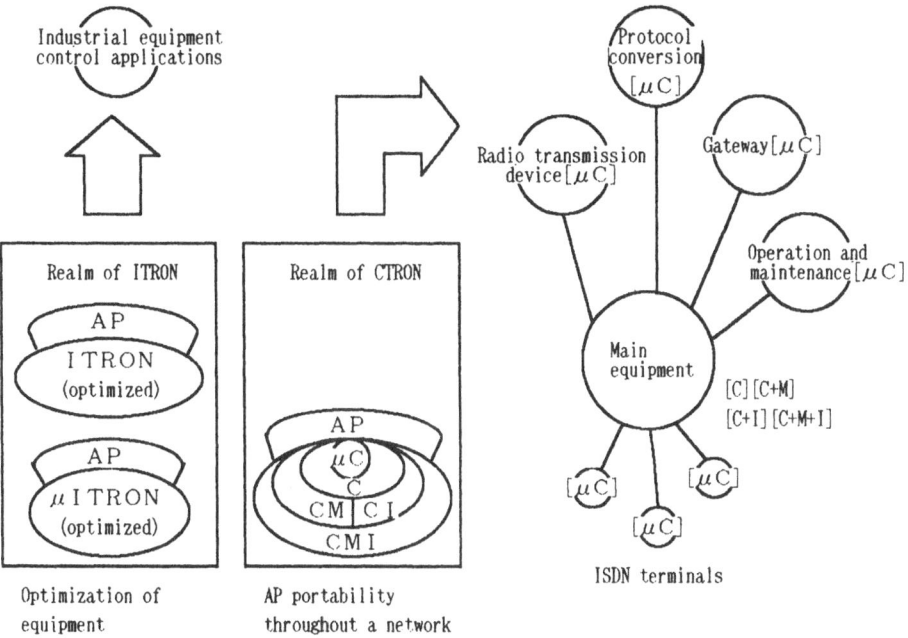

*Fig. 5   Relative positions of CTRON and ITRON*

2) The functions for building a Basic OS (I/O Control) are provided.

3) Slimming down is done in terms of interface primitives.

4) There are no limits peculiar to microsubset [mC] regarding use of functions. A simplification was made within the range of implementation-dependent items, and improved performance was sought.

5) In the case of interchangeable functions, primitive functions were chosen and duplication was avoided. (For cyclic wakeup functions, WUP_TSK and WAI_TSK are used.)

6) Treatment of each interface primitive:

   (i)   In task management, task state transitions are basic elements of tasks, which from the standpoint of compatibility and training are not to be changed.

   (ii)  In task synchronization and communication, semaphores and serially reusable resources are deleted as part of the slimming down effort.

   (iii) In interrupt management, instead of the two-dimensional management of classes and sources, only class management is specified.

   (iv)  System calls for exception management are omitted, with this function made implementation dependent (e.g., by registering of exception handlers at the time of system generation).

**(d) List of system calls**

System calls defined in the microsubset are listed in *Table 1*. The entire microsubset consists of 44 system calls, compared with 84 in the common interface unit [C], for a reduction by nearly half. The result is a minimal kernel that still preserves portability of application programs and the Extended OS to upper subsets. In principle CTRON makes no stipulations as to implementation method, since it is an interface specification. In selecting functions for the microsubset, however, performance aspects were considered to the extent that upward portability would not be hindered even if a speeding up was attempted in cases when the kernel's general implementation method is employed. The elimination of exception management and statistical information management in particular ease the implementer's burden and are effective in speeding up the kernel.

## 4. MODELS OF ARCHITECTURE-DEPENDENT INTERFACES

A detailed study was made of interface models for architecture-dependent features, and these models were the basis for a more thorough specification in this area.

### 4.1 Means of absorbing architectural variations

At the kernel level, the three pertinent classes of architecture are those of the processor, system configuration, and software configuration. Each of these three is subject to many different variations. In devising a method for absorbing these variations, specification is conceivable on any of the following levels (see *Fig. 6*).

1) [Level A] Specify only object names
2) [Level B] Specify also operation names
3) [Level C] Specify also parameters
4) [Level D] Specify also parameter semantics

In Version 1, specification was at Level A, while Level D is the level for ordinary system calls. The issue in drawing up detailed specifications for the architecture-dependent interfaces was to decide the actual level of specification to be applied. The approach taken was to devise specific interface models and study their suitability from the standpoint of common applicability. The models served to clarify the objects of system call operations and the operations themselves, and were also used to extract input and output information from the attributes of the objects of operations.

*Table 1  List of system calls in common interface unit [C]  (cont.)*

| Class | Name | Semantics | μC |
|---|---|---|---|
| | LOC_SRR | Serially reusable resource lock | × |
| | UNL_SRR | Serially reusable resource unlock | × |
| | GET_RID | Serially reusable resource identifier acquisition | × |
| Interrupt | DIS_INT | Interrupt disabling | ○ |
| Management | ENA_INT | Interrupt enabling | ○ |
| | SET_INM | Interrupt mask setting | × |
| | RST_INM | Interrupt mask resetting | × |
| | REF_INS | Interrupt disable state referencing | ○ |
| | REF_IMS | Interrupt mask state referencing | × |
| | DEF_INH | Interrupt handler definition | ○ |
| | EXT_INH | Exit from interrupt hadler | ○ |
| | RAS_INT | Interrupt raising | × |
| | REF_INT | Interrupt occurrence state referencing | × |
| | GET_INH | Interrupt handler information acquisition | × |
| Exception | ENA_EXC | Exception generation enabling | × |
| Management | DIS_EXC | Exception generation desabling | × |
| | REF_EXM | Exception mask state referencing | × |
| | GET_EXH | Exception handler information acquisition | × |
| | DEF_EXH | Exception handler definition | × |
| | CAN_EXC | System default exception handler resetting | × |
| | EXT_EXH | Exit from exception handler | × |
| | REF_EXD | Exception code referencing | × |
| | RAS_EXS | Same task exception raising | × |
| | RAS_EXC | Other task exception raising | × |
| Timer | GET_TIM | Time acquisition | ○ |
| Management | SET_TIM | Time setting | ○ |
| Memory | CRE_MPL | Memory pool creation | ○ |
| Management | DEL_MPL | Memory pool deletion | ○ |
| | GET_MID | Memory pool identifier acquisition | ○ |
| | GET_MPI | Pool information acquisition | × |
| | REF_MRA | Available memory space referencing | ○ |
| | ALC_MEM | Memory block allocation | ○ |
| | FRE_MEM | Memory block release | ○ |
| | ALC_MMS | Memory block (system space) allocation | × |
| | FRE_MMS | Memory block (system space) release | × |
| | GET_MBS | Memory block size acquisition | ○ |
| | GET_MBI | Memory block information acquisition | × |
| Statistical | REF_SIN | Statistical information referencing | × |
| Information | STA_SIN | Start statistical information gathering | × |
| Management | STP_SIN | Stop statistical information gathering | × |

*Table 1  List of system calls in common interface unit [C]*

| Class | Name | Semantics | μ C |
|---|---|---|---|
| Task | CRE_TSK | Task creation | ○ |
| Management | STA_TSK | Task starting | ○ |
| | CAS_TSK | Task creation and starting | × |
| | EXT_TSK | Task exit | ○ |
| | EXD_TSK | Task deletion | ○ |
| | SUS_TSK | Task suspension | ○ |
| | RSM_TSK | Task resumption | ○ |
| | WUP_TSK | Task wakeup | ○ |
| | SLP_TSK | Task sleep | ○ |
| | TER_TSK | Task termination | ○ |
| | DEL_TSK | Task forced deletion | ○ |
| | CYC_WUP | Task cyclic wakeup | × |
| | CAN_CYC | Task cyclic wakeup cancelation | × |
| | WAI_TSK | Task delayed wakeup | ○ |
| | CAN_WUP | Task wakeup cancelation | ○ |
| | DEF_EXT | Task exit routine definition | ○ |
| | ABO_TSK | Task abort | ○ |
| | GET_TID | Task identifier acquisition | ○ |
| | REF_ABD | Abort code referencing | ○ |
| | GET_TSI | Same task information acquisition | ○ |
| | CHG_TSI | Same task information change | ○ |
| | GET_TIF | Other task information acquisition | ○ |
| | CHG_TIF | Other task information change | ○ |
| Intertask | CRE_EVF | Event flag creation | ○ |
| Synchronization | DEL_EVF | Event flag deletion | ○ |
| and | SET_EVF | Event flag setting | ○ |
| Communication | WAI_EVF | Event waiting | ○ |
| | REF_EVF | Event flag referencing | × |
| | GET_EID | Event flag identifier acquisition | ○ |
| | CRE_SEM | Semaphore creation | × |
| | DEL_SEM | Semaphore deletion | × |
| | SIG_SEM | Semaphore signal | × |
| | WAI_SEM | Semaphore waiting | × |
| | REF_SEM | Semaphore referencing | × |
| | GET_SID | Semaphore identifier acquisition | × |
| | CRE_MBX | Message box creation | ○ |
| | DEL_MBX | Message box deletion | ○ |
| | REF_MBX | Message box referencing | × |
| | SND_MSG | Message transmission | ○ |
| | REM_MSG | Message reception (move mode) | × |
| | REL_MSG | Message reception (locate mode) | ○ |
| | GET_BID | Message box identifier acquisition | ○ |
| | DEF_SRR | Serially reusable resource definition | × |
| | CAN_SRR | Serially reusable resource definition cancelation | × |

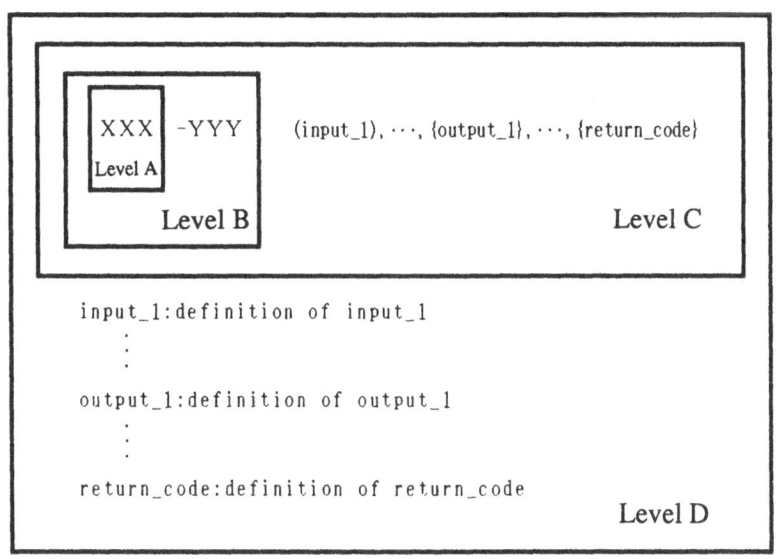

*Fig. 6   Architecture-dependent interface specification levels*

## 4.2 Processor architecture-dependent model

Items of processor architecture related to the kernel interface are listed in *Table 2*. For most of these it is possible to specify a processor-independent kernel interface by devising a virtual processor model. It is not possible, however, to create a virtual processor model that covers all the different kinds of interrupts, or memory protection functions. In other words, a single model of kernel interface specification cannot be made.

### 1) Memory protection functions

Memory protection functions depend greatly on processor architecture, but from the standpoint of subject and object of access they can be classified broadly as either key method or ring method. There are also many different units defining the range of protection, such as page or segment, etc.

Considering only memory protection operational functions, however, the following can be specified.

- Setting and changing memory protection attributes with respect to an allocated memory unit.
- Referencing memory protection attributes set for an allocated memory unit.

*Table 2   Processor Architecture and System Resources*

| Architecture item | Method for achieving invisibility | Corresponding system resource |
|---|---|---|
| Interrupt | Logicalization of type/format | Interrupt, Exception |
| Executive mode, Order set, Timer | Setting logical levels, Creation of soft timer | Task Timer |
| Control register | Hiding by program/ system status | Program, System |
| Memory management | Separating real/virtual memory function | Memory |
| Addressing, Address translation | Dynamic linkage of logical space | Task, Memory, Program |
| Memory protection | Providing exclusive interface | Memory |
| CPU/Memory configuration | Exclusive access, Logical configuration | Communications medea, System |

If an interface model is devised based on these operations, the differences between key method and ring method will not be reflected, permitting a consistent naming of system calls. It is also possible to adopt a hierarchical structure for units of memory designation, but in many cases a simple designation is sufficient, and there is little advantage in terms of common applicability. Therefore specification of memory protection functions is made on Level B.

## 2) Interrupt-related control

The interrupt management interface in the CTRON kernel common interface unit classifies interrupt factors on two levels, and provides mask and handler control functions (see *Fig. 7*). Classification of interrupt factors, however, is clearly dependent on processor architecture, so that it is difficult to draw up common specifications as with exception classes. Interrupt factors are thus systematized broadly along the following two lines (see *Fig. 8*).

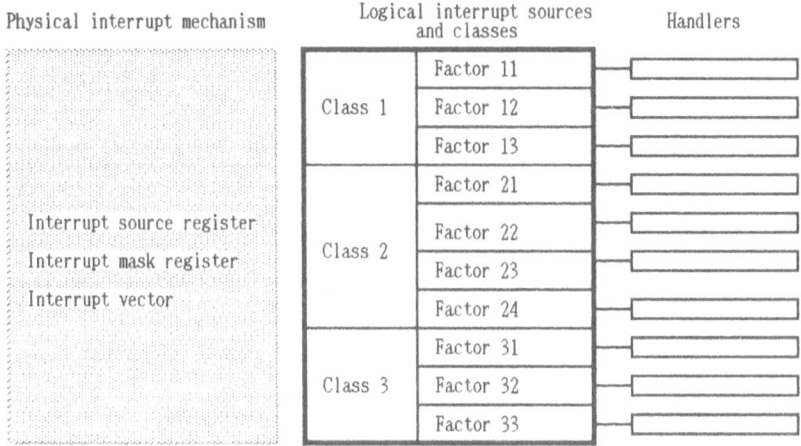

*Fig. 7  CTRON logical interrupt management*

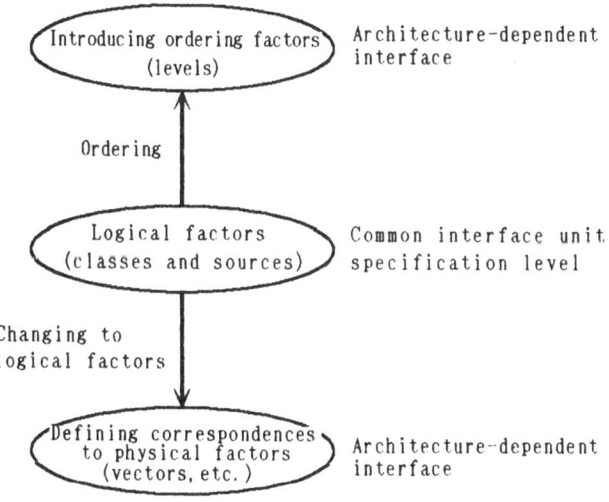

*Fig. 8  Systematization of interrupt factors*

- Logical interrupt factor system
    (A) Model defining logical interrupts
- Ordered interrupt factor system
    (A) Model defining interrupt vectors
    (B) Model defining interrupt levels

The first system defines the actual correspondences between logical and physical factors, and is aimed at portability of the interrupt handlers themselves. The second introduces order to interrupt enable/disable designations.

The interface model defining logical interrupts cannot specify the system of physical factors which are its object, and thus Level B is suitable.

In the interface model for interrupt level control, on the other hand, there is only one set of attributes (although the content is system dependent), so that for a clear interface it is possible to specify on Level C. The interface model defining interrupt vectors, however, specifies only system call names, since in some cases special information is required.

In order to make possible more detailed control of interrupts, the following interface models are created.
- Model for changing interrupt exit point
- Model for referencing interrupt information

In both of these interface models there are variations in format and semantics of the information passed, but the operation model itself is clear, so specification can be made on Level C.

### 4.3 System architecture-dependent model

System configuration problems for the kernel interface arise specifically from the diversity of connection patterns between the CPU and memory. Having a number of CPU-memory combinations improves performance and reliability, but there are many different ways in which these combinations can be arranged. If, however, the environment on which one kernel runs is seen as a CPU-memory combination, each CPU and memory can be divided into either "in use" or "standby." This includes cases when the CPU in use is subject to so-called multiprocessor control. Multiprocessors are of two kinds, the tight coupling type and loose coupling type, depending on the range of control by one kernel. The first type is covered by specifications for the kernel common interface unit. The second type, however, should be specified as part of an Extended OS interface for communication control, communication I/O control, or the like. The system architecture-dependent interface is for control of the "in use" and "standby" status of so-called main unit devices such as CPU and memory, but does not include multiprocessor control.

1) Multiplex system control

Provision of standby equipment is essential for building a highly reliable system, which means that control of "in use" and "standby" status is also required. Since the interface model is not limited to only one standby device, the concept of lineage is valid. The concept of lineage is not required in every case, however, so specification on Level B is suitable for this interface.

2) Control peculiar to special types of hardware

This model specifies operations peculiar to special kinds of hardware which are not standby devices. It is difficult, however, to specify attributes and operation methods for hardware configuring a system (e.g., communication devices between processors, or synchronized operation and supervision devices). For this reason the specification here is on Level A as before, with only part of the system call name being specified.

3) Initialization control

Besides the initialization that takes place when the system is started up, reset instructions are required, for example, after fault processing, for restart processing, and in operation and maintenance processing; and completion notice is necessary to indicate Extended OS initialization. The initialization and starting level, however, depends on system configuration and software architecture. It would be difficult, therefore, to standardize the parameters that are passed, and so Level B specification is suitable.

**4.4 Software architecture-dependent model**

An interface involved with software architecture is intrinsically difficult to include in OS interface standardization efforts, but is necessary as a way of preserving knowhow built up in various application fields. Some sort of mechanism should also no doubt be provided for the sake of future expansion.

1) Transaction control functions

A transaction is, like a task, a unit of parallel processing. Unlike a task, however, the work area is managed not by the OS, but by the application program itself (see *Fig. 9*). The difference, in other words, has to do with whether a program is made re-entrant at the OS level or at the application program level. Among the advantages of using a transaction are that, since the application program manages the work area, the application program can manage restart information independently and memory can be used more efficiently.

Specification of the interface for transaction-related control includes also the semantics of parameters (i.e., Level D), since the model is very clear. In the revision of the interface specification in Version 2, in order to avoid duplication with task management functions this interface was changed from the optional part to the software architecture-dependent part.

2) System call extension functions

Providing an interface for creation of individual system calls allows dynamic system addition for Extended OS use, and makes it easy to encode a kernel in a ROM. Although the necessary information cannot be decided uniformly, standardization of parameter names is possible. The interface model is thus specified on Level C.

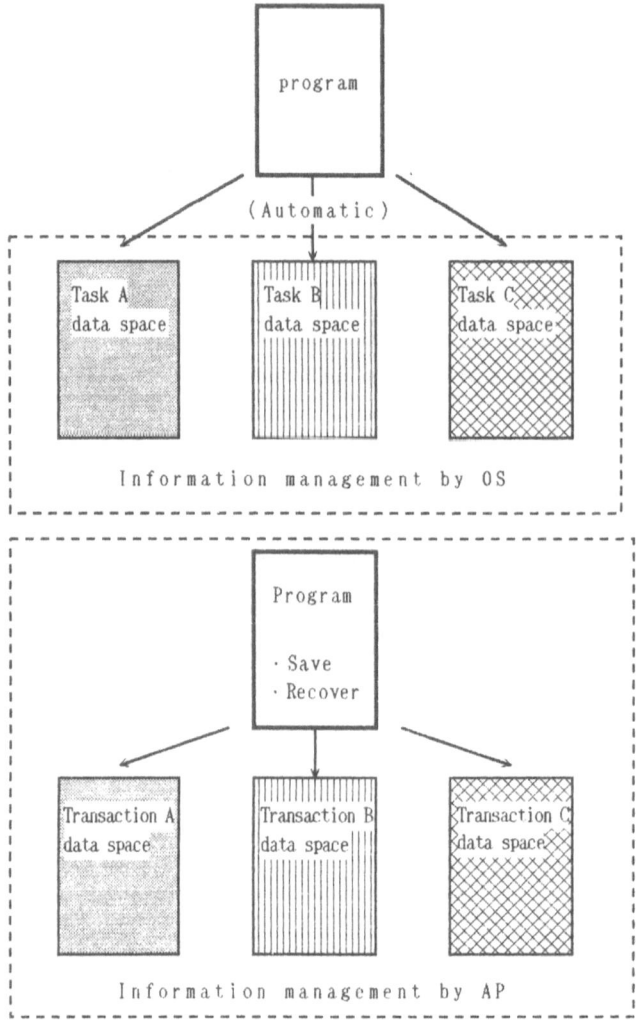

*Fig. 9   Tasks and transactions*

**4.5  List of architecture-dependent interfaces**

The results of the Version 2 revision of architecture-dependent features are summarized in *Table 3*.

**5.  IN CONCLUSION**

The revisions to the CTRON Kernel Interface Specification described here include two major topics, that of the subsetting revision and a more detailed modeling of architecture-

*Table 3  Summary of Architecture-dependent Interface Specifications*

| Application (purpose for use) | Functions | Specification level | System calls |
|---|---|---|---|
| Memory protection* | Prevent improper access | B | MEMORY_PROTECTION_SET<br>MEMORY_PROTECTION_REFER |
| Interrupt related* | Define correspondence between logical and physical interrupt factors | B | INTERRUPT_CORRESPONDENCE_DEFINE |
| | Define correspondence between interrupt vectors and interrupt handlers | B | INTERRUPT_VECTOR_DEFINE |
| | Disable and enable external interrupts in accord with interrupt factor level | C | INTERRUPT_LEVEL_DISABLE<br>INTERRUPT_LEVEL_ENABLE |
| | Change interrupt exit point peculiar to system | C | INTERRUPT_EXIT_CHANGE |
| | Refer to detrailed interrupt information | C | INTERRUPT_DETAIL_REFER |
| Multiplex system control | Control main multiplexed devices (detaching, switching, embedding, state referencing, etc.) | B | MULTIPLE_HARDWARE_CONTROL |
| Control peculiar to speceal hardware* | Perform control functions peculiar to special hardware other than standby equipment | A | PHYSICAL_HARDWARE_CONTROL |
| Initialization control* | Indicate initial settings, and give completion notice of Extended OS initialization | B | SYSTEM_INITIATE<br>SYSTEM_START |
| System call expansion | Register special system calls | C | SYSTEMCALL_DEFINE |
| Transaction related control | Control transaction creation, deletion, queueing, etc. | D | (Omitted) |

Note 1:Specification levels are indicated as follows:
   **A** :Partial system call name specification only (as in Version 1)
   **B** :Specification of system call name only
   **C** :Specification up to and including parameter names
   **D** :Specification of parameter semantics as well (as with ordinary system call specification)
Note 2:An asterisk(*)in the Application column indicates a functional category in the original architecture dependent interface.

dependent features. These issues are very closely related to the applicability of CTRON as a whole. This paper has attempted to describe the approach and methods applied in the revisions.

The concept of subsetting, which aims to satisfy at once both applicability and portability, distinguishes CTRON from other attempts at OS interface standardization. POSIX[11], for example, at present has no such concept. MOSI[10] includes subset units known as functional modules, but they are many in number, so that the subsets created by combining these modules are very large. This makes portability more difficult.

The modeling of architecture-dependent aspects is an attempt to standardize the OS interfaces to the greatest extent possible. This concept is also one not found in POSIX or MOSI. The present models, however, have been created by referring to present examples of implementation, and will need further refinement in the future.

## ACKNOWLEDGMENTS

The authors wish to thank Dr. Ken Sakamura of the University of Tokyo Faculty of Science, and Dr. Fukuya Ishino of NTT's Information and Communication Processing Laboratory, for their kind advice and assistance. Appreciation is due also to members of the CTRON Technical Committee, and especially to those on the Kernel Working Group.

## REFERENCES

[1]  Ohkubo T, Wasano T, Kogiku I, "Configuration of the CTRON kernel". IEEE Micro 7(2):33-44, 1987

[2]  CTRON Technical Committee, "CTRON KERNEL interface specifications. TRON Association", Tokyo, 1987

[3]  Kogiku I, Ohrui T, Ohkubo T, Hamada Y, "A Real-time Portable Operating System Common to Switching and Information Processing Applications", Proc. International Switching Symposium '87. IEEE, New York, B.4.4.1, 1987

[4]  Wasano T, Ohminami M, Kobayashi Y, Ohkubo T, Sakamura K, "Design Principles and Configuration of CTRON", Proc. FJCC '87. IEEE and ACM, New York, pp 159-166, 1987

[5]  Wasano T, Ohminami M, Kobayashi Y, Ohkubo T, Sakamura K, "Design of CTRON", Proceedings of the Third TRON Project Symposium, pp 157-172, 1987

[6]  Suda K, Kubota M, Ohrui T, "Realtime Portable Operating System for ISDN", Proc. COMPSAC 87. IEEE, New York, 1987

[7] Ohrui T, "The DEX-CTRON Operating System Applicable to ISDN Switching and Communications Processing Systems", Proc. GLOBECOM '88. IEEE, New York, 1988

[8] Ishizuka M, Ikeda Y, Fukuyoshi M, Ogawa T, Sakuma T, Matsushita M, "An Implementation of CTRON Basic OS", Proceedings of the Fifth TRON Project Symposium (this volume), 1988

[9] Oda K, Shimizu N, Inoue N, Iba Y, "Implementation of CTRON basic OS on a laptop workstation", Proceedings of the Fifth TRON Project Symposium (this volume), 1988

[10] Jackson DL (chair),"IEEE Trial-Use Standard Specification for Microprocessor Operating Systems Interfaces" IEEE, New York, 1985

[11] Issak J (Chair), "IEEE Trial-Use Standard Portable Operating System Environment P1003/D6", IEEE, New York, 1985

[12] Narimatsu S, "Design of CTRON Input-output Control Interface", Proceedings of the Third TRON Project Symposium, pp 183-196, 1987

[13] Kumazaki K, "Design of the CTRON File Management", Proceedings of the Third TRON Project Symposium, pp 173-182, 1987

[14] Kobayashi Y, Wasano T, Sakamura K, "Configuration and design concepts of CTRON interface", Proceedings of the Fifth TRON Project Symposium (this volume), 1988

[15] Shimizu Y, "Design of CTRON Communication Control Interface", Proceedings of the Fifth TRON Project Symposium (this volume), 1988

[16] Baba Y, Ohminami M, Kusumoto H, Kosugi H, "Design of CTRON Execution Control Interface", Proceedings of the Fifth TRON Project Symposium (this volume(, 1988

**Ichizo Kogiku**: A senior research engineer, supervisor in the Third Project Team, NTT Communication Switching Laboratories. There, he is conducting research on operating system architectures. Previously, he had engaged in developmental research on DIPS operating systems and relational database retrieval systems at NTT Communications and Information Processing Laboratories. He received his BS and MS degrees in mathematics from Tohoku University in 1975 and 1977. He is a member of the IEICE, of the IPS, of the IEEE, and of the ACM.

**Toshikazu Ohkubo:** A senior research engineer, supervisor, team leader in the Third Project Team, NTT Communication Switching Laboratories. There, he conducts research into operating system architectures. Since joining the company in 1971, he has been engaged in developmental research on DIPS operating systems and communication control systems. He received the BE degree in 1969 and the ME degree in 1971 at Waseda University in Tokyo. He is a member of the IEICE, of the IPS, and of the IEEE

Above authors may be reached at: Third Project Team, NTT Communication Switching Laboratories, 3-9-11 Midori-cho, Musashino, Tokyo 180, Japan.

**Masayoshi Matsushita:** A manager of Software Engineering Section in Software Engineering Department, Switching Systems Engineering Division, Telecommunications Group at Oki Electric Industry Co., Ltd. He joined the company in 1971 after graduating from Doshisha University in Kyoto. Since then, he has been engaged in the development of the basic software and microprocessor architecture. He is a member of the IEICE and the IPS.

Above author may be reached at: Microprocessor Development Labolatory, OKi Electric Industry Co, Ltd.,10-3, Shibaura 4-Chome,Minato-ku, Tokyo 108, Japan.

# An Implementation of the CTRON Basic OS

Masaru Ishizuka, Yoshimichi Ikeda, Makoto Fukuyoshi,
Tsukasa Ogawa, Tetsuo Sakuma, Masayoshi Matsushita
Oki Electric Industry Co., Ltd.

ABSTRACT

CTRON designed in the TRON project is an operating system which can be used commonly for various kinds of network nodes such as information processing nodes and switching processing nodes.
The CTRON-based operating system named "RG68K" has been developed as a company-wide standard operating system.

This paper describes the implementation and some evaluation of the RG68K Operating system and also proposes a standard implementation of the CTRON basic operating system using the MC68000 microprocessor family.

Keywords: CTRON, RG68K, MC68020, Realtime Operating System, Fault Tolerance

## 1. INTRODUCTION

The interface specification for a high performance realtime operating system applicable to various kinds of information network nodes such as switching nodes, communication processing nodes, information processing nodes, and workstation nodes are being studied as CTRON in the TRON project [1].

There are various scales and types of network nodes. Namely, network nodes range from microprocessors to mainframes in terms of their scales and also range from switching systems which require super-multiple processing capability and high reliability to information storing and processing systems represented by database systems.

With the arrival of a full-scale ISDN age in the future, these network nodes are expected to be more diversified and the amount of application programs (AP) will become enormous. CTRON aims to permit common use of software resources by standardizing operating system interfaces.

We are developing the CTRON-based realtime OS named "RG68K" as the next-generation standard OS used for our switching systems and communication equipment [2, 6, 7]. The RG68K is an operating system using our MC68020 processor board. We aim at implementing a distributed realtime OS in the super-cluster configuration at our final development stage.[3]

This paper describes overall configuration of the RG68K, and that of hardware in the chapter 2. In the chapter 3, we describe the structure, features and implement specification of the **RG68K** Realtime Kernel, System Interfacer (SIC) and I/O Control (IOC). In particular, we emphasize unspecified items in the CTRON Specifications. And we also propose the standard implementation of the implement-dependent part of the CTRON interface Specifications using MC68000 microprocessor family. In the chapter 4, we describe some evaluation results of the **RG68K** Basic OS for real storage version.

## 2. OVERALL CONFIGURATION OF THE RG68K

### 2.1 SOFTWARE CONFIGURATION

*Fig. 1* shows the final overall configuration of the **RG68K**.

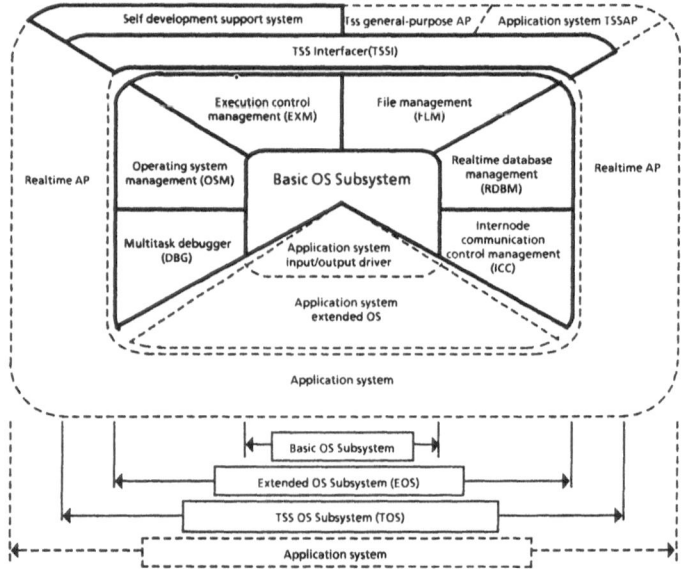

*Fig.1 Overall Configuration of the RG68K*

The **RG68K** Operating system consists of Basic OS (BOS), Extended OS (EOS) and Time-sharing OS (TOS). In this chapter, we describe the overall configuration and feature of each OS part and we also give the hardware configuration and feature. The EOS, TOS and BOS (virtual storage version) are being studyed.

### (a) BASIC OS SUBSYSTEM (BOS)

The BOS is a subsystem to hide the processor architecture (processor configuration, interrupts, exceptions, control registers, memory management, etc.) and input/output device architecture from the upper level software. The BOS is described in the chapter 3.

### (b) EXTENED OS SUBSYSTEM (EOS)

The EOS is a subsystem to provide the virtual interface for system resources to the upper level application program (AP) and uses the minimum subset of the BOS .

### 1) Execution Control Management (EXM)

The EXM has process management, program management, and interactive control and manages the allocation of processor resources.

## 2) File Management (FLM)

The FLM is a distributed file management with a tree structure directory and is designed to have high realtime and high fault tolerance.

## 3) Realtime Database Management (RDBM)

The RDBM is a high speed memory-oriented database to secure the realtime handling capability. It provides a general-purpose access method for a great variety of data at network nodes. And the RDBM permits easy AP development.

## 4) Internode Communication Control (ICC)

The ICC is a internode communication control for distributed resource accessing (interprocess communication, file transfer, etc.).

## 5) Operating System Management (OSM)

The OSM is a standard operating system management to operate and maintain common equipments on the OP68KS, consisting of processors, memories, hardware timer and input/output equipments (fixed disks, flexible disks, printers, etc.).

## 6) Multitask Debugger (DBG)

The DBG is a debugger to perform efficiently AP self debugging in the multi-tasking environment. In addition to general debugging functions such as read/write-memories and registers, break, instruction trace, and disassemble, it provides break function performed on the occurrence of events such as interrupts, exceptions, messages, event flags and semaphores, and task scheduling trace of a specific task.

### (c) TSS SUBSYSTEM (TOS)

The TOS is a subsystem to execute the self development support program and the information processing application program and also provides a high level human/machine interface in combination with a realtime system. The AP in the TOS can communicate with the realtime AP and can utilize the EOS. The realtime AP can utilize the TSS application program, so that high-grade network node services can be provided using the information processing systems such as expert and language translation systems.

### (d) APPLICATION SYSTEM

The RG68K is a common OS that contains only the functions common to all types of node. Consequently, the functions unique to application system, such as subscriber line control and speech path control for circuit switching systems, and various types of communication line control for packet switching systems, will be implemented by adding input/output drivers, EOS, and operation and maintenance management to each application system. In this way, the RG68K secures its independence. According to their respective purpose, the application programs can be built as realtime tasks on the kernel, realtime processes on the EXM, and TSS processes on the TOS.

### 2.2 HARDWARE CONFIGURATION AND FEATURE

The RG68K has been implemented aiming at the application to the OP68KS fault-tolerant processor system (real storage version). To implement the fault tolerance which is one of unique features of CTRON, a hot-standby duplicated processor system is adopted. The processors run active/standby, in which a fault in the active processor causes a switchover to standby processor without any degradation in processing power. This typical fault-tolerant system has been mainly used in many telephone switching systems and has high reliability. The OP68KS configuration is shown in *Fig. 2* and its features are as followings:

- Self-checking
- Watchdog timer
- Memory protection
- Error correcting code (ECC)
- Duplicated main memory
- Emergency circuit (EMA)
- Duplicated VME bus

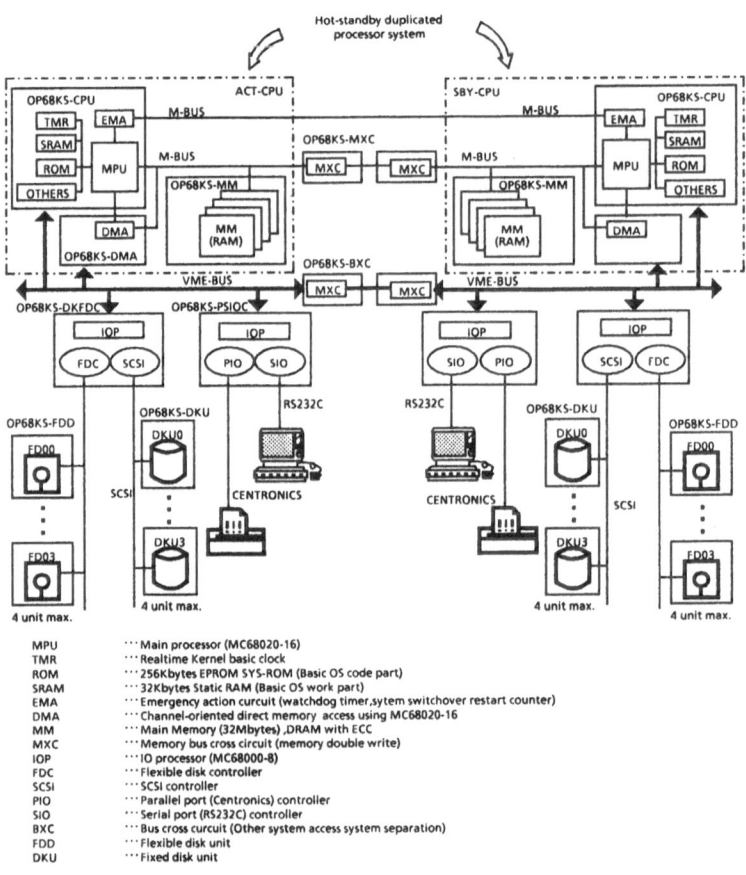

| MPU | ··· Main processor (MC68020-16) |
| --- | --- |
| TMR | ··· Realtime Kernel basic clock |
| ROM | ··· 256Kbytes EPROM SYS-ROM (Basic OS code part) |
| SRAM | ··· 32Kbytes Static RAM (Basic OS work part) |
| EMA | ··· Emergency action curcuit (watchdog timer,sytem switchover restart counter) |
| DMA | ··· Channel-oriented direct memory access using MC68020-16 |
| MM | ··· Main Memory (32Mbytes) ,DRAM with ECC |
| MXC | ··· Memory bus cross circuit (memory double write) |
| IOP | ··· IO processor (MC68000-8) |
| FDC | ··· Flexible disk controller |
| SCSI | ··· SCSI controller |
| PIO | ··· Parallel port (Centronics) controller |
| SIO | ··· Serial port (RS232C) controller |
| BXC | ··· Bus cross curcuit (Other system access system separation) |
| FDD | ··· Flexible disk unit |
| DKU | ··· Fixed disk unit |

*Fig.2 OP68KS Processor System Configuration*

## 3. THE RG68K BASIC OS

*Fig. 3* shows the structure of the RG68K Basic OS.

The Realtime Kernel and the System Interfacer (SIC) provide the CTRON kernel interface. Architecture dependent part of the interface is implemented in the System Interfacer (SIC) and the other part is implemented in the Realtime Kernel.

The I/O Control (I/O client, I/O servers and drivers) provide the CTRON I/O control interface.

These are designed according to the CTRON SPECIFICATION KERNEL INTERFACE Ver.1(Nov. 1987)[4] and the CTRON SPECIFICATION I/O CONTROL INTERFACE Ver.1(Nov. 1987)[5].

System loader, off-line monitor and system call library are also provided as parts of the BOS.

To enhance the system performance, the BOS was written in an assembler language and provided as ROMs.

Following sections describe the structure and major features of the Realtime Kernel, the System Interfacer (SIC) and the I/O Control (IOC).

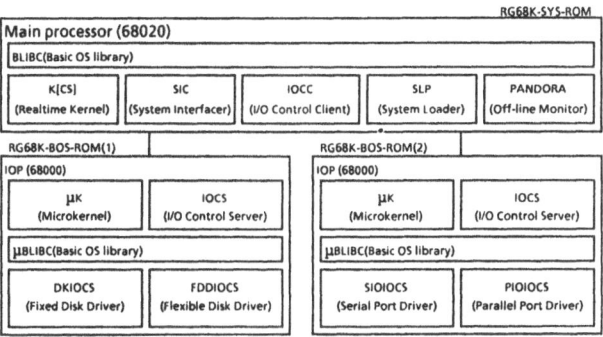

*Fig.3 Structure of the Basic OS Subsystem*

### 3.1 REALTIME KERNEL

#### (a) STRUCTURE AND FEATURE

*Fig. 4* shows the RG68K Realtime Kernel structure, and *Table 1* shows Realtime Kernel specifications. Upon implementing the CTRON kernel, we payed the following considerations.

1) We adopted "common part [C] + task management option part [S]" subset, aiming at the application to switching and communication processing fields. However, we have not implemented the transaction-related control function of the task management option part [S]. We considered that the transaction-related function was not needed because all programs to be developed in the CTRON environment will be implemented as tasks. (The transaction-related control function is a programming style used in the conventional switching processing.)

2) The hardware-dependent processing of the target system, such as system timer interrupt and interrupt controller, is separated from the kernel itself as a hardware-dependent procedure so that the kernel itself can run on the virtual processor consisting only of a CPU and a memory. Therefore, each target system having the same type of CPU can be generated easily by recoding only the hardware-dependent procedure linked to the configuration table (C_TBL).

3) The parameter checking grade, the execution level, the system timer basic cycle, and the presence/absence of time slices can be selected by the C__TBL to build an optimum execution environment in the application system.

4) Various systems ranging from a small-sized system to a large-sized system can be designed using the same kernel running on the MC68000 family (MC68020 and MC68000). Consequently, the instruction set and architecture with high grade of compatibility are selected. For example, the MSP (Master Stack Pointer) for the MC68020 is not used to secure compatibility with MC68000.

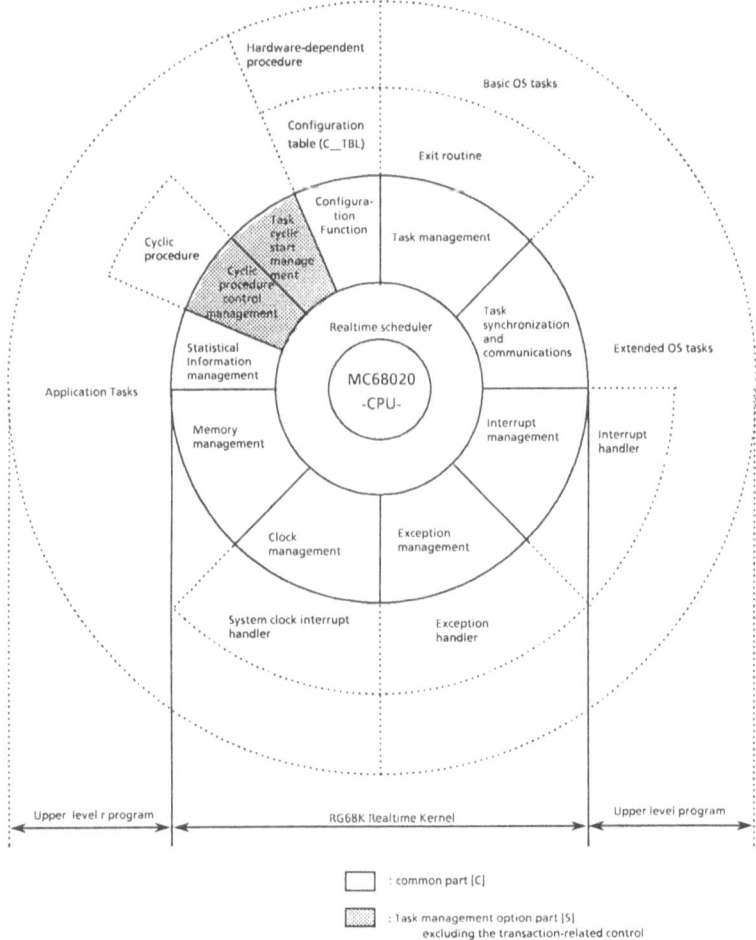

*Fig.4 Realtime Kernel Structure*

**(b) IMPLEMENT SPECIFICATION AND FEATURE**

*Fig. 5* illustrates the concept of the **RG68K** Realtime Kernel execution control.

**1) Task management**

—Execution level and priority

*Table 1 RG68K Realtime Kernel Specifications*

| Item | Description |
|---|---|
| Target processor | MC68020 (MSP is not used.Without MMU)<br>(The Realtime Kernel can run also on the MC68000.) |
| Maximum number of Task | 65,535 |
| Execution level and priority | Execution levels(Four patterns, 0~31, 0~63, 0~95 and 0~127, can be selected.)<br>priorities (1~31, A priority can be specified for each execution level) |
| Scheduring | Execution level + Priority ( + Time slice) |
| Task status | 7 statuses<br>①Non-Existent　　②Ready<br>③Running　　④Waiting<br>⑤Dormant　　⑥Suspended -waiting<br>⑦Suspended-ready |
| Synchronization and communication | Eventflag,Semaphore,Message box,Serially-reusable Resource(65,535 max. per item) |
| Interruption | Basic level 1~7 (Expansion is possible by interrupt controllers) |
| Number of system call | 90 |
| Subset in the CTRON Specifications | [C] + [S] (common part + Task management option part; but, excluding transaction-related control) |
| System generation | The user can perform system generation by setting the information in the configuration table (C__TBL) |
| Kernel programing language | Assembler language |
| User programing language | C language or assembler language (MOTOROLA standard mnuemonics) |
| Program size | Kernel code area　: (30~35K bytes)<br>Kernel work area　: (5K bytes) |

In the CTRON Specifications, a task is a minimum unit that can be executed in concurrent environment and is scheduled by the two-dimensional scheduling algorithm using execution levels and priorities. Event-driven preemption can be performed between the tasks having different execution levels. The same execution level tasks are scheduled in priority order. There is no specification for the range of execution levels and priorities.

In the **RG68K**, execution levels (0-31, 0-63, 0-95, and 0-127) and priorities (no priority, 1-31) can be selected by the configuration table (C__TBL). A system requiring only the event-driven scheduling can select the one-dimensional scheduling using only execution levels. The lowest execution level is assigned to the idle task (user specific idle task can be registered in the C__TBL) to be used for the measurement of the CPU idle time.

—Time slice

In the CTRON Specifications, the time slice is not prescribed specifically. The **RG68K** Realtime Kernel, however, will adopt the round robin scheduling method based on priorities by registering desired execution levels and time slice interval in the C__TBL.

—Exit routine

When the abort condition arises for the task (issue of TER__TSK, DEL__TSK, or ABO__TSK system call), the task exit routine is started to garbage the resource held during the execution of the task. The exit routine is executed as the same context of the task. In the **RG68K**, this execution level can be changed by the C__TBL. To garbage correctly, it is necessary to inhibit preemption temporarily. In the CTRON Specifications, there is no system call for the preemption disable/enable functions. Therefore, it is required to set the execution level to the highest one or to use the interrupt mask.

— Exception handler

The non-task exception handler is not specified in the CTRON Specifications. In the **RG68K**, the non-task exception handler is used to handle internal exceptions (CPU exceptions and system call exceptions) that occur in the interrupt handler or cyclic procedure. This non-task exception handler can be registered in the C_TBL and only one non-task exception handler is provided in the system.

— Abort handler

The **RG68K** contains the abort handler that is not specified in the CTRON Specifications. This handler is started together with the abort code and abort detail information when the initialization of the kernel is failed, when a user stack overflow is detected during the execution of a task, or when the system returns from the interrupt handler or exception handler to the system fixed point. Only one abort handler in the system is registered in the C_TBL.

— Task identifier

In the CTRON Specifications, when a task is created, the kernel returns the task identifier (task_id). In the **RG68K**, the task-id is the address of the task control block (TCB) to reduce the system call execution time. When a task is created, the task name can be specified and any 16-bit value (1 to 65,535) can be used as a task name. This can also apply to other resources (EVF, SEM, MBX, SRR, MPL).

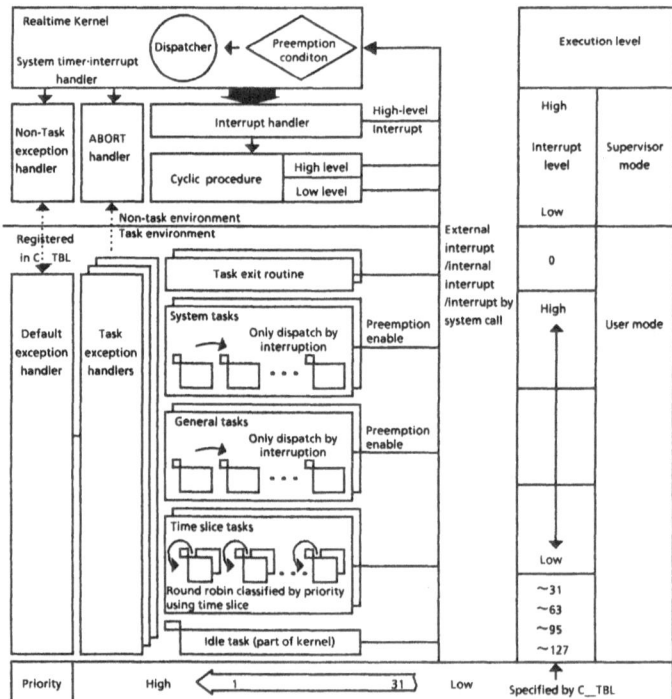

*Fig.5 Concept of Realtime Kernel Execution Control*

## 2) Task synchronization and communications

The **RG68K** contains the four types of synchronization and communication resources (i.e., event flags, semaphores, message boxes, and serially-reusable resources). It can create up to 65,535 resources for each type of resource. In implementing the semaphore and massage box, we paid attention to the following points.

When the execution level and the priority are changed using the system call (CHG__TIF), the task waiting queue of the semaphore will be rescheduled according to the new execution level and priority.

In the CTRON Specifications, the message box can be deleted even when there are messages unreceived or waiting tasks in the message box. In the **RG68K**, when the message box is deleted, the message buffer is released in the move mode, so that the messages are also released. On the other hand, in the locate mode, the message can be transmitted in the area other than that obtained from the memory pool, so that the messages cannot be released. Asynchronous deletion of the message box is inhibitive and it is necessary to pay attention to the deletion of the message box.

## 3) Interrupt management

### — Interrupt class and interrupt source

In the **RG68K**, seven interrupt levels of the MC68000 family processors are made to correspond to the interrupt class. The each input of interrupt controller (PIC) connected to the processor is made to correspond to the interrupt source. The interrupt disable/enable operation for each interrupt class can not be controlled by the internal registers of the CPU. In this way, interrpution source are implemented by adding special hardware, but the logicalization of interrupt is not realized from the point of view of overhead and necessity.

### — Information to interrupt handler

In the CTRON Specifications, there is no specification for the information to the interrupt handler. In the **RG68K**, the interrupt handler corresponding to a interrupt class needs to analyze the interrupt source number. The interrupt class number and the interrupt source number are passed to the interrupt handler via a stack as input parameters.

### — System call in the interrupt handler

In the CTRON Specifications, there is no specification for the system calls that can be issued from the interrupt handler. In the **RG68K**, issuing system calls for the creation/deletion of each resource is prohibited in order to minimize the interrupt mask time.

## 4) Exception management

### — Non-task exception handler

In the CTRON Specifications, exceptions are classified into the following two classes.

· Internal exceptions:      CPU exceptions and system call exceptions

· External exceptions:      External asynchronous post for tasks

In the CTRON Specifications, only the exceptions that occur in the task part is specified. However, in the **RG68K**, the system exception handler for the non-task part can be registered in the C_TBL so that internal exceptions that occur in the non-task part (interrupt handler and cyclic procedure) can be handled in the same way as in the task part.

— Exception nesting

In the CTRON Specifications, there is no specification for the inhibition of exception nesting. In the RG68K, the following is specified to prevent unlimited use of the stack area.

· CPU exception

When a CPU exception occurs while exception handler for other exception is being executed, the CPU exception will be started in the nesting mode. When a CPU exception occurs again while the CPU exception is being started, the abort handler will be started.

· System call exception

When a system call exception occurs while the relevant exception handler is being executed, the newly generated system call exception will be automatically masked and an error information will be returned.

· External exception

When an external exception occurs while the relevant exception hander is being executed, the external exception will be temporarily held. After the excuting exception handler finishes, the external exceptions being held will be started in order.

— External exception in a waiting status

If an external exception occurs in a waiting status task, the waiting status is cancelled when the relevant exception handler is raised. Upon returning from the exception handler, the system call in the waiting status is executed again to return the task to the waiting status. The waiting time is stored in a stack when the exception handler is raised so that the waiting time for reexecution of the system call can be adjusted.

It is also possible for the task to wake up forcedly without returning to the waiting status. This can be done by issuing the forced wake up system call (WUP_TSK) to the task itself during the exception handler processing. In the RG68K, the WUP_TSK system call for the task itself can be issued only in the exception handler.

— Information to exception handler

In the CTRON Specifications, there is no specification for the information to the exception handler. In the RG68K, the information can be passed to the exception handler via a stack as input parameters. *Fig. 6* shows the information to be passed to the exception handler. In case of the system call exception, the additional information is used as input parameters in order to reexecute the system call in the exception handler.

## 5) Timer management

The RG68K timer management providing absolute/relative time control for the tasks, is controlled by the interval timer interrupt. The system requiring precision of the absolute time need to compare the timer with the external high precision hardware timer via upper level software and correct it by the absolute time setting system call(SET_TIM).

— Absolute-time wake up and system timer

In the CTRON Specifications, the absolute time can be changed by the absolute time setting system call (SET_TIM), but there is no specification for effectness of changing time on the

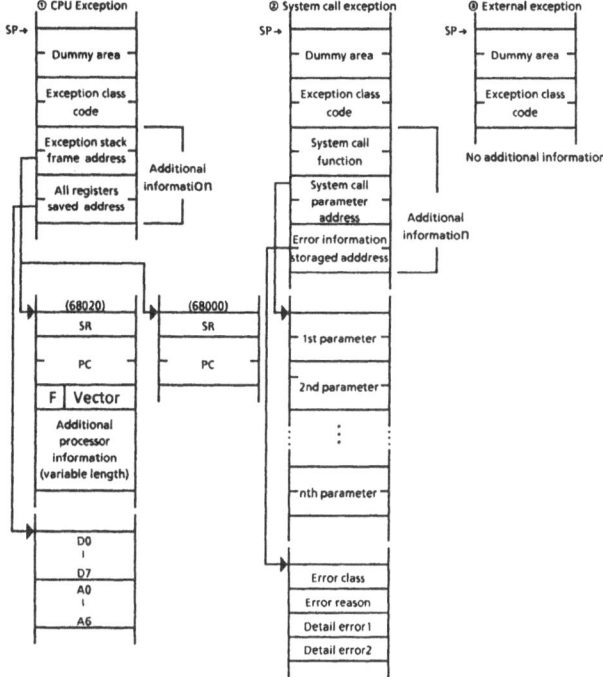

*Fig.6 Information to Exception Handlers of the RG68K*

absolute time wakeup requested by the cyclic wakeup (CYC_WUP) system calls before. The RG68K timer management is specified as follows:

— Relative time

When relative time is specified by the CYC_WUP system call, the cyclic time interval and the number of wakeup times will be guaranteed.

— Absolute time

When absolute time is specified by the CYC_WUP system call, wakeup time will be guaranteed (adjusted to a new time axis).

When the wakeup time is guaranteed by the absolute time, either the absolute time containing the date or the absolute time of the day can be selected by the C_TBL. The CTRON Specifications should specify such item to guarantee the portability of upper level software.

### 6) Memory management

RG68K provides the dynamic memory allocation/deallocation in the real storage system. This memory management handles a memory pool and memory block as a system space with no limitation. We do not have to be aware of the system/user space.

— Flagmentation

RG68K employs only variable length memory management by heap method. If the memory is used as a fixed length pool, the unit size is set to the minimum allocation size to enable high speed allocation. When the memory block is deallocated, it is deallocated in unity to prevent fragmentation caused by allocation and deallocation.

— Reservation of Kernel resouce

For each resource (TCB, EVF, SEM, ⋯) in the kernel, an area is allocated from memory pool #0 corresponding to the number registered in the C＿TBL in advance at kernel initialization, and management queue is separated, thereby reducing overheads for creation/deletion of each resource as much as possible.

## 7) Statistical information management

**RG68K** fully implemented the statistical information items specified in the CTRON Specifications. The feature of the implementation is that dedicated hardware for measurement of CPU usage time is used for each task and the running time under task/non-task environment are measured separately.

## 8) Cyclic procedure management

This cyclic procedure is executed in the non-task environment and is directly started by timer interrupts (cyclic value can be selected by the C＿TBL) other than the system timer. The cyclic procedure is suited to the multiple input/output control with severe realtime requirement. We considered that it is a standard function in switching and communication fields.

### 3.2 SYSTEM INTERFACER (SIC)

#### (a) STRUCTURE AND FEATURE

In the CTRON Specifications, the SIC is treated as part of the kernel interface. However, **RG68K** defines as the architecture-dependent part of the whole basic OS and provides the system calls for the operation and maintenance (device status management and fault recovery of duplicated processors and I/O devices, test and diagnosis and access method to peripheral circuits, etc.). *Fig.7* shows the structure of the SIC and its description.

#### (b) IMPLEMENT SPECIFICATION AND FEATURE

The SIC consists of following four functions: memory protection control, basic system control, interrupt management and hardware-specific control. We describe implement specification and feature of each function as below:

## 1) Memory protection control

In the OP68KS, the memory key method is used for the main memory protection. **RG68K** provides four system calls for the operation of the memory protect key and the memory key representing the attributes of the main memory in units of 4K bytes.

## 2) Basic system control

In the CTRON Specifications, the basic system control is specified as the function to initialize the kernel. In the **RG68K**, the initialization of the total Basic OS (including I/O Control and SIC) is implemented by the SIC.

## 3) Interrupt management

In the CTRON Specifications, the conversion between physical/logical interrupt sources is specified for the portability of the interrupt handler. In the **RG68K**, the interrupt sources are not logicalized because the target processor is limited to the MC68000 family CPU and it

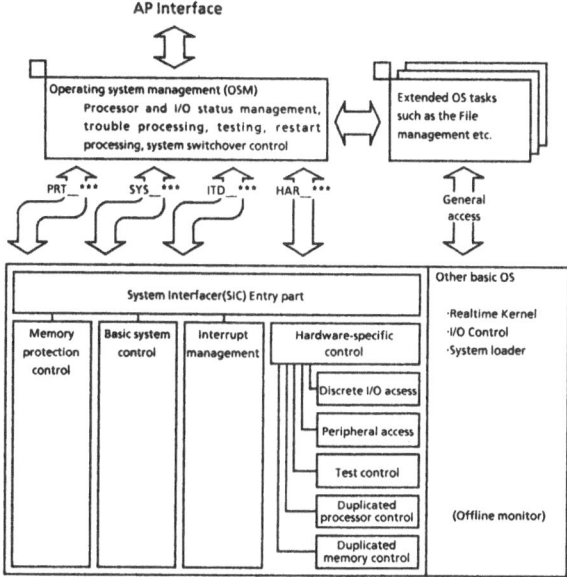

*Fig.7 Structure of the SIC*

is difficult to use the interrupt handler commonly among different CPU architectures, and the physical interrupt sources are indicated directly to the upper level software.

### 4) Hardware-specific control

The hardware-specific control provides the access method regarding operation and maintenance of the fault-tolerant system. The functions are shown as below:

- Duplicated memory control
- Duplicated processor control
- Test control
- Peripheral access
- Discrete I/O access

### 3.3 I/O CONTROL (IOC)

#### (a) STRUCTURE AND FEATURE

*Fig. 8* illustrates the concept of the RG68K I/O Control (IOC) and the outline of software modules are described below:

### 1) I/O manager

The I/O manager manages device identifiers in the I/O Control, and provides the interface with each logical device driver (each client part), and instructs the initialization of each client part.

### 2) Logical device driver (client)

The logical device driver is the I/O access module which handles device status, transfers mass data, notifies faults and asynchronous events to the upper level software.

### 3) I/O packet controller (client/server)

The I/O packet controller is the communication control and management between main processor and IOPs. It manages IOP status and transfers packet using the direct memory access controller (DMAC). In addition, it has the functions of starting up and diagnosing the IOP.

### 4) Physical device driver (server)

Each physical driver receives the I/O packets from each logical device driver and controls the physical device.
The physical architecture differences are hidden in this module.

### 5) Microkernel

The **RG68K** microkernel is a realtime monitor for high-speed execution in the IOP and is implemented by 17 system calls of the lower subset of the **RG68K** Realtime Kernel. It has been designed placing emphasis on its throughput to support more critical processing such as I/O Control and communication control. The high-speed feature of this microkernel has been achieved by eliminating the dynamic task and resource creating and reducing the functions to the minimum concurrent processing functions. The software developed in this microkernel can be ported easily to the **RG68K** Realtime Kernel.

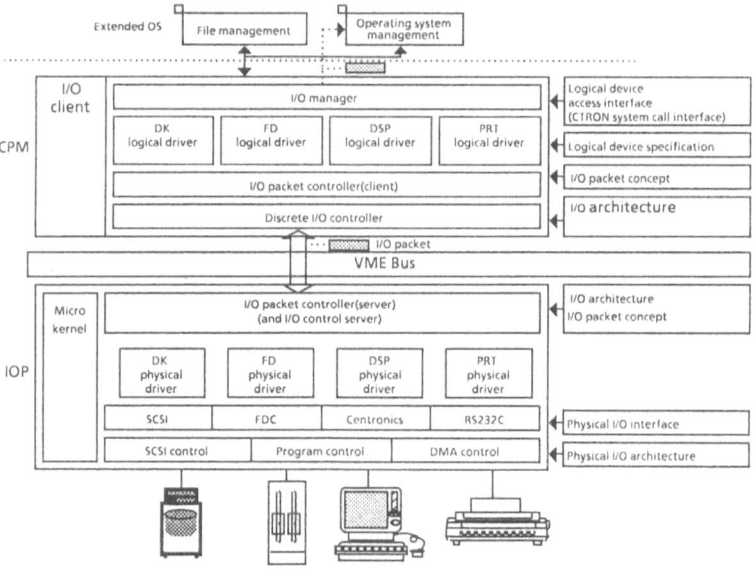

*Fig.8 Concept of the RG68K I/O Control*

### (b) IMPLEMENT SPECIFICATION AND FEATURE

### 1) I/O processor system

The **RG68K** adopts the I/O processor system isolated from the main processor. This system is intended to reduce the load to the main processor and prevent a fault in an IOP from affecting other IOPs. I/O requests are transfered to the IOP in a unified I/O packet form. The information between the main processor and the IOP is trnsfered via the common memory by the DMAC. The DMAC contends with the main processor at the bus cycle, so that the transfer of a long packet by DMAC will not disturb the main processor.

## (b) Control subcommand specification

The CTRON Specifications specifies that the control functions other than the I/O access (REA__BIO/WRI__BIO) are provided using the CTL__BIO system call.

The control functions are specified as a subcommand of the system call. Subcommand numbers 1 to 50 are reserved as common subcommand numbers. But there is no specification to extend implement dependent control functions. Therefore, we assigned other subcommand numbers(51, 52,...) to extend them. In the RG68K, the following two subcommands are provided additionally.

### — Device control block control (subcommand number 51)

This subcommand is used to refer and change the system-specific part of device control block (DCB) provided in the RG68K.

### — I/O block allocation in storage media (subcommand number 52)

This subcommand is used to format a storage medium corresponding to the specified logical device.

The I/O control functions for undefined devices are all provided by the REQ__GIO system call, which is not required at present in the RG68K.

## 3) Error processing

### — Retry

The option parameter of the read/write I/O request system call (REA__BIO/WRI__BIO) is used to appoint whether or not the retry for the I/O access is required according to the CTRON Specifications.

### — Alternate block

The alternate block can be changed by the relevant subcommand of the CTL__BIO. However, this alternate block can not be applied to the FD (flexible disk unit).

### — Verify read

In the CTRON Specifications, the verify read is treated as an internal implementation matter. RG68K provides the verify read control in the system specific-part of DCB.

### — Diagnosis

To diagnose a device terminated by some cause such as a fault, it is necessary to issue the INT__DEV system call again. In this case, the system tries to initialize the faulty device by means of hardware. But it may result in abnormal termination. In the RG68K, the device can be controlled even if a hardware initialization error occurs, so that the diagnosis can be performed using the relevant CTL__BIO subcommand.

## 4) Control of IOP

In the CTRON Specifications, the connection devices between various I/O devices and main processors are hidden within the I/O Control. However, the connection device control is necessary for the operation and maintenance control. In the **RG68K**, the IOP is defined as a GIO (undefined I/O).

### 5) DCB configuration

The device control block (DCB) is composed of the following three parts in the CTRON Specifications.

– Common part:            Common part to all logical devices

– Device-specific part:       Specific part for each logical device

– System-specific part:      Specific part for each system

In the **RG68K**, the system-specific part is further subdivided into the system common part and the system device-specific part. The system common part specifies the information on the IOP and the system device-specific part specifies the implementation dependent information. *Fig. 9* shows DCB configuration in the **RG68K** I/O Control.

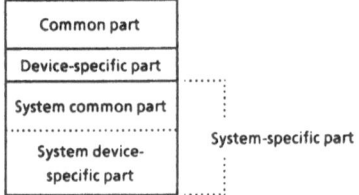

*Fig. 9  Device Control Block Configuration*

### 6) Asynchronous events

An asynchronous event is a notification from a logical device and sent to the upper level software asynchronously except for a completion notification. In the **RG68K**, asynchronous events are handled as follows:

– **Magnetic disk unit (DK)**

The RG68K is applied to fixed disk unit but not to pack type disk unit. Therefore, the asynchronous event is not notified. (In the pack type disk unit, asynchronous events may occur for the mounting control.)

– **Flexible disk unit (FD)**

The asynchronous event is notified as a device status change caused by the medium mounting operation. However, when the motor control is used for prolonging the device life (appointed by the DCB system dependent part), no device status change is notified.

– **Printer (PR)**

Notification of the status change by the operator's manipulation (paper end, power turn-off, not ready, etc.).

– **Display unit (DSP)**

Notification of the request by pressing the break key.

### 7) I/O extension

*Fig. 10* shows the concept of the I/O extension. Only the GIO in the **RG68K** is the IOP used as a connection device. Various I/O devices required for each application system can be supported easily by developing the physical/logical device drivers. The logical device drivers can be dynamically incorporated from the EOS of application systems into the system by using the device creation system call (CRE_DEV). Consequently, the system generation is not required in the **RG68K**. The standard format of the internal interface is specified to implement device drivers easily.

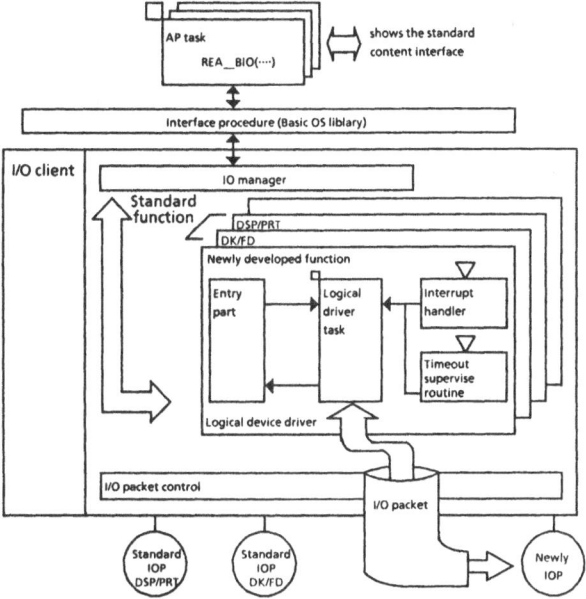

*Fig.10 Concept of I/O extension*

### 8) Initialization

The data used for the I/O Control are initialized by the request from OSM. After this initialization, the system calls for the I/O Control become available. In the CTRON Specifications, the initialization of each logical device is specified, but initializing the I/O Control software module is not specified. In the **RG68K**, the SYS_GIO (I/O Control initialization) system call is provided in the SIC. This initialization is a basic function in the **RG68K** basic OS.

### 9) Master DCB information

The I/O Control programs in an IOP are implemented in ROM, which has the master device control block (MDCB) corresponding to each device. Consequently, when a upper level software creates logical devices, it is necessary to refer the MDCB information in the ROM. The SYS_DCB (master DCB information reference) system call is provided in the SIC in order to refer the MDCB information.

## 4. CONSIDERATIONS

### 4.1 EVALUATION OF THE RG68K BASIC OS

We have implemented the Basic OS based on the CTRON SPECIFICATION KERNEL INTERFACE Ver. 1 and I/O CONTROL INTERFACE Ver. 1 (November, 1987), for switching and communication processing products, placing emphasis on its high throughput. The detailed evaluation (performance and memory size) of the Basic OS is under way.

## (a) KERNEL PROGRAM SIZE

*Table 2* shows the program size of the **RG68K** Realtime Kernel. The program size of the kernel varies according to the generating conditions and is about 30K to 35Kbytes.

*Table 2 Program Size of RG68K Realtime Kernel*

| Function module | Size (Kbyte) |
|---|---|
| 1. Task Management | 6.3 |
| 2. Task Synchronization and Communications | 3.6 |
| 3. Interrupt Management | 1.8 |
| 4. Exception Management | 3.2 |
| 5. Clock Management | 1.3 |
| 6. Memory Management | 5.0 |
| 7. Statistical Information Management | 0.9 |
| 8. Cyclic Procedure | 1.6 |
| 9. Common Subroutine | 1.2 |
| 10. Others (Initialization,System-depend, etc.) | 4.8~10 |

## (b) PERFORMANCE

The context switch time is less than 32 microseconds and the message exchange time is 62 to 90 microseconds in the **RG68K** Realtime Kernel. These values are satisfactory ones in comparison with the multitask OS for OKI developed switching system [8] and the ITRON. However, as for the memory overhead, the TCB requires 256 bytes and message box, semaphore, serially-reusable resource and event-flag needs 32 to 48 bytes. These values are required to fully implement a realtime kernel based on CTRON. However, further improvement will be required to apply this basic OS to middle-scale or small- scale realtime systems.

## 4.2 CTRON INTERFACE SPECIFICATIONS

We wish to point out the items to be improved or modified in the CTRON SPECIFICATION KERNEL INTERFACE Ver. 1 and I/O CONTROL INTERFACE Ver. 1, based on the results of the **RG68K** Basic OS implementation .

To summarize, consideration should be given to the standardization of the following unspecified items required as the more detailed-design information. (For further **RG68K** detailed design information, refer chapter 3)

### (a) KERNEL

— Definition of kernel architecture-dependent part.

— Definition of exeption handler for non-task.

— Definition of detailed information to exception handler.

— Limitation of exception handler nesting.

— Treatment of received messages when the message-box is deleted.

— Treatment of cyclic wake-up tasks when absolute system timer is set.

— Review of kernel subset specification.

### (b) I/O CONTROL

— Definition of the extended-control subcommand.

— Treatment of connection devices.

- Initialization of I/O Control program.
- Definition of system-specific part of DCB.

(C) OTHERS

- Definition of symbols.

The symbol names for parameters, exception codes and error information should be specified in consideration of portability of the EOS and the AP built on the BOS.

The specifications for semantics of system calls should be more strict and more detailed ones so that a variety of products to be implemented in the future can perform perfectly the same operations (for example, motivations of preemptions, etc.).

The CTRON Specifications do not deal with the standard specifications based on specific processor architectures. However, the standard and detailed specifications for typical processors should be included in the CTRON Specifications in order to promote the standardization and diffusion of CTRON and to reduce the load of implementers.

## 5. CONCLUSION

In this paper, we describe mainly an overview of the RG68K Basic OS being developed based on the CTRON Specifications. In particular,we emphasize our implementation that does not appear in the specifications. This paper includes some items to be standardized for the implementation of a CTRON basic OS using MC68000 family processors. We wish to propose these items as standard implement specifications.

To achieve a wide use of CTRON as the standard OS for information communication network, we consider that it is necessary to improve and prescribe more strictly the specifications based on various implementation results in the future.

The throughput is one of the most important factors required for a realtime OS. We achieved satisfactory results on the implementation of the RG68K Basic OS. However, our implementation results still have problems from the standpoint of application to small-scale equipment (for example, terminal equipment). It is therefore expected to specify smaller subset (micro) than that of the CTRON Specifications, placing emphasis on the performance.

In the future, we will make more detailed evaluations on the RG68K Basic OS. Furthermore, we will implement the RG68K Basic OS (virtual storage version), EOS and TOS and apply them to the parallel processing system. We plan to report the results of the detailed evaluations and new implementations succesively.

Finally the authors wish to thank the members concerned of the CTRON project for their valuable guidance and cooperation in the implementation of the CTRON basic OS.

## REFERENCES

[1] T. Wasano, M. Ohminami, Y. Kobayashi, T. Ohkubo, and K. Sakamura, "Design Principles and Configuration of CTRON," 2nd TRON Temporary Study Group, Institute of Electronics Information and Communication Engineers of Japan, July 1987, pp. 25-39.

[2] Nikkei Electronics, "Special Issue on TRON," January 25, 1988, Nikkei MacGRAW-HILL

[3] M. Matsushita, H. Ueda, E. Nagashima, K. Sakuma, and K. Kawanishi, "A Study of the Fault-Tolerant Processor on CTRON," SE87-163

[4] CTRON Technical Committee, "CTRON SPECIFICATION KERNEL INTERFACE," November 1987

[5] CTRON Technical Committee, "CTRON SPECIFICATION I/O CONTROL INTERFACE," November 1987

[6] M. kobayashi, M. Ishizuka, S. Takenouchi, and K. Sakuma, "CTRON Kernel Common Design (Design Methodology)," Proc. (1), 36th National Conference, Information Processing Soc., Japan, P284

[7] T. Ogawa, K. Sakuma, M. Sawada, and R. Hama, "CTRON Kernel Common Design (Implementation to the MC68020)," Proc. (1), 36th National Conference, Information Processing Soc., Japan, P284

[8] M.Matsushita, K. Sakuma, K. Kawanishi, and M. Joh, "Application of the Realtime OS to Switching Processing," Proc., National Conference, Information System Group, Institute of Electronics Information and Communication Engineers of Japan, S6-4, November 1987

233

**Masayoshi Matsushita:** Manager of Software Engineering Section in Software Engineering Department, Switching Systems Engineering Division, Telecommunications Group at Oki Electric Industry Co., Ltd. He joined the company in 1971 after graduating from Doshisha University in Kyoto. Since then, he has been engaged in the development of the basic software and micro processor architecture. He is a member of the IEICE and the IPS.

**Masaru Ishizuka:** Assistant manager of Software Engineering Section in Software Engineering Department, Switching Systems Engineering Division, Telecommunications Group at Oki Electric Industry Co., Ltd. He joined the company in 1974 after graduating from Meiji University in Tokyo. Since then, he has been engaged in the development of the basic software and switching software.

**Yoshimichi Ikeda:** Assistant manager of Software Engineering Section in Software Engineering Department, Switching Systems Engineering Division, Telecommunications Group at Oki Electric Industry Co., Ltd. He joined the company in 1974 after graduating from Toin Technical College in Kanagawa. Since then, he has been engaged in the development of the basic software.

**Makoto Fukuyoshi:** Assistant manager of Software Engineering Section in Software Engineering Department, Switching Systems Engineering Division, Telecommunications Group at Oki Electric Industry Co., Ltd. He joined the company in 1979 after graduating from Kyushu Institute of Technology in Fukuoka. Since then, he has been engaged in the development of the basic software.

**Tsukasa Ogawa:** Engineer of Software Engineering Section in Software Engineering Department, Switching Systems Engineering Division, Telecommunications Group at Oki Electric Industry Co., Ltd. He joined the company in 1980 after graduating from University of Electronics and Communications. Since then, he has been engaged in the development of the basic software and switching system. He is a member of the IPS.

**Tetsuo Sakuma:** Engineer of Software Engineering Section in Software Engineering Department, Switching Systems Engineering Division, Telecommunications Group at Oki Electric Industry Co., Ltd. He joined the company in 1980 after graduating from University of Osaka Prefecture. Since then, he has been engaged in the development of the operating systems. He is a member of the IPS.

Above authors may be reached at: OKi Electric Industry Co., Ltd.
10-16, Shibaura 4-chome, Minato-ku, Tokyo 108 Japan

# An Implementation of CTRON Basic OS on a Lap-Top Workstation

Kazuhiro Oda, Nobuo Shimizu, Norio Inoue, Yoshiaki Iba
Toshiba Corporation

## ABSTRACT

We have been developing a CTRON basic OS on a lap-top
workstation. This OS(called as OS/CT) is based on the
interface specification  of CTRON basic OS(kernel and input/
output control).

We also prepared some demonstration programs to verify our
design principles as follows:
1)To hide characteristics of hardware as much as we can.
2)To use the full power of i80386 hardware.
3)To develop programs for verification of our
   CTRON basic OS implementation.

We will continue to enhance the functions of our CTRON basic
OS for workstation.

Keywords:CTRON,Lap-Top Workstation,Basic OS,Memory Management
        Software Development Environment

## 1.INTRODUCTION

In this paper we explain our implementation of CTRON basic
OS which complies with CTRON interface specifications.
We have been developing our OS according to the following
design principles:
1)To hide the differences of hardware architectures.
2)To make maximum use of the performance of target CPU.
3)To do test implementation and verification of our OS.
Up to now,we have implemented the common kernel interface unit
(C) of CTRON basic OS.
However,we will continue to enhance these functions such as
virtual memory system,human-machine interface and others to
fulfill the needs of workstation applications.

## 2.IMPLEMENTATION PRINCIPLES

We have decided to follow the implementation principles
stated as below:
1)To hide the differences of hardware architectures
   In CTRON,the operating system is configured in two layers,
   basic OS and extended OS. The extended OS is considered to
   achieve its higher portability and the basic OS is designed
   to make the extended OS portable by hiding the differences
   of various hardware architectures.

For our OS/CT,we thought that to hide the differences of
hardware architecture is the most important item to be
treated in the implementation of CTRON basic OS.

We therefore decided to implement OS/CT without showing the
differences of hardware architecture as much as we can.
In other words,we didn't consider the degree of
accomplishment of functions in basic OS,but we concentrated
our efforts on how to enable each functions to be
independent of an architecture.

The CTRON interface specifications are now on  development
stage and therefore we avoided an unnecessary additions to
the CTRON interface specification even if we need some
interfaces which have not yet been defined in the CTRON
specification.
2)To make maximum use of the performance of target CPU
  If the performance degradation is caused by hiding the
differences of hardware architecture,it is meaningless.
We therefore considered to implement our OS in order to make
maximum use of the target microprocessor.
We payed the special attention on the handling of the
address space and the memory management.
3)To do test implementation and verification of our OS
The principles stated above show sometimes inconsistency
between them. We therefore implemented actually the subset
of CTRON basic OS,called OS/CT,in order to verify the
realization of hiding of hardware architecture and the
performance achievement.  The reason why we implemented the
subset is only to shorten the implementation period.
This test system is desirable to provide the suitably small
system configuration which is widely used and to have enough
address space suitable for software development.

Actual conditions of implementation are as follows:
-To use a lap-top workstation,J-3100 SGT(based on i80386
 microprocessor)
-To implement the system-calls which are the smaller part
 of CTRON basic OS interface in this test implementation.
 (Additional functions which are duplicated with CTRON
 specification are not allowed.)
-Enhancement of these functions is done synchronizing with
 the evaluation and investigation of this test system,and
 investigation of the extended OS and application software.


3.STRUCTURE OF OS/CT SYSTEM

We used the protect mode of i80386 because we want to
provide the large address space and to use hardware
memory protection mechanism.

The C compiler used does not generate segment information,
therefore the segmentation mechanism of i80386 is used only
for separating the basic OS and the others.
We considered that it is sufficient for our purpose because
it could support 4GB address space and no overhead might be
caused by segment exchange.

The model of structure of address space for tasks defined in
CTRON specification is as follows:

1)Common space for all tasks(system space)
  In this space,there are system programs common to the
  basic OS and extended OS,system data such as TCBs,message
  buffers and system constant and so on.
2)User space(local space for tasks)
  In this space,there are user's program and data.
  This space is allocated for each task.

On our implementation,the structure of address space is
defined shown in Fig.1.
The address space of each task are automatically generated
by the basic OS at the task creation.
This implies that the page directory and page table used for
paging are maintained at that time.
Local address space of tasks are implemented by using paging
mechanism. By this method,each task could have 4GB address
space and the future extention to the demand paging becomes
possible. Besides,the memory protection function is provided
to application programs.

Therefore allocation of 4GB address space becomes important.
Because the address space should be managed by the extended
OS layer in order to support various extended OS parts in
future,the address space is divided into two part,the region
of basic OS and extended OS/application program,and the basic
OS does not participate the internal allocation of address
space in the region of extended OS/application program.

According to this situation,we have not yet implemented the
function which allocates the user work area at task creation.
 The relation between system space and local space of task is
considered as described below.
The problem still remains in the case that if the system
space were allocated in the region of the extended OS/
application program,how should we share the function between
common space and system space.

This problem could be described as follows:
By using the common space mechanism,the space could be shared
among tasks and also the same purpose could be done using
the system space. This conflict has not solved in our
implementation. This remains for further study.
By this reason,we decided that no system spaces exist in the
region of the extended OS/application program.

The region of the basic OS consists of the system space and
the task local space. In the task local space of this region,
we allocate the region which has control data of basic OS
such as stack area for basic OS.
This area is also allocated by paging mechanism and only data
of task is allocated to the fixed address. This makes the
structure of the system simple.
Besides,the isolation between tasks can be established
easily.

As for the task switching,the i80386 has the sophisticated
and rapid task switching mechanism. By using this mechanism,
the task switching can be done very quickly in our
implementation.

In the case of implementation of the cyclic waking up task
function,the overhead of unnecessary interrupt handling
might be caused by usage of interval timer.

Therefore,we used the alarm clock function of specific time
definition and reduced the overhead of unnecessary interrupt
handling. The alarm clock function is used to wakeup tasks
or cause interrupt when it reaches the time defined in this
function previously.
However,we are not confident whether this method is suitable
for the extended OS or not in the future.
This is for further study.

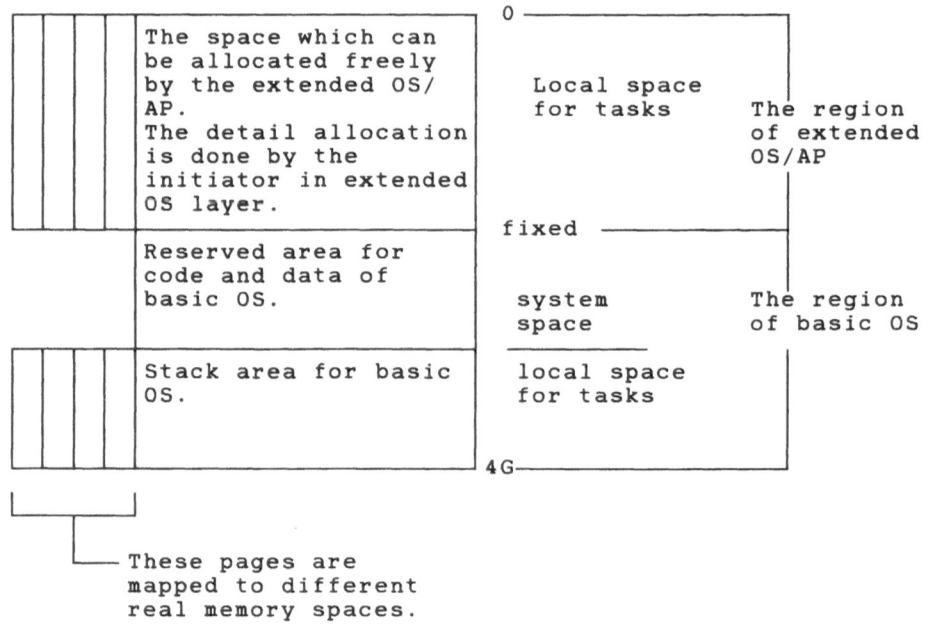

Fig.1   Memory Map of OS/CT


4.HARDWARE CONFIGURATION

   The hardware configuration used for OS/CT implementation is
Toshiba's lap-top workstation called J-3100SGT. The detail
features are stated as below:

1)CPU
   main processor :i80386 16MHZ clock
2)Main memory
   ROM : 96Kbytes for BIOS,1Mbytes for fonts of Japanese
         characters
   RAM : 2Mbytes as standard(maximum 4Mbytes)
   video RAM :256Kbytes
3)Display
   graphic presentation : 640 x 400 pixel,plasma display
   Japanese character presentation : 40chracters x 25 lines
                                      character 16 x 16 dots
                                      JIS 1st and 2nd level
                                      standard fonts are
                                      supported.
4)Input device
   keyboard : JIS key arrangement,84 keys

5)Secondary storage
　3.5inchies floppy disk drive : 1 drive
　　　　　　　　　　　　　　　 use 2DD(720KB) and 2HD(1.2MB)
　　　　　　　　　　　　　　　 disket
　3.5inchies harddisk drive : 1 drive
　　　　　　　　　　　　　　 40MB/drive(formatted)

Photo.1　Lap-Top Workstation J-3100SGT

## 5.SOFTWARE DEVELOPMENT ENVIRONMENT

We used some number of J-3100SGT which connected each
other via LAN to develop our system for efficient
implementation.
The main features are as follows:
1)UNIX(*1) System V/R3.0
　This UNIX runs on our J-3100SGT.
2)LAN system
　TCP/IP protocol is supported via Ethernet(*2) optical
　cable.
　Distribution and sharing of file by RFS(Remote File
　Share).
3)Software development tools
　C compiler : standard C compiler for i80386
　Assembler  : standard assembler for i80386

We used many and powerful tools,such as vi,ld,make etc.,
provided by UNIX system.


(*1)UNIX is the trademark of AT&T in the USA and other
　　countries.
(*2)Ethernet is the trademark of Xerox Co..

# 6.DEMONSTRATION PROGRAMS

We implemented some demonstration programs to test and
verify our implementation.
Our demonstration programs are as follows:
 1)To display image data to CRT
  The image data was input to this system previously
  by flexible disk in which the image data had been stored
  by another computer. Our system does not have an input
  device for image data.
  The I/O interface with bitmap display has not yet been
  defined in CTRON,therefore we implemented it by our own
  interface.
 2)To show the system statistical data to operator.
  The information relating with tasks such as the name of
  task,status and so on,and some statistical data such as
  the number of page faults occurrences and I/O activities
  are displayed to CRT for operator.
These programs run directly on the basic OS using the basic
OS interface.

By these programs,we confirm that the functions of basic OS
is suitable for our workstation applications and also the
performance is sufficient.


# 7.CONCLUSIONS

The following results was obtained from our implementation:
 1)To hide the differences of hardware architectures
  Because of the time limitation of implementation and needs
for more time to investigate the hiding the hardware
architectures,in our implementation,the management such as
the memory and  task context management which are highly
dependent on CPU architecture could not be implemented as an
architecture independent interface.

 Essentially,to hide some concepts is not to avoid mention of
that concept,but to establish an abstract or virtual model.
Generally,when we raise the level of abstraction,the gap
between target hardware and model becomes bigger and the
performance problem may occur.
When we select architecture dependent method,software in
higher layer could not be portable.
However,this problem has to be solved by the abstraction of
data object and abstract operation to them,and if we avoid
this abstraction,the portability of extended OS could not be
obtained.

 The current implementation has many architecture dependent
parts because of highlighting the performance and the
constraint of development time.

 The concept of CTRON is to integrate and standardize OS
interface and realization of open-ended system by this
integration and standardization.
The management of address space and task are very important
issues to be solved in OS. Therefore we will continue our
study on this items cooperating with CTRON technical
committee in order to establish the system which continues to
exist beyond the advance and evolution of hardware
technology.

Our implementation moves now to actual implementation stage and we are going to built a workstation system which is high realtime oriented and suitable for network system.

2)To make maximum use of the performance of target CPU
 We satisfied the performance of our implementation.
However,after the extended OS is implemented on this basic OS
 we should verify the performance again.

3)To do test implementation and verification of our OS
 As for the basic OS,this test implementation is
considered satisfactory results.

To fulfill the requirement of workstation application fields, we need more investigation and standardization of such items stated bellow.

OSI has now being developed on upper application layer,but the distributed file system which is essential to workstation has not been standardized yet. Rapid standardization is considered necessary. Besides,we must pay much attention to various activities being done in the world in order to make our system open-ended.

The human-machine interface is also very important issue in the workstation application fields and HMI ad-hoc group has just begun its study.
When a workstation is connected to information processing nodes and switching nodes in the network system,both programs on the workstation and on the host computer which communicate with users via workstation must have the same human-machine interfaces and also this interface is transparent to users in the network system.

We have many problems to be solved,but we will continue our study to overcome these problems. We have just begun the first steps to establish the integration and standardization of OS interface. Our responsibility would be to make a maximum efforts on this matters.


## 8.ACKNOWLEDGMENT

The authors wish to express our deep appreciation for the valuable advice given by Dr.Ken Sakamura,Dr.Fukuya Ishino and members of CTRON technical committee.


## REFERENCES

[1]I.Kogiku,T.Ohrui,T.Ohkubo,and Y.Hamada,"A Real-time
 Portable Operating System Common to Switching and Information
 Processing Applications,"Proc.ISS87,Phoenix,1987.
[2]T.Ohkubo,T.Wasano and I.Kogiku,"Configuration of the CTRON
 Kernel,"IEEE Micro,April 1987,pp33-44.
[3]T.Wasano,M.Ohminami,Y.Kobayashi,T.Ohkubo and K.Sakamura,
 "Design Principles and Configuration of CTRON,"Proc.FJCC'87,
 Dallas,1987.

[4]K.Sakamura,"CTRON:An Overview,"TRON Project 1987,Springer-
Verlag,1987,pp153-156.
[5]T.Wasano,M.Ohminami,Y.Kobayashi,T.Ohkubo and K.Sakamura,
"Design of CTRON,"TRON Project 1987,Springer-Verlag,1987,
pp157-172.
[6]K.Kumazaki,"Design of the CTRON File Management,"TRON
Project 1987,Springer-Verlag 1987,pp173-182.
[7]S.Narimatsu,"Design of CTRON Input-Output Control
Interface,"TRON Project 1987,Springer-Verlag 1987,pp183-196.
[8]"CTRON SPECIFICATION KERNEL INTERFACE,"CTRON Technical
Committee,Nov.1987.
[9]"CTRON SPECIFICATION I/O CONTROL INTERFACE,"CTRON Technical
Committee,Nov.1987.

**Kazuhiro Oda** is a chief specialist in Personal Computer Design Department at the Ome Works of Toshiba Corporation. He is now a member of BTRON and CTRON technical committee of TRON Association. He received his BE from Kyuusyuu University at Fukuoka in 1964. He is a member of ACM, the Information Processing Society of Japan(IPSJ) and the Institute of Electronics, Information and Communication Engineers of Japan(IEICE).

**Nobuo Shimizu** is an engineer in Personal Computer Design Dept. at the Ome Works of Toshiba Corporation. He received his BE in mathematics from Waseda University in 1983. He has been engaged in software design and development of micro-processors. He is a member of Information Processing Society of Japan.

**Norio Inoue** is an engineer is Personal Computer Design Dept. at the Ome Works of Toshiba Corporation. He joined Toshiba Corporation after graduated from electric engineering of Todatsu Technical high school. He has been engaged in software design and development of large and medium scale general purpose computers and an office computer.

**Yoshiaki Iba** is an engineer in Personal Computer Design Dept. at the Ome Works of Toshiba Corporation after graduated from the image science and engineering of Chiba University in 1984. He received his BE from Chiba University in 1984. He has been engaged in software design and devlopment of an office computer. He is a member of Information Processing Society of Japan.

Above authors may be reached at : Personal Computer Design Dept. in Ome Works, Toshiba Corporation 2-9, Suehiro-cho, Ome , Tokyo 198, Japan

# Chapter 5: TRONCHIP

# Architectural Features of OKI 32-Bit Microprocessor

Noriyoshi Ito, Hiromi Nojima, and Yoshikazu Mori
Oki Electric Industry Co., Ltd.

**ABSTRACT**

A 32-bit microprocessor to be used as a processor for a communication network node or engineering work station is being developed. In order to improve processor performance, various techniques, such as six-stage pipelining, two internal caches for instruction codes and operand data, and full-associative address translation look-aside buffer, have been integrated. The average throughput for instruction execution will be up to ten million instructions per second by means of 33 MHz machine clock. Careful consideration have been given to the support of highly reliable systems or multiple processor systems. As a result, a processor bus comparator, partial cache invalidation function, stack exception mechanism, and powerful debug support facilities have also been integrated in the chip.

**Keywords:** 32-bit microprocessor, pipelining, high reliability, multi-processor, debug support

## 1. INTRODUCTION

OKI 32-bit microprocessor (hereafter called O32) is being developed whose external specification is based on TRONCHIP architecture [1], which is proposed to give a standard of 32-bit microprocessors extensible to future 64-bit architecture. The primary target of O32 is implementation of high-performance, single-chip processors for communication network nodes or engineering work stations, which require not only high performance and virtual memory support, but also the capability to support highly reliable systems or multiple processor systems. To improve performance, therefore, various speed-up techniques have been adopted, and various support functions for these requirements have also been integrated in a single chip.

Architectural features of O32 is given in Section 2, and its internal architecture and pipeline structure are described in Section 3. Section 4 discusses the high reliability support function and Section 5 discusses the multiple processor support function. Finally, the debug support function is described in Section 6.

## 2. ARCHITECTURAL FEATURES OF O32

*Table 1* gives a brief description of the O32 specification. As shown in the table, O32 supports an instruction set of <<L1>> specification, a virtual memory support version of TRONCHIP architecture. This instruction set is very powerful and there are 102 instructions from the basic instructions to the high-level instructions.

The various speed-up techniques have been adopted. They include a six-stage pipeline structure to increase throughput, branch prediction table to reduce branch penalty, and separate cache memories for instruction codes and operand data to increase the internal bus bandwidth. The capacity of both cache memories is 1KB. In addition to these techniques, a high-speed machine clock (33 MHz) is used, to achieve 10 million instructions per second (MIPS) at the average throughput for instruction execution.

The chip also has 32 full-associative address translation look-aside buffer (TLB) entries for virtual memory support. To support the efficient context switching needed in real-time systems, such as the network switching nodes, a four-bit logical space identifier (LSID) have been provided.

*Table 1  Specification of O32*

| | |
|---|---|
| Performance  MAX | 15 MIPS |
| TYP | 10 MIPS |
| Spec.  Level | L1 + <L2> |
| Number of Instructions | 102 |
| General Registers | 16 |
| TLB | 32  Entries |
| Memory  Protection | 4 Levels |
| Interrupt  Level | 7  Levels |
| Min. Bus Cycle | 2 Clocks, 1 Clock(Burst) |
| Pipeline | 6  Stages |
| Branch  Table | YES |
| Instruction Cache | 1 K Bytes |
| Data  Cache | 1 K Bytes |
| LSI Package | 176 pin PGA |
| Number of Transistors | 700 K Tr. |
| Process | 0.8 micron CMOS |
| Features | Fault Tolerant Support<br>Powerful Debug Support<br>Stack Boundary Check |

The LSID is used to support efficient multiple processing environments by assigning a unique LSID to each active process. The LSID field can be assumed to be an extension of logical address space and eliminates cache or TLB invalidation on process context switching [5]. The cache or TLB hit ratio will thus be kept high even if frequent context switching occurs. The size of each logical address space is 4GB and 16 such logical spaces can be resident on the chip.

O32 support a burst data transfer mode. That is, on cache mishit, 16-byte cache block data are loaded from the external memory in a single external bus operation sequence (5 clock cycles), in which the memory address is output within the first machine clock cycle, and the 16-byte block is loaded during the remaining four machine clock cycles at the rate of 4 bytes per clock. Other external data transfer is performed on a normal data transfer mode at the rate of 4 bytes per 2 machine cycles.

The chip is fabricated into 176-pin PGA (Pin Grid Array) package and about seven hundred thousand transistors will be integrated by means of 0.8 micron CMOS process technology.

The outstanding features which differs from other TRONCHIPs [4] [5] are:
- processor bus comparator;
- stack boundary checker;
- partial cache invalidation function;
- debug support.

Our major design target is on the support of high-performance, highly reliable systems, where non-stop, real time processing is needed. The processor bus comparator is used to construct highly reliable systems, such as majority decision systems or pair-and-spare systems, in which multiple redundant processors synchronously executing the same programs check the one another's bus data. The stack boundary checker is used to increase software reliability. The partial cache invalidation function is used for maintenance of local cache consistency of multiple processor systems, in which more high performance is needed than single processor systems. There are also four independent break point registers, two branch history registers, and jump instruction trap facilities for debug support.

## 3. INTERNAL ARCHITECTURE

In order to shorten the chip design time, a top-down design approach is being carried out. The complex internal structure is divided into ten functional units. The behavior models of these functional units have been described in the hardware description language and simulated. In this section, the detailed description of these functional units are given, and then the pipeline structure to achieve very high performance is described.

## 3.1 HARDWARE CONFIGURATION OF O32

*Fig.1* shows the internal architecture of O32 which is divided into ten functional units, as listed below:

- instruction prefetch unit (IPU);
- instruction decode unit (IDU);
- instruction address unit (IAU);
- data address unit (DAU);
- micro-ROM unit (MRU);
- execution unit (EXU);
- instruction cache unit (ICU);
- data cache unit (DCU);
- memory management unit (MMU);
- bus interface unit (BIU).

The IPU prefetches instruction codes to the 16-byte internal instruction buffers. The 16-byte instruction codes are loaded into the instruction buffers on the burst mode.

The IDU decodes a prefetched instruction code from the IPU and generates two types of decoded information. One is for operand address calculation and the other is for micro execution. TRON instructions are variable length and composed of one or more opcodes followed by optional multiple indirect addressing codes. These opcodes constituting the instructions are called atomic instruction codes (AICs). Each AIC consists of a half-word (16-bit) opcode followed by an optional half-word or word (32-bit) immediate or displacement field.

The IDU decodes one AIC at a time and sends the optional displacement or immediate field to the address calculation or execution stage in this decode cycle. Therefore, each short instruction, such as MOV:L, MOV:S, MOV:Z, MOV:Q, or MOV:I, is decoded in a single decode cycle if it has no multiple indirect addressing codes. Each long instruction, such as MOV:G or MOV:E, however, is decoded in more than two decode cycles. The detailed description of these instructions will be given in reference [2]. Because the long instructions is not so frequently used by means of the compiler optimization, most instructions will be decoded in a single decode cycle.

The IAU generates the next instruction code address, which is calculated by the addition of the current program counter (PC) value and instruction length or branch offset obtained by the IDU.

The DAU generates the operand address, which is then sent to the data cache. In order to support multiple indirect addressing, the DAU controls indirect memory reference, index register scaling, and index and displacement addition. The DAU also has a cache

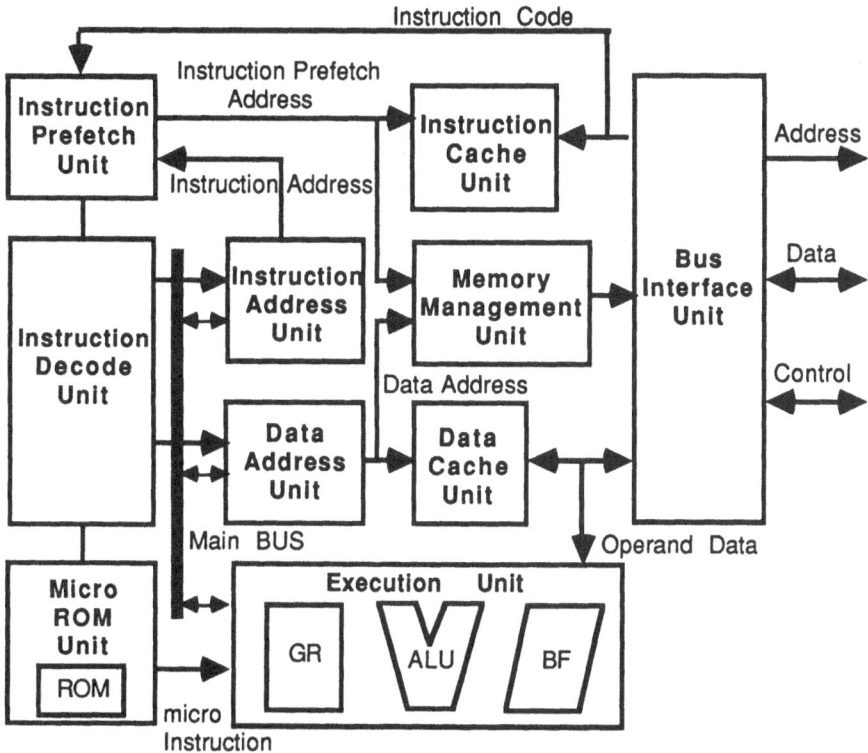

*Fig.1 Block Diagram of O32*

block boundary and page boundary detector to control double accesses to cache blocks or TLB entries.

The MRU consists of a micro-program read only memory (ROM) and a micro-program sequencer. The sequencer is activated by the completion of AIC decode in the IDU or by the occurrence of an exception condition. After activated, it fetches micro instructions from the micro-ROM and sends control signals to the other units.

The EXU performs instruction execution under the control of micro instructions from MRU. It consists of a general register file (GR), arithmetic and logic unit (ALU), bit field operation module (BF), barrel shifter, multiplier/divider, and so on.

The ICU is a two-way set-associative cache for instruction codes and has a capacity of 1KB (32 blocks x 16 bytes x 2 ways). It is responsible for instruction prefetch requests from the IPU. If a cache miss occurs, the external memory fetch is performed by a burst data transfer mode.

The DCU is also a two-way set-associative cache for operand data and has a capacity of 1KB (32 blocks x 16 bytes x 2 ways). It is responsible for operand prefetch requests from the DAU or operand load/store requests from the EXU. The operand store operation is performed by a store-through method. A store buffer is used in order to avoid performance degradation because of a conflict between the store operations and other memory operations. If the external bus is busy, the store operation is completed by leaving the store operand to the store buffer and the actual memory store is performed after the external bus becomes available. If a cache miss occurs on the prefetch or read operation, the external memory load of the missed cache block is performed by a burst data transfer mode. A cache miss in the store operation, on the other hand, does not invoke this cache load operation.

The MMU has 32 TLB entries to translate virtual addresses into physical addresses. As shown in *Fig.1*, the ICU and DCU are logical address caches and are accessed parallel to MMU accesses. The operand fetch operation, therefore, will successfully complete if the caches are accessed without mis-hit even if the MMU access mis-hits occur. The replacement algorithm for TLB entries employs the least recently used (LRU) method. The MMU has a simultaneous TLB reset function which enables an single clock cycle invalidation of all TLB entries or a subset of TLB entries specified by the logical space identifier (LSID) field.

The length of the LSID field is four bits. The 4-bit LSID length (which means the maximum number of resident processes is 16) will fit on 32 TLB entries if each resident process accesses two different pages (one for the instruction codes and one for the local stack) without page faults.

The BIU coordinates the external memory access requests from the ICU and DCU. It controls the normal single-word data transfer or burst data transfer, the external memory access retry sequence, and the external bus arbitration.

In order to achieve 30 nano second clock period (33 MHz clock frequency), the detailed circuit design is being carried out. The SPICE simulation results of micro-program ROM in MRU, carry select adder (CSA), which is a basic component of EXU, are shown in *Table 2*. Because half clock cycle is used for precharge timing, these modules must output valid data within the remaining half cycle (15 nano second). *Table 2* shows that propagation delays of these modules satisfy the target clock cycle time (33 MHz clock frequency).

*Table 2 SPICE Simulation Result*

| simulated modules | delay time(typical) |
|---|---|
| ROM | 6.5 nano second |
| 32-bit Adder CSA | 6.7 nano second |

CSA : Carry Select Adder

## 3.2 PIPELINING

In order to achieve a high performance, a six-stage pipeline structure shown in *Fig.2* has been adopted and several queues are used among the pipeline stages. Mechanisms to detect pipeline hazards and to stall the pipelining have been implemented.

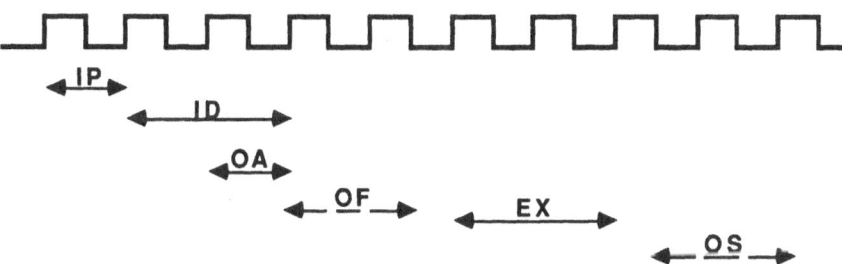

*Fig.2  Pipeline Stages and Timing of O32*

The first pipeline stage is an instruction prefetch (IP) stage in the IPU and the second is an instruction decode (ID) stage in the IDU. The third is an operand address generation (OA) stage in the DAU, in which memory operand addresses are calculated. The fourth one is an operand fetch (OF) stage, in which memory operand data are prefetched from the DCU. The fifth one is an execution (EX) stage in the EXU and the sixth is an operand store (OS) stage in the DCU.

In order to absorb temporal mismatching of pipeline timing between these stages that is caused by the execution of time-consuming instructions or by address calculation of multiple indirect addressing operands, several queues are inserted between these stages and the EX stage. They include a decoded instruction queue (DIQ) which holds decoded instructions from the ID stage, an operand address queue (OAQ) which holds calculated operand addresses from the OA stage, a fetched operand queue (FOQ) which holds prefetched operands from the OF stage, and a program counter queue (PCQ) which holds program counter values of the decoded instructions from the IAU. On completion of instruction execution, the contents of these queues are shifted out under the micro-program control and the next entries are supplied to the EXU.

Among these stages, resource confliction may occur between the OF and OS stages because both of them access the DCU. An instruction at the OS stage, therefore, may conflict with another instruction at the OF stage. One of them will be suspended until the other operation is finished. As shown by the broken lines in *Fig.2*, however, these two stages are optional and the average percentage of such conflicts is less than 25%, which is the average percentage of the memory store instructions. Furthermore, because a store buffer enables deferred cache store, the performance degradation caused by such conflicts is negligible.

Register hazard and memory hazard caused by pipelining are resolved by IDU and DAU, respectively. A register hazard is detected when an instruction which modifies an register is already decoded but is not executed while the same register is being used as the index register of the succeeding instruction whose index register is going to be fetched for the operand address generation. In this case, the OA stage of the succeeding instruction should be deferred until the EX stage of the former instruction is completed.

In order to detect such conditions, the DIQ has destination register number fields which are compared to the index register number currently in the operand address generation stage. If the comparison succeeds, the operand address generation stage is stalled until the decoded instructions are shifted out of the DIQ by the completion of the execution stages.

Some instructions, such as high-level instructions, may modify implicit registers not specified as their operands. Such implicitly modified register information is also specified in the DIQ and is used to detect the register hazard instead of performing a pipeline purge after the completion of such instructions.

A memory hazard is detected when an instruction which modifies a memory operand is already decoded but is not executed while the same memory operand is being used as the source operand of the succeeding instruction. In this case, the operand prefetch stage of the succeeding instruction should be deferred until the former instruction is completed, or the prefetched operand of the succeeding instruction should be purged. In the latter case, the memory operand should be refetched from the DCU in the execution stage. We have selected the operand purge method instead of the deferred operand prefetch because of simplicity of the hardware.

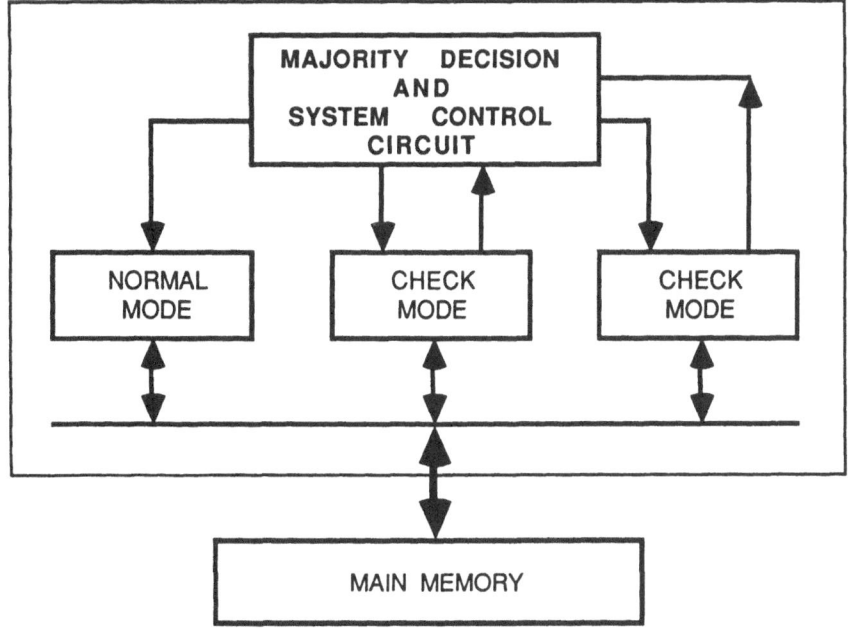

Fig.3  A Majority Decision System

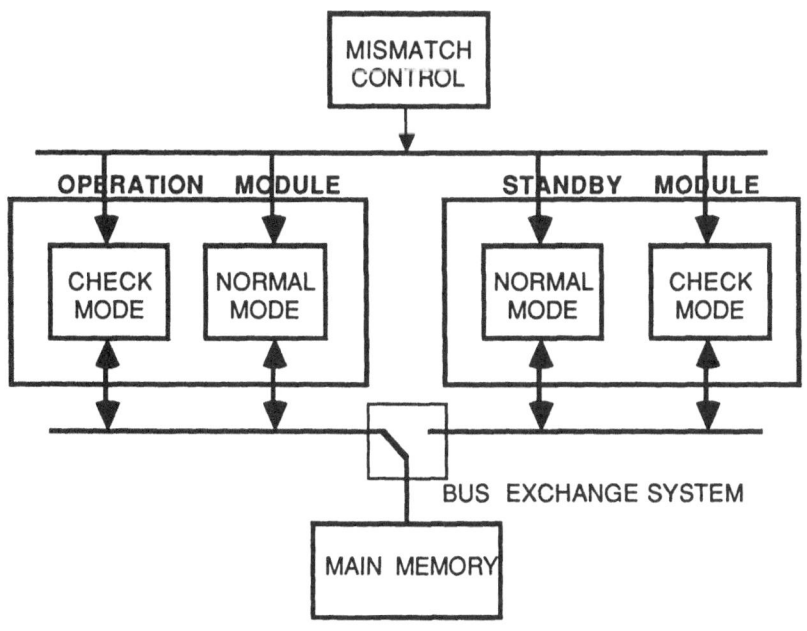

Fig.4  A Pair-and-Spare System

## 4. HIGH RELIABILITY SUPPORT

Two features to support highly reliable systems are described in this section. One is hardware reliability support and another is software reliability support.

### 4.1 BUS COMPARATOR

O32 will be applied to the application area where a main-frame or a mini-computer was needed. Those systems such as on-line transaction processing systems or real-time processing systems need high reliability. Typical methods to construct highly reliable systems are majority-decision method and pair-and-spare method. To realize these methods, it is necessary to compare results of multiple processors executing same program on each machine cycle. Problems to realize this function on board with no reliability support processors are:

- longer machine cycle time because of delay-time caused by external circuit;
- LSI implementation difficulty of bus comparator because a vast number of pins is needed.

O32 support this function on chip. So highly reliable systems can be easily implemented.

In the majority decision systems or pair-and-spare systems, a single master processor and one or more slave processors, which have processor bus comparators with their internal data at their external bus interface units, are connected to a common processor bus and all of these processors perform the synchronized execution of the same programs [6]. Only the master processor drives the processor bus, the other slave processor(s) input the bus data instead of driving the bus and compare the contents of internal data with the bus data. A system malfunction is detected when a mismatch occurs because either the bus data or internal data is wrong.

The majority decision system uses two or more slave processors, as shown in *Fig.3*. The external circuit decides which processor is wrong according to the mismatch signals from the slave processors. If a majority of slave processors activates the signals, the master processor is switched to one of the slave processors whose mismatch signals are active. Otherwise, the processing is continued without such processor switching.

The pair-and-spare system uses two pairs of master-slave processor modules (an operation module and a standby module), as shown in *Fig.4*. Only the master processor of the operation module drives the main memory bus. If a mismatch is detected in the operation module (i.e., if a bus mismatch signal is active at the operation slave processor), the bus exchange system switches the main memory bus to the standby module and the processing is continued.

## 4.2 STACK EXCEPTION

Stack boundary detection is very useful for detection of program bugs.Wrong stack pointer manipulation or infinitive procedure calls may be detected if the hardware stack boundary detection is supported.

It is also useful for support of a vast number of processes in systems with limited memory space. In the multiple processing system, th instruction codes can be shared among the processes. The stack spaces, however, should be localized to each process.

In the network switching node system, for example, thousands of processes may be simultaneously created. If stacks are allocated in page sizes, more than four million bytes of memory space are necessary for stack space even if only one page stack is allocated to each process because the page size of the TRONCHIP is 4KB.

O32 enables a more flexible stack allocation in which each stack space is specified in 256-byte memory address boundaries. The total stack space needed, therefore, is significantly reduced when compared to the page allocation system. If a stack exception occurs, the operation system can allocate extra stack space for the process or can kill such a process.

*Fig.5.* shows the stack boundary check mechanism in the O32. There are five stack pointers and five stack boundary word registers that correspond to the interrupt mode and the current ring level, which specifies the privilege level of the executing programs and is value of from zero to three. The current stack pointer and stack boundary word are selected from these stack pointers and stack boundary word registers according to the current interrupt mode and ring level specified by the program status word.

The stack boundary is specified by the current stack boundary word,which consists of a 16-bit stack segment number (SSN), 8-bit stack boundary bottom offset (SBO), and 8-bit stack boundary top offset(STO). The SSN specifies a 64-KB segment number where the stack area is resident. Two offsets specify the offset addresses in 256-byte blocks of the upper and lower limit address of the stack boundary in the segment. The stack boundary is specified by a single word, which is enough to check the normal stack area, instead of two words. Because a stack boundary word is given for each stack pointer, the stack boundary for all the stack pointers can be checked.

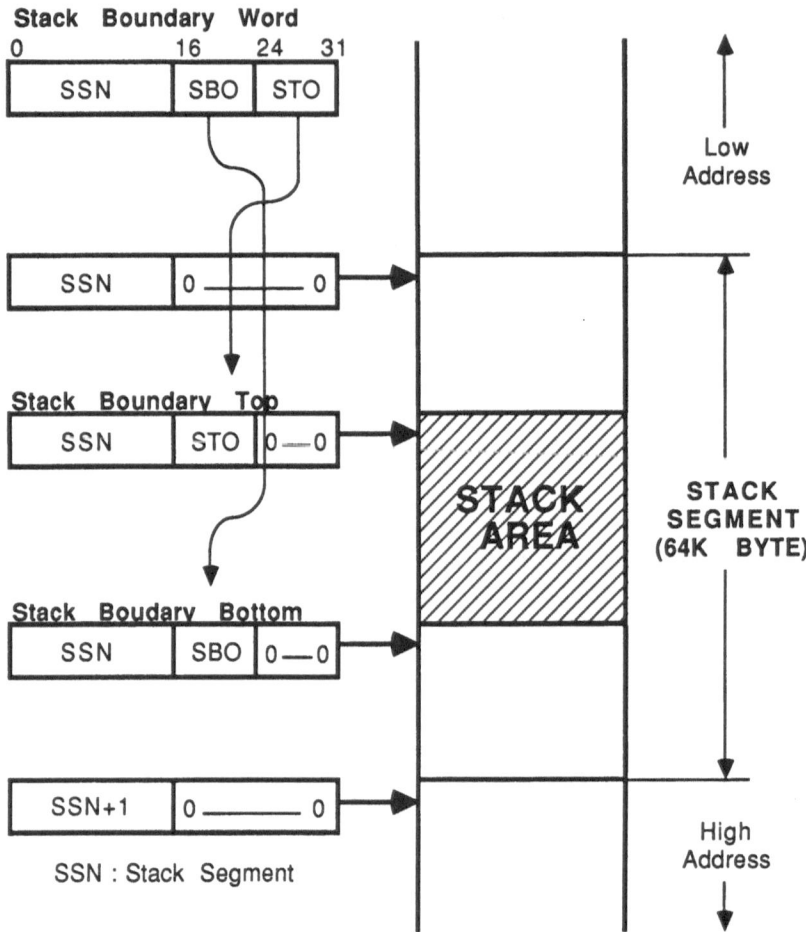

*Fig.5  Stack Boundary Check Mechanism*

## 5. MULTIPLE PROCESSOR SUPPORT

A load-sharing multiple processor system is one of the target application areas of O32. To realize a multiple processor system, it is necessary to maintain consistency between local cache memories and external common memory [3]. There are two typical methods to maintain the consistency. One is all cache purge method that invalidates all the contents of the local cache memory when a external device or another processor modifies data in common memory. Another is partial cache purge method to invalidate only one cache entry corresponding to the modified data address. Because all cache purge method will significantly reduce cache hit ratio and system performance, we have chosen the partial cache purge method.

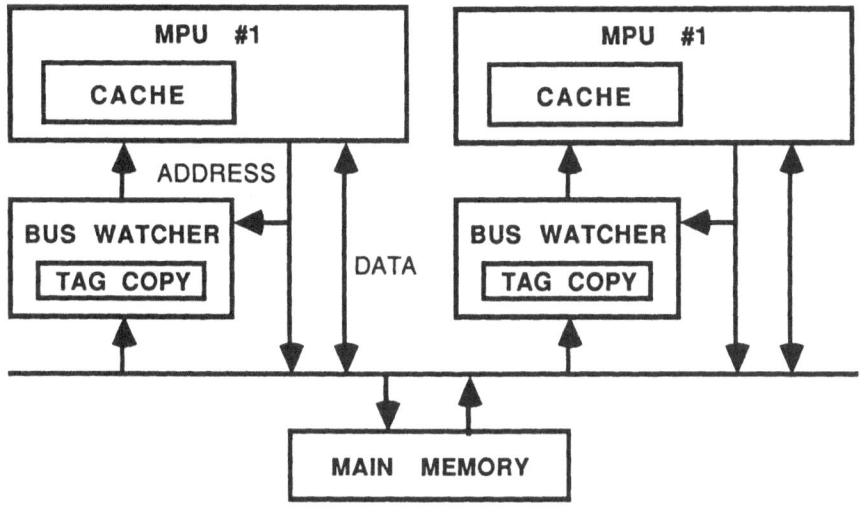

*Fig.6 Cache Invalidation Control*

*Fig.6*. shows an example system that performs such invalidation control. Each processor has an external cache directory circuit which includes the internal cache directory and monitors the system bus to detect whether a modification of the internal cache is being performed by the other processors. When a modification has been made, the external circuit activates an invalidate signal and the cache block number is input to the processor. The processor then invalidates its internal cache block with the block number that has been specified.

## 6. DEBUG SUPPORT

In order to simplify software debugging, O32 has powerful debug support:
- four break point and mask registers;
- two jump history registers;
- jump trap facilities.

Four 32-bit break point registers enable programmers to specify up to four addresses to cause exception when memory accesses whose addresses are matched with these registers are performed. Of these, two registers are used to monitor the instruction addresses and the remaining two registers are used to monitor the operand data addresses. The break point addresses are also maskable: a 32-bit mask register is associated with each break point register and comparison is performed between the contents of the break point register and the memory address masked with the mask register. Four regions of break point address spaces can thus be specified. The debug control register selectively enables these break points.

There are two jump history registers. One register holds the last-executed jump instruction address and the other holds the next-to-last executed jump address. They are very useful in analyzing the reasons where and why unexpected exceptions occur.

In addition to the normal instruction trace facilities, such as single step trace, which causes an exception on completion of every instruction execution, and the jump trap, which causes an exception on completion of a jump or branch instruction, a special inter-ring jump trap, which causes an exception on completion of an inter-ring jump instruction, has been provided. The inter-ring jump instructions are used for operating system calls and returns. This final trap facility is very useful for the operating system debug.


## 7. CONCLUSION

The features and internal structure of O32 microprocessor have been described. In order to improve performance, various implementation techniques, such as six-stage pipelining, two cache memories, and full-associative TLB have been adopted and high speed machine clock is used. The average throughput for instruction execution will be 10 million instructions per second (MIPS) and the peak will be 15 MIPS. In addition to these, various support functions for highly reliable systems, multiple processor systems, and debugging have been integrated.

The chip design is being performed by the top-down design approach, in which the design is proceeded from the abstract functional design stage to the detailed circuit design or layout design stages. In addition to the application of this top-down design approach, the bottom-up design approach, in which the full custom module layout is designed to evaluate the module sizes or propagation delays, is also being carried out.

The functional design stage, in which the ten functional units constituting the whole chip structure are described in the behavioral models and verified by simulation, has been completed and the current design stage is in the detailed circuit design stage. In the bottom-up design approach, the time-critical, full custom modules, such as high-density ROM, RAM, and programmable logic array(PLA), are designed and evaluated. As a result, it becomes prospective to implement a high-speed microprocessor chip with 33 MHz clock frequency.

ACKNOWLEDGEMENTS

The authors give thanks to Mr. Uehara, Director of the Microprocessor Development Laboratory, for his daily encouragement to the project, and the other laboratory members for their fruitful discussions and chip design.

REFERENCES

[1] Sakamura, K., "TRON VLSI CPU: Concepts and Architecture," TRON Project 1987, Springer-Verlag, pp.199-238.

[2] Sakamura, K., "Architecture of the TRON VLSI CPU," IEEE Micro, Vol.7, No.2 (Apr.1987), pp.17-31.

[3] Smith, A.J., "Cache Memories," Computing Surveys, No.14, Vol.3, Sep. 1982, pp.483-530.

[4] Inayoshi, H., et al., "Realization of Gmicro/200," IEEE Micro, Vol.8, No.2 (Apr.1988), pp.12-21.

[5] Itoh, M., "Architecture Characteristics of Gmicro/300," TRON Project 1987, Springer-Verlag, pp.273-280.

[6] Johnson, D., "The Intel 432: A VLSI Architecture for Fault-tolerant Computer Systems," Computer, Vol.17, No.8, 1984, pp.40-48.

**Noriyoshi Ito** is a manager of Microprocessor Development Laboratory, OKI Electric Industry Co.,Ltd. He recieved a B.S. degrees in electrical engineering from Kumamoto University in 1976 and an M.S. degrees in information engineering from Tokyo University in 1978. He joined OKI Electric Industry Co.,Ltd in 1978. From 1982 to 1985, he joined ICOT(Institute of New Genaration Computer Technology ) Project and was engaged in research of parallel inference machine. He is currently engaged in development of VLSI microprocessor.

**Hiromi Nojima** is a manager of Microprocessor Development Laboratory, OKI Electric Industry Co.,Ltd. He received a B.S. degrees in electrical engneering from Kyusyu Institute of Technology in 1973 and an M.S. degrees in electorical engineering from kyusyu University in 1975. He joined OKI Electric Industory Co., Ltd. in 1975. Since then, he has been working on mini-computer design. He is currently engaged in development of VLSI microprocessor.

**Yoshikazu Mori** is a researcher of Microprocessor Development Laboratory, OKI Electric Industry Co., Ltd. He received a B.S. degrees in electrical engineering from Housei University in 1981. He joined OKI Electric Industry Co., Ltd. in 1981. Since then, he has been engaged in research and development of the VLSI digital signal processors and application systems at Research Laboratory. He is currently engaged in development of VLSI microprocessor.

Above authors may be reached at: Microprocessor Development Labolatory, OKi Electric Industry Co, Ltd.,10-3, Shibaura 4-Chome,Minato-ku, Tokyo 108, Japan.

# Design Considerations of the Matsushita 32-Bit Microprocessor for Real-Memory Systems

Tokuzo Kiyohara, Takashi Sakao
Matsushita Electric Industrial Co., Ltd.


Kozo Adachi, Osamu Nishijima
Matsushita Electronics Corporation

**ABSTRACT**

A high-speed, high-performance 32-bit microprocessor for real-memory systems is described that is now being developed based upon TRONCHIP specifications. The principle applications of this processor are as a high-performance controller for control devices, communications, networks, graphics, etc.; as a high-performance specific LSI core; and as a CPU for personal computers, word processors, etc. It has been designed to achieve a performance of 8 MIPS (million instructions per second) at a 20 MHz clock rate within the chip size which makes future ASIC development possible. As a result, design is now progressing toward one-clock execution of register-to-register instructions, speeded up load and store instructions, reduced number of pipeline stages (4 stages and a store buffer), and incorporation of the instruction cache.

**Keywords:** Microprocessor, Pipeline, Cache memory, Real-memory system

## 1.INTRODUCTION

VLSI technology has enabled recent microprocessors to obtain remarkable improvements in high-speed operation frequency and provide more powerful hardware performance. The applications of 32-bit microprocessors can be classified into two categories. One of them is computer-oriented such as workstations and personal computers. The other is controller-oriented such as laser printers and network controllers. In the future, the 32-bit microprocessor can be expected to be specialized in these fields, and it can also be expected that the approach for high performance will also be differentiated. For processors specializing in computer-oriented applications, an overall performance improvement is expected for general applications. The approach will be toward larger capacity of the cache memory and the address translation buffer, and an advanced pipeline configuration. Moreover, for processors specializing in controller-oriented applications, there is expected to be higher performance for specific applications and an improved cost-performance ratio for systems incorporating the hardware accelerator, memory, peripheral circuitry, etc.

Considering these future prospects, Matsushita is now engaged in the development of a processor for controller-oriented applications as well as for some computer-oriented applications. This processor is a high-speed, high-performance 32-bit microprocessor for real-memory systems based upon TRONCHIP specifications. The principle applications of this processor are as a high-performance controller for control devices, communications, networks, graphics, etc.; as a high-performance specific LSI core; and as a CPU for personal computers, word processors, etc. It has been designed to achieve a performance of 8 MIPS at a 20 MHz clock rate within the chip size which makes future ASIC development possible. The design is now progressing toward one-clock execution of register-to-register instructions, speeded up load and store instructions, reduced number of pipeline stages (4 stages and a store buffer), and incorporation of the instruction cache.

After an explanation of the design concept in section 2, section 3 concerns the operating speed of this processor. In section 4, the processor's configuration and pipeline operation are explained.

## 2. DESIGN CONCEPT

In the design of a microprocessor, the configuration is directly and substantially influenced by the applications and target performance of that microprocessor. This microprocessor was designed for the following applications:

1) As a high-performance controller

   This is an application for an embedded controller requiring high performance for control devices, communications, networks, graphics, etc.. Since real-time performance is required, the system is structured as a real-memory system rather than as a virtual-memory system.

2) As a high-performance, specific LSI core

   The directions of customization can be classified into two categories. In the first category, the hardware accelerator required for network engines and graphics engines is incorporated and is tuned to give the best performance for each application. This category can be thought of as an application-specific general-purpose processor. The memory and peripheral circuitry are incorporated in the second category, as for a 4-bit or 8-bit microprocessor, to improve the cost-performance ratio of the system.

3) As a CPU for personal computers, word processors, etc.

   This is an application in the CPU for personal computers and word processors. These systems generally require highly efficient operation of one, or a few, application programs, although support for graphics, etc. must also be given consideration in order to minimize system costs.

When considering embedded applications, and particularly ASIC development, the clock frequency must be minimized for low power consumption, and the following design objectives were set:

- 8 MIPS target average performance
- 20 (- 25) MHz target clock frequency
- A chip size compatible with future ASIC development

To achieve these objectives involved one-clock execution of register-to-register instructions, speeding up load and store instructions, reducing the number of pipeline stages (4 stages and a store buffer) and incorporating the instruction cache.

The result, with a simple configuration, is an average execution time of approximately 2.5 CPI (clocks per instruction) and an average performance of 8 MIPS with a clock frequency of 20 MHz.

### 3. PRINCIPLES INVOLVED IN ACHIEVING HIGH-SPEED PROCESSING

Speeding up a processor can be achieved by optimizing the object codes, reducing the average CPI and improving the clock frequency. The relationship indicated in *Table 1* exists between the CPI and the clock frequency, and to realize the target performance of 8 MIPS at a clock frequency of 20 (- 25) MHz, it can be thought that a CPI range of 2.5 to 3.0 is reasonable.

*Table 1    CPI and clock frequency relationship (target performance of 8 MIPS)*

| CPI | Clock  frequency |
|-----|------------------|
| 2.0 | 16 MHz |
| 2.5 | 20 MHz |
| 3.0 | 24 MHz |
| 3.5 | 32 MHz |

There are two approaches to achieve high speed relative to the CPI and clock frequency. The first involves simplifying the configurational structure and improving the clock frequency, while the other approach involves reducing the CPI with a complex configurational structure. It is also important to decide whether to select one-clock or two-clock execution for the register-to-register instructions, which has a significant effect on achieving high speed.

If one-clock execution of register-to-register instructions is selected, the execution time for memory-to-register instructions and branch instructions is satisfactory at about three clocks in order to achieve a CPI between 2.5 and 3.0, but it is then necessary to speed up the execution circuit. This corresponds to the first approach.

If two-clock execution of register-to-register instructions is selected, this corresponds to the second approach for achieving high speed. From the perspective of achieving high processing-circuit speed, it is preferable to consider the processor's clock frequency as being one-half, thus making possible higher-speed processor operation. If, however, the execution time for memory-to-register instructions and branch instructions must be within three clocks, it is necessary to consider an advanced pipeline configuration, and incorporating branch prediction, data cache, etc..

Based upon the present level of VLSI technology, one-clock execution of register-to-register instructions can be accomplished at a clock frequency of approximately 20 MHz. If, on the other hand, two-clock execution of register-to-register instructions is selected, the clock frequency is restricted to approximately 20 (- 25) MHz for a reasonable power dissipation.

Bearing all these points in mind, one-clock execution of register-to-register instructions was selected for this processor.

## 4. PIPELINE AND CONFIGURATION

### 4.1 Pipeline

The objectives for the design of the pipeline were to achieve one-clock execution of register-to-register instructions, approximately three-clock execution of memory-to-register instructions and branch instructions, and a chip size compatible with future ASIC development. The pipeline incorporates the following features:

1) Inclusion of the instruction cache

    Together with speeding up instruction transfer, the problem of a bus bottleneck has also been resolved. The internal bus configuration is divided into the instruction and data channels as a result of incorporating the instruction cache, and an instruction ROM can be easily incorporated in connection with future ASIC evolution by simply substituting it for the instruction cache.

First stage  Second stage  Third stage  Fourth stage Store  buffer

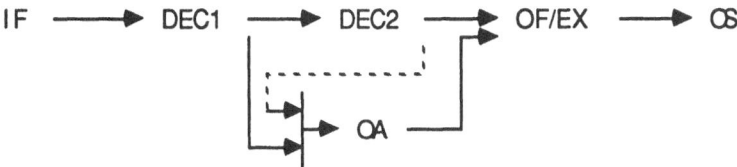

*Fig. 1 Pipeline stages*

2) Reduction of the number of pipeline stages

   Speeding up branch instructions has been accomplished with the simplified arrangement.

3) Implementation of operand address generation as a pipeline stage

   The target performance can be achieved without operand pre-fetching; operand fetching and execution are performed sequentially, so that the mechanism for maintaining memory consistency has been reduced.

4) Improving speed of load and store instructions

   Higher speed is achieved by making use of the fact that frequently used load and store instructions do not require execution.

As a result, the pipeline of this processor has four stages, and a store buffer is provided to speed up storing (*Fig. 1*). In addition, the number of decoder elements has been reduced by dividing decoding into two stages.

The first pipeline stage is called the IF stage, and is used for fetching instructions. The second pipeline stage for decoding is called the DEC1 stage. The third is called the OA and DEC2 stage, and is used for operand address generation and decoding. The fourth pipeline stage is called the OF/EX stage, and is used for sequentially fetching operands and execution. After the operand has once been written into the store buffer at the OF/EX stage, it thereafter operates independently of the OF/EX stage.

**4.2 Configuration**

This processor consists of three major units, IU, CU and EU (*Fig. 2*), with the functions explained below.

1) Instruction-fetch Unit (IU)    IF stage

   This unit incorporates the instruction cache and can pre-fetch instructions simultaneously with data transfer. Pre-fetched instructions are cued to the instruction buffer.

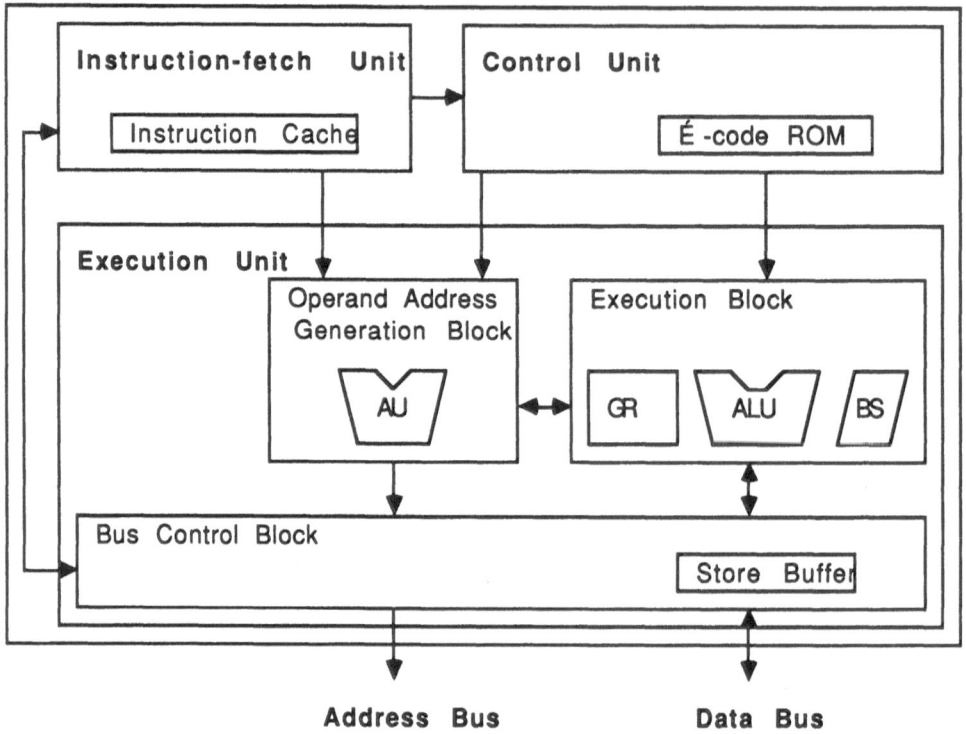

*Fig. 2 Structural configuration*

2) Control Unit (CU)                    DEC1 and DEC2 stages

This unit incorporates PLAs, for decoding instructions, and a micro-code ROM. Instruction codes supplied from the instruction-fetch unit (IU) are decoded here, and control signals are produced. Instruction decoding is divided into two stages.

3) Execution Unit (EU)                 OA and OF/EX stages

This unit incorporates an address generation adder, an ALU, a barrel shifter, general-purpose registers, etc., and address generation and execution are performed according to control signals supplied from the control unit (CU). Address generation and execution are performed simultaneously. In order to speed up loading, the general-purpose registers simultaneously perform the read operation of the current execution and the write operation of the previous operation. A store buffer is incorporated to speed up storing.

All the control devices are concentrated together in this processor, so that except for pre-fetching instructions and storing operands, all IU and EU operations are controlled by CU.

## 4.3 Pipeline Behavior

Timing charts for the pipeline flow of basic instructions are provided below, with "n" indicating the bus access time.

*Fig. 3* shows the pipeline flow when executing register-to-register instructions. In this instance, the execution time is one clock. *Fig. 4* shows the pipeline flow when the executing memory-to-register instructions. In this case, operand address generation is executed in the pipeline, and operand fetching and execution are sequentially performed, the execution time being "1+n" clock. *Fig. 5* shows the pipeline flow when the load instruction is executed. In this instance, operand address generation and operand fetching are executed in the pipeline, the execution time being "n" clock.

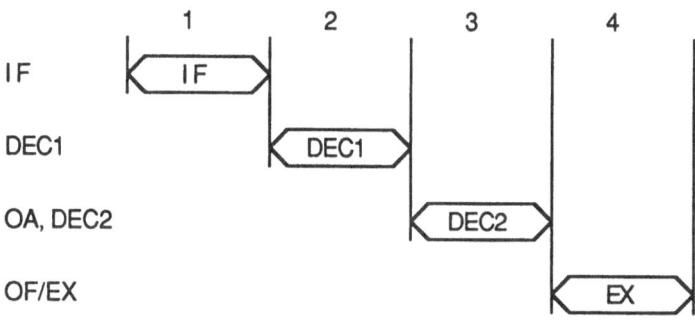

Fig. 3 Pipeline flow of register-to-register instructions

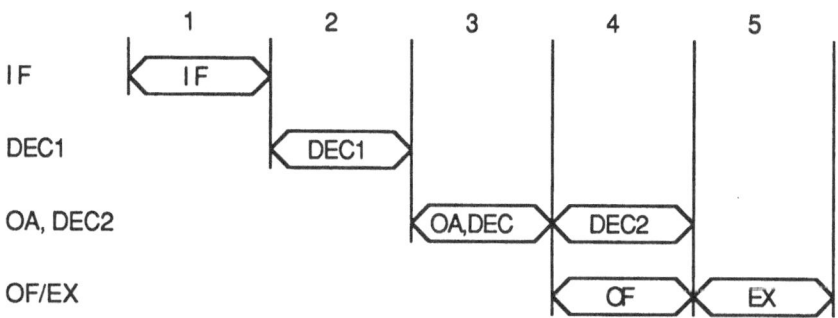

Fig. 4 Pipeline flow of memory-to-register instructions

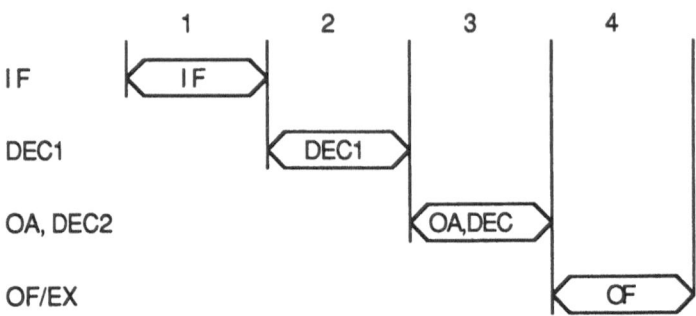

Fig. 5 Pipeline flow of load instructions

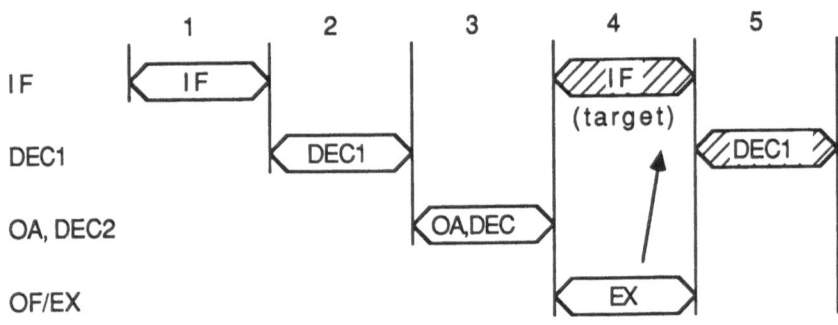

Fig. 6 Pipeline flow of branch instructions being taken

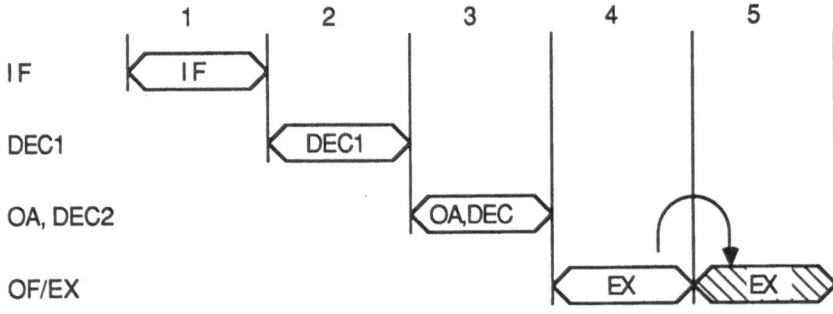

Fig. 7 Pipeline flow of branch instructions being not taken

*Fig. 6* shows the pipeline flow when the branch instruction being taken is executed. In this case, it is necessary to cancel the following instruction within the pipeline at the same time as the branch operation. For this reason, the execution time is three clocks. *Fig. 7* shows the pipeline flow when a branch instruction being not taken is executed. In this case, the following instructions within the pipeline perform continuously and the execution time is one clock.

### 4.4 Performance Evaluation

The average CPI depends upon the instruction mix ratio, this ratio varying widely according to the subject program and the method of optimization.

As indicated in ref. 5, when the mix ratio is about 60% register-to-register instructions, 20% load and store instructions and 20% branch instructions, the CPI of this processor is evaluated between 1.3 and 1.5 (when the instruction cache hit ratio is 100%.).

If, however, powerful addressing modes and high-level instructions featuring the TRONCHIP instruction set are used, high speed and compression of the instruction code size can be achieved. As a result, an instruction mix ratio of about 25% load and store instructions, 25% register-to-register instructions, 20% instructions in conjunction with memory reference, 20% branch instructions, and 10% other instructions (multiplication instructions, etc.) is assumed. In this case, the CPI of this processor is approximately 2.5 (when the instruction cache hit ratio is 100%.).

### 5. CONCLUSION

We have reported the design concepts of a new microprocessor that is currently under development, as well as its applications and performance.

This processor offers one-clock execution of register-to-register instructions, speeded up load and store instructions, reduced number of pipeline stages (4 stages and a store buffer) and incorporation of the instruction cache, so that it is possible to achieve, with a simple pipeline structure, an average CPI of approximately 2.5. As a result, we have met the target performance of 8 MIPS at a 20 MHz clock rate in a chip size compatible with future ASIC development. Furthermore, the bus access time influences the execution time of instructions with memory operations, and, if a one-clock-accessible high-speed memory is integrated through ASIC development, the average performance can further be improved.

This processor is now in the LSI design stage, and it is expected that a family, with this processor as the core, will be developed in the future.

**REFERENCES**

[1]   Sakamura K "Architecture of the TRON VLSI CPU," IEEE Micro April, pp.17-31, 1987.

[2]   Kiyohara T, Deguchi M, Sakao T "A Study of Microprocessor Implementation Based on TRON Specifications," Proc. of the Second TRON Symposium, pp.34-39 (in Japanese), 1987.

[3]   Sakamura K "Architecture of VLSI CPU in the TRON Project," Proc. of the Second TRON Symposium, pp.1-33, 1987.

[4]   Kiyohara T, Deguchi M, Sakao T "Pipeline Structure of Matsushita 32-bit Microprocessor," TRON Project 1987 (Proc. of the Third TRON Project Symposium), Springer-Verlag, pp 281-289, 1987.

[5]   Namjoo M, Agrawal A, Jackson D, Quach L "CMOS Gate Array Implementation of SPARC Architecture," IEEE COMPCON Spring 88, pp.10-13, 1988.

273

**Tokuzo Kiyohara:** He received the M.E. degree from Kyoto University in 1982. After joining Matsushita Electric Industrial Co., Ltd. in 1982, he has been engaged in the development of the VLSI processor and application systems.

**Takashi Sakao:** He received the B.E. degree from Osaka University in 1968. After joining Matsushita Electric Industrial Co., Ltd. in 1972, he has been engaged in the development of the VLSI processor and application systems.

Above authors may be reached at: Information Systems Research Laboratory, Matsushita Electric Industrial Co., Ltd., Yagumo-nakamachi Moriguchi, Osaka, 570 Japan

**Kozo Adachi:** He received the B.E. degree from Kyoto Technical University, Kyoto, in 1978. After joining Matsushita Electronics Corp., Kyoto, in 1978, he has been engaged in the development of MOS LSI.

**Osamu Nishijima:** He received the M.E. degree from Kyoto University in 1970. After joining Matsushita Electronics Corp., Kyoto, in 1970, he has been involved in the development of MOS LSI.

Above authors may be reached at: Semiconductor Group, Matsushita Electronics Corporation , Nagaokakyo, Kyoto, 617 Japan

# An Examination of the Fundamental Configuration of the Microprocessor for Virtual Memory Systems

Yukinobu Nishikawa, Masashi Deguchi, Takashi Sakao
Matsushita Electric Industrial Co., Ltd.

ABSTRACT

The fundamental configuration of a high-performance microprocessor for virtual memory systems is described, which was designed to TRON specifications[1]. This microprocessor has a pipeline configuration that is separated into register-to-register operations and load/store operations; this enables high performance to be achieved, together with the provision of high-speed on-chip resources such as stack cache and data cache. By separating into the register-to-register operation pipeline and the memory access pipeline, it is possible to execute register-to-register operations and memory access in parallel, and to reduce the number of instruction execution clocks. High performance has been additionally achieved by splitting the on-chip operand cache into stack data and other-than-stack data portions, which enables the cache for stack data to be operated as a virtual register.

Keywords: Microprocessor, TRON VLSI CPU, Pipeline, Cache

## 1. INTRODUCTION

According to the advances of semiconductor technology, it will be possible for microprocessors to integrate millions of transistors in the 1990s. Moreover, the clock frequency is also progressively increasing so that operation at frequencies of 30 MHz and higher is currently becoming a reality. As a consequence, it is important for microprocessors of the 1990s to achieve higher operating speeds that take advantage of enlarged on-chip resources, and a configuration that can take full advantage of higher clock frequency. With these two objectives in mind, we are examining the basic configuration of a high-performance microprocessor for virtual memory systems based upon TRON specifications.

RISC processors use on-chip resources to increase the number of registers so that higher executing speeds can be obtained[2]. Our approach is to split the on-chip cache into stack data and other-than-stack data and then to tune each appropriately. A speed-up mechanism is also provided in the stack cache so that the stack can be used as a virtual register with regard to access to the stack by specific addressing modes. To enable the clock frequency to be higher, we have adopted a pipeline configuration which is separated into register-to-register operations and load/store operations, so that each clock rate can be set independently. This pipeline configuration is effective in CISC architecture such as TRON VLSI CPU architecture, as well as RISC architecture.

The basic configuration of this microprocessor is first described and then the pipeline configuration and the cache organization will be studied.

## 2. OVERVIEW

*Fig. 1* shows the configuration of this microprocessor, which can be broadly classified into seven blocks: the instruction cache unit, the decode unit, the register-to-register operation unit, the load unit, the store unit, the data cache unit, and the bus control unit.

### (a) Instruction cache unit (ICU)

This unit supplies instructions to the instruction buffer (located within the decode unit) by a pre-fetch operation.

### (b) Decode unit (DU)

This unit decodes instructions and transmits the control signals of the three execution units (RRU, LDU and STU). In addition, this unit is also provided with a branch prediction mechanism to speed up the execution of branch instructions.

### (c) Register-to-register operation unit (RRU)

This unit comprises the arithmetic and logical unit (ALU), general-purpose registers (GR) and the high-level stack cache (STK), and executes register-to-register operation instructions. For an instruction that has a memory operand, an address calculation is performed in this unit. For an instruction that has a stack operand, however, execution that is equivalent to register-to-register operation is possible by the high-level stack cache. Register-to-register operations are executed by the three-stage (transfer - operation - transfer) pipeline.

### (d) Load unit (LDU)

This unit loads memory operands by using addresses calculated in the RRU, and operates as the load channel to execute a load instruction independently of register-to-register operations.

### (e) Store unit (STU)

This unit stores data by using addresses calculated in the RRU. The unit, in the same way as the LDU, operates as the store channel to execute the store instruction independently of register-to-register operations, and is also provided with the store buffer (STB).

### (f) Data cache unit (DCU)

This unit is the other-than-stack data cache, and an entry is not replaced when there is a write miss; a new entry is created at the time of read access.

### (g) Bus control unit (BCU)

The bus control unit arbitrates data transfer requests from the STU, DCU and ICU; it performs, via the external bus, data transfer with the memory. This unit has a high-speed address translation buffer for virtual memory support.

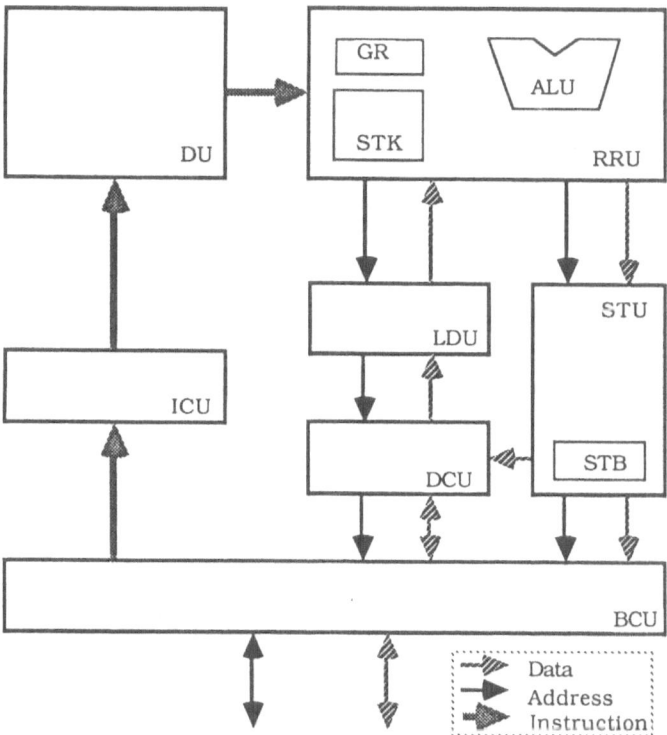

*Fig. 1 Configuration of the microprocessor*

## 3. PIPELINE CONFIGURATION

The pipeline configuration of this microprocessor was determined by following two principles: first, a configuration that makes it possible to easily improve performance according to higher clock frequency; second, avoiding overhead caused by a speed gap between the CPU and the memory .

In order to achieve these objectives, the following operating features were selected:

1) Register-to-register operations processed in three stages
2) A pipeline configuration that separates register-to-register operations and load/store operations.
3) Parallel execution of register-to-register operation and load/store processing.
4) Delayed flag reflection for overlapping load operations.

In other words, register-to-register operations are executed in three stages (transfer - operation - transfer), and by separating into register-to-register operations and load/store operations, each operation rate can be set independently.

This has made it possible to match the performance to a higher clock frequency. Moreover, any internal execution delay due to memory access has been reduced through parallel execution of the register-to-register operation and the load/store operations. In order to execute in parallel a load instruction ("mov:L") and the register-to-register operation that immediately follows, flag changes on a load execution are reflected in the processor status word (PSW) by the delayed flag reflection mechanism, after the flags from a load execution have been determined.

*Fig.* 2 shows an outline of the pipeline stages of this microprocessor, which are separated into the register-to-register operation pipeline and the load/store operation pipelines. The register-to-register operation pipeline comprises the instruction fetch stage, the decode stages (two stages), the register read stage, the execution stage, and the register write stage. In the load/store operation pipelines, the address calculated by using the ALU is sent to the load channel and the store channel, and thereafter each channel performs load/store operations independently. By employing this type of pipeline configuration, it is possible to execute register-to-register operations and load/store operations in parallel.

*Fig.* 3 illustrates the pipeline flow that shows the status of the delayed flag reflection at the load instruction and the register-to-register operation  instruction that follows it. The delayed flag reflection mechanism is the mechanism that reflects flag changes, caused by a load instruction, to the PSW after the flag decision.

In *Fig.* 3, the instruction sequence of (1) "mov @(exp,R0), Rl",  (2) "sub R2, R3" and  (3) "add R3, R4" is shown. The flag change by (2) is reflected to the PSW earlier than the flag

279

change by (1). The flag change by (1) is reflected to the PSW at the same time as the flag change by (3), and only the flags not renewed at (2) and (3) are then renewed. When, however, there is a conditional branch instruction, or an instruction with a PSW operand or instructions that accumulate the flag effect (addx or subx) following the "mov" instruction, the delayed flag reflection does not occur and execution of the subsequent instruction is deferred until the flag decision resulting from the "mov" instruction.

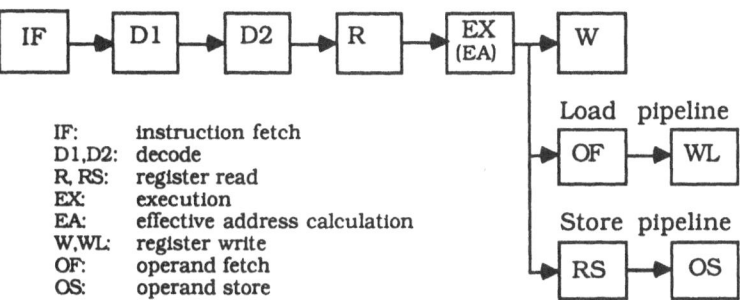

IF: instruction fetch
D1,D2: decode
R, RS: register read
EX: execution
EA: effective address calculation
W,WL: register write
OF: operand fetch
OS: operand store

*Fig. 2 Pipeline outline*

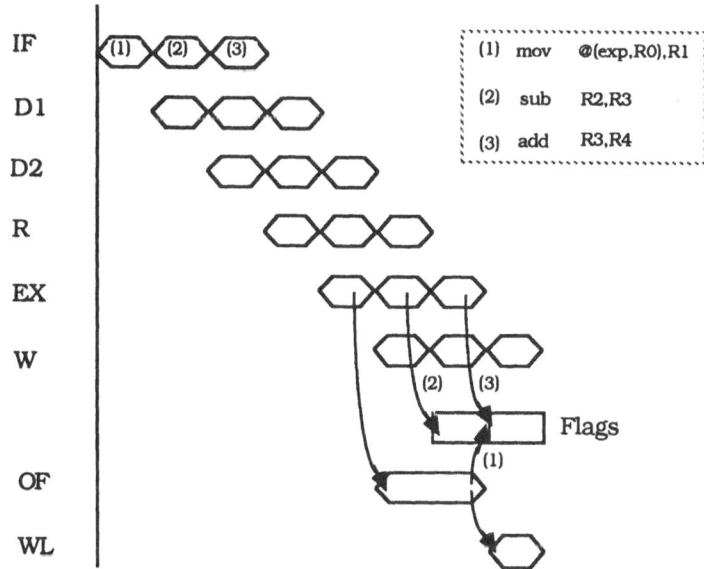

*Fig. 3 Pipeline flow when the delayed flag reflection is performed*

## 4. CACHE ORGANIZATION

Achievement of increased speeds to take advantage of on-chip resources is important with regard to the performance of a processor. In our microprocessor, this speeding up is accomplished by such steps as providing the store buffer, and by separating the operand caches according to their target functions, and tuning each appropriately. In other words, memory traffic is reduced by separating the operand caches into the cache for stack data and the cache for other-than-stack data, and faster memory access can be accomplished by the store buffer. Furthermore, a speeding up mechanism is provided in the stack cache so that the stack can be used as a virtual register with regard to access to the stack by specific addressing modes.

Memory operands can be divided into stack data and other-than-stack data. Data characteristics differ for stack data and other-than-stack data; usually, local variables are allocated to stack data, and global variables are allocated to other-than-stack data. Therefore, stack data are peculiar to the context, and for other-than-stack data, there is the possibility that such data are shared between contexts. Therefore, for other-than-stack data, there is the necessity to maintain consistency relative to access from another master. In contrast, for stack data, there is no necessity to consider maintenance of consistency relative to access from another master. In addition, with regard to access to data, other-than-stack data have a high tendency that same data are read several times, whereas, stack data are read only after the data have been written. Moreover, for stack data, the creation and deallocation of stack frames affect the data characteristics.

Consequently, a suitable cache organization differs for stack data and for other-than-stack data, so that by separating each and adopting the most suitable organization for each, it is possible to improve performance. The cache for other-than-stack data implements the method whereby an entry is not replaced when there is a write miss, and write-through occurs when there is a write hit. The cache for stack data, on the other hand, implements the method whereby an entry is replaced when there is a write miss, and a unique copy-back occurs when there is a write hit; for stack area deallocated by the "pop" instruction and so on, the entry is invalidated. Memory traffic can be reduced by employing this method.

With regard to whether a physical cache or a logical cache is created, a distinction is made between stack data and other-than-stack data. For other-than-stack data, because there are instances in which data are shared, there is the necessity to maintain consistency with regard to other master accesses. Therefore, for other-than-stack data, a physical cache is used, and consistency with regard to other master accesses is dealt with by the bus monitoring mechanism. In contrast, because stack data are intrinsic to the context, a logical cache is used for stack data. The result of separating the caches as just described enables a cache organization to be adopted according to the characteristics of the data. Thus, performance can be improved such as increasing the overall hit ratio for the caches and reducing the memory traffic.

However, it is not possible by these methods alone to eliminate the delays in executing instructions, which occur as a result of writing to the memory. Such delays affect performance to a greater extent as the speed difference between the CPU and the memory increases. In our microprocessor, the store buffer is provided to resolve this problem. Because a write to memory is terminated by a write to the store buffer, the execution of the next instruction can overlap the memory access. It is therefore possible to reduce execution delays resulting from the speed gap between the CPU and the memory.

## 5. ENHANCING THE STACK OPERATION

The stack operation is enhanced in this microprocessor in order to co-operatively support high-level languages. For a stack operand using the SP relative indirect addressing mode (@(exp:4,SP)) and the FP relative indirect addressing mode (@(exp:4,FP)) on TRON Level 2 specifications, the register-to-register operation pipeline is used, and it is possible to perform stack access without effective address calculation.

*Fig. 4* shows the configuration of the high-level stack cache. For access to within the the upper and lower limit address ranges maintained in the address control block, high-speed stack access using @(exp:4,SP) and @(exp:4,FP) is performed. The entry of the stack cache is determined in parallel with the decode stage by the special hardware that employs these addressing modes, and the stack operation is executed in the register-to-register operation pipeline.

Stack access by addressing modes other than @(exp:4,SP) and @(exp:4,FP) is performed in the load/store operation pipelines. If access by @(exp:4,SP) and @(exp:4,FP) is not within the upper and lower limit address ranges maintained in the address control block, an overflow or underflow operation is performed. For overflow and underflow operations, the area that includes the address that is being accessed is taken into the stack cache, and the upper limit address and lower limit address maintained in the control block are renewed.

By evaluating with "Dhrystone" benchmark program, 50% of the instructions with memory operands can use these addressing modes, and 24% of their execution clocks can be reduced.

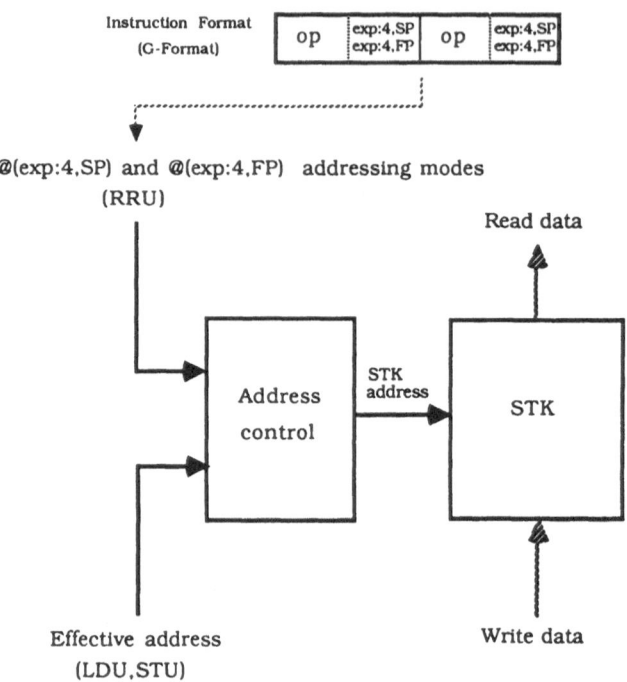

Fig. 4 *Configuration of the high-level stack cache*

## 6. CONCLUSIONS

The high-performance microprocessor described is based on TRON specifications, and achieves its performance by utilizing on-chip resources and taking full advantage of a higher clock frequency. A pipeline configuration is employed in which register-to-register operations and load/store operations are separated, and the provision of a store buffer and a cache configuration can be separated according to the application.

It was confirmed by simulation that the average performance would be 18 MIPS or higher at a clock frequency of 30 MHz ( when hit ratios of on-chip cache memories are 100%). We are presently making a detailed performance evaluation and examining an implementation design.

### REFERENCES

[1]   Sakamura K "TRON VLSI CPU: Concepts and Architecture," TRON Project 1987 (Proc. of the Third TRON Project Symposium), Springer-Verlag, pp 200-238, 1987.

[2]   Patterson DA "Reduced Instruction Set Computer," Comm. of the ACM, 28 (1), pp.8-21, 1985.

**Yukinobu Nishikawa:** He received B.E. and M.E. degrees from Osaka University in 1982 and 1984. After joining Matsushita Electric Industrial Co., Ltd. in 1984, he has been engaged in the development of the VLSI processor and application systems. He is a member of IPSJ.

**Masashi Deguchi:** He received B.E. and M.E. degrees from the Nagoya Institute of Technology in 1974 and 1976. After joining Matsushita Electric Industrial Co., Ltd. in 1976, he has been engaged in the development of the VLSI processor and application systems. He is a member of IECEJ.

**Takashi Sakao:** He received B.E. degree from Osaka University in 1968. After joining Matsushita Electric Industrial Co., Ltd. in 1972, he has been engaged in the development of the VLSI processor and application systems. He is a member of IECEJ and IPSJ.

Above authors may be reached at: Information Systems Research Laboratory, Matsushita Electric Industrial Co., Ltd., 3-15 Yagumo-nakamachi Moriguchi, Osaka, 570 Japan

# Implementation and Evaluation of the TRONCHIP Specification for the TX1

Jun Iwamura, Hidechika Kishigami, Aya Ishii, Kimiyoshi Usami
Toshiba Corporation

**Abstract**

Features of the TRONCHIP specification were analyzed and implemented to a newly developed 32-bit microprocessor, the TX1. Performance of the TX1 was measured from the view point of verification of the effectiveness of the TRONCHIP specification.

**Keywords:** TX1, Performance, Implementation, Instruction format, Addressing mode

## 1. INTRODUCTION

TX1 is the first 32-bit microprocessor of Toshiba TX series microprocessors[1], which is fully based on the TRONCHIP specification[2]. The TX1 supports 92 instructions and executes basic instructions in 2 cycles at 25MHz. The average performance of the TX1 exceeds 5MIPS[3]. This paper describes the hardware architecture of the TX1 featuring the TRONCHIP specification. Discussions are focused on implementation of the address generation scheme and the instruction decoder. Effectiveness of the short-format and the chained-addressing both are distinctive for the TRONCHIP specification is qualitatively measured by using several benchmark programs. Performance of a single board computer which installs the TX1 is also demonstrated.

## 2. OUTLINE OF THE TX1

The TX1 was designed to exploit the characteristics of the TRONCHIP specification to its full extent. Especially, the short-format and the chained addressing were considered as a key. Therefore, our strategy was focused on to make address generating scheme stronger and to enhance the capability of the instruction decoding. In this chapter, outline of the TX1 is described highlighting the Operand Address Generator and the Instruction Decoder.

TX1 consists of five blocks, as shown in Fig.1; Instruction Fetch Unit (IFU), Instruction Decoder(ID), Operand Address Generator (OAG), Execution Unit (EXU) and Operand Management Unit (OMU) [3]. The IFU prefetches instructions and submits them to the Instruction Decoder. After decoding, the ID generates the first address of a corresponding microprogram and transfers it to the EXU. Simultaneously, the ID distributes related operand information to the OAG. When the ID recognizes displacement or immediate data should follow, the ID requests the IFU to move them directly to the OAG. When the OAG receives the related operand information, displacement and address-index which is written in a general register in the EXU, generation of an effective address which is sent to the OMU starts. The OAG also calculates a target address for a branch instruction and contributes to speeding up branch operations. The OMU manages prefetch of instructions as well as prefetch and store of operand data. The EXU executes instructions under the control of microprograms.

Pipeline scheme of the TX1 is shown in Fig.2. The pipeline has two streams. One stream is instruction fetch, decode & microprogram address generation, and execution. In parallel with this stream, a corresponding operand address is generated, and the operands are prefetched.

Photograph 1 shows the chip photograph of the TX1. Characteristics of the chip are summarized in Table 1 [4].

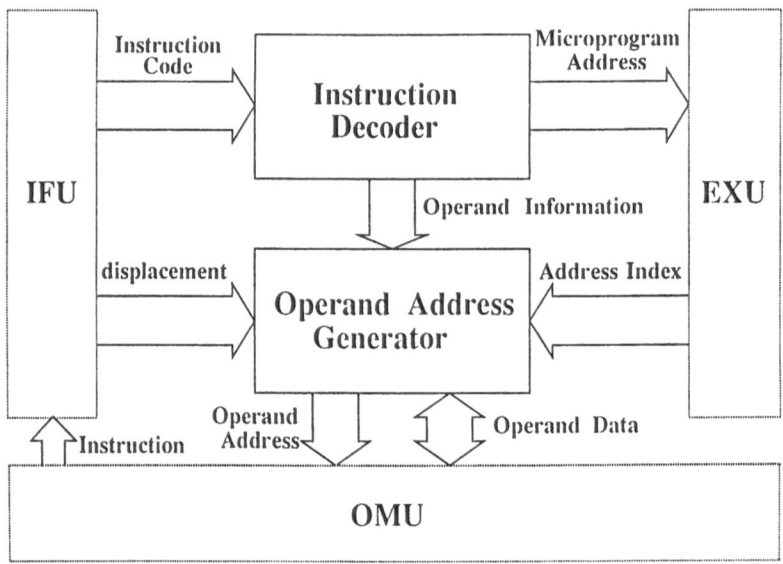

Fig. 1. Block Diagram of the TX1

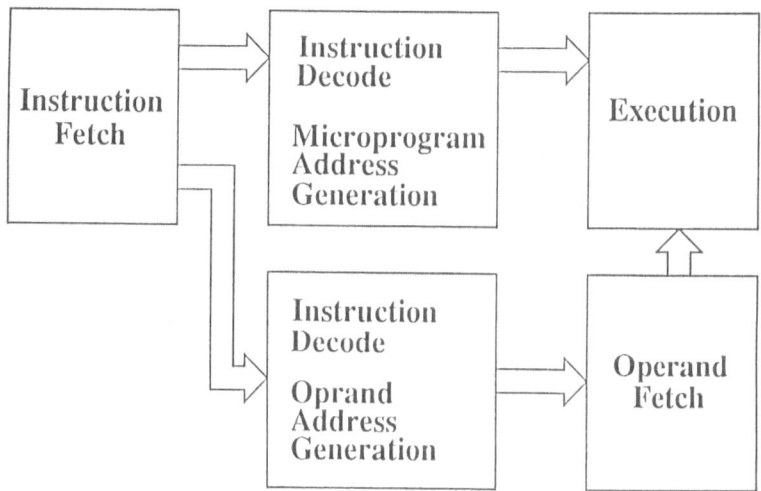

Fig. 2. Pipeline of the TX1

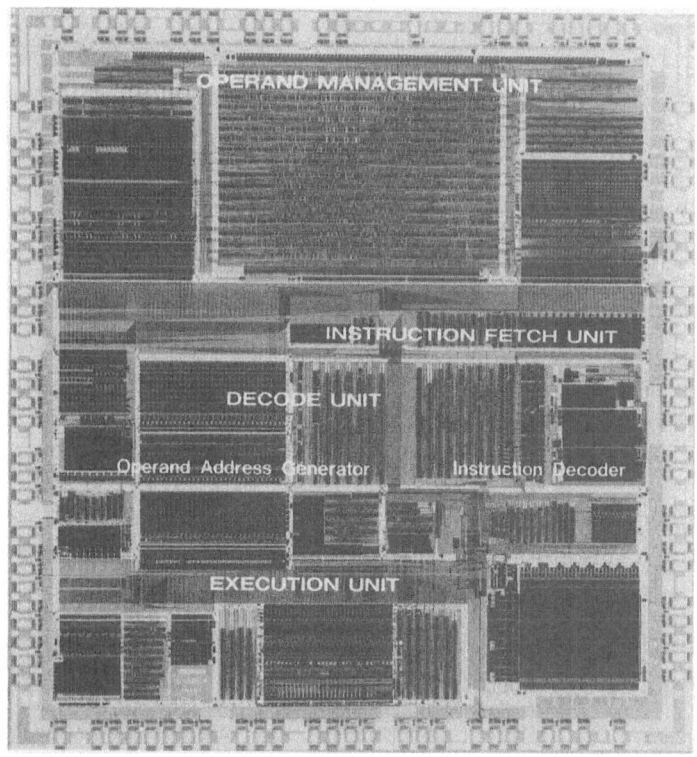

Photo. 1. The TX1 Chip

Table 1. Characteristics of the TX1

| Target System | Controller |
|---|---|
| Performance | 5MIPS |
| Clock Frequency | 25MHz |
| Minimum Bus Cycle | 2 clock access |
| Process Technology | 1.0μm 2AL CMOS |
| Number of Transistors | 450,000 |
| Die Size | 10.89mm × 10.27mm |
| Package | 155 pin PGA |
| Number of Instructions | 92 |

## 3. IMPLEMENTATION OF THE KEY FEATURES

### 3.1 Instruction Decoder

#### (a) Features of the TRONCHIP Instruction Codes

The TRONCHIP instruction codes are designed as a multiple of 16-bit length. Consequently we designed the Instruction Decoder of the TX1 to decode a 16-bit code as a unit. In the TRONCHIP specification, most of 16-bit codes which specify operands have attribute information such as addressing mode in the same code unit. But in some cases, information of the operands are specified by more than two 16-bit codes. In such case, necessary information is provided as a "feedback-code" to the decoder.

The main features of the TRONCHIP instructions are as follows;

(1) Various addressing modes

There are 10 basic addressing modes and 3 chained addressing modes.

(2) Various Short-format instructions

18 instructions such as MOV, CMP, ADD, ..., have the short format.

There are 6 types of short-formats such as Z-format, I-format, ... etc.

Examples of the short-format instruction and the chained-addressing are shown in Fig.3[5] and Fig.4[5], respectively.

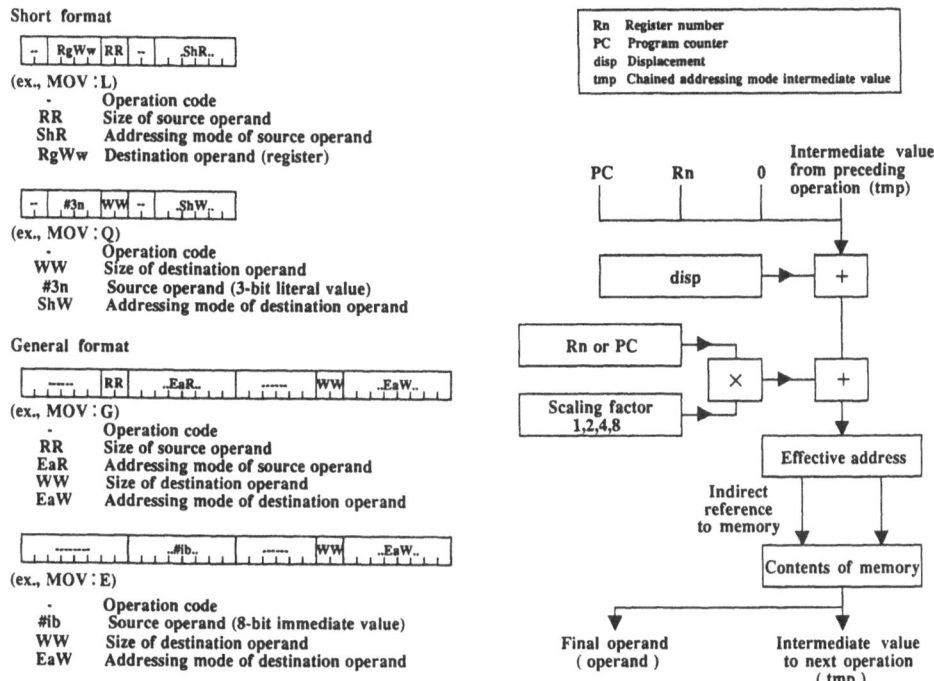

Short format

(ex., MOV : L)

- Operation code
RR Size of source operand
ShR Addressing mode of source operand
RgWw Destination operand (register)

(ex., MOV : Q)

- Operation code
WW Size of destination operand
#3n Source operand (3-bit literal value)
ShW Addressing mode of destination operand

General format

(ex., MOV : G)

- Operation code
RR Size of source operand
EaR Addressing mode of source operand
WW Size of destination operand
EaW Addressing mode of destination operand

(ex., MOV : E)

- Operation code
#ib Source operand (8-bit immediate value)
WW Size of destination operand
EaW Addressing mode of destination operand

Rn Register number
PC Program counter
disp Displacement
tmp Chained addressing mode intermediate value

Fig. 3. Examples of instruction formats    Fig. 4. Chained-addressing Mode

## (b) Design of Instruction Decoder

In a high-level instruction set microprocesser such as the TRONCHIP, careful considerations are required to implement the instruction decoder. One of the typical problems is that the decode PLA tends to be too large. As a result, the PLA operates so slowly that it cannot be used in a high speed microprocessor. In order to obtain a smaller and faster decode PLA, we used some optimizing techniques for PLA implementation. They are "parallel dividing" of the PLA and "separating some logics" from the PLA.

Firstly, "the parallel dividing" of a PLA is described. We found that the number of product-terms of the PLA would become more than 700 without dividing, and the number was too large to obtain sufficient operating speed. Therefore, the "parallel dividing" technique was applied, by which the large PLA was divided along the output signals into smaller 4 PLAs. Each PLA has the same input signals. They are,

PLA1 having 30 outputs for the microprogram address,
PLA2 having 44 outputs for the information of operand,
PLA3 having 1 output for RIE (Reserved Instruction Exception), and
PLA4 having 12 outputs for the addressing mode.

By dividing the PLA, maximum number of the product-terms is reduced to 211 which enables the TX1 to operate at 25MHz.

Another technique, "separating some logics" from PLAs will be discussed. It is well known that PLA is a two-level AND-OR logic and in principle every logic can be realized as a PLA. In actual design however, we have to select which part of the logic should be implemented by PLA and which part is suitable for random logic implementation. This is because the PLA is basically a two-level logic, and designing a multi-level logic only by PLAs tends to generate huge PLAs. One example is the decode logic for addressing mode of the TRONCHIP. In the TRONCHIP specification, there are three types of addressing mode formats; the general format, the short format and the addressing mode which is implicitly indicated by the instruction such as BRA, BSR, TRAP or WAIT. Furthermore, there are several "kinds" of addressing modes such as register-direct, immediate, absolute, etc., for each addressing mode "format". If the decode logic for the addressing modes was implemented only by PLAs, the number of terms which were involved in boolean equations exceeded hundreds of thousands and the size of PLAs would be unacceptable. Therefore we had to try to implement the decode logic for addressing modes by a structure which comprises PLAs and a selector logic, as shown in Fig.5. Logics which were implemented by PLAs are as follows.

Logic-A : A logic to distinguish the kind of addressing mode such as register-direct, immediate, absolute, etc., assuming that the addressing mode format is the "general format".

Logic-B : A logic to distinguish the kind of addressing mode as same as above, assuming that the addressing mode format is the "short format".

Logic-C : A logic to distinguish the kind of addressing mode as same as above, assuming that the addressing mode is implicitly indicated by the instruction.

Logic-D : A logic to distinguish the addressing mode "format" among the general format, the short format and the case in which addressing mode is implicitly indicated.

In addition, a selector logic in a random logic style is placed at the output side of the PLAs to select one addressing mode. Actually, the Logic-A and the Logic-B composes PLA2 and the Logic-C and the Logic-D are in PLA4. As a result, decode PLAs in the TX1 occupy less than 3% of the chip area and satisfy the 25MHz operation.

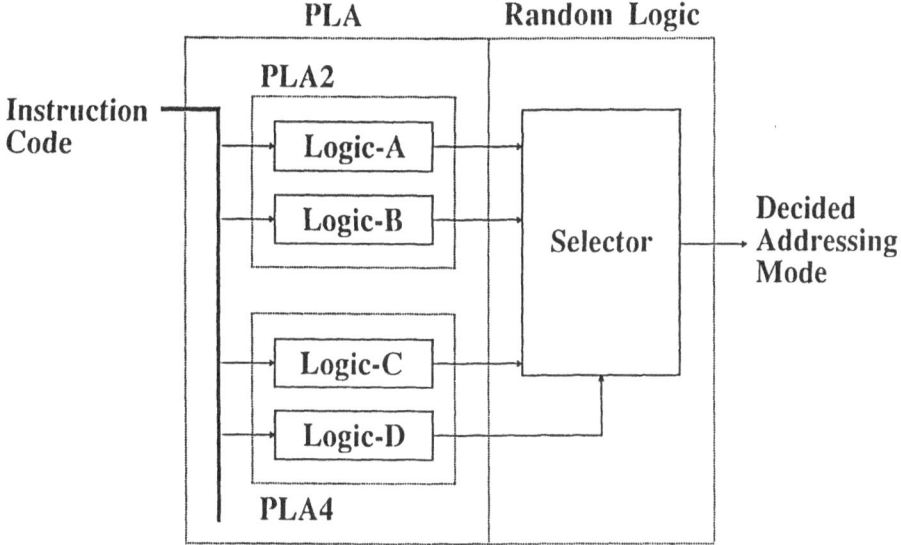

Fig. 5. Decode Logic for Addressing Mode

## 3.2 Operand Address Generator

One of the characteristics of the TX1 is a hardware dedicated to address generation is provided, which enables that the operand address can be generated in parallel with instruction decoding and execution. A block diagram of the Operand Address Generator (OAG) is shown in Fig.6.

### (a) Scheme of Address Generation

A three-input-adder is provided for the OAG in order to achieve higher performance in the address generation of the chained-addressing. For the chained-addressing, the following process is repeated. Firstly, three parameters such as index, displacement and a content of the temporary register (TMP_reg) are added. The index is given by a specified register or by the program counter. Secondly, the external memory is optionally referenced using the address which is obtained by the above-mentioned addition.

The OAG can add three of those data with the three-input-adder and send them to the OMU via Operand-bus (O-bus) in one cycle. The O-bus is used for transferring the operands between the OAG and the OMU. It is also used to carry data from general registers to the OAG. The general registers are implemented as a register file in the TX1.

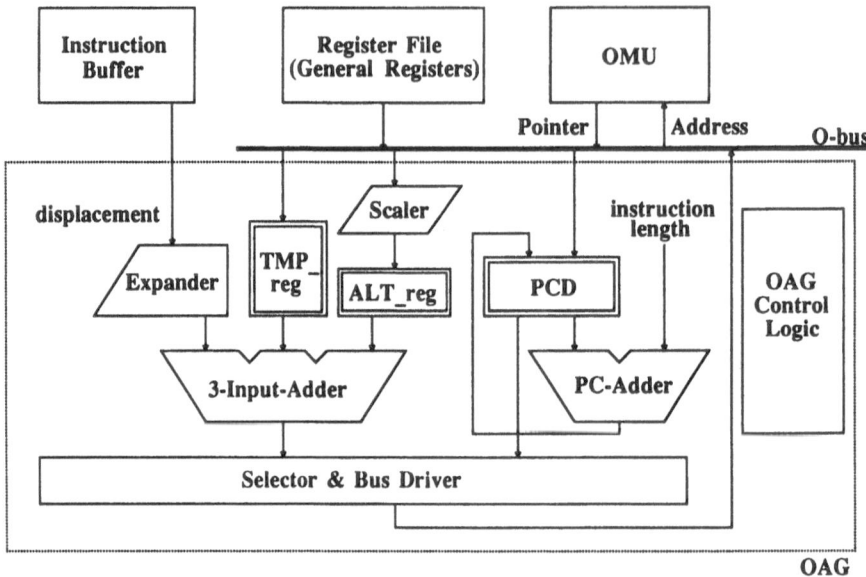

Fig. 6. Block Diagram of Operand Addressing Generator in the TX1

## (b) Hardware for Operand Address Generation

Details of hardware for the above-mentioned address generation are described.

### (1) Hardwired Control Logic

Control logic of the OAG manages address generation for various addressing modes and target addresses of branch instructions. Although it is a complicated finite state machine, it is implemented in a hardwired style to realize high speed operation.

### (2) Adders

Adder for the program-counter in the OAG is implemented using a two-input-adder with Carry-Look-Ahead (CLA) circuits. The three-input-adder for the address generation is designed based on the above mentioned two-input-adder.

### (3) Three-port Register File

The register file in the EXU has three ports. Two of them are for execution and the rest for address generation, so that the address generation can be performed in parallel with the execution. Figure 7 illustrates the connection of the three ports to three busses. L-bus port and R-bus port are controlled by microinstructions. When the OAG requests the data in the register file on the course of the address generation, it is read out via O-bus port. If an instruction under execution intends to modify the content of the register file and the next instruction under decoding process uses the same data in the register file simultaneously, which is so-called register hazard, the Instruction Decoder detects and arbitrates the hazard.

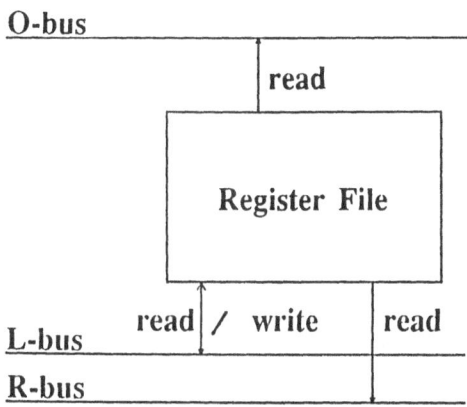

Fig. 7.  3-port Register File

(c) **Cost-performance of Operand Address Generator**

As described above, the Operand Address Generator is implemented in the TX1 and the operand addresses are generated in parallel with the processes of instruction decode and execution. We discuss here the cost as the chip area and the performance of this implementation.

As for the area, the Operand Address Generator which consists of the control part and the datapath part including the three-input-adder occupies 6% of the total chip area.

Next, it is described how much the performance is improved with this implementation. The ratio of address generation in the OAG in parallel with the execution in the EXU was investigated by function simulation. Dhrystone benchmark program [6] was used. The result shows that the OAG and the EXU are operating simultaneously during 18% of the total cycles. In other words, the total number of cycles would be increased by 18% if the TX1 does not equip with the OAG. As a result, the TX1 could improve the performance with a reasonable area increase by providing the Operand Address Generator.

## 3.3 Cost of the TRONCHIP specification

The short-format and the chained-addressing both are important features of the TRONCHIP specification. The impact of these characteristics onto area increase is investigated and estimated, respectively.

In the TRONCHIP specification, every code except for defined instruction codes is treated as Reserved Instruction Exception (RIE). Therefore, the effects of the short-format and the chained-addressing mode onto area increase can be estimated by supposing those formats as RIE.

### (a) Short-format

Existence of the short-format affects only the size of PLAs in the Instruction Decoder. As described above, the decoder consists of 4 PLAs. By excluding the short-format, the sizes of all these PLAs are reduced ranging from 9% to 17% as summarized in Table 2. As a result the area of the PLAs decreases 13% however, that corresponds to only 0.3% of the TX1 as a whole.

Table 2. Effect of Short-format and Chained-addressing to PLA

| PLA name | | TX1 | Short-Format | | Chained-Addressing | |
|---|---|---|---|---|---|---|
| | | | Short-Format →RIE | decrease (%) | Chained Addr. →RIE | decrease (%) |
| PLA1 | inputs | 22 | 22 | | 21 | |
| | outputs | 30 | 30 | | 30 | |
| | product_terms | 211 | 177 | | 210 | |
| | area (mm2) | 0.70 | 0.60 | 14 | 0.68 | 3 |
| PLA2 | inputs | 22 | 22 | | 21 | |
| | outputs | 44 | 43 | | 44 | |
| | product_terms | 204 | 173 | | 199 | |
| | area (mm2) | 0.79 | 0.68 | 14 | 0.76 | 3 |
| PLA3 | inputs | 23 | 23 | | 22 | |
| | outputs | 1 | 1 | | 1 | |
| | product_terms | 145 | 129 | | 139 | |
| | area (mm2) | 0.34 | 0.31 | 9 | 0.32 | 6 |
| PLA4 | inputs | 7 | 7 | | 7 | |
| | outputs | 12 | 6 | | 12 | |
| | product_terms | 18 | 18 | | 18 | |
| | area (mm2) | 0.06 | 0.05 | 17 | 0.06 | 0 |
| total area (mm 2) | | 1.89 | 1.64 | 13 | 1.82 | 4 |

## (b) Chained-addressing

If the chained-addressing mode is removed, the Instruction Decoder and the Operand Address Generator would be affected from the view point of chip area. The size of the PLAs in the Instruction Decoder is estimated to be 4% smaller mainly due to elimination of feedback codes for the chained-addressing mode. Details of the reduction are also described in Table 3. The 4% of the PLAs equals to about 0.1% of the TX1 chip in the area. Besides PLAs, 7% of random logics in the decoder are found to be related to the chained-addressing mode by counting the number of lines of the functional description [7][8], that corresponds to 0.3% of the total chip area.

The Operand Address Generator involves extra hardware for the chained-addressing mode such as the temporary register, the three-input-adder and their control logics. The additional circuits amounts to 17% of the OAG, or 1% of the TX1 in the area. As a result, 1.4% of the chip area are spent in order to realize the chained-addressing mode.

## 4. EVALUATION

In order to evaluate the performance of the TX1 as a computer system, three common benchmark programs were executed on a TX1 board computer. Effectiveness of the short format instructions and the chained addressing was mainly studied.

### 4.1 TX1 system performance

#### (a) Abstract of TX1 board computer

TX1 board computer consists of the TX1 as a CPU, 32Kbyte SRAM(0wait access), 32Kbyte EPROM(0wait access) and 4Mbyte DRAM (4wait access). It also has two channel RS232C in order to communicate with a host computer(AS3260) and one channel sentronics interface. Interrupt control part is composed of TTLs and as a result it occupies one fourth of the board. This part will be replaced by one ICT(Interrupt controller & timer) LSI in the next edition. Photograph of the board is shown in Photo. 2. Because this board computer is yet under adjustment stage, stable operating frequency is limited to 10MHz. Accordingly, results described hereafter are obtained by converting raw data measured at 10MHz into 25MHz.

#### (b) Benchmark programs

Dhrystone[6], Sieve[9] and Fibonacci[9] benchmark programs are used to evaluate the system performance. Dhrystone is a general purpose benchmark testing processor performance except floating-point operation. Sieve finds 1899 primes using Sieve of Eratosthenes algorithm. Fibonacci computes the Fibonacci sequence f(24). Machine codes are obtained by using a C compiler for the TX1.

Photo. 2. The TX1 Board Computer

Although the C compiler does not have an optimizing function yet which is under development, performance evaluation of the TX1 in a system discussed below is demonstrated as the first step.

### (c) Performance of the TX1 system

Table 3 shows the execution time of the three benchmark programs executed on the TX1 board computer. The TX1 board computer executes 9649 Dhrystone loops in a second. It also executes Sieve in 4.24 seconds and Fibonacci in 25.0 seconds. Much higher performance will be expected after the optimizing function of the compiler is available.

Table 3. The TX1 System Performance

| Dhrystone/sec. | 9649 times |
|---|---|
| Sieve | 4.24 sec. |
| Fibonacci | 25.0 sec. |

## 4.2 Effect of TRONCHIP features

### (a) Effect of the short-format instructions

The short-format instructions are prepared for frequently used instructions in order to not only decrease code size but to enhance the performance. The effectiveness of the short-format was examined in the TX1 system. The results are shown in Table 4. The performance ratio and the code size ratio are calculated as follows;

$$\text{Performance ratio} = \frac{\text{MIPS of using only General-format instruction}}{\text{MIPS of using all instructions}}$$

$$\text{Code size ratio} = \frac{\text{Code size of using only General-format instruction}}{\text{Code size of using all instructions}}$$

Table 4.  Effect of Short-format instruction

|  | | Performance ratio | Code size ratio |
|---|---|---|---|
| Dhrystone | (SRAM; 0 wait)<br>(DRAM; 4 wait) | 0.95<br>0.87 | 1.47 |
| Sieve | (SRAM; 0 wait)<br>(DRAM; 4 wait) | 0.89<br>0.84 | 1.60 |
| Fibonacci | (SRAM; 0 wait)<br>(DRAM; 4 wait) | 0.89<br>0.80 | 1.53 |

From the results, it is found that performance will be degraded by 5 to 20 percent and the code size will increase by 47 to 60 percent if no short-format instruction is used in the benchmark programs. The results also show the improvement in performance is more remarkable in DRAM memory system. This is because the slow speed of instruction fetches in DRAM memory system causes the chip bus bottleneck more when the code size increases.

## (b) Effect of the chained addressing

Another characteristics of the TRONCHIP specification is to have chained addressing modes which permit multi-level indirection with scaling and offsets. For example, a sequence of instructions shown here,

```
mov @(8,fp),r1
mov @(r1),r1
mov @(r1),r1
```

can be replaced by one instruction using the chained addressing as follows;

```
mov @(@(@(8,fp))),r1.
```

Table 5 shows the comparison of the performance and code size between programs using chained addressing "(used)" and not using chained addressing "(not used)" in these benchmark programs. The results show that the chained addressing improves the performance 2 percent in Dhrystone and 4 percent in Sieve in the TX1 system. As for code size, 6 percent of total code area can be saved in Dhrystone and 1 percent in Sieve. There is no chance to use chained addressing in Fibonacci. The difference between the result in Dhrystone and that in Sieve is due to different use ratio of the chained addressing. In Dhrystone, chained addressing is used by 8 percent of total instructions both in dynamic and static. On the other hand in Sieve, it is used by 20 percent in dynamic but 8 percent in static. In these benchmark programs, there is no chance to use the chained addressing of adding three address data simultaneously with the three-input-adder in the OAG of the TX1. More improvement in performance will be expected in other programs treating complex data structure such as multi-dimensional array.

Although we could see the effectiveness of short-format instructions and chained addressing of the TRONCHIP specification to some extent, further investigation is needed to discuss the effectiveness in detail especially for chained addressing.

Table 5.  Effect of Chained-addressing

| | | Performance ratio | Code size ratio |
|---|---|---|---|
| Dhrystone | (not used) | 1.00 | 1.00 |
| | ( used) | 1.02 | 0.94 |
| Sieve | (not used) | 1.00 | 1.00 |
| | ( used) | 1.04 | 0.99 |

# 5. CONCLUSION

Features of the TRONCHIP specification were carefully analyzed and implemented to a 32-bit microprocessor, the TX1. The Instruction Decoder and the Operand Address Generator are reinforced. It is estimated that the installation of the OAG hardware enhances the performance of the TX1 by 18%.

It is qualitatively found that the short-format is very cost-effective to improve the performance of the TX1 from the view points of MIPS number and the code-size. Although benchmark programs used here such as Dhrystone or Sieve could not prove the effectiveness of the chained addressing significantly, overhead for installing the addressing costs just 1.4% of the TX1 in the area. Suitable application must be developed and demonstrated.

Performance of the TX1 was investigated as a single board computer. It should be noted that higher performance is expected after the compiler for the TX1 has an optimizing function.

# 6. ACKNOWLEDGEMENT

The authors would like to thank Dr. Ken Sakamura of University of Tokyo for his many helpful suggestions.

# REFERENCES

[1] K.Namimoto et al.,"TX series Based on TRONCHIP Architecture", TRON Project 1987, Springer-Verlag, pp.291-308.
[2] K.Sakamura,"The TRON Project", IEEE Micro, vol.7, no.2, pp.8-14, Apr. 1987.
[3] M.Miyata, H.Kishigami, K.Okamoto, and S.Kamiya, "The TX1 32-Bit Microprocessor: Performance Analysis and Debugging Support", IEEE Micro, vol.8, no.2, pp.37-46, Apr. 1988.
[4] T.Tokumaru, E.Masuda, C.Hori, K.Usami, M.Miyata, and J.Iwamura, "Design of a 32Bit Microprocessor, TX1", 1988 Symposium on VLSI Circuits Technical Digest, III-5, Aug. 1988.
[5] K.Sakamura, "Architecture of the TRON VLSI CPU", IEEE Micro, vol.7, no.2, pp.17-31, Apr., 1987.
[6] R.P.Weicker, "Dhrystone : A Synthetic System Programming Benchmark", Communications of the ACM, vol.27, no.10, Oct. 1984, pp.1013-1030.
[7] M.Miyata, I.Yamazaki and S.Nishio, "A Hierarchical Hardware Description Language", Proc. of Electronic Design Automation Conf. (EDA84), 1984.
[8] M.Miyata, Y.Masubuchi, K.Murai and M.Yoshimura, "Automatic Logic Synthesis from $H^2DL$ Description", Proc. of ISCAS85, 1985, pp.643-646.
[9] Editorial staff, "High-Tech Horsepower", BYTE, July, 1987, pp.101-108.

**Jun Iwamura:** He is a manager of VLSI design in the department of Advanced Microprocessor Development at the Semiconductor Device Engineering Laboratory(SDEL) of Toshiba Corporation. After he received the B.S degree in physics from Nagoya University, Japan, in 1971, he joined the R&D center of Toshiba Corporation, where he was involved in the research and development of MOS devices. Since 1978, he has been engaged in the design of MOS LSI's and VLSI's at the SDEL. His current interests include design methodology of VLSI processor, design for testability and CMOS circuitry for high-speed operation. He is a member of the information Processing Society of Japan.

**Hidechika Kishigami:** He is a researcher in the same laboratory. He received his BS and MS degrees in electronics engineering from Kyoto University in 1983 and 1985, respectively. Since joining the department, he has been engaged in research and development of 32-bit microprocessor design. His current interests include performance analysis of 32-bit microprocessors. He is a member of the information Processing Society of Japan.

**Aya Ishii:** She is a researcher in the same laboratory. She received her BS and MS degrees in applied chemistry from Keio University in 1984 and 1986,respectively. Since joining the department, she has been engaged in research and development of 32-bit microprocessor design. Her current interests are VLSI circuit design, including PLA optimization.

**Kimiyoshi Usami:** He is a researcher in the same laboratory. He received his BS and MS degrees in electrical engineering from Waseda University in 1982 and 1984, respectively. Since joining the department, he is engaged in research and development of 32-bit microprocessor design. His current interests are design methodology of VLSI processor, VLSI circuit design, including PLA optimization. He is a member of the institute of electronics, information and communication engineers of Japan.

Above authors may be reached at: Advanced Microprocessor Technology, Semiconductor Device Engineering Laboratory, 580-1, Horikawa-cho, Saiwai-ku, Kawasaki, 210 Japan.

# A Floating Point Processing Unit for the GMICRO CPU

Hiroyuki Kida, Mitsuru Watabe, Tetsuaki Nakamikawa,
Shigeki Morinaga, Shumpei Kawasaki, Hideo Inayoshi
Hitachi Ltd.

ABSTRACT

This paper describes the architecture and implementation of a newly developed floating point processing unit (FPU). It was developed as a high performance 32-bit coprocessor of the 32-bit GMICRO microprocessor, which satisfies the IEEE 754 Standard for Binary Floating-Point Arithmetic.

High performance was achieved by the high speed coprocessor's interface with the GMICRO CPU and the pipeline processing. The coprocessor's interface was designed to minimize CPU-FPU communication overhead caused by transferring commands, operands and coprocessor information. Furthermore, to improve operation speed, the FPU performs pipeline processing named command pipeline. The FPU has three main elements, the bus control unit, format conversion unit, and execution control unit. In order to perform high speed calculations, each element in the chip is designed to operate in parallel. Thus the FPU command pipeline operation can execute up to three instructions concurrently. In addition to pipeline processing, the FPU has a powerful execution control unit. It contains a multiplier and two arithmetic units; one is used for exponent value calculations, and the other for mantissa value calculations.

As a result, the FPU executes floating point addition in 0.5 µs and floating point multiplication in 0.45 µs at a 20-MHz clock rate. The FPU with the GMICRO CPU is expected to achieve 4 MWIPS performance.

Keywords: Floating Point Processing Unit, Floating Point Arithmetic, Coprocessor, Coprocessor Protocol, GMICRO CPU.

## 1. INTRODUCTION

IN RECENT YEARS, rapid progress in semiconductor technology, particularly metal oxide semiconductor (MOS) technology, has made it possible to fabricate highly integrated microprocessors that are constituted of several hundred thousand MOS transistors and high performance microprocessors are appearing on the market. However, many applications are beginning to require new generation microprocessors with higher performance which advanced semiconductor technology helps to provide.

GMICRO CPU is a high performance 32-bit microprocessor which has been developed using the standard architecture defined by TRON (The Real time Operating system Nucleus) project [1]. Its major target application is for engineering workstation systems. In such an application, powerful floating point processing is required.

The floating point processing unit (FPU) is developed as a coprocessor of the 32-bit GMICRO microprocessor family based upon TRON specifications. The FPU is provided as a VLSI chip for performing floating point arithmetic operations at high speed based on the IEEE 754 Standard for Binary Floating-Point Arithmetic ( Draft 10.0 ) [2]. This FPU's target performance is 4 MWIPS (Whetstone benchmark Instructions Per Second) at a 20-MHz clock rate. This paper discusses the FPU specifications and its micro chip architecture which achieves this target performance.

## 2. ARCHITECTURAL CONCEPT

### 2.1 High Performance

The GMICRO CPUs are noticeable 32-bit microprocessors that satisfy TRON specifications and have their own family peripherals. The FPU is a device to process floating point arithmetic. It is designed to interface with the GMICRO CPU as a coprocessor. The GMICRO CPU and FPU are targeted for the high end workstation market and they will work as a high speed graphic engine. Thus we want to design the FPU with the following features:
1) high speed floating point processing;
2) high speed coprocessor protocol with the GMICRO CPU; and
3) high level instructions to support graphics.

### 2.2 Full Conformation to the IEEE Standard

It is very important to facilitate the transportation of numerically oriented programs and to encourage the development of high quality numerical software. Therefore, the FPU is designed to perform floating point arithmetic operations based upon the IEEE 754 Standard for Binary Floating-Point Arithmetic. It fully conforms to the IEEE Standard, including all requirements and suggestions. It supports many binary floating point arithmetic operations and various data formats employing floating point and binary integer expressions.

## 3. ARCHITECTURE SPECIFICATIONS

### 3.1 New Coprocessor Interface

The FPU has a tightly coupled coprocessor protocol with the GMICRO CPU. The protocol sequence is implemented in the hardware in both the CPU and the FPU. The coprocessor protocol has the following features:

1) The FPU command set is included in the CPU instruction set so that programmers can use the FPU as one of several CPU resources.

2) Direct data transfer between the FPU and memory is available under the CPU bus control to reduce operand transfer time.

3) Up to eight FPUs can be connected to the CPU to realize overlapping operations on multiple FPUs.

With the above features, the new coprocessor protocol can be performed at a high speed.

## 3.2 High Speed Operation

The FPU employs pipeline processing to improve floating point operation processing speed. Pipeline processing allows concurrent operations. The FPU has three main elements, the bus control unit, format conversion unit, and execution control unit. In order to perform high speed calculations, each element in the FPU chip is designed to operate in parallel. Therefore, the FPU commands can be executed in the three stages of the pipeline. We named this pipeline **command pipeline**. The FPU command pipeline operation can execute up to three instructions concurrently.

## 3.3 High Level and Large Instructions
## (a) Large Instructions

The command set for the FPU is included in the CPU instruction set. The FPU has 52 instructions which are made up of arithmetic, transcendental function, data transfer, system control and graphic instructions. The FPU command set is shown in Table 1.

Table 1   FPU command set

| | | | | |
|---|---|---|---|---|
| ARITHMETIC | FADD | FSUB | FMUL | FDIV |
| | FABS | FNEG | FSQRT | FSCALE |
| | FREM | FMOD | FINT | FINTRZ |
| | FEXTE | FEXTM | | |
| TRANSCENDENTAL | FSIN | FCOS | FTAN | FSINCOS |
| | FASIN | FACOS | FATAN | |
| | FSINH | FCOSH | FTANH | FATANH |
| FUNCTION | FEXP2 | FEXPE | FEXP10 | |
| | FLOG2 | FLOGE | FLOG10 | |
| DATA TRANSFER | FLD | FST | FMVR | |
| | FLDI | FSTI | FLDUI | FSTUI |
| SYSTEM CONTROL | FNOP | FCMP | FTST | FBcc |
| | FSAVE | FREST | FABT | FLDM |
| | FLDC | FSTC | FSTMN | FSTMU |
| GRAPHICS | FDOTPR | | FLIMIT | |

Add, subtract, multiply, compare and remainder operations are compatible with the IEEE Standard. The results of these arithmetic functions can be obtained exactly in accordance with the defined specifications. Furthermore 17 transcendental functions including trigonometric, hyperbolic, exponential and logarithmic functions are implemented and are defined for the entire range of all floating point data representations. But these transcendental functions do not give a result with the same error limit as the standard arithmetic functions because of the relationship between a arithmetic unit and a algorithm [3]. The worst-case accuracy of any transcendental function corresponds to that of double precision.

*(b) High Level Instructions*

Aside from supporting the IEEE Standard, the FPU has instructions aimed for three-dimensional graphics; i.e. an instruction to aid in clipping operation and an instruction to aid in coordinates transformation.

*3.4 IEEE Standard Data Format*

*(a) Data Format*

The FPU supports three floating point data formats: single precision, double precision and extended double precision as defined in the IEEE Standard. Also all integer formats of GMICRO family processors are supported. The FPU data format is shown in Table 2. The data format conversion among all of the floating point data formats and the integer data formats are defined in the instruction set.

*(b) Data Type*

The floating point data must be able to express normalized and denormalized numbers, zeros, infinities and not-a-number (NAN). The FPU supports the above data types as defined in the IEEE Standard.

Table 2   FPU data formats

| | | |
|---|---|---|
| BINARY FLOATING POINT | | SINGLE PRECISION (32-BIT) |
| | | DOUBLE PRECISION (64-BIT) |
| | | EXTENDED DOUBLE PRECISION (80-BIT) |
| INTEGER | SIGNED | BYTE (8-BIT) |
| | | HALF-WORD (16-BIT) |
| | | WORD (32-BIT) |
| | UNSIGNED | BYTE (8-BIT) |
| | | HALF-WORD (16-BIT) |
| | | WORD (32-BIT) |

## 4. NEW COPROCESSOR INTERFACE

### 4.1 Tightly Coupled Coprocessor Protocol with the GMICRO CPU

Fig. 1 shows a standard system configuration using the GMICRO CPU and the FPU. The FPU has a tightly coupled coprocessor protocol with the GMICRO CPU. The FPU can be used as one of the CPU resources. The protocol is designed to minimize CPU-FPU communication overhead during command or operand transfers and to secure data-coherency between the CPU internal cache and external memory.

Fig. 2 shows the processing flow of the new coprocessor protocol. The GMICRO CPU and FPU have the following four procedures in this protocol.

1) Command transfer: This transfers a command to be executed by the FPU along with necessary information such as operation type and data transfer type, operand size and operation precision.

2) Input operand transfer: This transfers the operands necessary to perform the operation and data transfer by the FPU.

3) Floating point instruction address (FIA) transfer: This transfers a floating point instruction address corresponding to the FPU command. The FIA is used to get the address of the instruction in an application program when exception processing has occurred in the FPU.

4) Output operand transfer: This transfers the operation and data transfer results when the destination is specified as an external resource of the FPU.

Fig. 3 shows a new coprocessor protocol sequence. In the coprocessor protocol, FPU status is reported to the CPU through a **coprocessor status** (CPST) signal. The CPST indicates the operational status of the FPU. Conventional FPUs do not have such a signal used exclusively for reporting the operational status [4] [5]. FPU status is as follows:

1) ACC: This indicates that the FPU accepts the defined command.

2) CERR: This indicates that the FPU accepts the undefined command.

3) BUSY:This indicates that the FPU can not accept the command or operand.

4) EXCP: This indicates that the FPU occurs the exceptional operation.

5) DTR: This indicates that the FPU requests the operand transfer.

6) TRUE: This indicates that the FPU has set true status as a result of FBcc command execution.

In this protocol, since the CPU and FPU determine processing using coprocessor instructions and commands, i.e., transfer control information and data to each other in a dynamic fashion, the coprocessor operation can be executed in high speed.

On the other hand, the FPU can be used with a CPU having no coprocessor protocol as a peripheral device. In this case, the CPU supplies commands and data to the FPU by emulating transfer of protocol used for coprocessor operation, since CPUs other than GMICRO CPUs do not have coprocessor connecting pins for the FPU. In the peripheral protocol, the FPU status is loaded into the CPU during the CPST transfer bus cycle.

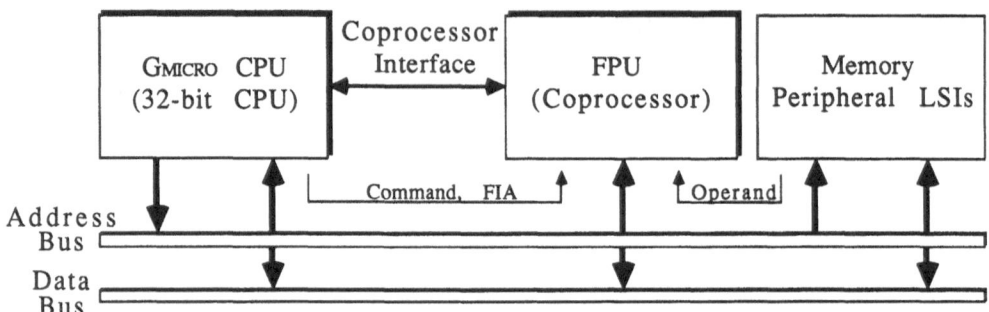

Fig. 1  Standard system configuration used in the GMICRO CPU and FPU

Fig. 2  Processing flow of new coprocessor protocol

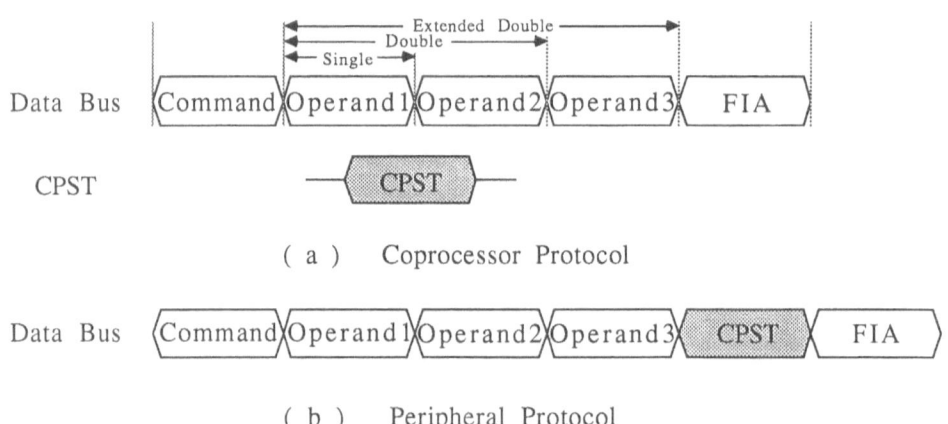

Fig. 3  New coprocessor protocol sequence

*4.2 Overlapping Operation on Multiple FPUs*

Overlapping operations on multiple FPUs can be achieved by connecting multiple FPUs to one CPU. Fig. 4 shows the system configuration of a multiple FPU application. Each FPU has an input signal, named CPID (**coprocessor identification**) to carry out overlapping operations on multiple FPUs. The CPID provides a coprocessor ID number. In such a configuration, it is enough that the signals output from the CPST of each FPU are wired-OR and supplied to the CPU.

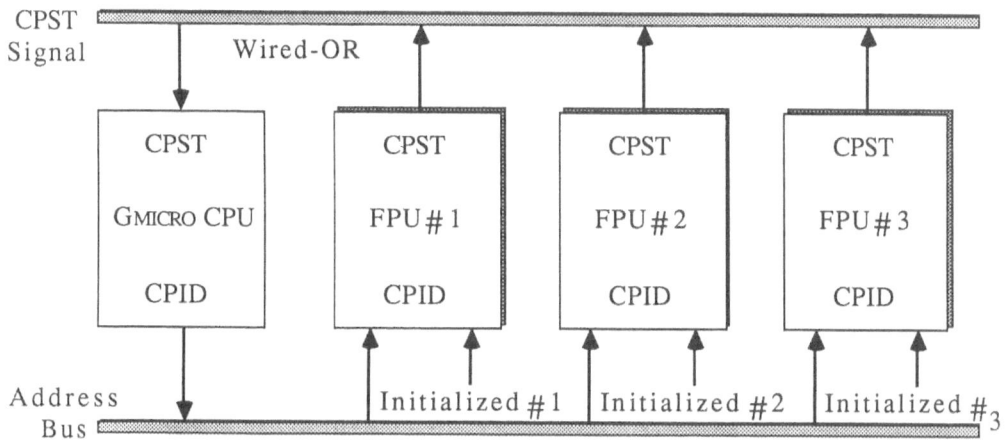

Fig. 4    System configuration of a multiple FPU application

*4.3 The Protocol in Floating Point Processing*

Fig. 5 outlines the protocol in floating point processing between memory and the FPU's register. In this protocol, the CPU and FPU behave as follows:

1) The CPU fetches a floating point instruction and decodes it. Then the CPU generates a command for the FPU. Next, it transfers the command and CPID to the FPU.

2) The FPU tests the CPID and gets the command.

3) The CPU reads out the operand from the main memory.

4) The FPU reports the internal status through the CPST signal.

5) The CPU recognizes the CPST signal.

6) The FPU gets the operand on a data bus.

7) The CPU transfers the floating point instruction address (FIA) through the data bus.

8) The FPU gets the FIA on the data bus and executes floating point arithmetic.

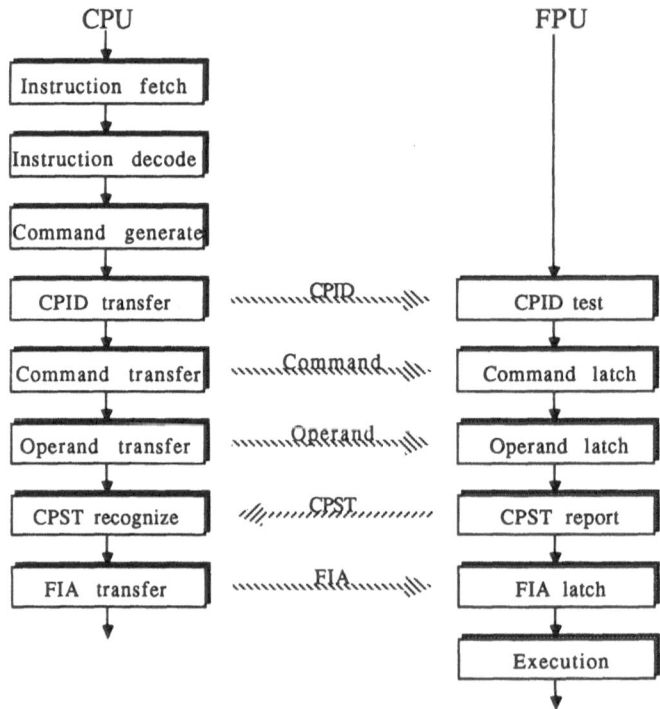

Fig. 5    Protocol in floating point processing

As described above, the FPU internal status is provided to the CPU through the CPST signal without using the system bus.    It is reported to the CPU when the CPU transfers an operand to the FPU.    Operand transfer between memory and the FPU is directly performed under CPU bus control.    Therefore the FPU can quickly obtain the operand to execute floating point arithmetic.    Thus, high speed coprocessor operation can be realized.

## 5. HIGH SPEED FLOATING-POINT OPERATION

### 5.1  Basic Architecture

#### (a) Registers

The FPU is based on a general register machine.    The FPU has sixteen 80-bit floating point data registers (FR0-FR15) which are completely general purpose.    Fig. 6 shows the FPU programming model.    In addition to FR0-FR15, the FPU has several registers which can be accessed by FPU transfer command execution.    These registers are three control registers containing FSR, FMCR and FQR, and a constant ROM in which ten constants are stored.

Functional summary of each register is given below.

1) FR0-FR15: Floating point registers to store floating point data.

2) FROM$0-FROM$15: Constant ROM to store fixed constants used frequently for floating point operations, e.g. $\pi$ .

3) FMCR: Mode control register to specify trap enable bits and mode bits to set the rounding modes.

4) FSR: Status register to store condition codes and accumulated exception status.

5) FQR: Quotient register to store the quotient after executing a remainder instruction.

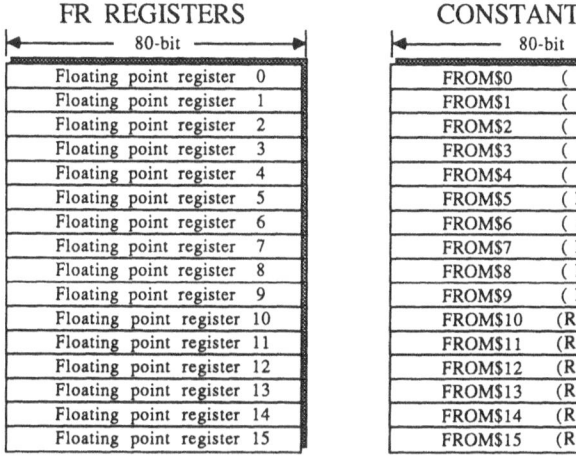

FR REGISTERS — 80-bit

| Floating point register | | CONSTANT ROM — 80-bit | |
|---|---|---|---|
| Floating point register 0 | | FROM$0 | ( +0.0 ) |
| Floating point register 1 | | FROM$1 | ( +1.0 ) |
| Floating point register 2 | | FROM$2 | ( $\pi$ ) |
| Floating point register 3 | | FROM$3 | ( $\pi/2$ ) |
| Floating point register 4 | | FROM$4 | ( e ) |
| Floating point register 5 | | FROM$5 | ( $\log_e 2$ ) |
| Floating point register 6 | | FROM$6 | ( $\log_e 10$ ) |
| Floating point register 7 | | FROM$7 | ( $\log_{10} 2$ ) |
| Floating point register 8 | | FROM$8 | ( $\log_{10} e$ ) |
| Floating point register 9 | | FROM$9 | ( $\log_2 e$ ) |
| Floating point register 10 | | FROM$10 | (Reserved) |
| Floating point register 11 | | FROM$11 | (Reserved) |
| Floating point register 12 | | FROM$12 | (Reserved) |
| Floating point register 13 | | FROM$13 | (Reserved) |
| Floating point register 14 | | FROM$14 | (Reserved) |
| Floating point register 15 | | FROM$15 | (Reserved) |

CONTROL REGISTERS

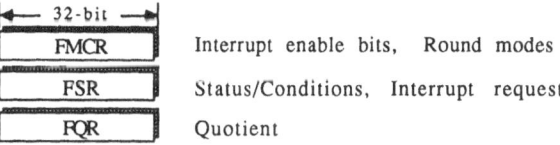

— 32-bit —

| FMCR | Interrupt enable bits, Round modes |
| FSR | Status/Conditions, Interrupt request |
| FQR | Quotient |

Fig. 6    FPU programming model

*(b) Internal Structure*

Fig. 7 shows the FPU's internal structure. The FPU chip has three main elements, **a bus control unit** (BCU), **a format conversion unit** (FCU) and **a floating point execution control unit** (ECU).

1) Bus Control Unit: The bus control unit is responsible for handshakes with the main processor. The response to the bus cycles, initiated by the main processor, and the protocol carried out in order to complete the necessary data/status transfer between the main processor and the FPU are all administered by this unit.

2) Format Conversion Unit: In the FPU, all floating point data are represented in one internal data format. The operands sent from the main processor or the memory are all converted to the internal floating point data format before the actual arithmetic operation starts. Once the store operation of the floating point data is completed, the data are again converted into the external format as defined in the IEEE Standard. The format conversion unit carries out the above conversion operations.

3) Tag Logic Unit: The floating point data format can express those values such as infinities, zeros and not-a-number. The arithmetic operations involving these special values are done in the tag logic unit. In addition, the sign of a result can be decided in this unit.

4) Exponent Arithmetic Unit: The addition/subtraction operations for the exponent calculations are done in the exponent arithmetic unit.

5) Mantissa Arithmetic Unit: The addition, subtraction, shifting and other operations necessary for the mantissa of floating point values are done in the mantissa arithmetic unit.

6) Multiplier: The multiplier can carry out high speed floating point multiplication operation.

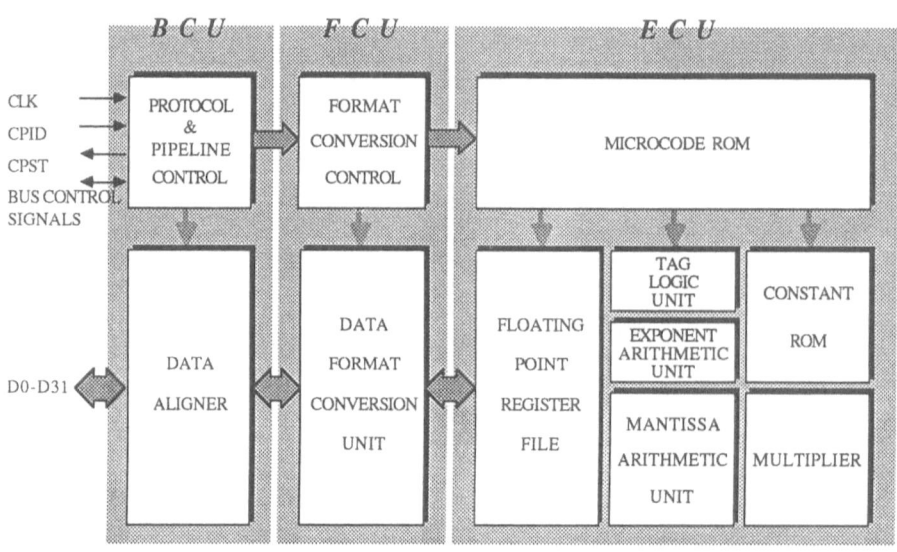

Fig. 7    FPU's internal structure

## 5.2 Command Pipeline

### (a) Pipeline Operation

The FPU performs pipeline processing to improve floating point operation speed. When the FPU executes floating point instructions, each of the three main elements, BCU, FCU and ECU in the FPU chip performs multiple instructions concurrently.

Fig. 8 shows the basic mechanism of the command pipeline. When a floating point instruction is executed in the FPU after the CPU performs instruction fetch and effective address calculation, the operation sequence is divided into three phases as described below.

1) In the BCU processing phase, the BCU fetches the command and operand. Next the BCU fetches FIA.

2) In the FCU processing phase, as soon as the FCU gets the operand, it converts data of the IEEE Standard format into data of the original format.

3) In the ECU processing phase, the ECU performs floating point arithmetic.

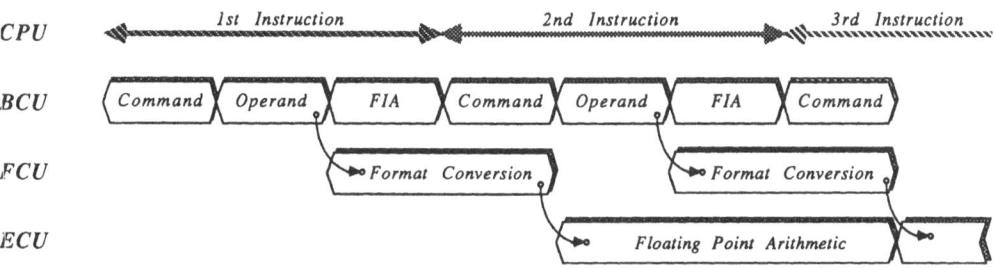

Fig. 8    Basic mechanism of the command pipeline

In order to perform high speed calculation, the FPU chip is designed so that the three processing phases operate in parallel within the FPU command pipeline operation. The status of each processing phase in command pipeline operation is as follows:

1) The first instruction executes the ECU processing phase.

2) The second instruction executes the FCU processing phase.

3) The third instruction executes the BCU processing phase.

Accordingly, the FPU command pipeline operation can execute up to three instructions concurrently.

*(b) Performance*

Table 3 shows the operating speed of basic floating point instructions and the frequency of each instruction in the Whetstone benchmark program. As shown in the table, the FPU executes floating point addition in 0.5 µs and floating point multiplication in 0.45 µs at a 20-MHz clock rate. The FPU executes floating point instructions in this benchmark program in about 0.119 s. The GMICRO/200 takes about 0.091 s and communication overhead between the FPU and GMICRO/200 is 0.025 s. When we take the GMICRO/200 or GMICRO/300 CPU's performance into consideration, the system performance with the FPU and either GMICRO CPU is expected to achieve 4 MWIPS performance at a 20-MHz clock rate.

Table 3    Operating speed of basic floating point
instructions and their frequency

| INSTRUCTION | OPERATING SPEED (μs) | FREQUENCY | RATES (%) |
|---|---|---|---|
| ADDITION | 0.5 | 36890 | 21.54 |
| SUBTRACTION | 0.5 | 4160 | 2.43 |
| MULTIPLICATION | 0.45 | 22900 | 13.37 |
| DIVISION | 1.6 | 11400 | 6.65 |
| SINE | 6.2 | 3200 | 1.87 |
| LOAD | 0.3 | 40120 | 23.43 |
| STORE | 0.85 | 44640 | 26.07 |

### 5.3  High Level Instructions for Graphics

Aside from supporting the IEEE Standard Floating-Point Arithmetic, the FPU has special commands for graphics applications.   They are FDOTPR and FLIMIT.

FLIMIT is a command to aid in limit check for clipping operation in graphics applications.   Fig. 9 shows an FLIMIT command example.   FLIMIT compares AX with XMIN and AX with XMAX.   The result of the comparison is stored in the FSR.   When a comparison of the abscissa AX and a comparison of the ordinate AY are completed, it can be judged whether the point A exists in the window or not.   In the example such as shown Fig. 9, it can be judged easily by using this command whether segment AB exists in the window or not.

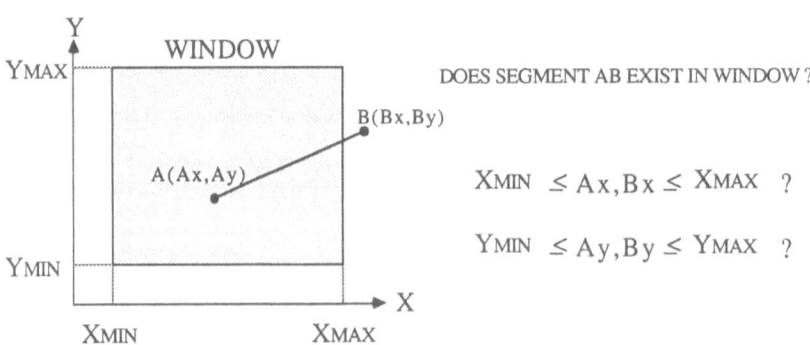

Fig. 9    FLIMIT  command  example

FDOTPR is a command to aid in calculating a convolution of row and column matrices for coordinates transformation in three-dimensional graphics applications. It can specify up to eight dimensions. An example of four dimensions is as follows:

$$[\,FR0\ \ FR1\ \ FR2\ \ FR3\,]\begin{bmatrix} FR4 \\ FR5 \\ FR6 \\ FR7 \end{bmatrix} = FR8$$

By making use of these commands, high speed processing of clipping operation and coordinates transformation for graphics applications is expected.

## 6. CHIP DESIGN

Photo. 1 shows a microphotograph of the FPU. The FPU can be fabricated with advanced 1.0-micron CMOS design technology to operate at a 20-MHz machine cycle. It is implemented in a 14.05 mm × 13.37 mm die. It has integrated five hundred forty thousand transistors. The sixteen 80-bit general registers, two arithmetic units, multiplier, constant ROM and the microcode ROM are all implemented in this chip.

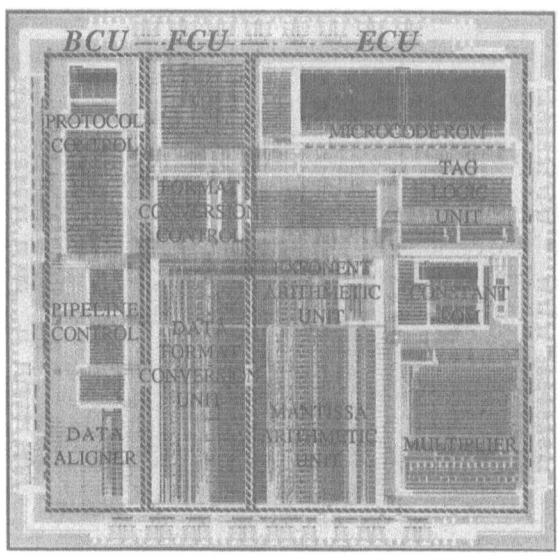

Photo. 1   Microphotograph of the FPU

## 7. CONCLUSION

We have developed a floating point processing unit (FPU) which has the following features:

1) The FPU is a coprocessor of the 32-bit GMICRO microprocessor family based on TRON specifications.

2) The FPU is provided as a chip for performing floating point arithmetic operations based upon the IEEE 754 Standard for Binary Floating-Point Arithmetic and high level arithmetic operations for graphics applications.

3) The FPU employs pipeline processing to improve floating point operation speed. The FPU command pipeline operation can execute up to three instructions concurrently. As a result, the FPU executes floating point addition in 0.5 µs and floating point multiplication in 0.45 µs at a 20-MHz clock rate. The FPU with GMICRO CPU is expected to achieve 4 MWIPS performance.

This architecture should be effective for high speed floating point arithmetic.

## ACKNOWLEDGEMENTS

We would like to extend our sincere thanks to Messrs. H. Yasuda, T. Kihara, Y.Tominaga, Dr. I. Masuda, Dr. T. Bando and Dr. H. Maejima for giving us the opportunity to develop this FPU and for their useful suggestions during the work.

## REFERENCES

[1] TRON Project 1987, Open-Architecture Computer Systems, Proceedings of the Third TRON Project Symposium.

[2] "A Proposed Standard for Binary Floating-Point Arithmetic", (Draft 10.0 of IEEE Task P754) IEEE Floating Point Subcommittee Working Document, Dec. 2, 1982.

[3] J.S. Walther, "A Unified Algorithm for Elementary Functions", AFIPS 1971 Spring Joint Comput. Conf., 1971, pp.379-385.

[4] C. Huntsman et al., "The MC68881 Floating-point Coprocessor", IEEE Micro, Vol.3, No.6, Dec. 1983, pp.44-54.

[5] R.J. Simcoe et al., "A Floating Point Unit for a 32-bit Microprocessor System", Proceedings of the IEEE 1984 Custom Integrated Circuits Conference, May 1984, pp.478-481.

**Hiroyuki Kida**: He is a researcher of the Hitachi Research Laboratory, Hitachi Ltd. He has been engaged in research and development on microprocessor. He received a B.E. and a M.E. degrees in electronic engineering from Ibaraki University in 1980 and 1982 respectively.

**Mitsuru Watabe**: He is a researcher of the Hitachi Research Laboratory, Hitachi Ltd. He has been engaged in VLSI architecture of machinery control. His interests include electro-machinery control with microcomputer. Watabe received a B.E. and a M.E. degrees in electrical engineering from Musashi Institute of Technology in 1981 and 1983 respectively.

**Tetsuaki Nakamikawa**: He is a researcher of the Hitachi Research Laboratory, Hitachi Ltd. He has been engaged in research and development on architecture for microprocessor. He received a B.E. and a M.E. degrees in information science from Utsunomiya University in 1983 and 1985 respectively.

**Shigeki Morinaga**: He is a senior researcher of the Hitachi Research Laboratory, Hitachi Ltd. He has been engaged in research and development on control LSI. He received a B.E. and a M.E. degrees in electrical engineering from Kyushu University in 1970 and 1972 respectively.

Above authors may be reached at: Hitachi Research Laboratory, Hitachi, Ltd., 4026 Kuji-cho, Hitachi-shi, Ibaraki, 319-12 Japan

**Shumpei Kawasaki**: He is a VLSI design engineer of the Microcomputer Engineering Dept. at Musashi Works, Hitachi Ltd. He is presently engaged in development of 32-bit microprocessor LSIs. He received B.A. degree in mathematics from Knox College in 1978 and M.S. degree in Computer Science from the University of Illinois at Urbana-Champaign in 1980.

**Hideo Inayoshi**: He is a senior engineer of the Microcomputer Engineering Dept. at Musashi Works, Hitachi Ltd. He is presently engaged in development of 32-bit microprocessor and peripherals. He received a B.S. and a M.S. degrees in applied physics from the University of Tokyo in 1969 and 1971 respectively.

Above authors may be reached at: Microcomputer Engineering Dept., Musashi Works, Hitachi Ltd., 5-20-1 Josui-Honcho, Kodaira, Tokyo, 187 Japan

# High Performance Bus Interface of GMICRO/300

Takeshi Kitahara, Masanobu Yuhara, Atsushi Fujihira,
Masato Mitsuhashi, Matao Itoh
FUJITSU LIMITED

## ABSTRACT

This paper shows external interface of GMICRO/300 which is a high performance 32-bit microprocessor based on the TRON architecture. External interface has block-fetch function to achieve high- performance and address monitor function to keep internal cache's consistency on multi-CPU system. Block fetch has 64 Mbytes/second transmission rate at a 20 MHz CPU machine clock.

**Keywords:** Physical cache, Address monitor, Block-fetch, Multi-processor, External-TAG

## 1. INTRODUCTION

In proportion to the advances of semiconductor technology, micro- processors have become very powerful. More functions have been integrated on one chip, moreover, the clock rate has become very higher. A gap, however, between access time of main memory and CPU clock cycle is left as a restriction of system performance. In order to solve this problem, we use cache memories, which are high speed associative memories. *Fig.1* shows the configurations of GMICRO/300 CPU. The GMICRO/ 300 CPU has cache memories, 2 Kbytes of instruction cache and 2 Kbytes of operand cache. For a cache system, it is very important that the external bus interface has high-speed data transfer. We implemented block-fetch protocol. From another point of view, on a multi processor system, cache memories must be kept consistent with the external common memory.

This paper explains two major characteristics of GMICRO/300 CPU's external interface that are high-speed bus interface and mechanism to keep cache consistency.

## 2. HIGH-SPEED BUS INTERFACE

We designed GMICRO/300 CPU bus specification so that it has a high speed data transfer performance. This chapter shows the fundamental bus specification, and the specification for high-speed data transfer (block- fetch).

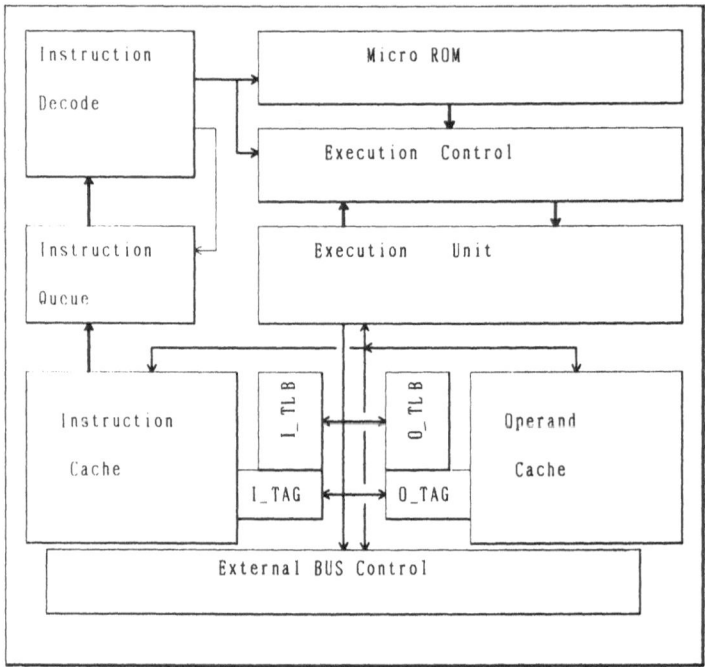

*Fig.1  Block Diagram*

## 2.1 Fundamental Bus Interface

GMICRO/300 CPU has bus interface which is based on asynchronous protocol. We chose this protocol because when synchronous protocol is adopted, it is difficult for external devices to have the interval time between bus command and response to be adapted to CPU bus cycle, or run at the same clock rate as CPU. *Fig.2* shows fundamental bus interface of GMICRO/300 CPU. This processor executes one bus cycle in 2 machine-cycles without memory wait cycle. There are two typical strobe signals. The first signal, named *AS (Address Strobe), indicates the validity of Address, R/W (Read/Write), BC0-3 (Byte controls), and BAT0-2 (Bus Access Type like Function Code of MC68020). The second signal, named *DS (Data Strobe), indicates the end of bus cycle and the validity of write data in write cycle. GMICRO/300 CPU has two types of ready-signals, *SDC (Synchronous Data transfer Complete) and *ASDC (Asynchronous Data transfer Complete). A device which is near to the CPU may use *SDC which has 1/4 machine cycle margin more than *ASDC. On the other hand, a device which is far from the CPU that it is unable to run on the CPU's synchronized clock may use *ASDC. *SDC or *ASDC indicates the validity of the Read Data, *BERR (bus error status signal), and *RETRY (request signal to retry bus cycle).

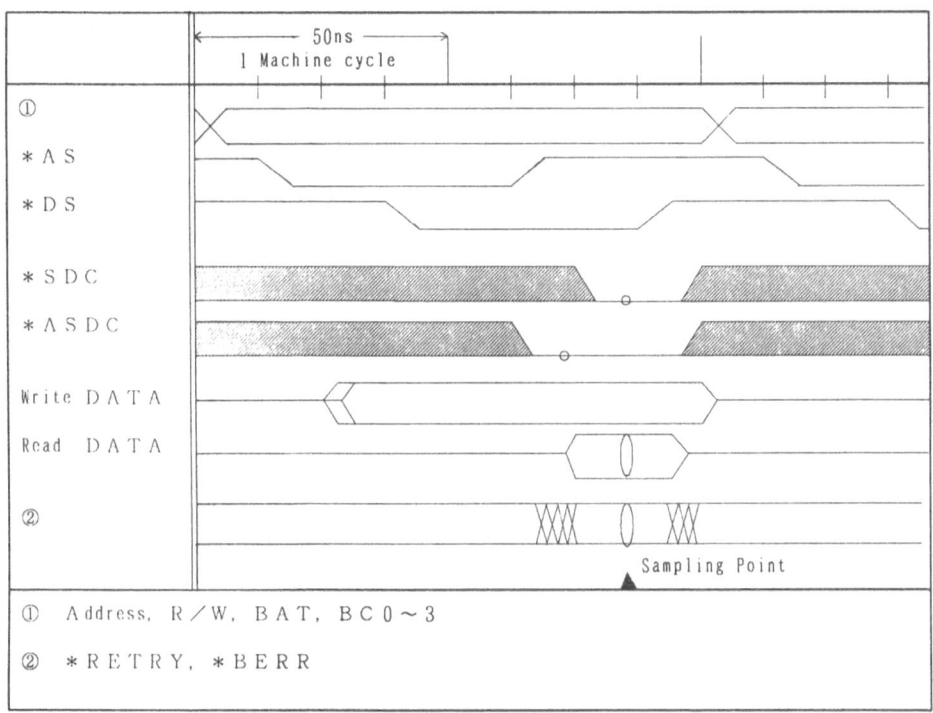

*Fig.2  Fundamental BUS CYCLE*

## 2.2 Block Fetch Protocol

Block size is an important parameter of cache memories. The larger the block size is the more effective the cache is, on condition that memory access time is short. GMICRO/300 CPU has two caches which consist of two sets of 64 blocks (**16 bytes/block**) each. Block size was decided for reasons of data bus width and nibble mode of Dynamic RAM which may be used in main memory. In order to make the memory access time short, we implemented block-fetch function. We estimated two level cache memory system shown in *Fig.3*. The first cache memory is an internal cache, and the second cache memory is an external large cache whose speed is higher than main memory's. So that we implemented two modes of block-fetch function such as synchronous mode and asynchronous mode. The two modes are able to be selected in a bus cycle dynamically by two acknowledge signals. ( *BLACKF: Block Access ACKnowledge for Fast mode or *BLACKS: Block Access ACKnowledge for Slow mode.)

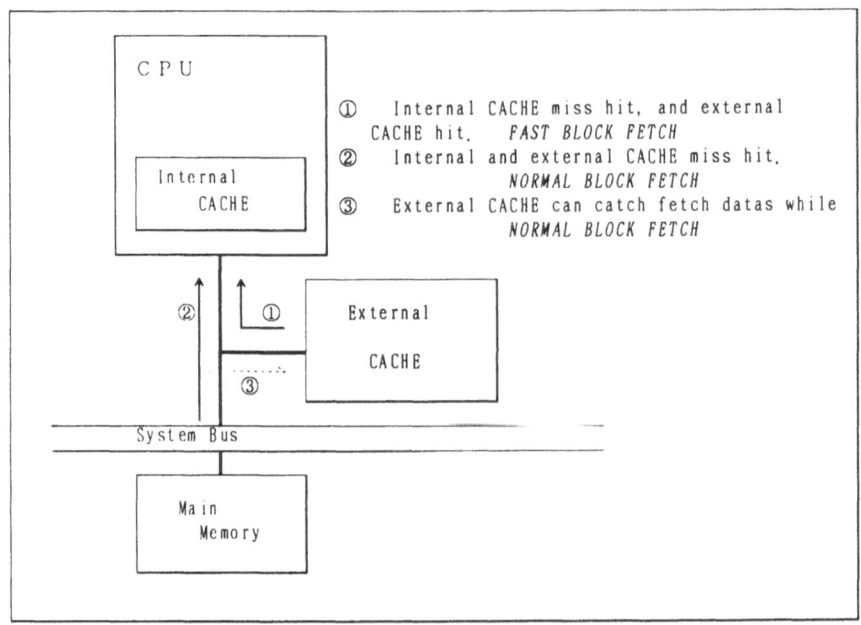

Fig.3   2 Level CACHE System

## (1) Synchronous mode

When the internal cache miss occurs, synchronous block fetch would be taken and data would be fetched from external cache memory which may be near to the CPU and can run on the synchronized clock of CPU. This mode has a **64 Mbytes/second** rate. In this mode, the first word needs at least two machine cycles (able to be kept waiting by *SDC, or *ASDC), and from the second word to the fourth word are transmitted on every machine cycle. One block (16 bytes) is transmitted in a minimum of 5 machine cycles ( 250 ns at a 20 MHz CPU clock). This protocol is shown in *Fig.4*. GMICRO/300 CPU has two bus clocks (BCLK1 and BCLK2). These two output clocks give the timing of data fetch to the external devices. Therefore users can implement easily synchronous block-fetch mode with these clocks.

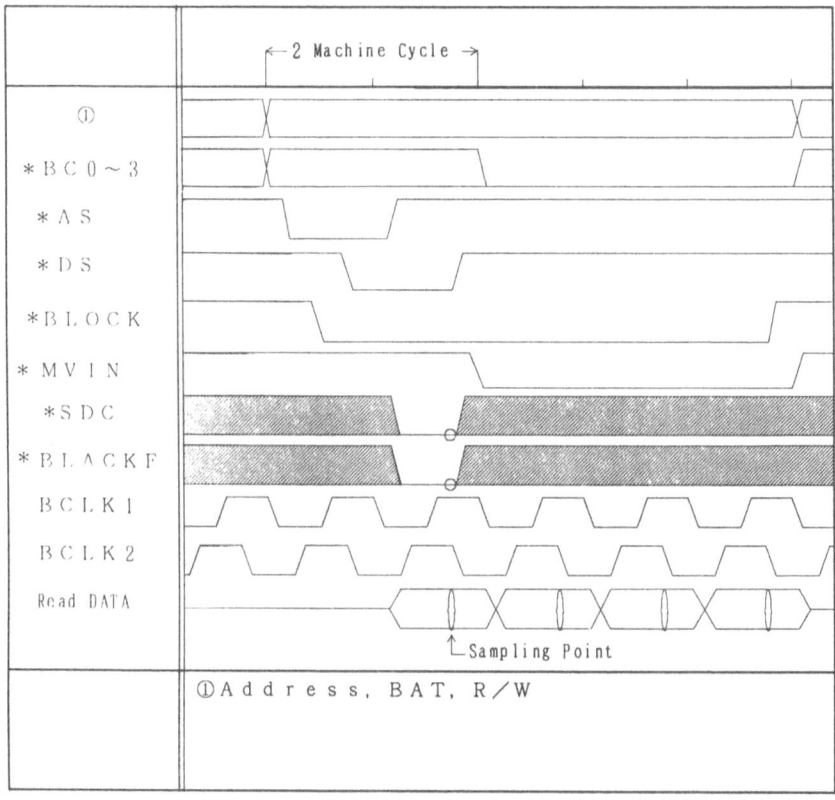

*Fig.4  Synchronous BLOCK Fetch*

## (2) Asynchronous mode

When external cache memory also misses, asynchronous block-fetch is used and data is fetched from the External common memory. This mode has a **40 Mbytes/second** rate. In this mode, transmit from the first word to the fourth word need at least 2 machine cycles, and each cycle can be kept waiting by *SDC or *ASDC. This protocol is shown in *Fig.5*. In this protocol , the CPU and the External cache can catch the fetched data simultaneously without exclusive hardware to make bus sequence for transmitting data to the external cache.

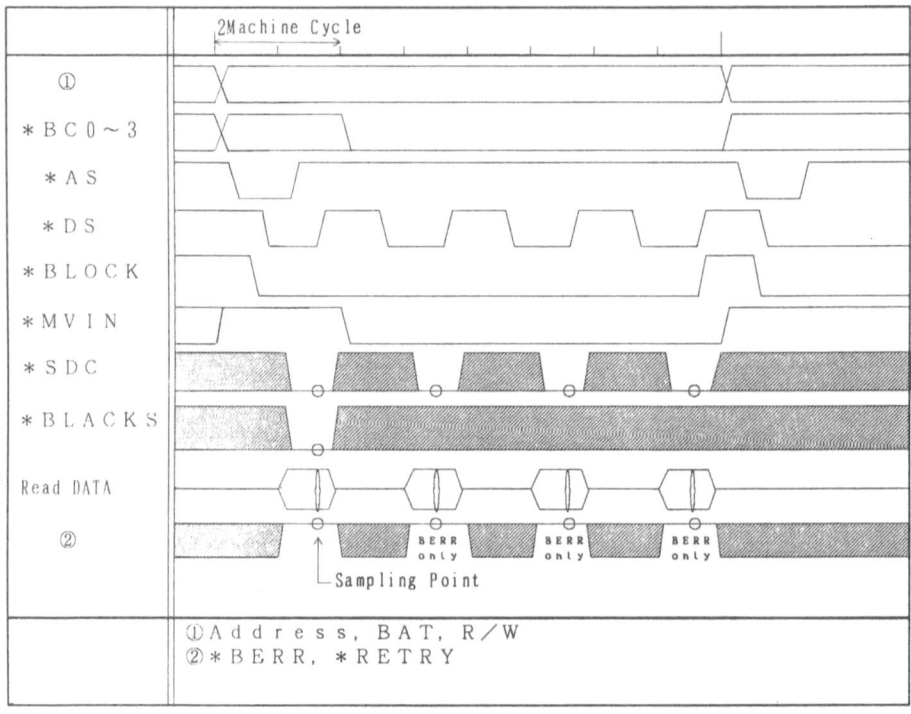

*Fig.5  Asynchronous BLOCK Fetch*

## 2.3 Examples

Concerning with **D-RAM** cycle time, a typical sample has 180 ns as cycle time, 80 ns as access time, and 45 ns as cycle time of nibble mode.

### (1) Non block-fetch

When block fetch is not used, four accesses must be executed, each access spends 200 ns ( > 180 ns) at a 20 MHz CPU clock. One block transfer spends at least **800 ns** (200 ns x 4).

### (2) Asynchronous block-fetch

When asynchronous block fetch is used, the first word may be transmitted in 200 ns and from the second word to the fourth word may be transmitted in 100 ns each in D-RAM nibble mode. One block is transmitted in **500 ns** (200 ns + 100 ns x 3 ).

## (3) Synchronous block-fetch

When synchronous block fetch can be used, the first word may be transmitted in 200 ns, and from the second word to the fourth word may be transmitted in 50 ns each in synchronized mode. One block is transmitted in only **350 ns** (200 ns + 50 ns x 3 ).

Block fetch makes the access time of one block to be 1.6 - 2.3 times faster than non block-fetch. We can see that the block-fetch function is effective to the cache system.

## 3. CACHE CONSISTENCY ON MULTI PROCESSOR SYSTEM

It is a very important subject to keep consistency between cache memory and the external common memory on multi processor system. There are two typical ways to realize the consistency. The first is software control. Under the software control, overhead of operating system lets system performance go down, and the operating system software must know the timing to recover consistency, and must manage to purge or invalidate cache memories after some device writes data to external common memory. The second is hardware control. Under hardware control, software doesn't have to be conscious of cache's consistency at all and the operating system software doesn't need to know the

### 3.1 Physical cache or Logical cache

The two cache memories of GMICRO/300 CPU which has address translation function, are composed as physical caches, because it is easy to recover consistency with the external common memory when an external device writes data to external common memory. If we composed these caches as logical caches, and tried to keep consistency automatically, we would have needed an inverted table to look up logical address from external physical address, but this table needs a large number of transistors or logic gates, and the implementation of this table is very difficult for a one chip device.

### 3.2 Address Monitor Function

The GMICRO/300 CPU monitors external bus, while it isn't a bus master. In bus slave mode, the processor watches *DS signal, and when the signal is asserted by an external device, the processor latches Address, R/W, BAT0-2 on the external bus. Only when R/W indicates write (='0') and BAT0-2 indicates CPU Data, CPU Instruction, or Co-processor Data (='000', '001', '100'), the processor compares external address with addresses in internal cache TAGs. If the address matches, the processor invalidates one corresponding block (internal caches are implemented as a store through cache). This can be done every machine cycle.

Also in bus master mode, on the operand store cycle, the corresponding block of the internal instruction cache is invalidated when store address is hit on the instruction.

We designed internal cache **TAGs as 2 port memories,** so that this CPU can execute instructions and monitor external addresses simultaneously while the instruction and its operand hit on internal caches. Therefore users can implement easily the consistency of the cache memory with the external common memory by use of the Address Monitor Function which the GMICRO/300 CPU has.

### 3.3 External TAG interface

In addition to the address monitor function, we prepared a method to decrease the frequency of address monitor in the system shown in *Fig.6*. Address monitor has to be executed whenever an external device writes a data to external common memory. Each processor can't use only local-bus while the address monitor is executed.Then the merit of local memory decreases and the processor's performance decrease.

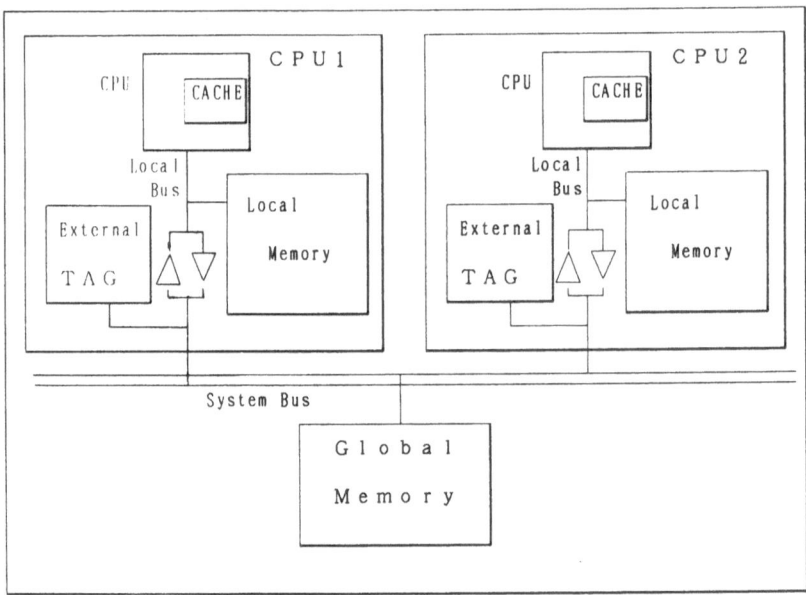

*Fig.6 Multi Processor System*

In order to avoid this problem, the External TAG ( that is a copy of each processor's internal TAG indicating certain addresses that their internal caches hold) may be provided beside the outer local memory.

A mechanism to decrease the frequency of address monitor is shown in *Fig.7.1* and *Fig.7.2*.

*Fig.7.1* shows a replacement mechanism of the internal cache and the External TAG. GMICRO/300 CPU reads one block data from the Global Memory, when the External TAG latches the block address. In the CPU, it waits for whole block data to record the block data into the internal cache. When the whole block data reaches to the internal Buffer, the data is memorized into the internal cache, and the CPU sends signals to indicate replaced set and timing strobe to the External TAG. The External TAG records the latched block address into the internal memory.

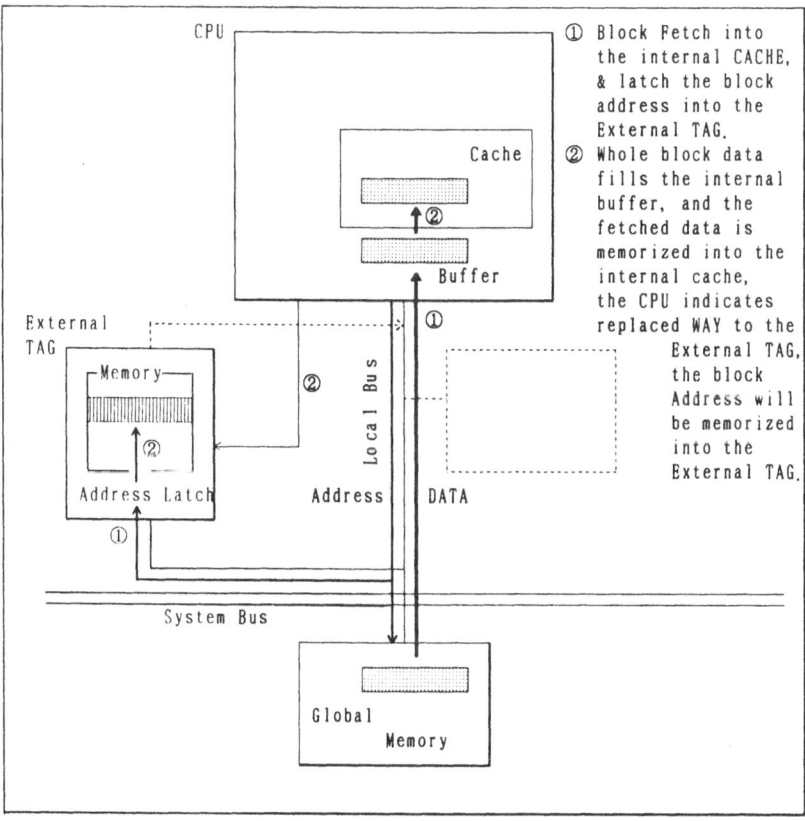

*Fig.7.1  Replacement Mechanism*

326

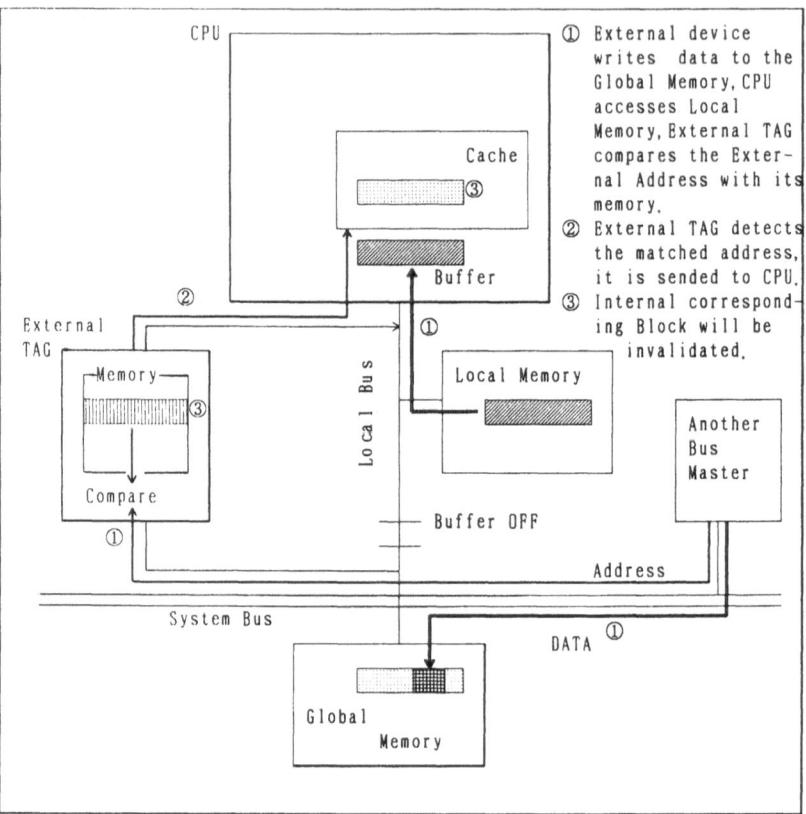

*Fig.7.2  Invalidation Mechanism*

*Fig.7.2* shows an invalidation mechanism of the internal cache. The CPU is running with the Local Memory while an external device writes data to the Global Memory. The External TAG watches the store address, and compares the address with the addresses in its internal memory. Only if the store address matches the internal address, the External TAG requests bus master to the CPU, and sends the matched address in the form of Address Monitor Function. The GMICRO/300 CPU has four output signals to interface the External TAG.

-   A signal to indicate the set to be changed (internal cache has two sets )
-   A signal to indicate the timing of changing the internal TAG
-   A signal to indicate that the internal instruction cache is purged
-   A signal to indicate that the internal operand cache is purged

The address monitor function and this interface to the External TAG memories are very useful to make the system performance higher in a multi-processor system.

## 4. CONCLUSIONS

1) High-speed bus interface (2 types of block-fetch mechanism) is supported to use internal caches effectively.

2) A mechanism (address monitor function) to make the consistency of internal caches with external common memories is supported for multi processor system.\

3) An interface to external TAG is supported to decrease the frequency of the address monitor for high-performance multi processor system.

We designed GMICRO/300 CPU to be adapted to high performance workstation, or multi processor system.

## ACKNOWLEDGEMENTS

The authors would like to thank Ken Sakamura, professor of the University of Tokyo and the members of the GMICRO group, Hitachi Ltd., and Mitsubishi Electric Corp, for their cooperation.

## REFERENCES

[1] K. Sakamura, "Architecture of the TRON VLSI CPU", IEEE Micro, April 1987, pp.17-31.

[2] A. J. Smith, "Cache Memories", Computing Survey , Vol.14, No.3, September 1982.

[3] K.Sakamura, "TRON VLSI CPU: Concepts and Architecture", TRON Project 1987, Springer-Verlag, pp. 200-238.

[4] "MC68020 32-Bit Microprocessor User's Manual", MOTOROLA Inc., 1984.

**TAKESHI KITAHARA** received the B.S. in applied physics from the University of Tokyo in 1980. He has been engaged in Gmicro/300 logic design group.

**MASANOBU YUHARA** received the B.S. in electronics engineering and the M.S. in electrical engineering from the University of Tokyo in 1982 and 1984, respectively. He has been engaged in Gmicro/300 logic design group.

**ATSUSHI FUJIHIRA** received the M.S. in electrical engineering from Chiba University in 1984. He has been engaged in Gmicro/300 logic design group.

**MASATO MITSUHASHI** received the B.S. and the M.S. in electrical engineering from Kanagawa University in 1984 and 1986, respectively. He has been engaged in Gmicro/300 logic design group.

329

**MATAO ITOH** received the B.S. in electrical engineering from the University of Tokyo in 1970. He is a manager of Gmicro/300 logic design group.

Above authors may be reached at: Microcomputer Development Department, MOS Division, Semiconductor Group, FUJITSU LIMITED. 1015, Kamikodanaka, Nakahara-ku, Kawasaki, 211 Japan

# A 40 MB/s 32 Bit DMA Controller with 3411 Product Terms PLA

Masaharu Kimura, Tomonobu Iwasaki, Shosuke Mori,
Koichi Fujita, Sagoro Hazama
FUJITSU LIMITED

## ABSTRACT

A 32 bit DMA controller with the maximum data transfer rate 40 MB/sec implemented with 380K transistors on a 11.14 mm x 10.46 mm chip in a 1.2 µm, 2 metal layers CMOS process, is reported. This paper describes the design of large (28 inputs, 30 outputs and 3411 product terms) and high speed access (12.1 ns typ.) PLA.

**Keywords:** DMA, DMAC, PLA, Peripheral LSI

## 1. INTRODUCTION

This chip has been developed as a peripheral LSI for 32 bit Gmicro CPU which based on TRON architecture[1] and supports data transfer between 8 / 16 /32 bit width peripheral device and memory, and between memories. There are four 32 bit DMA channels, which can be set independently to single or dual address mode and to cycle steal mode or burst mode. Descriptor chaining allows continuous transfer among multiple blocks. Byte, half word, word, or long word(64 bit) transfer units may be selected. The byte control signal and word assembly / disassembly function allow transfer from any byte address boundary and transfer between peripheral devices or memories of different data sizes. There are several DMA BUS interface implementations exist for various system applications . Asynchronous BUS interface method is adopted to this DMAC chip specifications. This interface does not depend on specific synchronous CPU clock signals, and thus provides much flexibility to system designers. This chip also supports data transfer between two isolated buses and may reside between two microprocessor buses and control the data transfer between them. An interrupt control function and message buffer are built in for communications between the CPUs in each of the two buses.

## 2. OUTLINE OF PLA DESIGN

Implementing above various specifications of DMA transfer mode functions and high performances, following three design methodologies had been discussed.

1) random logic gate design

2) micro program

3) PLA

In the case of random logic gate design, this DMA transfer mode functions were estimated to correspond to about 15K gate random logic. At this level of gate number size, the sum total wiring area will become serious problem rather than its sum total cell area. In the case of micro programming, there exist some critical path that micro programming method cannot achieve its operation within the requested cycle time. We reached to a conclusion that PLA design method is the most proper way to satisfy both area size reduction and high access speed.

*Fig.1* shows the block diagram of this chip. 37 PLAs exist in this chip totally and several problems arise along with these PLAs development. The largest original PLA which we called the Gate control PLA had 28 inputs, 30 outputs and 7306 product terms at the beginning stage. Minimization, compression and partition DA tools reduced this to the level of 3411 total product terms consisted of 26 clustered PLAs.

First, we partitioned the Gate control PLA into two groups by each output function categories. One PLA has 7 outputs and other has 23 outputs. And next, we subdivided each of them into ten kinds of PLAs by each AND-OR terms.

And then, we tried the minimization for each of them incrementally and got the final PLA including 13 x 2 =26 clustered PLAs.

## 3. PLA CIRCUIT IMPROVEMENTS

A compact and efficient PLA architecture is a necessary requirement of any PLA based LSI system to maximize packing density and hence increase of performance and yield. *Fig.2a* shows a part of circuit diagram of our dynamic logic circuit based PLA. PLA elements such as AND array driver, OR array driver, sense amplifier are requested minimum area size, but these parameters are also the trade off for the determination of PLA access speed. The ordinary pre-charge control circuit such as shown as *Fig.2b* causes much consumption of chip area because of its imbalance of their layout pitch with each AND array outputs and OR array inputs. In the case of this chip, since the precharge control circuit shown as *Fig.2a* is constructed by simple logic, it can be possible to layout all of them with same layout pitch height. This new improved circuit

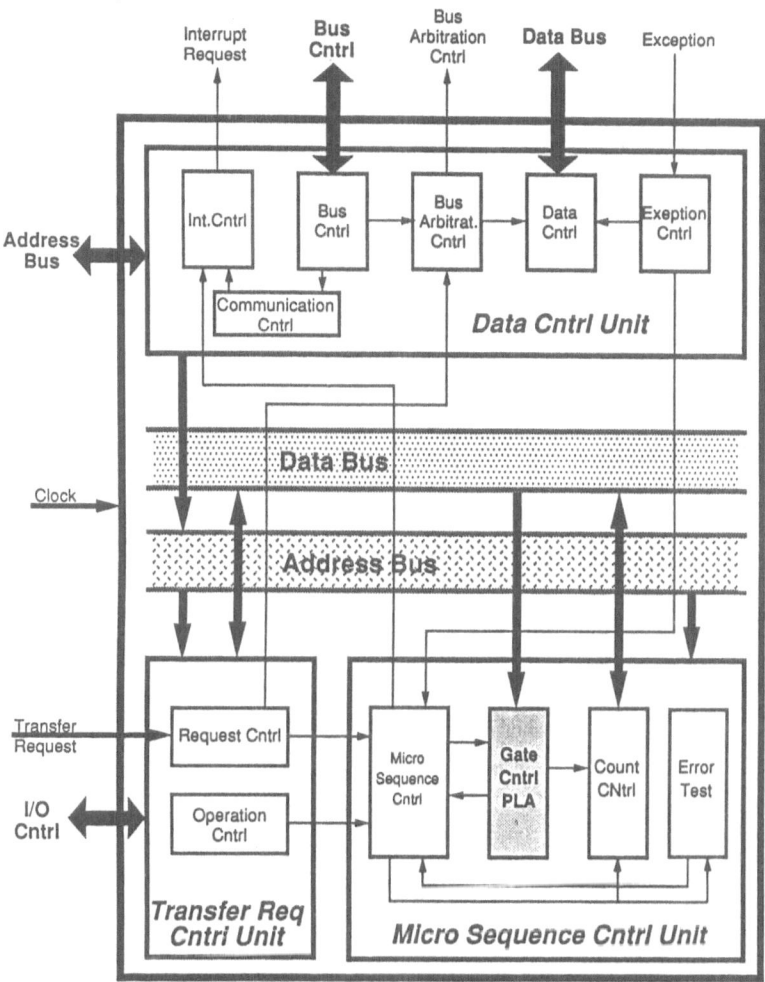

**Fig. 1 Dmac Block Diagram**

also provides the merit for reducing the area size of the pre-charging transistors which drive PC2 and PC2# signals and hence makes a contribution to improve the PLA access speed. In *Fig.2b* circuit, the value of loading capacitance of pre-charge signal (PC2#) shows large sum number of their connected inputs of NAND gate and this causes the increase of area size of pre-charge signal driver transistor.

*Fig.2a* shows an improved OR array driver circuit. This circuit has less number of transistors and achieved to reduce the block area size to the level of one per three to one per four of *Fig.2b* circuit. And another important merit is that only the active OR array drivers will become as load capacitance, so we can reduce the driving capability of pre-charge transistor and then this contributes the improvement of the PLA access speed.

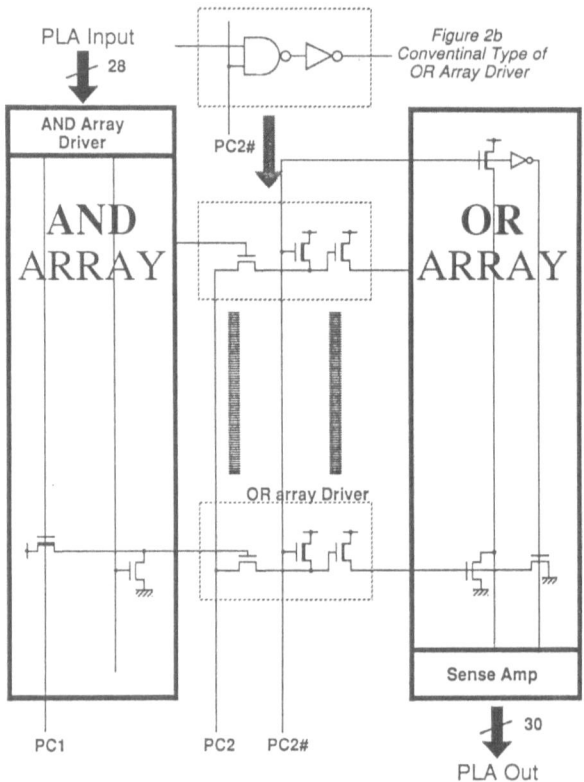

**Fig. 2a   PLA Block Diagram**

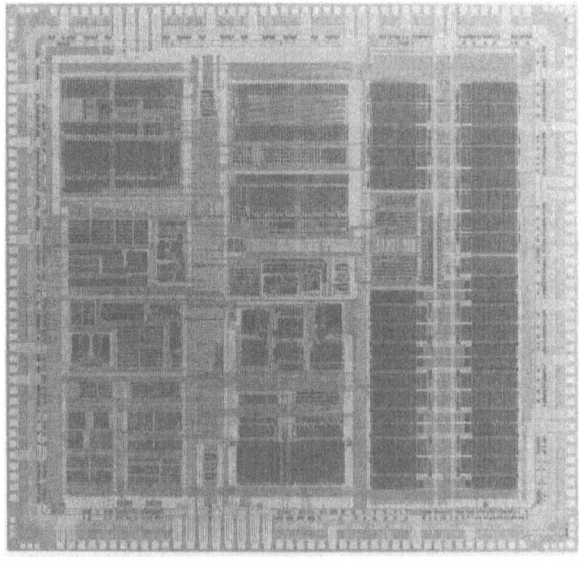

**Fig. 3   Photomicrograph of Chip**

## 4. PLA LAYOUT DESIGN

Layout design with each above mentioned clustered PLAs was performed to be configured on a same height level in that each of them has 132 product terms. *Fig.4a* shows the layout structure of each PLAs before optimization. On this state, sizes of AND-OR terms are different by different PLAs and therefore this imbalance causes the increase of wasteful layout dead area. To solve this problem, the method of layout design shown as *Fig.4b* was employed. The total number of AND array inputs increased from 12 to 20 inputs. These increased 8 inputs signals are utilized for decoding PLA#1 and PLA#2 or PLA#4 and PLA#2. Although the number of AND array inputs are increased, homogeneous height of merged PLA itself has no wasteful layout area, and then this contributes to the cut down of total LSI chip size.

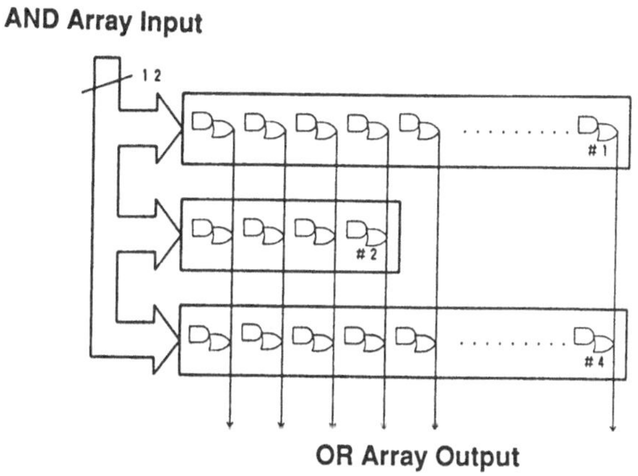

**Fig. 4a   PLA Before Optimization**

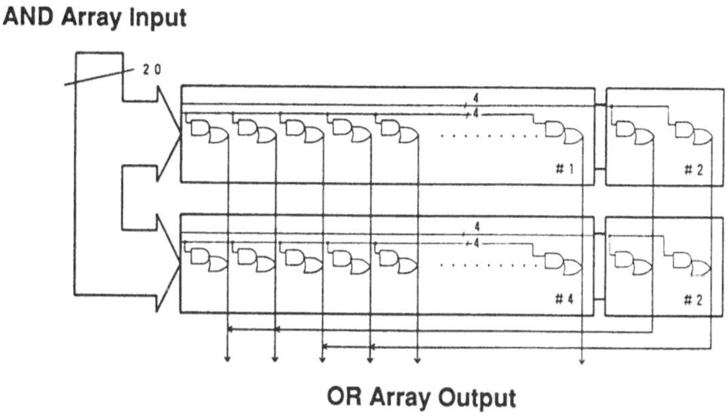

**Fig. 4b   Optimized PLA Configuration**

## 5. CONCLUSION

*Fig.3* shows the photomicrograph of this chip. The total access time 12.1 nsec(typ.) from the AND array driver inputs to the OR array sense amplifier outputs after each period of precharge cycle is achieved (See *Fig.5*). This value shows about 70% faster than our previous designed conventional type of PLA. A rough area size estimation has also been done if in the case of ordinary random logic design was employed instead of above mentioned PLA design method. According to this estimation, this PLA block is equivalent to consisted 15,000 logic gates and because of its increase of wiring area, the block area size will be at least 1.5 times larger than the original PLA block if random logic design was employed. This chip characteristics summary is shown in *Table 1*.

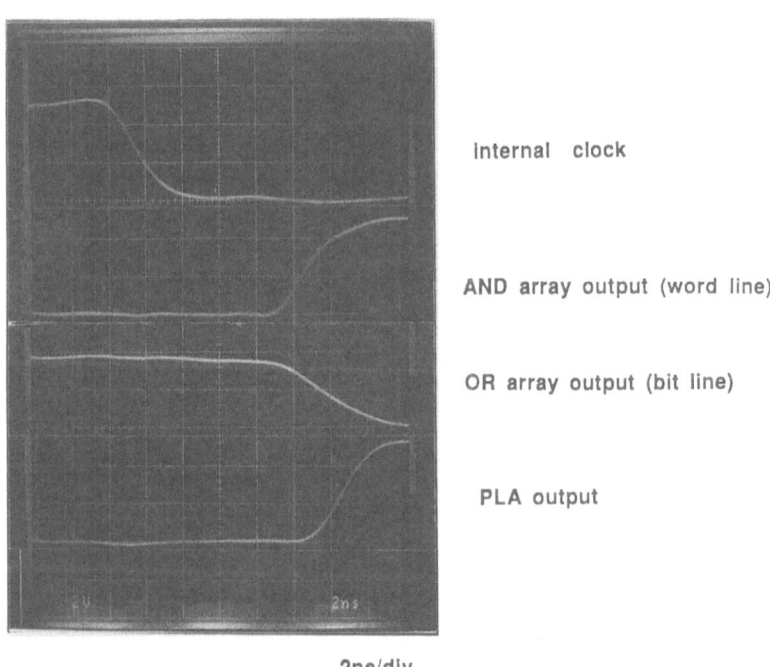

Internal clock

AND array output (word line)

OR array output (bit line)

PLA output

2ns/div.

**Fig. 5 Oscilloscope Pictures of PLA Output Waveform**

**Table 1.  Chip Characteristics**

| | |
|---|---|
| Process | Double - metal layer CMOS |
| Design Rule | 1.2 μm |
| Transistors | 380,000 |
| Chip size | 11.14 mm x 10.46 mm |
| PLA size | 28 inputs, 30 outputs |
| | 3411 product terms |
| Clock Rate | 20 MHz |
| Microcycle | 50 nsec |
| Transfer Rate | 40 MB/sec |
| Power Dissipation | 1.0 W |
| Power Supply | + 5 V |
| Package | 179 pin PGA |
| #Signal Pads | 128 |
| #Pwr / GND Pads | 18 / 26 |

ACKNOWLEDGMENTS

This accomplishment was a team effort. Acknowledged are ; Yoshinori Hatano for his timely tools development ; Hidenori Hida for his logic designs. Many people with many skills were associated with this project. To all who helped, our thanks.

REFERENCE

[1]  K. Sakamura, "Architecture of the TRON VLSI CPU", IEEE Micro, April 1987, pp.17-31.

338

**Masaharu Kimura** is a senior engineer of GMICRO peripheral LSI design group at Microcomputer Development Division, FUJITSU LIMITED in KAWASAKI, JAPAN. He joined FUJITSU LIMITED in 1969. He was engaged in logic design of LSI and support tools. He is engaged in development of 32 bit peripheral LSI and logic design methodology of full custom LSI.

**Tomonobu Iwazaki** is a senior engineer of GMICRO LSI design group at Microcomputer Development Division, FUJITSU LIMITED in KAWASAKI, JAPAN.He was engaged in development of MCUs and peripheral LSIs, and has been engaged in development of GMICRO LSI.He received a B.E. degree in electrical engineering from Tohoku University in 1978.

**Shosuke Mori** is a manager of GMICRO peripheral LSI design group at Microcomputer Development Division, FUJITSU LIMITED in KAWASAKI, JAPAN. He was engaged in process engineering of bipolar memories, and in development of personal computer systems. He received a M.E. in chemical engineering from Tokyo Institute of Technology in 1973.

**Koichi Fujita** is a manager of GMICRO LSI design group at Microcomputer Development Division, FUJITSU LIMITED in KAWASAKI, JAPAN. He was engaged in development of MPU and MCU LSIs, and has been engaged in development of GMICRO LSIs and layout design methodology of full custom LSI.He received a B.E. degree in electronics engineering from University of Electro-Communications in 1972.

339

**Sagoro Hazama** is the director of GMICRO project group at Microcomputer Development Division, FUJITSU LIMITED in KAWASAKI, JAPAN. He was engaged in CAD systems engineering of LSIs, and in development of personal computer systems. Since then, he has been engaged in development of microprocessor LSIs, softwares and systems. He received a B.E. and M.E. degrees, both in electronics and communication engineering, from Tohoku University in 1966 and 1968 respectively.

Above authors may be reached at: Microcomputer Development Department, MOS Division, Semiconductor Group,FUJITSU LIMITED 1015 Kamikodanaka, Nakahara-ku, Kawasaki, 211 Japan

# Development of a C Compiler for Gmicro Microprocessor Based on TRON Architecture

Yugo Kashiwagi, Hideaki Chaki, Masachika Narushima
Hitachi Ltd.

**ABSTRACT**

Hitachi Ltd. has developed a C compiler for Gmicro microprocessor which is based on TRON architecture. The compiler implements the language specification based on the ANSI standard draft, and constitutes unified programming environment with other cross development tools.
This paper describes high-level-language oriented features of Gmicro architecture which facilitates the generation of efficient object code and optimization techniques of the compiler to utilize these features.

**Keywords:** C Compiler, Chained Addressing Mode, Gmicro Microprocessor, Optimization, Pipeline Control

## 1. Introduction

We have adopted the C language as the main language for system software development of Gmicro microprocessor and have implemented its compiler. The compiler constitutes a unified cross software development environment for Gmicro with other tools such as assembler, linkage editor, and simulator/debugger. The compiler has the following features:

1) Language specification based on ANSI (American National Standard for Information Systems) draft standard of the Programming Language C[1]
2) High performance object program
3) Output of debugging information to enable symbolic debugging
4) Generation of ROMable object programs

In the following chapters, we will discuss the generation of high performance object code for Gmicro microprocessor in detail. At first, high-level-language oriented features of the Gmicro architecture from the viewpoint of C compiler implementation are discussed, and then optimization techniques of the compiler are presented.

## 2. High-level-language Oriented Features of Gmicro Architecture

Gmicro architecture has many features which facilitates the implementation of high level languages. These features are derived from extensive investigations of high-level-language behavior. In this chapter, we list these features and discuss them from the viewpoint of the compiler implementation.

(a) Sixteen general registers
The CPU and FPU each have 16 general purpose registers. This facilitates flexible register assignment by the compiler.

(b) Orthogonal operands
Each combination of addressing modes and data sizes may be specified in both the source and destination operands of arithmetic instructions. This enables unified processing by the compiler of arithmetic operations, including type conversion.

(c) High-level addressing mode
Up to four levels of address indirection, displacement, and index register can be specified in one high-level addressing mode (chained addressing mode). This facilitates the implementation of pointer operations or array references in the C language.

(d) Data type support for high-level languages
Arithmetic instructions are provided for both signed and unsigned data. Mixed-type operations are easily implemented by the orthogonality of the operand specification, where data conversion is automatically performed.

(e) Efficient implementation of frequently used instructions
Frequently used instructions (e.g., MOV instruction) are provided in short format that executes at high speed and reduces program size.

(f) Support of function call/return instructions
Standard function (procedure) entry and exit operations are performed at high speed by ENTER and EXITD instructions. These instructions significantly reduce the overhead of subroutine call.

(g) High-level instructions
Fixed-length bit field instructions or character string handling instructions enable the operation of bit fields or struct type data in one instruction.

(h) High-level jump instructions
High-level jump instructions (ACB and SCB instructions) which increment or decrement loop counter and perform conditional jump are implemented as one instruction.

With these features, even a simple code generation scheme can attain fairly efficient object program performance. Each basic operation of the C language (not only simple arithmetic operations but also bit field and struct assignment operations) has a corresponding Gmicro instruction, and these correspondences are almost optimal.

But there remain further possibilities of code optimization. For example, simple code generation scheme cannot generate high-level instructions which does not correspond to basic operations of the C language. We have studied these possibilities of optimization and implemented them in our compiler.

## 3. Optimization by the C Compiler Utilizing Gmicro Features

Our C compiler implements various optimization techniques to improve the execution speed of the object code. Table 1 shows the optimization techniques which we have adopted and common with other microprocessors.

### Table 1 General Optimization Techniques of the C Compiler

| No. | Optimization Technique | Effect |
|-----|------------------------|--------|
| 1 | Constant folding | Constant expressions are calculated at compile time |
| 2 | Elimination of common subexpressions | Common expressions are evaluated only once |
| 3 | Strength reduction of operation | All operations are converted for optimal speed (e.g. converting multiplication to a shift operation) |
| 4 | Deletion of unnecessary instructions | Unexecuted instructions are deleted |
| 5 | Deletion of unnecessary branches | Redundant branch instructions are deleted |
| 6 | Elimination of common code sequences | Duplicated code sequences are merged |

Besides these general optimization techniques, we have developed several techniques specific to Gmicro architecture.

We will present three Gmicro specific optimization techniques here. Two of them extract the full possibility of high-level features of Gmicro architecture: high-level addressing modes and high-level instructions. The third one is the optimization for the pipeline control of instruction execution.

### 3.1 Generation of High-level Addressing Mode

In this section, we will discuss how the C compiler generates the high-level addressing mode for Gmicro to improve the execution speed of the object program.

The Gmicro architecture has a high-level addressing mode called chained addressing mode. This addressing mode can specify indirection, index, and displacement up to four levels. It expresses accesses to arrays, pointers, and more complicated data structures such as list or tree structure efficiently. In performing complicated address calculations, chained addressing mode avoids storing temporary results in registers and improves execution speed of object programs.

The following examples show how chained addressing mode is specified in Gmicro assembly programs.

**Example**

        MOV        @(@(R0,R1*4,10),R2,R3*2,10),R4

In Gmicro assembly program, we can specify complicated operands. In the specification of the operands, "@" indicates one level indirection, and "*" indicates the scaling factor of the index value.

The first operand of the above example indicates the contents of the address "@(R0, R1*4, 10) plus R2 plus R3*2 plus 10", where "@(R0, R1*4, 10)" specifies the contents of addresses "R0 plus R1*4 plus   10".

This may be written in C-like notation as:

*(*(R0 + R1*4 + 10) + R2 + R3*2 + 10)

Since one level of chained addressing mode consists of an index register and a displacement value, the first operand consists of three levels of chained addressing mode.

The following example shows object codes with and without chained addressing mode.

**C Program Example** (Underlined part compiled)

```
char *a;
f()
{
        register int b, c;
        char d[80];
             ⋮
        a = &d[b+c+1]+1;
             ⋮
}
```

**Object Program Example without Chained Addressing Mode**

        MOV        R14,R0
        ADD        R13,R0
        ADD        R12,R0
        SUB        #78,R0
        MOV        R0,@__a

                                        Execution time: 10 (cycles) *

**Object Program Example with Chained Addressing Mode**

        MOVA        @(R12,R13,-78,R14),@__a

                                        Execution time: 8 (cycles)


*: Machine cycles are that of Gmicro/200

To generate optimal object code, the compiler examines the expression tree from its leaves and synthesizes the corresponding addressing mode from the locations of each operands leaves. Fig. 1 shows how the final complex addressing mode is synthesized from the expression tree.

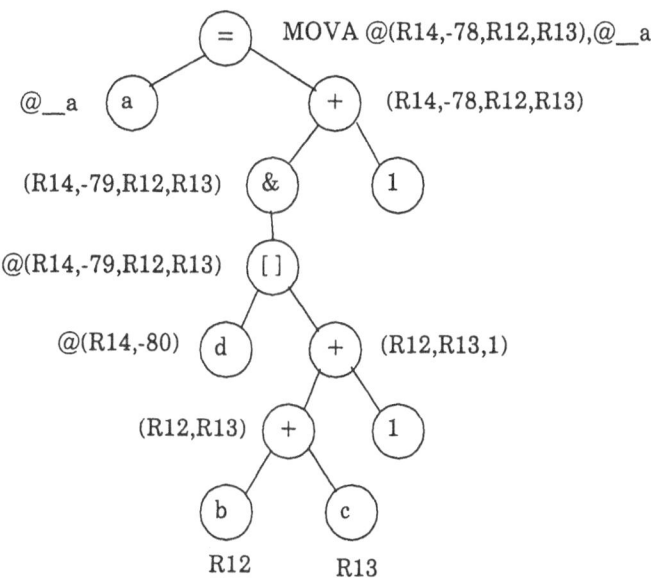

Fig. 1 Generation of Chained Addressing Mode

Since chained addressing mode provides functions such as addition, subtraction and multiplication, it may be used not only for pointer or array access but for normal arithmetic operations. The following is an example of this technique:

**C Program Example** (Underlined part compiled)

```
int a;
f()
{
        register int b;
        ⋮
    a = b*12;
        ⋮
}
```

**Object Example without Chained Addressing Mode**

```
MOV    R13,R0
MUL    #12,R0
MOV    R0,@_a
```

Execution time: 13 (cycles)

**Object Example with Chained Addressing Mode**

        MOVA      @(R0*4,R0*8),@__a

                                        Execution time: 6 (cycles)

Multiplication of a variable and a small integer, which frequently appears in usual programs, can be efficiently implemented without using MUL instruction, as shown above.

However, the selection of the chained addressing mode is not always optimal. As the chained addressing mode does not leave intermediate results on registers, the subsequent object code cannot make use of these intermediate results. So our compiler performs common subexpression detection and register allocation before the generation of chained addressing mode. When an intermediate expression result is detected as a common subexpression and allocated to a register, the compiler stops the generation of chained addressing mode there, and assigns the intermediate result to the register.

## 3.2 Generation of High-level Instructions

Some of the Gmicro high level instructions do not correspond to basic C language operations. Among these instructions, string handling instructions correspond to string handling standard library functions. In usual implementation, these library functions are implemented as subroutines. In our implementation, to use these high-level instructions effectively, the C compiler recognizes library calls and generates these instructions in line.

Table 2 lists the library functions which is implemented by inline expansion.

### Table 2  Library Functions and Corresponding Gmicro Instructions

| No. | Function Name | GMICRO Instruction | No. | Function Name | GMICRO Instruction |
|---|---|---|---|---|---|
| 1 | memcpy | SMOV | 8 | strncmp | SCMP |
| 2 | strcpy | SMOV | 9 | memchr | SSCH |
| 3 | strncpy | SMOV | 10 | strchr | SSCH |
| 4 | strcat | SSCH, SMOV | 11 | strrchr | SSTR |
| 5 | strncat | SSCH, SMOV | 12 | memset | SSTR |
| 6 | memcmp | SCMP | 13 | strlen | SSCH |
| 7 | strcmp | SCMP | -- | ---------- | ------------- |

An example of the object code for an inline expansion of a library function is shown below.

**C Program** (Underlined part compiled)

```
char *a;
f()
{
        register int x;
          ⋮
        x = strlen(a);
          ⋮
}
‘
```

**Object Example**

```
        MOV       @__a,R0
        MOV:Z     #0,R2
        MOV:Z     #0,R3
        SSCH.B/EQ
        ADD       #1,R2
        NEG       R2
        MOV       R2,R13
```

Inline expansion of library functions reduces function call overhead and enables efficient allocation of registers before/after a library call.

### 3.3 Optimization for Pipeline Control of Instruction Exectuion

The compiler includes optimization for pipeline control of instruction execution and parallel processing between the FPU and CPU. The compiler improves execution speed of the object program by reordering the instruction sequence to eliminate sequences that disturb pipeline control or FPU and CPU parallel execution. There are following two cases in which this optimization is effective.

1) Pipeline control is disturbed when a register is used for address calculation just after being set.

2) If a CPU instruction is executed just after an instruction whose destination is an FPU register, the instruction can be executed in parallel.

Instructions are reordered in the following stages.

1) Instruction sequence is re-constructed into a directed graph which reflects the mutual dependence of each instruction.

2) The instruction sequence which disturbs pipeline control is reordered under the conditions indicated by the dependency graph.

The following is an example of instructions reordered by the compiler.

**C Program** (Underlined part compiled)

```
f()
{
        register int b, c, *d;
        int a;
            ⋮
        c = a + b;
        d = &a;
        b = *d;
        c + +;
            ⋮
}
```

**Object Sequence before Reordering**

| ① | MOVA | @(@(R14,-4), R13),R12 |
|---|------|------------------------|
| ② | MOVA | @(-4,R14),R11 |
| ③ | MOV  | @R11,R13 |
| ④ | ADD  | #1,R12 |

In the above example, the dependence relation between the instructions is first re-constructed into a directed graph. Instructions are dependent if they access to the same registers, memory areas, or flags. Fig. 2 shows the dependence relation of the instructions for this example.

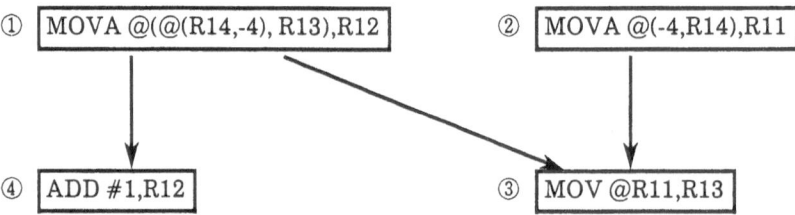

**Fig. 2 Dependence Relation Graph of Instruction Sequence**

According to this graph of dependence relations, the compiler generates the most suitable instruction among the candidates for the next instruction. Instruction sequence ② and ③ uses the same register for address calculation just after it is set, and executing these instructions sequentially disturbs pipeline control. So the compiler selects the instruction ② rather than ① as the first instruction in this sequence, which is possible because there is no dependency relation between ① and ②. The final output from the compiler is as follows.

**Final Output Instruction Sequence**

| ② | MOVA | @(-4,R14),R11 |
| ① | MOVA | @(@(R14,-4), R13),R12 |
| ③ | MOV | @R11,R13 |
| ④ | ADD | #1,R12 |

This output instruction sequence avoids disturbance of pipeline control between ② and ③, which took one extra machine cycle.

## 4. Conclusion

This paper discussed the implementation of a C compiler on a 32-bit Gmicro microprocessor. Being the main language for Gmicro system software development, the implementation emphasizes standard language specification, a unified environment for program development, and high-speed object code.

Gmicro architecture can execute the C language at high speed. This is accomplished not only by the high-level language oriented features of its architecture itself, but also by the extensive optimization by the C compiler utilizing addressing modes and instruction sets for high-level languages. Besides, optimization for pipeline control improves the generated object code.

We are now preparing to evaluate the performance of the object programs and effects of each optimization technique for real-world programs in various application fields. And planning to implement further optimizations based on the result of evaluation.

## REFERENCES

[1] ANSI(1986), Draft Proposed Standard - Programming Language C. ANSI X3J11 Language Subcomitee, X3J11/86-0074 May 1986.

[2] Inayoshi H, Kawasaki I, Nishimukai T, Sakamura K(1988), Realization of Gmicro/200. IEEE micro, pp12-21, april 1988.

[3] Kida H, Watabe M, Nakamikawa T, Morinaga S, Kawasaki S, Inayoshi H(1988), A Floating Point Processing Unit for the Gmicro CPU. In: TRON Project 1988, Springer-Verlag, Tokyo Berlin Heidelberg New York.

**Yugo Kashiwagi** is an engineer in the Microcomputer System Engineering Department at Musashi Works, Hitachi Ltd. He is presently engaged in development of C compilers for microprocessors. He received B.S. in mathematics from the University of Tokyo in 1981.

**Hideaki Chaki** is an engineer in the Microcomputer System Engineering Department at Musashi Works, Hitachi Ltd. He is presently engaged in development of compilers and operating systems for microprocessors. He received B.E. in mathematical engineering from Kyoto University in 1979.

**Masachika Narushima** is a senior engineer in the Microcomputer System Engineering Department at Musashi Works, Hitachi Ltd. He is presently engaged in product planning of supporting tools for microprocessors. He received B.E. in printing engineering from Chiba University in 1971.

Above authors may be reached at Microcomputer System Engineering Department, Musashi Works, Hitachi Ltd. 5-20-1 Josuihon-cho, Kodaira, Tokyo, 187 Japan

# Development Support System for TX Series

## Shuichi Ishimaru, Kiichiro Tamaru
Toshiba Corporation

**Abstract**

This paper describes the functions and features of a Development Support System for 32-bit TX Series microprocessor. This System provides several functions for development such as a language processing tool, a debugging support tool, and other software tools as well as a single-board computer, a real-time operating system. This paper introduces software tools that support the development of application program. Moreover, the software to be described in this paper can be applied to AS series workstations and J-3100 series lap-top personal computer, and this paper outlines the development procedures of application programs using these tools.

**Keywords:** TX Series, Software Tools, Object Module Format, Function, Feature

## 1. Introduction

The development support system is characterized by its high level language processing function. This function is provided by the TX Series microprocessor, an optimization processing function that effectively uses instructions for real-time processing, and a detailed user-specification function which allows for easy adaptation to an application system. This system has an important role in the development of any application system used with a microprocessor. It is especially important for a high performance microprocessor such as the TX1 to have a high performance development support system so as to make fullest use of the chip's performance capabilities on the user's application system. High level language is often used for describing application programs that are designed to run an high performance microprocessors. The reason is that both the performance of the microprocessor itself and its effective performance on the application system described in high level language are important.

The Development Support System for TX Series supported an optimization through user controllability, and has been realized a high-quality, performance system. The TX Series Development Support ranging from a software development tool to a system for configuring program parts. This paper reports on the basic support tools developed for these software tools.

Figure 1 shows the basic configuration of the software tools in the TX Series Development System. The software tools consists of C compiler, assembler, linkage editor, librarian, software simulator, debugging monitor ,and performance analyzer. The basic configuration can be divided into a language processing tool which supports programming and a debugging support tool. The section above the executable object in the figure corresponds to the language processing tools and the section below the object to the debugging tools. In this paper, the linkage editor and the debug monitor particularly is explained in detail.

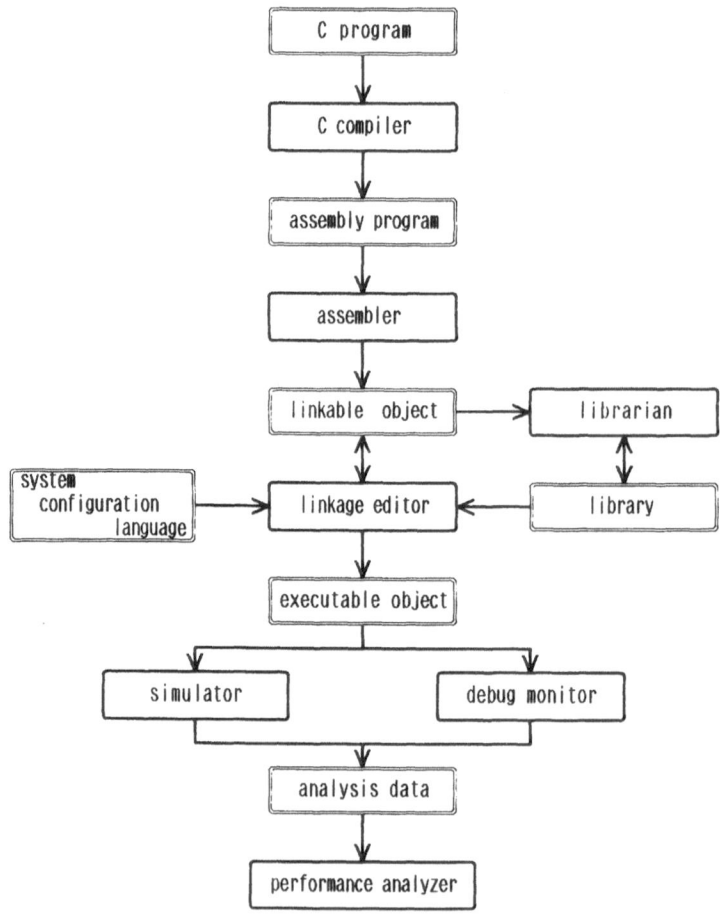

Figure 1  System Configuration of TX Series Development Support System

## 2. Language Processing Tools

The language processing tool is comprised of a C compiler, an assembler, linkage editor, and a library which are needed for developing application programs in C and assembly language.

### 2.1 Compiler

The C compiler is based on the UNIX*System V Portable C Compiler (PCC) specifications. It is characterized by chained addressing mode (multilevel) in TRONCHIP, effective execution of high performance instructions, and high execution and memory efficiencies due to optimized processing. Moreover, it contains function for generating symbolic information for symbolic debugging and the ROMable codes. The most distinctive characteristic of the TRONCHIP instruction set, when viewed from the standpoint of high level language processing, is its chained addressing mode. The chained addressing mode is an addressing mode capable of specifying multiple levels of relative registers with a single instruction. C compiler for TX1 allows up to four stages of multilevel addressing. This characteristic is particularly effective for C language programming where variable access is often made through pointer variables since chained addressing mode can execute a variable access usually requiring several instructions with a single instruction. While the chained addressing mode is advantageous with respect to execution time and memory size, it is disadvantageous in term of its real-time response. This is because all interrupts are disable during the chained addressing mode. The TX Series compiler makes it possible to tailer programming to the specific requirement of an application program by allowing the user to select the maximum stage number of the chained addressing mode.

### 2.2 Assembler

The assembler processes the TRONCHIP standard machine instruction mnemonics and assembly language of the IEEE-694 compatible assembler directives. The TRONCHIP instruction set has several instruction formats for each instruction. The MOV instruction (a data transfer instruction) has the greatest number (7 types) of instruction formats. For example, a MOV instruction for transferring a value of the source field to the destination field can be selected out of 7 instructive formats, from the shortest 2-byte instruction to the longest 8-byte resource. However, in view of instruction execution time and memory requirements it is necessary to select the shortest instruction format. The TX Series assembler has a function that automatically selects the optimal instruction format.

The object module format that is to be used by TX tools is based on the IEEE-695 standard, and includes extensions. An object file is divided into eight component parts including the debug information. Therefore TX tools are able to support debugging for the high level language.

* UNIX is the name of operating system developed by AT&T.

## 2.3 Linkage Editor

The linkage editor can process several linkable objects to generate linkable/loadable objects. The TX Series linkage editor has adopted a specification system which uses system configuration language (SCL). The SCL enabled the user to easily make program arrangements which correspond to the hardware configuration of the application system. It is considered to make ROMable object, therefor it provides three characteristics as follows;

1)specify the memory configuration of the application system,
2)decide the application program module layout,
3)define the EIT and jump-ring table.
(The EIT means Exception, Interrupt and Trap)

Figure 2 shows the SCL example. In this example, the memory declaration defines the available memory area as ROM or RAM. Since the program object divided into section parts, it is assigned to memory area by the section declaration in the SCL. The each section in Figure 2, named sample1 and sample2, is assigned to memory address 0 and 20000(hexadecimal). The table declaration can provide the EIT vector table and the Jump vector table on the available memory area. The EIT is used to represent phenomena that change the program flow. The linkage editor assigns the EIT processing program to a program counter(PC) in the EIT vector table entry by the declaration of the SCL. The EIT vector table entry consists of a processor status halfword for system(PSS) and the PC for executing the EIT processing program. The PSS and PC is specified each the operation mode of the processor and the program counter after execution of JRNG instruction.

Moreover, the linkage editor can provide the jump vector table. In the case of the jump vector table, the linkage editor processes like the EIT vector table processing. Figure 4 shows the EIT vector table entry and Figure 5 shows the jump vector table entry. A value of the PSS, vector ring(VR), and access ring (AR) in the each table entry may be designated by the SCL. The VR is ring level of destination, and the AR is outermost ring level that allows JRNG instructions.

```
begin;
  memory:
        rom  := (    0 -   FFFF) ,
        ram  := (10000 - 1000000) ;
  section:
        sample1 (base :=      0) ,
        sample2 (base := 20000);
  table:
        EIT (base := 0F00000 ,
          entry1 := sample1 ,
          entry2 := sample2 ) ;
  end;
```

Figure 2  System Configuration Language Example

Figure 3 shows the memory definition sample using the SCL in Figure 2. In this way, the SCL can declare the memory layout, the program layout, and table definition in detail.

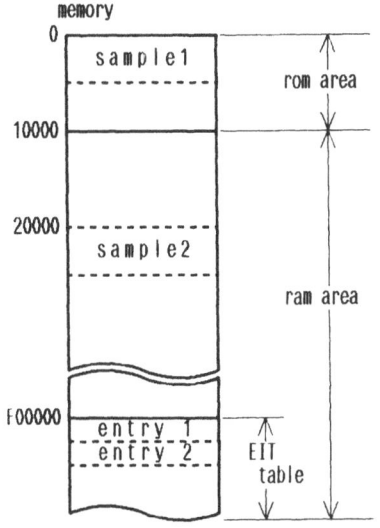

Figure 3  System Memory Layout Example

```
 0            16           31
┌──────────────┬──────────────┐
│     PSS      │   Reserved   │
├──────────────┴──────────────┤
│            P  C             │
└─────────────────────────────┘
```

PSS  :  Operation mode of the processor
PC   :  Program counter

Figure 4  EIT Vector Table Entry

```
 0            16           31
┌──┬────────┬──┬──────────┐
│VR│Reserved│AR│ Reserved │
├──┴────────┴──┴──────────┤
│          VPC           │
└─────────────────────────┘
```

VR   :  Ring level of destination
AR   :  Outermost ring level that allows JRNG instruction
VPC  :  PC after execution of JRNG instruction

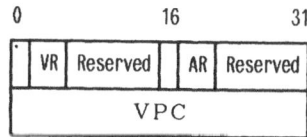

Figure 5′  Jump Vector Table Entry

## 2.4 Librarian

The librarian is a utility that manages library files. The library file organizes object modules made by other tools. The librarian for the TX series can treat several object file types except for the boot-loadable type and it has two operation modes. The one is conversational mode that can allows execute of processing in a lump, and the other is command mode that allows serial processing. The librarian for TX series provides 13 commands which include "add", "delete", "replace", and "extract" etc.

## 3. Debugging Support Tool

The debugging support tool is comprised of a simulator and a debug monitor. The tool provides both cross debugging and self-debugging environments with an identical command.

## 3.1 Simulator

The simulator is a software simulator which operates on the host system. Using an environment set file, the application system memory configuration, input/output device layout and access protection (read/write/executable) can be specified. Another characteristic of the simulator is that it can be used to set up an operand access content which is difficult to resize using actual hardware, or to set up a break condition in response to a combination complicated conditions. Moreover, the debug monitor can be applied to debugging a program having a built-in debug support system which is restricted due to the use of the tool itself. On the other side, processing speed is a problem in the software simulator. This is particularly the case in processor having a complicated instruction format which requires extended processing time for decoding instructions. Given that approximately 80% of the instructions in an ordinary program can be processed with simple decoding using a maximum of the first 10 bits, the TX Series simulator realizes high speed decoding by adopting a table type decoder drive system based on the first 10 bits.

## 3.2 Debug monitor

The debug monitor provides a self-debugging environment which carries out program debugging on the application system by connecting with the host system through the communications port (RS232C, etc.) of the application system. Debugging in both real-time and single step modes is possible using the debugging function built into the TX Series. The debug monitor is superior to the simulator in processing speed and is suitable for program debugging during operation of the application system hardware. Moreover, though its function is more limited than an emulator, this debug monitor can also be used for debugging the application system hardware.

The debug monitor for TX series uses 12 debug registers; DBC, DBS, BA0-BA3, BPC, EXS, FC0-FC1, and FD0-FD1 (Figure 6) and three on-chip debugging support features. The TX's debug feature is as follows;

1) instruction execution breakpoints and data breakpoints,
2) a single-step or multistep (N-step) break, and
3) a flow trace.

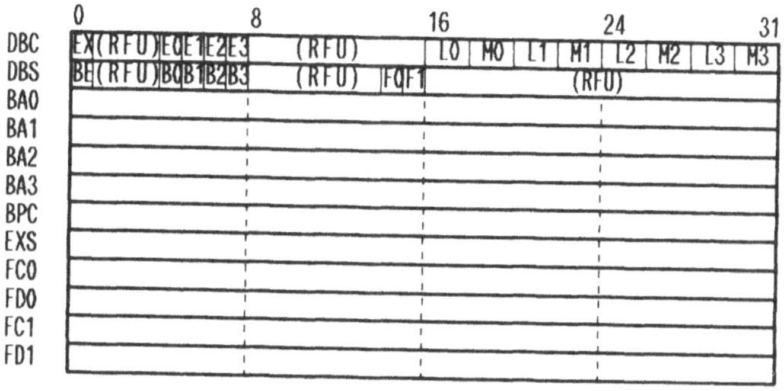

Figure 6  Debug registers

## (a) Breakpoints

The TX1 supports data access breakpoints as well as instruction execution breakpoints by using the BA0-BA3, DBC, and DBS fields. Each of the BA0-BA3's can be loaded with an instruction or data address. Instruction execution breakpoints can be set not only in RAM areas but also in ROM, since memory does not have to be modified to place a breakpoint. For instruction execution breakpoints, the debug EIT occurs before the instruction is executed.

Data breakpoints can be set not only in memory areas but also in memory-mapped I/O areas. For data breakpoints, the debug EIT occurs after the instruction and data access is complete. Data access breakpoints can be set to occur for 1) data reading only, 2) data writing only, or 3) data reading or writing.

The selection among one type of instruction execution breakpoint and three types of data breakpoints(read, write, read or write) is specified by setting the 2-bit M0-M3 fields in debug control register(DBC).

The data breakpoints can be specified to span a 1-byte, 2-byte, 4-byte, or 8-byte region by using the L0-L3 fields in the DBC; any reference within the region causes a trap. Instruction breakpoints must be specified to the exact byte.

When the TX1 detects a debug EIT due to a breakpoint, it sets the bit Bi corresponding to the debug register BAi causing trap.

The action of the 0th breakpoint, specified in the BA0, can be modified by the breakpoint counter (BPC). If the BPC contains a nonzero number K, the BPC is decremented when the BA0 is matched, and no trap occurs. When the BPC is zero, the BA0 breakpoint becomes active.

358

## (b) Single-step or multistep breaks

The TX1 can trap after the Nth instruction. The execution step register (EXS) is set to N + 1 and is decremented after an instruction completes. A debug EIT occurs (provided debugging is enabled) when the EXS reaches zero. The debug EIT program reloads the EXS (with an arbitrary value) before exiting.

## (c) Flow trace.

The TX1 can retain both the byte addresses of the last two executed branch instructions and the byte addresses of their targets. There are two flow current registers (FC0, FC1) and two flow destination registers (FD0, FD1). When the branch instruction is executed, and when debugging is enabled:

1)the contents of FC0 move to FC1, the contents of FD0 move to FD1,
and the contents of F0 (of DBS) move to F1; and
2)the address of the current branch is placed in FC0 and the target
address in FD0; F0 (of DBS) is set to 1.

We classify branch instructions into three types: unconditional branch instruction, including subroutine call and Return, successful conditional branch instructions, and EIT operations (except the debug EIT).

Figure 7 is an example of the flow trace procedure. A program begins from an instruction Ig of an address Ag. The first branch occurs at an address Ai for a branch instruction Ii. At this time the program branches to an address Aa of a branch target instruction Ia. The second branch action for a branch instruction Ij occurs from an address Aj to an address Ab of a branch target instruction Ib. Finally, the program stops at an address Ac of an instruction execution breakpoint. At this time, FC0 is Aj, FD0 is Ab, FC1 is Ai, and FD1 is Aa, and both F0 and F1 are 1.

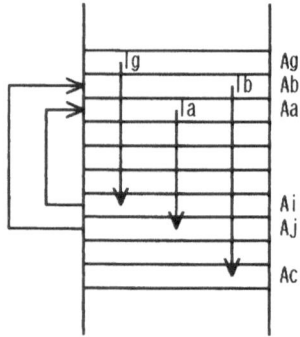

Figure 7  Example of a flow trace

## 3.3 Performance Analyzer

The performance analyzer is used with the simulator or debug monitor and it provides the available function to analyze the performance for the application program. The major function of the performance analyzer is display the calling pass of the routine, the number of executed routine and instruction, condition of register, status of memory access, and coverage in the routine etc.

## 4. Development Procedures for Application Programs

The development cycle of an application program can be typical divided into six basic processes; namely, the decisions specifications, basic systems design, program design, programming, program debugging, and system debugging. The software tool described in the present paper supports the processes form the programming to the system debugging stage of development. The complete programming support environment is available on the AS Series UNIX workstations and others as a host system. Moreover, it can be used on the host system in combination with a general-purpose program, development tool such as a text editor, source code control system, etc.

Processes before program design are supported by the abovementioned general purpose tool. In the actual programming process, the application program is described in either C or assembly language and is translateed into object code by a C compiler or assembler on the host system. Each complete program module is then assembled by the linkage editor into object code in an executable form. Program debugging can thus be executed using the simulator before the actual application hardware has been completed. In this case, if it is not feasible to simulate detailed operation of the hardware equipment, logical operation including interrupts can still be debugged. If the application hardware is completed, system debugging of the application program can begin on this hardware. The debug monitor connects the application program using either the program as ROM or by downloading. Upon completion of system debugging, the application program is completed.

However, MPU is on the high performance and speed trend, and it is difficult to develop the high level emulator and other device correspond to the high speed. Therefore the development support system for TX series aim at the target without complex hardware device. It is a simple system, but it can support by using the debug function on chip.

## 5. Conclusion

This paper reported the function and characteristics of the TX Series Development Support System, focusing mainly on the language processing tool and the debugging support tool. At present, in addition to these basic support tools, the development of other tools is currently underway.

These tools consist of an object translator that support ROMable programs, a real-time emulator and other which support hardware debugging. Moreover, libraries are currently being developed for built-in program as part of the application program.

## 6. Acknowledgment

We would like to thank Ken Sakamura of the University of Tokyo for his helpful suggestions.

## References

[1] M.Miyata et al., "The TX1 32-Bit Microprocessor Performance Analysis and Debugging Support," IEEE MICRO Apr. 1988 p.37-46.

[2] K.Tamaru et al., "Development Support System for TRON TX Series," Toshiba Review Nov. 1988.

361

**Shuichi Ishimaru:** He is a researcher in the Semiconductor Device Engineering laboratory(SDEL) of Toshiba Corporation. He is engaged in development of Support System for 32-bit microprocessor. He graduated from Nihon University in electrical engineering. His current interests include design of Language Processing Tools.

**Kiichiro Tamaru:** He is a specialist at Advanced Microprocessor Technology Department of the Semiconductor Device Engineering Laboratory in Toshiba Corporation. He received the BS, MS, and PhD degrees in electrical engineering from Keio University in 1976, 1978 and 1981, respectively. After joining Toshiba Corporation in 1981, he has been engaged in research and development of the VLSI processor and the software systems for microprocessors.

Above authors may be reached at: Advanced Microprocessor Technology, Semiconductor Device Engineering Laboratory, 580-1, Horikawa-cho, Saiwai-ku, Kawasaki, 210 Japan.

# An Integrated Software Development Toolkit for the GMICRO/200

Antonio Bigazzi, J. E. Lillge, D. E. Jaskolski

Microtec® Research, Inc.

**Abstract**

The GMICRO/200 is a high performance 32-bit microprocessor developed using the standard architecture defined by the TRON (The Realtime Operating System Nucleus) project. The power of the TRON architecture results from its clean design and CISC (Complex Instruction Set Computer) instruction set. Unlike many other compilers that support CISC architectures, the GMICRO/200 C Compiler from Microtec Research, Inc. (MRI) generates code that takes full advantage of the rich CISC instruction set provided by the TRON architecture.

The MRI GMICRO/200 toolkit consists of an ANSI standard C language optimizing compiler, a TRON association syntax-compliant assembler, a linker, an object module librarian, and an innovative source-level debugger/simulator.

This paper presents an overview of the MRI GMICRO/200 Software Development Toolkit and demonstrates its use through a simple application example.

**Keywords:** ANSI C compiler, TRON assembler, source debugger, GMICRO

## 1. Introduction

Microtec Research, Inc. is a company based in Santa Clara, California that provides software development tools such as compilers, assemblers, linkers, simulators, and debuggers. These tools are designed as integrated toolkits, and operate on a variety of popular computer systems.

In the second quarter of 1987, MRI started the development of a GMICRO/200 toolkit. The GMICRO family of microprocessors is being produced as a result of the cooperative effort of three leading semiconductor companies: Hitachi Ltd., Fujitsu Ltd., and Mitsubishi Electric Corporation. Assisted by advance information from these companies, MRI has achieved its goal of developing a complete, integrated set of tools for the GMICRO/200, similar to its popular Motorola/680X0 toolkit. These GMICRO/200 tools are now available on VAX/VMS$^{TM}$ and will be available on other host computers in the near future. Similar tools for other GMICRO processors will also be produced by MRI.

This paper presents an overview of the GMICRO/200 toolkit by employing a simple example of its use. The example is a program that controls an elevator for a six-story building.

The GMICRO/200 is a CISC (Complex Instruction Set Computer). It is often argued that compilers for CISC architectures do not take full advantage of their rich instruction sets. However, we will show that the MRI ANSI-C compiler takes advantage of the full power of the GMICRO/200. The compiler selects the most efficient sequence of instructions possible from the GMICRO/200 repertoire when translating each C statement and expression. Thus, the generated code can make use of architectural features such as special-purpose instructions and Chained Addressing Mode operands when appropriate. The Chained Addressing Mode is a generalized, indirect addressing mechanism unique to the TRON architecture. In general, any addressing expression consists of addition, indirect reference and a scaling operation. The Chained Addressing Mode allows for a cascading of these three operations within operand address calculations. In addition, an innovative feature of the MRI C compiler allows efficient access to the complete instruction set and registers — both for the main CPU and the floating-point coprocessor.

## 2. Toolkit Overview

Fig. 1 shows the GMICRO/200 toolkit and how its components communicate with each other and with the host computer system. The compiler, assembler, linker, librarian, and debugger provide an integrated chain of tools for developing software applications using the GMICRO/200 microprocessor.

## 2.1 Compiler

The C compiler, MCCG32$^{TM}$, is a complete implementation of the emerging ANSI standard. The ANSI standard extends the C language with function prototypes, "const" and "volatile" variables, preprocessor enhancements, and other features to aid development productivity. MCCG32 is designed to help users in their transition to ANSI-C. In particular, much attention has been given to producing informative error messages.

Many users of the C language will gradually upgrade their code from the older K & R C language to ANSI-C to take advantage of these new ANSI features. Although ANSI-C is largely upward-compatible with the older C language, a few incompatibilities do exist. MCCG32 can optionally ignore those ANSI features that conflict, or it can strictly enforce ANSI requirements to ensure conformity.

By combining the power of the TRON architecture with state-of-the-art optimization techniques, MCCG32 produces compact and efficient code. The orthogonal design of the GMICRO/200 allows efficient code to be generated because every addressing mode can be used with every opcode. It also allowed the MCCG32 code generator to be designed in a more straightforward manner so that more focus could be placed on the production of highly optimized code.

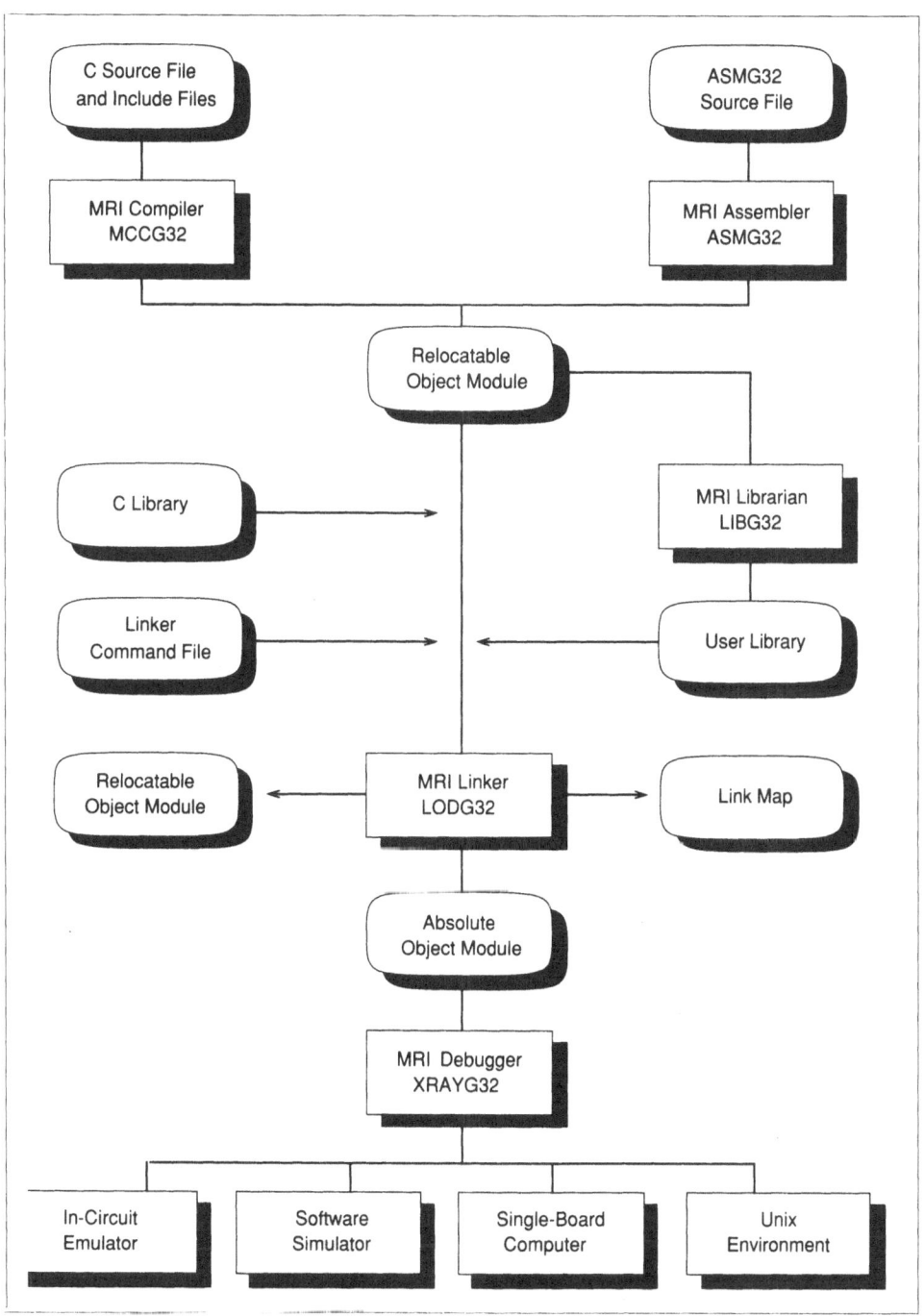

*Fig. 1  Microtec Research GMICRO/200 Toolkit*

Among the many optimizations that MCCG32 employs, the following are particularly significant:

- allocating registers by graph-coloring
- eliminating loop induction variables
- moving invariant code out of loops
- eliminating common sub-expressions
- factorizing frequently used static addresses

The use of a global optimizer as part of MCCG32 results in the generation of much faster and smaller object code than would be possible without it. However, certain optimizations create significant problems for debuggers that are not as well integrated as that of the GMICRO/200 tools. Of particular concern are optimizations for resource use that attempt to maintain the most commonly used variables, addresses and sub-expressions multiplexed in a set of registers rather than in slower main memory. At different points in time, the registers' contents must be associated with the correct program construct. Code movement optimizations merge common code at the beginning and end of conditionals and move code out of loops to avoid unnecessary recomputation. Target-specific code optimizations move or schedule instructions to improve pipeline performance.

It is not possible to completely hide the effects of such optimizations from the user who is trying to follow the flow of a program, so the debugger must present the program information in a manner that can be easily understood. This is possible only if the compiler has transmitted the relevant optimization information to the debugger.

MCCG32 performs an important function by generating key information for the XRAYG32™ source debugger. With this information, the user can debug highly optimized programs at the C language level.

## 2.2 Assembler

The GMICRO/200 macro-assembler, ASMG32™, complies with the standard syntax defined by the TRON association. In addition, many structured directives are provided to ease the assembly programmer's task.

ASMG32 produces an AT&T-compatible System V COFF object module format to facilitate the toolkit's use in a Unix® environment. Since most current object formats do not possess facilities for transferring the optimization information discussed previously, MRI has extended the AT&T System V COFF object formats to include the optimization information on register use. The extensions have been implemented so that existing software tools and applications will not be affected.

## 2.3 Linker

The compiler and assembler produce relocatable output which is organized in sections (e.g. code, data, constants). The GMICRO/200 linker, LODG32, allows these sections to be allocated to specific memory areas. Such control is often necessary for systems that use different types of memory (e.g. high speed ROM versus slower RAM). The LODG32 linker is a sophisticated tool that allows the user complete control over memory allocation. This control is accomplished through a powerful command language.

## 2.3 Librarian

An object module librarian is also provided to conveniently organize support routines. A standard C library and other support routines are supplied as part of the toolkit.

## 2.4 Debugger

The compiler, assembler, and object module librarian produce and manipulate debug information, such as symbol names, types, line numbers, and source files. This information is then used by the XRAYG32 source-level debugger/simulator to allow a user to non-intrusively debug a program.

Various debugging execution environments can be used throughout the debugging and hardware/software integration phases of an embedded microprocessor system. In the early stages of development, when a hardware prototype system is not available, a simulator or stand-alone emulator can be used. If the simulator environment provides simulation for I/O, timer, and interrupts, the general functionality of the software system can be verified on a host system.

We have developed a simulator for the GMICRO/200 instruction set (including floating-point instructions) and have been executing programs on it for many months. The simulator itself is driven and monitored by XRAYG32, a screen-oriented, high-level/assembly-level debugger.

The simulator played a key role in the quality assurance and testing processes during the development of the GMICRO/200 toolkit. Since the compiler, assembler, and linker were developed in advance of the silicon manufacture of the GMICRO/200, we needed an execution environment to validate the tools that we were developing. The simulator is delivered as an integral part of XRAYG32.

In the later phases of development, a hardware prototype system is often available. This allows debugging and testing to be accomplished by using a monitor, a target board, or an in-circuit emulator in the target environment. XRAYG32 is a source-level debugger that is adaptable to all of these target environments.

XRAYG32 provides a full debugging environment by allowing the user total control at both the source level and the assembly level. The user can monitor variables and expressions, simulate peripheral devices, set and condition breakpoints to various events, patch code, and invoke powerful macros on execution conditions. Moreover, maximum control and measurement capabilities are provided by the simulator environment. As already mentioned, XRAYG32 will also be available to control other execution environments such as in-circuit emulators, single board computers, and real-time operating systems.

## 3. The Application

To illustrate the MRI GMICRO/200 toolkit, we will define a very simple application. We shall describe a C program, **otis**, that controls a simplified six-story building elevator. To maintain our emphasis on the toolkit and TRON architecture, details have purposefully been kept to a minimum and part of the program has been omitted.

The program **otis** continuously monitors a certain memory byte location and controls the actions of the elevator by activating either an external "motor" or a "door manager." When one of the elevator buttons (see Fig. 2) is depressed, circuitry will cause the control byte to reflect the event by setting one of the 8 bits, according to the function map shown in Fig. 3.

In **otis**, a controlling "switch" statement will monitor the control byte and select one of two possible actions:

1. If a floor button is depressed, a relative number will be sent to the "motor" that indicates how many floors and in which direction to move the elevator. For example, if the elevator is currently on floor #4 and the floor #1 button is depressed, the "motor" will receive the value -3, meaning "go down 3 floors". It is easy to see that this value can be computed by the formula:

   motor command = destination floor - current floor

   The external "motor" is constantly watching its own memory location for non-zero values, and it will execute the command by moving the elevator appropriately. At the end of this non-interruptible operation, the motor will set a shared variable to the current floor number.

2. If a door button is depressed, the program will check the status of the door (a byte in some memory location) and send the "door manager" a command to either open or close the door. Trying to open an already opened door, or to close it when it is already closed will activate an acoustic signal (a bell), by TRAPping the event and invoking a special routine.

   To keep the example short, the "motor", the "door manager", and the "bell" components are not shown.

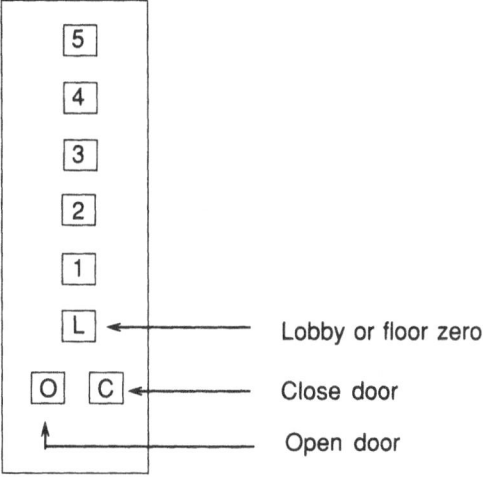

Fig. 2 Elevator Buttons

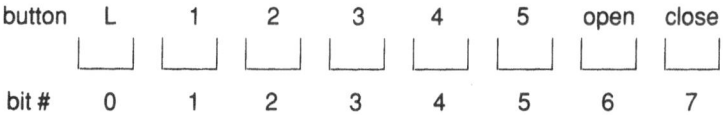

| button | L | 1 | 2 | 3 | 4 | 5 | open | close |
|--------|---|---|---|---|---|---|------|-------|

| bit # | 0 | 1 | 2 | 3 | 4 | 5 | 6 | 7 |
|-------|---|---|---|---|---|---|---|---|

Fig. 3 Function Map

The program, **otis**, relies heavily on the ability of MCCG32 to insert assembler pseudo-function calls at any point in a program that a regular function could be used. In other words, the implementors of **otis** have taken advantage of the fact that MCCG32 can provide access to the complete instruction set and registers of the chip. The user can call the ASM function with one or more strings containing valid assembly language code. MCCG32 will place these ASM strings into the code generated by its processing of other C language statements to replace the invocation of the function. To the software engineer, this seems to take place at the C statement level. By merely being aware of MCCG32's calling conventions, the user has *total* access to the main CPU and to any coprocessors.

Consider the following examples, remembering that ℗ denotes a memory location, # denotes an immediate value, and **H'** introduces a hexadecimal sequence.

**Example 1:**

```
register5 = ASM("  mov r5,r0");
```

Since ASM externally behaves exactly like a function, the above call will return an "int" value in **r0** as specified by calling conventions. Since the value of **r5** is moved to **r0**, the C code is effectively accessing the value of **r5**.

The following code will be generated:

```
mov r5,r0
mov r0,@_register5
```

**Example 2:**

```
register0 = ASM();
```

generates

```
mov r0,@_register0
```

The example above shows an extreme case in which ASM returns whatever is already in **r0**.

**Example 3:**

```
const long double pi = ASM(long double, "  fmvr from2,fr0");
```

This declaration shows how to access the floating point coprocessor. The instruction **fmvr from2,fr0** moves the constant $\pi$ contained in **from2** into the floating point register **fr0**. The first (optional) parameter to ASM makes the function locally behave as if it had been declared as:

```
long double ASM(const char*, ...);
```

A long double as specified by calling conventions is returned in **fr0** (if the coprocessor is present). Code similar to that shown below will be generated:

```
fmvr from2,fr0
fmov fr0,(-12,fp)
```

**Example 4:**

```
char *os_buf_ptr = ASM(char*,"  mov #H'02FE,r0");
```

This example assigns an absolute value to a pointer. Notice the instruction which prepares **r0** for return. According to the calling conventions, pointers are returned in **r0**.

While assigning an absolute address is easy to do by using ASM, it is better practice to use the linker to place variables at absolute memory locations. In fact, should these absolute addresses change, it will not be necessary to recompile or reassemble the application — relinking would suffice.

The C source code for **otis** is shown in Fig. 4.

```
/*  This program controls an elevator for a 6 story building.  */
typedef unsigned char BYTE;
extern volatile BYTE buttons;
extern volatile BYTE motor;
extern volatile int current_floor;
extern volatile enum { CLOSE,OPEN } door_status;

extern void Open_Door(void);
extern void Close_Door(void);

main()
{
buttons = 0; motor = 0;       /* initialize control areas */
current_floor = 0;            /* start at the lobby level */
door_status = OPEN;           /* with open door */

while(1)
    {
    int n;

    switch( n = ASM( int, /* hence must return in r0 */
                "loop:    mov        #0,r0",
                "         bsch/f/1.b@_buttons,r0",
                "         bvs        loop" ) )
         {
         case 0:
         case 1:
         case 2:
         case 3:
         case 4:
         case 5:  motor = n - current_floor;
                  while ( motor )
                             /* wait for motor to be finished */ ;
                  break;
         case 6:                      /* open if not already open */
                  if ( door_status == OPEN )
                      ASM( void, "trap/eq" ); /* beep! */
                  else
                      {Open_Door(); /* wait for complete opening */
                      while( door_status == CLOSE ) ;}
                  break;
         case 7:                      /* close if not already closed */
                  if ( door_status == CLOSE )
                      ASM( void, "trap/eq" ); /* beep! */
                  else
                      {Close_Door(); /* wait for complete closing */
                      while( door_status -- OPEN ) ;}
                  break;
         }
    }
}
```

see Note 1

see Note 2

*Fig. 4  C Source Code for Otis*

Notes:

1. The new ANSI attribute "volatile" indicates to the compiler that a variable can be externally modified (for example by Direct Memory Access). Therefore, MCCG32's optimizer will avoid making assumptions on the value of such a risky variable.

2. The sequence:

```
loop:   mov         #0,r0
        bsch/f/1.b  @_buttons,r0
        bvs         loop
```

utilizes an advanced GMICRO/200 instruction: Bit Search (bsch). This instruction initiates a search at the byte (.b option) "buttons," at the bit 0 (according to r0). It will search forward (/f option) for a set bit (/1 option). At the end of the instruction, r0 will contain a value from 0 to 7 that represents the corresponding bit in "buttons" that was set, or the value 8, if the search failed (i.e. no "buttons" were depressed). In the latter case, the "v" flag will be set, and the "Branch on V Set" instruction will repeat the loop.

Especially for small tasks, the overhead associated with a procedure call and return may equal or exceed the time taken by the task at hand. The use of ASM avoids the overhead, and it is particularly advantageous in time critical sections of code.

MCCG32 incorporates a very powerful global flow optimizer which performs a variety of optimizations in addition to those performed by the code generator. To keep the output as easy to read as possible, we have chosen to turn off these optimizations. Fig. 5 shows the compiler output (edited) for **otis** in assembler form.

```
;           Microtec(R) Research Inc. G32 C Compiler 1.0
;           Host Operating System - SUN UNIX
;           Command Line Options Specified:
;                   -M -J/usr5/gmicro/proto_include -DG32=1 -ng otis

           .PROGRAM   otis
           .DISPSIZE  FWD=32,FBR=16
           .SECTION   initdata,data,ALIGN=4
           .SECTION   text,code,ALIGN=2
           .IMPORT    _buttons,_motor,_current_floor,_door_status
           .IMPORT    $Open_Door,$Close_Door
           .EXPORT    _main
_main:
;*** local symbols ***   n = r4
           enter      #0,(r4)
; buttons = 0; motor = 0;      /* initialize control areas */
           mov.b      #0,@_buttons
           mov.b      #0,@_motor
; current_floor = 0;           /* start at the lobby level */
           mov        #0,@_current_floor
; door_status = OPEN;          /* with open door */
           mov.b      #1,@_door_status
; while(1)
;     {
```

*Fig. 5 Compiler Output for Otis*

```
;     int n;
;     switch( n = ASM( int, /* hence must return in r0 */ ......
L1:
loop:      mov      #0,r0
           bsch/f/1.b@_buttons,r0
           bvs      loop
           mov      r0,r4
           cmpu     #H'7,r4
           bgt      L1
           jmp      @@(pc,4,r4*4)      ◄─────  Chained Addressing Mode
           .DATA.W  M5,M5,M5,M5,M5,M6,M7
;          {
;          case 0:
;          case 1:
;          case 2:
;          case 3:
;          case 4:
;          case 5:    motor = n - current_floor;
M5:        mov.b    r4,r0
           sub.b    @_current_floor+3,r0
           mov.b    r0,@_motor
;                   while ( motor )
;                           /* wait for motor to be finished */ ;
L6:        cmp.b    #0,@_motor
           bne:d    L6
;                   break;
           bra      L1
;          case 6:          /* open if not already open */
;                   if ( door_status == OPEN )
M6:        cmp.b    #1,@_door_status
           bne      L9
;                       ASM( void, "trap/eq"); /* beep! */
           trap/eq
           bra      L1
;                   else
;                       {Open_Door(); /* wait for complete opening */
L9:        jsr      @$Open_Door
;                       while( door_status == CLOSE ) ;}
L11:       cmp.b    #0,@_door_status
           beq:d    L11
;                   break;
           bra      L1
;          case 7:          /* close if not already closed */
M7:        ;..... omitted ......
;          }
;     }
; }
           exitd    (r4),#0
           .END
```

*Fig. 5 Compiler Output for Otis (cont.)*

After **otis** has been assembled producing a relocatable AT&T System V COFF file, LODG32 is invoked with the following command file:

```
ORDER text=0x0100,data=0xf000,bss,heap

PUBLIC stacktop=0x0

PUBLIC _motor=0xE0
PUBLIC _door_status=0xE4
PUBLIC _buttons=0xF0
PUBLIC _current_floor=0xFA

LOAD /usr5/gmicro/lib/start
LOAD otis
LOAD door_manager,motor_manager,bell_manager
LOAD /usr5/gmicro/lib/g32p.lib
LOAD /usr5/gmicro/lib/g32sys.lib
```

The ORDER command specifies in which order the various sections should be laid out. For "text" and "data," user-selected addresses will be used.

Through the PUBLIC directive, the "volatile" variables of the example are placed at particular addresses. If these addresses change, perhaps from one system or installation to another, there is no need to recompile — new directives will do the job.

The LOAD command specifies which objects have to be included, and which libraries should be used to resolve external references.

The library "g32p.lib" is the C library, while "g32sys.lib" provides low level functionalities on which "g32p.lib" relies. In MRI's case, for instance, "g32sys.lib" is a layer that "borrows" from the host's operating system (Unix or VAX/VMS). Both libraries have been previously created with the MRI object librarian.

### 3.1 Simulated XRAYG32 Execution of otis

We will now describe a simulated XRAYG32 execution of **otis**.

After activating the debugger/simulator, the following commands are supplied to XRAYG32:

```
LOAD otis.x
DEFINE button(floor)
     {
     $ CEXPRESSION buttons=1<<(7-floor) $;
     }
DEFINE open()
     {
     button(6);
     }
```

```
DEFINE close()
     {
     button(7);
     }
MONITOR buttons,door_status
MONITOR motor != 0
BREAKINSTRUCT #20
GO
```

After LOADing the program **otis**, the macro "button" is DEFINEd, enabling us to simulate the depressing of a button. Subsidiary macros "open" and "close" are also easily defined in terms of "button." XRAYG32 owes much of its power to its macro definition mechanism. For instance, macros can be conditionally associated with a specific event (for example, a counter becoming greater than a given value), or it can be used to patch code for the immediate verification of corrections.

We can also continuously display in the DATA viewport (see Fig. 6) a number of variables and conditions by using the MONITOR command. Then, to test the operation of the "switch" statement, we set a breakpoint on the "switch" instruction and order XRAYG32 to proceed.

Program execution is suspended as expected at line 20. The inverse video indicates the location of the program counter.

Notice the MONITORed values and the TRACE viewport at the top of Fig. 6.

By depressing a function key, we cause XRAYG32 to switch to low-level mode, as shown in Fig. 7. Here, GMICRO/200 assembly code is intermixed with the original C source. Notice the REGISTERS bank (which includes various flags, coprocessor registers, and cycle count) and the STACK viewport. There are fifty viewports that may be custom-designed by the user. User viewports can display information formatted by user-defined macros. Each viewport can be resized at will.

In order to proceed, the breakpoint at line 20 is cleared and the macro "button(3)" is invoked to simulate depressing button #3. This will be reflected in the DATA viewport as we MONITOR the value of "n" (in r4) after stepping execution by 4 (low-level) STEPs. We single step execution through the "switch" jump (notice the Chained Addressing Mode). We now find it useful to return to the C source-level view (see Fig. 8) to find ourselves computing the value of "motor." One (high-level) STEP, and we will be able to verify, through "PRINTVALUE motor == 3", that we actually computed the correct value.

By causing another single step execution, we find **otis** waiting indefinitely for "motor" to become zero. To force this condition, we can define and use a macro "done( )" which has no parameters, and which will also update "current_floor" as follows:

```
XRAYG32 Version 1.3d
                        ═DATA═                    ═3═            ═══════TRACE═══════    ═4═
1    buttons        00                            2. 00000130?START\<unknown>
2    door_status    <OPEN>                         1. 000002A4?MAIN\<unknown>
3    motor != 0     0                              0. 0000014E OTIS\main
4
5
6
                                        ═CODE═                                            2
     6
     7    extern void Open_Door(void);
     8    extern void Close_Door(void);
     9
    10    main()
    11    {
    12    buttons = 0; motor = 0;/* initialize control areas */
    13    current_floor = 0;      /* start at the lobby level */
    14    door_status = OPEN;     /* with open door */
.   15
.   16    while(1)
.   17       {
.   18       int n;
    19
*   20       switch( n = ASM( int, /* hence must return in r0 */
    21                   "loop:  mov            #0,r0",
    22                   "       bsch/f/1.b     @_buttons,r0",
    23                   "       bvs            loop" ) )
    24          {
    25          case 0:
    26          case 1:
    27          case 2:
    28          case 3:
    29          case 4:
    30          case 5: motor = n - current_floor;
    31                  while ( motor )
    32                      /* wait for motor to be finished */ ;
    33                  break;
    34          case 6:/* open if not already open */
Command         GM200   MODULE: OTIS              BREAK #: 1   HELP=F5   MRI 1.3d
                                     ═COMMAND═                                         ═1═
:          {
:          button(7);
:          }
: .
> MONITOR buttons,door_status
> MONITOR motor != 0
> BREAKINSTRUCT #20
> GO
  Break # 1 on instr module OTIS line 20
>
```

*Fig. 6  Setting a Breakpoint*

```
DEFINE done()
      {
      current_floor += motor;
      motor = 0;
      }
```

After we invoke "done" to terminate the wait loop, the command GO will send us back to the "switch" statement shown in Fig. 6 to wait for a new button to be serviced.

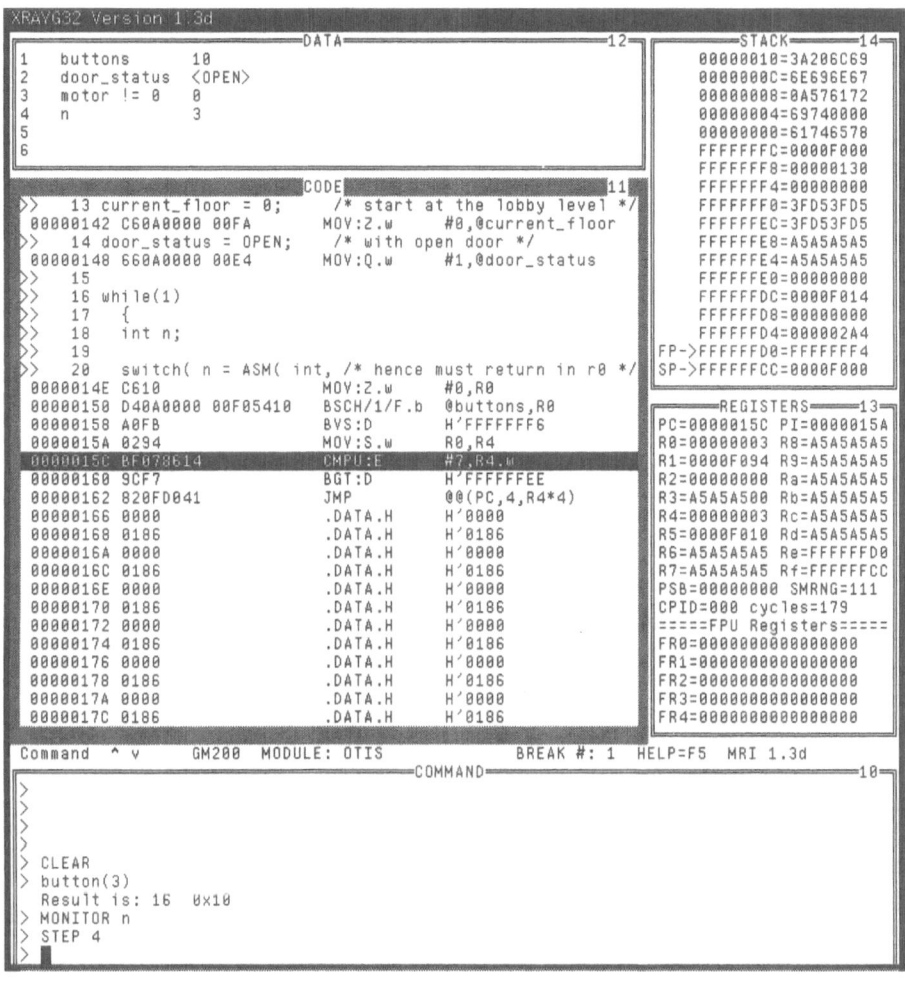

*Fig. 7  Assembly-Level Mode*

## 4.   Conclusion

The GMICRO/200 is a high performance 32-bit microprocessor based on the TRON architecture.   As such, it is a Complex Instruction Set Computer.   Despite its orthogonal instruction set, its variety of instructions, addressing modes and pipelining make the development of easy-to-use software tools a challenge.  In this paper, we have reviewed some of the features of a set of tools for the GMICRO/200 that exploit its power in innovative ways for both developing and debugging programs.   Some aspects of particular importance to the ANSI-C standard and the TRON architecture as embodied in the GMICRO/200 are also mentioned.

```
XRAYG32 Version 1.3d
=================DATA================3=    ==============TRACE==============4=
1   buttons      10                       2. 00000130?START\<unknown>
2   door_status  <OPEN>                   1. 000002A4?MAIN\<unknown>
3   motor != 0   1                        0. 0000019A OTIS\main
4   n            3
5
6
=============================CODE=======================================2
   16   while(1)
   17   {
   18   int n;
   19
   20   switch( n = ASM( int, /* hence must return in r0 */
   21                   "loop:  mov              #0,r0",
   22                   "       bsch/f/1.b       @_buttons,r0",
   23                   "       bvs              loop" ) )
   24      {
   25      case 0:
   26      case 1:
   27      case 2:
   28      case 3:
   29      case 4:
   30      case 5: motor = n - current_floor;
   31              while ( motor )
   32                      /* wait for motor to be finished */ ;
   33              break;
   34      case 6:/* open if not already open */
   35              if ( door_status == OPEN )
   36                  ASM( void, "         trap/eq"); /* beep! */
   37              else
   38                  {Open_Door(); /* wait for complete opening */
   39                   while( door_status == CLOSE ) ;}
   40              break;
   41      case 7:/* close if not already closed */
   42              if ( door_status == CLOSE )
   43                  ASM( void, "         trap/eq"); /* beep! */
   44              else
Command        GM200  MODULE: OTIS           BREAK #: 1  HELP=F5  MRI 1.3d
============================COMMAND===============================1=
>
>
>
>
>
> STEP
> PRINTVALUE motor == 3
      1
>
```

*Fig. 8 High-Level Mode*

## 5. Acknowledgments

The authors wish to express their appreciation for the cooperation and advice given by GMICRO members, especially Mr. N. Ito of Hitachi, Ltd., Mr. S. Hazama of Fujitsu Ltd., and Dr. T. Enomoto of Mitsubishi Electric Corporation. We would like to thank Professor Ken Sakamura of the University of Tokyo for his encouragement, and his laboratory for its assistance as a Beta site for the tools. We would also like to thank the members of Nihon Microtec Research, Tokyo, for their coordination efforts on our behalf with the TRON association.

**References**

[1]   Agarwal, Durga and Kimelman, Paul. "An Adaptable High-Level Debugging Environment for Embedded Systems", Proceedings of BUSCON 1988, New York, New York, October 1988.

[2]   Application Engineering Department, Hitachi Microcomputer Engineering, Ltd. (Ed.), "H32/200 Programming Manual", Worldwide Product Marketing Operations, Hitachi, Ltd., Tokyo, Japan, December 1987.

[3]   ANSI Accredited Standards Committee X3, "Draft Proposed American National Standard for Information Systems – Programming Language C," The American National Standards Institute, Washington, D.C., May 1988.

[4]   K. Sakamura (Ed.), "TRON Project 1987 (Proceedings of the Third TRON Project Symposium)", Springer-Verlag, Tokyo, Japan, November 1987.

**Antonio Bigazzi:** joined Microtec Research, Inc. in 1987 as a Software Development Manager for the GMICRO toolkit and for TRON architectures. He currently leads a team of 7 engineers. He developed the ANSI-C Front End, together with coauthor J. E. Lillge. He obtained his M.S. in Computer Science in 1974 from the University of Pisa, Italy. Since 1973, he has worked in compilers and language tools, at Olivetti, Intel, Xerox, and MRI. During the past five years, he has focused on the C language, particularly in the emerging ANSI standard.

**J. E. Lillge:** is a Software Engineer at Microtec Research, Inc. He joined MRI in 1987 after serving for three years on the Computer Science faculty at California Polytechnic State University. He received a B.S. degree from Iowa State University in 1981, and an M.S. degree from the University of Illinois in 1984.

**Daniel E. Jaskolski:** joined Microtec Research, Inc. in 1983. He is currently Executive Vice President and is responsible for the operation of the company and its subsidiaries. He received his B.A. in Mathematics from La Salle College, Philadelphia, PA., and his MBA from the University of Pittsburgh, Pittsburgh, PA., the latter in 1967. Prior to joining MRI, he was employed by IBM as a Systems Engineer and Medicus Systems Corporation in various software development and management roles.

Above authors may be reached at:
Microtec Research, Inc.
2350 Mission College Blvd.
Santa Clara, CA 95054
USA

# List of Contributors

The page numbers given below refer to the page on which contribution begins.

Kozo Adachi 263
Yasuhiko Baba 167
Antonio Bigazzi 363
Hideaki Chaki 341
Masashi Deguchi 275
Tatsuya Enomoto 55
Atsushi Fujihira 317
Koichi Fujita 331
Makoto Fukuyoshi 213
Sagoro Hazama 331
Yoshiaki Iba 235
Yoshimichi Ikeda 213
Hideo Inayoshi 301
Norio Inoue 235
Aya Ishii 285
Shuichi Ishimaru 351
Masaru Ishizuka 213
Noriyoshi Ito 247
Matao Itoh 317
Jun Iwamura 285
Tomonobu Iwasaki 331
D.E. Jaskolski 363
Kazuo Kajimoto 109
David Kalinsky 67
Yugo Kashiwagi 341
Shumpei Kawasaki 301
Hiroyuki Kida 301
Masaharu Kimura 331
Hidechika Kishigami 285
Takeshi Kitahara 317
Tokuzo Kiyohara 263
Manabu Kobayakawa 35
Yoshizumi Kobayashi 145
Ichizo Kogiku 189
Hiroshi Kosugi 167
Yoshiaki Kushiki 109
Hiromi Kusumoto 167

J.E. Lillge 363
Masayoshi Matsushita 189
Masayoshi Matsushita 213
Masato Mitsuhashi 317
James D. Mooney 135
Yoshikazu Mori 247
Shosuke Mori 331
Shigeki Morinaga 301
Robert T. Myers 93
Tetsuaki Nakamikawa 301
Kiyoshi Nakata 55
Masachika Narushima 341
Osamu Nishijima 263
Yukinobu Nishikawa 275
Hiromi Nojima 247
Kazuhiro Oda 235
Tsukasa Ogawa 213
Toshikazu Ohkubo 189
Masato Ohminami 167
James Ready 67
Kazunori Saitoh 55
Ken Sakamura 3, 21, 79, 93, 119, 145
Takashi Sakao 263, 275
Tetsuo Sakuma 213
Nobuo Shimizu 235
Tsuyoshi Shimizu 35
Masahiro Shimizu 109
Toru Shimizu 55
Yutaka Shimizu 157
Hiroaki Takada 119
Hiroshi Takeyama 35
Kiichiro Tamaru 351
Hideo Tsubota 55
Kimiyoshi Usami 285
Tetsuo Wasano 145
Mitsuru Watabe 301
Masanobu Yuhara 317

# Keywords Index

Address monitor 317
Addressing mode 285
ANSI C compiler 363
Architecture-dependent 189

Basic OS 235
32-Bit microprocessor 247
Block-fetch 317
BTRON 79, 119
– specification OS 109

Cache 275
– memory 263
C compiler 341
Chained addressing mode 341
Communication control 157
Coprocessor 301
– protocol 301
CTRON 135, 145, 157, 167, 189, 213, 235

Debug support 247
DMA 331
DMAC 331

Embedded computer systems software 67
Execution environment 167
External-TAG 317

Fault tolerance 213
Feature 351
Floating point arithmetic 301
– – processing unit 301
Function 351

Gmicro 363
– CPU 301
– microprocessor 341

HFDS 3, 21
High reliability 247

Implementation 285
Information communication networks 145
Instruction format 285
Intelligent building/house 21
– object 21
Interface specifications 189
Interrupt 35
ITRON 35
– operating system 67
$\mu$-ITRON 35
– specification 55

Kernel 35, 189

Lap-top workstation 235
Logical video data model (LVD model) 109

Machine translation 93
Macro language 3
MC68020 213
MELPS7700 55
Memory management software development
   environment 235
Micro language 79
Microprocessor 263, 275
MR7700 55
MTRON 3, 21
Multi-processor 247, 317
Multi-tasking 67

Natural-language processing 93
Network architecture 21

Object module format 351
Open systems interconnection 157
Operating systems 93
– – interface 135, 145
Optimization 341

Parametric type 119
Performance 285

Peripheral LSI 331
Physical cache 317
Pipeline 263, 275
– control 341
Pipelining 247
PLA 331
Portability 135
Process control 167
Program control 167
Programmable interface 3
Programming environment 79
– language 79

Real-memory system 263
Real-time 67
– operating system 55, 213
Reference model 145
RG68K 213

Self-contained type 119
Signature 119

Single chip microcomputer 35
Single-chip microcontroller 55
Software design 67
– portability 145
– tools 351
Source debugger 363
Subsetting 189

TACL 79
TAD 3
TIPE system 119
TRON assembler 363
– VLSI CPU 275
TULS 3, 21, 79, 119
TX1 285
TX Series 351

Video descriptor 109
– manager 109
– processor unit 109
Virtual processor 167

# TRON TOTAL ARCHITECTURE

Designed by Ken Sakamura

## New Computer Systems Construction

In TRON (The Realtime Operating system Nucleus) project, we try to build new computer systems architecture by foreseeing the technological breakthroughs in the future together with the demands on computer systems and then designing new systems accordingly. We feel the existing computer systems have many problems not fit for the future.

## The Objectives of the TRON Project

The TRON project aims to support a society structure where computers are used in every conceivable places and where these computer systems talk to each other without difficulty. The TRON project will support HFDS (Highly Functionally Distributed System), which will connect many computer controlled objects and is an important infrastructure of the future society, by providing methodology of how to build such computer systems and plan for acceptance of the computer systems by the society. The reason the TRON project covers many fields is to realize such environment.

The 21st century will come within two decades. It is certain that the number of computers used then will be much larger than today's figure. Because the computer will be used very widely, any problem associated with it, however small, should be eliminated as soon as possible. Not all the criticisms about today's computer systems are about technical matters but are about socioeconomical matters as well. Hence, the preparation for eliminating or reducing the problems of the computer systems in the future must be planned in a very broad context.

## TRON Subprojects

The TRON project covers many fields of computer system construction and application. Activities of the TRON project are divided into subprojects. The following software subprojects are running currently; ITRON (Industrial-TRON) for embedded computer systems, BTRON (Business-TRON) for workstations, CTRON (Central-TRON) for large file and communication servers, and MTRON (Macro-TRON) for distributed control of TRON computer systems in a large network. The TRON VLSI CPU CHIP subproject to design VLSI microprocessor which can support various TRON systems is also underway.

## The Features of the TRON Project

The TRON computer systems are designed as hierarchy of system layers. The TRON project provides specifications for interfaces among these layers. However, the realization of each layers is left to each implementor. While following the TRON Design Guideline, each implementor can freely compete in creating a concrete computer system based on the general TRON concept and specifications.

The TRON computer systems has the data compatibility and the program compatibility. In addition, the TRON computer systems have man-machine interface compatibility, which has rarely been discussed before.

The man-machine interface compatibility together with other TRON design principles have make it possible to use uniform design principles in computer systems and application design. These principles are valid for all TRON-based computer systems.

## TRON Association

TRON Association is an organization to provide a forum for discussions about the future computer systems among TRON project members and any interested parties. Please contact the address below if you are interested in joining the TRON Association. Annual membership fee is 500,000 YEN.

**TRON Association**
5th floor, Tomoecho Annex-II
3-8-27, Toranomon, Minato-ku
Tokyo 105 JAPAN
TEL. 81-3-433-6741
FAX. 81-3-433-5003